EMBODIMENT AND THE TREATMENT OF EATING DISORDERS

A NORTON PROFESSIONAL BOOK

EMBODIMENT AND THE TREATMENT OF EATING DISORDERS

The Body as a Resource in Recovery

CATHERINE COOK-COTTONE

FOREWORD BY TRACY TYLKA

W. W. NORTON & COMPANY
Independent Publishers Since 1923

Note to Readers: Standards of clinical practice and protocol change over time, and no technique or recommendation is guaranteed to be safe or effective in all circumstances. This volume is intended as a general information resource for professionals practicing in the field of psychotherapy and mental health; it is not a substitute for appropriate training, peer review, and/or clinical supervision. Neither the publisher nor the authors can guarantee the complete accuracy, efficacy, or appropriateness of any particular recommendation in every respect.

For information about permission to reproduce selections from this book, write to Permissions, W. W. Norton & Company, Inc., 500 Fifth Avenue, New York, NY 10110

For information about special discounts for bulk purchases, please contact W. W. Norton Special Sales at specialsales@wwnorton.com or 800-233-4830

Manufacturing by Sheridan Books
Production manager: Katelyn MacKenzie

ISBN: 978-0-393-73410-2 (pbk.)

W. W. Norton & Company, Inc., 500 Fifth Avenue, New York, N.Y. 10110
www.wwnorton.com

W. W. Norton & Company Ltd., 15 Carlisle Street, London W1D 3BS

1 2 3 4 5 6 7 8 9 0

I believe that each of us has within us the capacity for an embodied experience of this one beautiful and precious life.
This book is dedicated to the clients who are ready to leave disordered eating behind and take on the courageous path toward embodiment.
This is not the easy path. It means being-with and working-with all of the sensations, emotions, and experiences life offers.
It includes an authoring a life story that integrates vulnerability, failures, victories, and ease. Embodiment requires mindful self-care, the kind of self-care that is woven into each hour of each day.
It asks that relationships and love come from the whole self—body, heart, and mind. More, it means living into a life filled with meaning and purpose.
I dedicate this book to the clients who are realizing that the way out is not just through, but inward; toward the embodied human that they were truly meant to be.

I also dedicate this book to the beautiful practice of yoga.
The poem "What If?" captures the essence of the embodied possibility that
yoga has brought to my own recovery and growth.
Thank you yoga for all you have given me.

What If?
by Ganga White

What if our religion was each other?

If our practice was our life?

If our prayer was our words?

What if the Temple was the Earth?

If forests were our church?

If holy water—the rivers, lakes and oceans?

What if meditation was our relationships?

If the Teacher was life?

If wisdom was self-knowledge?

If love was the center of our being

CONTENTS

FOREWORD

What drew you to this book? Perhaps you feel limited by the clinical treatments available for eating disorders. Perhaps these treatments have been helpful, but you feel that something is missing that could facilitate and sustain progress and recovery. In her book, *Embodiment and the Treatment of Eating Disorders: The Body as a Resource in Recovery,* Dr. Catherine Cook-Cottone identifies this missing piece as *embodiment* and presents her embodied approach to treating eating disorders (EAT-ED).

Embodiment involves "being-with and working-with all of the sensations, emotions, and experiences life offers." Embodiment is experiencing the body, heart, mind, soul, and relationships as intertwined and living "a life filled with meaning and purpose." To be embodied necessitates regular and mindful self-care, as embodiment can be regularly disrupted by external and internal factors—for example, being objectified and internalizing societal beauty ideals.

How are embodiment and eating disorders connected? As the EAT-ED elucidates, eating disorders represent disrupted embodiment. Rather than being intertwined, the body (including its various needs and emotional experiences) becomes a *target* of the mind. The mind views the body as the enemy. Harsh criticism, withholding of nourishment, and excessive and harmful physical activity are punishments to a body believed to be weak and uncontrolled. The authentic, lived experiences of the body are avoided. Disrupted embodiment is a simplified yet destructive way of "being"—yet it makes sense to those with eating disorders. A life without symptoms is perceived as unmanageable and frightening.

How then can we help those with eating disorders move towards embodiment? Recovery extends beyond the process of decreasing symptoms to reconnecting with the body. The shift from disorder to positive embodiment is carefully explicated in the EAT-ED. The body comes to be viewed as a source of strength and wisdom rather than an object to control.

To clarify, the EAT-ED does not abandon what we know to be safe and effective interventions. Rather, it gives meaning to these interventions and the importance of recovery. While meal plans, regulated exercise, and avoidance of binges and purges can help decrease symptoms, they don't reveal the importance of recovery. Recovery can be more fully achieved by engaging in practices that promote positive embodiment. Vignettes and clinical tools are provided to facilitate positive embodiment through four pillars of embodied practice: (a) mindful self-care, (b) being-with and working-with what is present in the moment, (c) honoring effort and struggle (i.e., self-compassion) and (d) cultivating mission and purpose.

These pillars provide present-moment skills for being-with and working-with the overwhelm that emerges in treatment. Scheduled pleasant events (mindful self-care) create direction and predictability. Knowing a reason for being and/or mission (a *why*) serves as a "rescue line" toward recovery, as it guides the development of realistic, intentional plans that are based on values, purpose, and personal meaning. Mindful awareness and listening to and connecting with internal experiences promote interoceptive awareness. Clinical examples, practice guides, and scripts are integrated throughout to facilitate the development of these skills, and the content comes to life. Throughout, Catherine Cook-Cottone calls attention to and honors the various authors, researchers, and therapists who unknowingly contributed to its foundation.

Interacting with Catherine is one of the great joys my life. We regularly connect and present together at conferences. Catherine truly embodies her work—she welcomes her physical and emotional experiences, directs her efforts toward meaning and purpose, and fully embraces mindful self-care, even when it is difficult to "fit in" her busy life as a professor, researcher, licensed therapist, editor, advisor, mentor, yoga instructor, non-profit business creator, scale developer, and more. Catherine is genuine, insightful, brilliant, inspirational, and innovative. Our discussions are therapy for my work, body, mind, and soul, and I leave invigorated, ready to do embodied, meaningful work.

Reading this book was no exception. I waited for winter break, when I could fully immerse myself in it. The day I started reading, I found out that my (routine) mammogram was abnormal, which was followed by more imaging, an ultrasound, a fine needle aspiration, a biopsy, and then waiting for the results. During this trying time, I found Catherine's book to be a gift. I highlighted content on nearly every page. It helped me rediscover my *why* and view my body as a source of strength and wisdom rather than something to control, scrutinize, and manage. I ended the book feeling stronger and more embodied, even before knowing the (negative) biopsy results.

Quite simply, this book can revolutionize the treatment of eating disorders and help all individuals, even professionals in this field, toward embodiment.

Tracy L. Tylka, Ph.D., FAED
Professor, Department of Psychology
The Ohio State University
Fellow, Academy for Eating Disorders
Editor-in-Chief, *Body Image: An International Journal of Research*

ACKNOWLEDGMENTS

There are so many people to acknowledge for supporting my work on this book. I would like to acknowledge Dr. Niva Piran and Dr. Tracy Tylka and their work in the field of body image and embodiment as inspirational sources for this text. Niva, thank you for accepting my self-invitation to come and speak with you more than a decade ago. I had been following your work since graduate school, when I first read about your groundbreaking program at the Toronto School of Ballet, and was thrilled to share my ideas and research dreams with you. You have given me, and all of us in the field, paradigm-shifting leadership. You carved out the pathway for participants to have a voice and agency in eating disorder inventions and research. Your work, including the developmental theory of embodiment, has inspired so many of my projects, including my school-based yoga prevention intervention in which the girls, themselves define embodiment and their relationship with the media.

Tracy, I am extremely grateful for your wonderful foreword for this text. I remember many years ago when we connected to talk about my attunement model and possible ways we could work together to study what is now conceptualized as embodiment. Thank you for seeing and valuing my work. I love presenting with you and your ease in citing the growing body of research in the field of embodiment and body image. Your passion and commitment to the field are relentless, academically brilliant, and strategic in a way that has changed the world. You not only study and create new concepts but also design tools so that others might as well. I specifically want to recognize your work in body appreciation, positive body image, intuitive eating, and embodiment. Further, I am grateful for your empowerment of others. You have demonstrated true leadership as you put together panels, editorial boards, and edited books, honoring this important field of research and amplifying the voices around you. You do not just believe in embodiment; you live it and create spaces for others to live it.

To my research team, I could not do what I do without you. When people ask me how our team is so productive, cohesive, and single-minded, I try to explain your passion for this work. So many of you sought me out when you were undergrads, not because I am loaded with research dollars but because you, like me, had a drive for this work since you were old enough to understand the interface between yourself and the world. You, like me, wanted to do something to make this a safer, healthier, and more loving place for the little ones to unfold into their embodied selves. I am so lucky to work with each and every one of you. I always tell my daughters what a lucky mom I am. In the same way, I need to tell all of you more often what a lucky research team leader I am. Dr. Wendy Guyker, thank you for leading this powerful group of students with me and helping me create the interventions, studies, and scales that are cited in this book. I could not do this work without you.

To Allison Drake, my graduate assistant who so graciously agreed to read every word of this manuscript and give me feedback—it had to be you. You have the sense of humor and the attention to detail that I and this book needed as we nurtured it through the writing and rewriting process. Summer 2019 will hold a special place in my heart, and I am sure your heart as well, when both of us dedicated most of our time to making this book what it is. I don't know if you felt it, but every time I read your notes that said something like, "Did you mean this?" I stopped editing and sent a meditation of gratitude to you. Also a note to your father; it means a lot to me that you and he shared this book. Thank you both so very much.

To Deborah Malmud, vice president and editor at W. W. Norton & Company, thank you for believing in this project from day one, when I worked to explain it to you on the phone more than eighteen months ago. Thank you for your thoughts on the proposal, for the check-ins, and for the work it took to turn this manuscript into beautiful and accessible book pages.

Last, to Jerry, Chloe, and Maya, who love my passion and me: Jerry, thank you for being my person and the one who makes my life and work possible, as well as for listening and giving helpful feedback as I pitched the theories and connections that became the chapters of this book. Chloe, thank you for showing me what it is like to unapologetically explore what it means to embody who you are and to push the limits of thinking and doing in the world and in this book. Thank you for loving my writing so much you felt compelled to share it with your friends—it is a mom's highest honor. Maya, thank you for embodying vulnerability, strength, humor, and beauty: in song, as you played my grandmother's old piano and sang beautiful ballads as I wrote, the way you know how to make all of us laugh even when nothing seems funny at all, and in heartfulness, as you graciously listened to me read through sections of the text and encouraged me to share from my heart. I acknowledge and love you all.

PREFACE

Be who God meant you to be and you will set the world on fire.
—St. Catherine of Sienna

The embodied approach to treating eating disorders (EAT-ED) evolved over twenty years of working with and studying eating disorders (EDs). For decades I have lived the questions about unique vulnerabilities and circumstances that carve out the pathway to these incredibly challenging disorders: anorexia nervosa, bulimia nervosa, and binge eating disorder. I worked with client after client who came to therapy in a relentless fight with their body—the home of their experiential world. Over time I noticed that for many of my clients there was, at some point, a separation of the perceived self from the body. Following this separation, the body and all that it needed and wanted became the target, the enemy, or the thing to be controlled and managed. This manifested as relentless and harsh criticism, withholding of nourishment to the point of starvation or death, smothering and overwhelming with food, excessive and hurtful physical activity as a punishment or undoing, isolation, and self-hatred.

This is not a new phenomenon brought forth solely by our culture. EDs have been noted in the literature for many hundreds of years. For example, my namesake, St. Catherine of Siena (1347–1380), was said to eat only a handful of herbs each day and would shove twigs down her throat to bring up the food she was forced to eat (Brumberg, 2000). Buddhist literatures talk of a hungry ghost, an apparition that relentlessly consumes and is never satisfied (Kabatznick, 1998). This disembodied intermingling of potentially pathological altruism, reluctance or inability to feel, the notion of the perpetual and unsatisfied hunger, and the pathway to self-destruction through starvation and bingeing has manifested among saints as well as common citizens throughout history.

I ask myself, "How have there been centuries of so many bright, sensitive, empathic, and thoughtful individuals pathologically engaging in such a disembodied and ultimately self-violent set of behaviors, yet we still have not found a robustly effective treatment?" I believe this comes in part from a misunderstanding of the root causes of EDs, which leads to a lack of funding for research and to creation and use of interventions that do not sufficiently address embodiment. EDs are misunderstood by lay people as intentional, superficial drives to be the most attractive person in the room. I have yet to meet a client for whom this is true—each and every one of my clients was seeking something else: to be accepted, to quiet the thoughts in their head, to numb emotions, to avoid a path forward that seems terrifying at best, to obliterate the past and all of its memories, to engage in something in their life that feels like it has meaning, to experience a sense of agency and self-determination, or to comply with harassing and objectifying beauty and gender standards that they saw as a pathway to being good enough.

In their seeking, they left their self. The body became a separate, troublesome, disposable, and equally romanticized yet discounted entity. Ultimately, the body was abandoned in favor of a self-perpetuating struggle in which clients straddle the disembodiment inherent in their psychological and behavioral states and choices and, at the same time, their wholly human drive for genuine and integrated embodiment. They can never feel fully in or out of themselves. My clients seem to long for embodiment as desperately as they long to leave themselves. They are trapped in the in-between, with any attempt to fully leave risking their mortality, and any attempt to return to the body risking the only coherent sense of self they know.

It is often said among substance use recovery circles that no one sets out to be a substance abuser. The same is true for EDs—it is often a misstep in the effort to get something right or to push down something that seems not right, is feared, or feels overwhelming. In *Eating by the Light of the Moon* (2000), Anita Johnston takes the reader through the story of accidentally falling into a raging river. Drowning, you reach for something outside of you. You grab a log that takes you to safety. The water calms as you float downstream, yet you hold the log, afraid you might drown if you let go. As Johnston explains it, you see your family and friends on the shore yelling for you to let go of the log and to swim to shore. But to let go of the log you not only need to embody the will to learn how to swim but also need to develop the competency of swimming. The water will not hurt you—you simply need to learn to swim.

I remember reading Johnston's book for the first time just after I received my license as a psychologist. I had already read Dan Siegel's first book, *The Developing Mind* (1999), Mary Pipher's *Reviving Ophelia* (1994), and Kim Chernin's *The Hungry Self* (1994) and had just started my study of dialectical behavioral therapy (Linehan, 1993). I was wholly inspired by Niva Piran's (1999) work at the Toronto School of Ballet and Lori Irving's (1999) Boulder model of prevention. From these roots, and all of the research I could gather, I developed the model described in this book (Cook-Cottone, 2006). It would also inform the first in-school, yoga-based ED prevention program: Girls Growing in Wellness and Balance (Cook-Cottone, Kane, Keddie, & Haugli, 2013; Cook-Cottone, Talebkhah, Guyker, & Keddie, 2017c). With my research team, I would implement and study this program for the next ten years and extend it to supplement treatment.

Since that time, I have dedicated my personal life and my career at the University at Buffalo, State University of New York to offering pathways of positive embodiment to those who seek it. Inspired by the findings of our yoga-based prevention program, I trained to be a yoga teacher and am now certified and registered with Yoga Alliance at the E-RYT 500 level (experienced registered yoga teacher). My embodiment work extended to consulting for the Africa Yoga Project, United Nations Foundation, and Yogis in Service, Inc., creating trauma-informed mindfulness and yoga programs for community members and humanitarian workers experiencing chronic stress and trauma (Cook-Cottone et al., 2017b, Cook-Cottone et al., 2017c; Cook-Cottone, Giambrone, & Klein, 2017a; Giambrone, Cook-Cottone, & Klein, 2018; Klein, Cook-Cottone, & Giambrone, 2015). My team also created the Mindful Self-Care Scale as a pathway to positive embodiment beyond yoga and mindfulness approaches (Cook-Cottone & Guyker, 2018). I work with clients in private practice, supporting them as they negotiate the pathway to positive embodiment, and now serve as co-editor in chief of the peer-reviewed *Eating Disorder: Journal of Treatment and Prevention*. My passion has only grown, and I have come to view embodiment as a basic human right. I believe that it is our work to remove any obstacles obscuring access to this right.

The EAT-ED framework comes from an aggregate of scientific research, clinical work, and personal experiences. It is a set of practices that can serve as an adjunct to the empirically supported practices that promote recovery and save lives. The EAT-ED framework offers a process of building embodiment from the inside out. Part I of this text provides the theoretical and empirical justification for this approach, including a review of the psychological models of embodiment and the embodiment-of-self model on which the text is based. Part II introduces the actionable processes related to positive embodiment. Each chapter is filled with tools, practices, practice guides, and scripts for use with your clients. The examples offered throughout, although derived from actual clients I've encountered in my practice, are composites—they do not represent transcripts of actual sessions, and they use fictitious names. They nonetheless exemplify approaches and dialogue I have found effective in my practice. In sum, this book provides a comprehensive framework for applying embodiment practices in the treatment of EDs.

Within the EAT-ED framework, I ask you to live questions rather than seek immediate answers. Questions lived are contemplations in which truth can unfold into a knowing and a being. As you read this book, live and love questions like these:

- What would a fully embodied life be like for my clients?
- How can I help them begin to be with and trust their bodies again?
- How can I support them as they find a sense of meaning and purpose in their lives outside their disordered eating?
- What challenges and joys lie in that process?
- Am I a role model of embodiment?
- How can I be more fully embodied in my own life?

As you listen for answers to these questions, for your clients and for yourself, you may find that embodiment invites you into a richer, more textured, and more beautiful way of being that is full of feelings, complexities, and relationships. It is not an easy process, and it requires ongoing practice, but both you and your clients are worth the effort.

EMBODIMENT AND THE TREATMENT OF EATING DISORDERS

Introduction

A Pathway to the Embodied Approach

This is how a human being can change:
There's a worm addicted to eating grape leaves.
Suddenly, he wakes up . . .
and he's no longer a worm.
He's the entire vineyard,
And the orchard too,
The fruit, the trunks, a
Growing wisdom and joy
That doesn't need to devour.

—J. A. Rumi, *The Worm's Waking*

Anorexia nervosa (AN), bulimia nervosa (BN), and binge eating disorder (BED) are a set of complex disorders involving the ability to nourish, love, and care for the body. Although eating is one of the core features of eating disorders (EDs), they are not simply disorders of eating. As the diagnostic criteria and behavioral, emotional, and cognitive correlates reveal, central to EDs is a complicated and disordered mind-body relationship that goes far beyond the relationship with food and eating. These whole-self disorders extend beyond the cognitive and emotional experience of the body and food to something bigger, deeper, and much more profound: embodiment. Based on a body of work detailed in Chapters 2 and 3, embodiment is uniquely defined for this text as follows:

Embodiment is a way of being (non-dualistic conceptualization self) in which being is understood as residing in and manifesting from the body as one experiences the internal (i.e., physiological, emotional, cognitive), external (i.e., interpersonal, social, cultural), and existential dimensions of life.

EDs show us that embodiment can be a violent, self-destructive process. They show us that embodiment, or attempts to avoid all that comes with it, can also be a form of self-abandonment. What makes these self-perpetuating disorders so difficult to treat is that they involve a reliance on a set of behaviors, or an identity (e.g., "I am an anorexic" or "I am a bulimic"), that seek the objects and states of being that they ultimately destroy: the body, mind, spirit, and relationships, as well as the client's sense of safety, control, happiness, and peace. EDs show us that no amount of eating, starving, or compensating truly connects us to our body, serves our mind or spirit, or supports meaningful relationships. More, no amount of eating, starving, or compensating can make us feel happy, safe, satisfied, in control, or at peace.

For an ED intervention to work, it must offer the promise of what the client seeks and must be inconsistent and incompatible with ED thoughts and behaviors. Unlike ED symptoms, positive embodiment practices offer more than short relief from distress and are wholly compatible with happiness, safety, satisfaction, agency, and peace. With positive embodiment, the path to recovery extends beyond the reprieve from symptoms. It is a way of being that promotes a sense of well-being, agency, common humanity, and purpose in a person's life. These practices help develop skills for and offer direction toward a life that your clients want to be present in, a life in which the body is a resource and in which connection with the self is the center of a beautifully unfolding experience of being each and every day.

Consider Sarah, a 27-year-old, late for work again. She is a little hungover because she decided to "drink her calories" last night. She catches a glimpse of herself in the window as she passes by and vows to skip lunch and dinner. Briefly, she wonders if she'll ever feel okay. Refocusing, she thinks about her workout. It should be easy to not eat too much today, as she has booked a spinning class right after work and is meeting friends for drinks after. The person she is dating agrees that she looks best about five pounds thinner and tries to help her in her weight loss efforts. Sarah has been working as a clerk in a law office for six years now. She wants to go to law school. She needs to take the Law School Admission Test to apply. She is supposed to be studying. If she were being honest with herself, she would admit that she hasn't even thought about it in months. Lately, Sarah's nights end after five drinks and then bingeing and purging when she gets home because she is both starving and afraid she'll gain weight. Lost in her disorder, she is disconnected from her physiological and emotional self. Successfully avoiding any feelings she has about her career, her relationship, her past, or her future, each night she goes to bed, checking to be sure she can feel her hip bones, and lies there, promising she'll do better tomorrow.

Also 27, Mattie has been recovered from an ED for five years now. She has been preparing for her first big presentation at work. She and her partner have been going over her presentation for days. She has been carefully balancing her self-care and this big project. When the weather is fair, she walks to and from work and—quite literally—stops to smell the flowers. She has an informal hobby she calls "beauty hunting" (an embodiment practice) that she learned from a blogger online. Throughout the day she stops, presses her feet into the ground, takes a deep breath, and looks around for something beautiful. Mattie says this practice has helped her see what beauty really is—a little girl with an ice cream cone, an unlikely flower breaking free of pavement, or the eyes of a couple walking down the street as they share a gaze. She does not love cooking, loves to eat, and can tell you about all of the healthiest and yummiest places to eat in the city. She loves yoga and running— one for the contemplative practice and the other for the companionship of her fellow runners. She feels her feelings and sometimes needs the support of her friends to sort things out. Ultimately, Mattie makes decisions from her belly, her heart, and her mind, saying that her embodied guidance system never steers her wrong. Her day ends with chamomile tea and her gratitude journal (an embodiment practice). She writes down a few things she found that were beautiful and a few things for which she is grateful.

Sarah and Mattie illustrate two versions of embodiment. Sarah avoids and judges, failing to experience the world from and through her embodiment. Mattie embraces and appreciates her moment-by-moment experiences through a sensing, feeling, and embodied approach to her life. As shown by Sarah and Mattie, the degree to which we are embodied and the nature of embodiment can be deeply related to the manifestation of ED symptoms.

With people like Sarah and Mattie in mind, this text focuses on the three primary EDs, AN, BN, and BED (American Psychiatric Association, 2013), are often identified by several key features associated with four behavioral domains: (a) eating (i.e., restriction or bingeing of food), (b) the presence or absence of compensatory behaviors related to eating, (c) pursuit of thinness, and (d) the role of shape and weight in the evaluation of self. AN is characterized by a fear of gaining weight, a distorted sense of body size and shape, an exaggerated sense of the importance of size and shape in the assessment of self-worth, and efforts to lose weight, including food restriction, exercise, and in some cases purging and other behaviors compensate for the ingestion of food. BN involves a pattern of binge eating and compensatory behaviors (e.g., self-induced vomiting, excessive exercise, and laxatives) that is believed to relate to attempts at self-regulation. Further, BN involves an exaggerated valuing of size and shape in self-evaluation. BED is characterized by episodes of binge eating, which may be related to attempts at emotion regulation, without compensatory behaviors or an exaggerated sense of size and shape in self-evaluation. (Chapter 3 provides a more comprehensive diagnostic review.)

Although the characteristic features help detail the behaviors associated with each diagnosis, they do little to help us understand the experience of those struggling with these disorders, or the pathway from illness to well-being. The characteristic features allude to what is missing in the lives of those who have dedicating much of their thinking, feeling, and being to monitoring and managing their bodies. Still, without a discussion of what is missing and what is lost, recovery can seem deceptively simple. I have worked with parents truly dismayed by their child's behavior, asking, "Why doesn't my child just stop?" And there lies the question. In my years of research and work as a psychologist, I have come to believe that the promise of recovery must offer more than the reprieve experienced from the symptoms. I once heard it described this way: Having an eating disorder is hell, but it's a hell I know and a hell I can control.

For those lost in disordered eating, a life without symptoms is perceived as unmanageable and terrifying. They fear the loss of any sense of agency, control, or self-determination. Ironically, it is disordered eating that is unmanageable, that takes away a sense of agency, control, and self-determination, and that is truly terrifying given mortality rates and complications. Despite these known outcomes for those who are lost in the disorder, to just stop means to face the fear of losing the only sense of embodiment they know, no matter how self-destructive. As described by Ayelet in *In and Out of Anorexia* (Ronen & Ayelet, 1988),

I was suffering, but I resisted help. I knew I was in a bad state, but I was angry and resentful. I couldn't understand why people were interfering with what was going on between me and myself. It was not as if I were harming my environment. So why was it other people's business if I harmed myself? Didn't I have the freedom to make decisions about my own life? (p. 71).

Marissa Larocca, in her memoir *Starving: In Search of Me* (2018), listed the 20 reasons she starved herself. Entrenched in her symptoms, Marissa felt as if her ED met her psychological, emotional, relational, and existential needs. Each reason listed began with "I wanted": she wanted and needed relief from and expression of her emotions, validation from and connection to others, acceptance of her physiological experience, self-regulation, and a sense of agency and purpose—not one of them food specific and all speaking directly to embodiment and her role in the world. For Marissa, to get better meant more than a meal plan, regulated exercise, avoidance of a binge or a purge, or a cognitive reframe. It meant finding new ways to manage her long list of self-described needs that spanned across all areas of her embodiment. To fully recover, she would need to learn key aspects of positive embodiment.

Gabor Maté (2010) and Tara Brach (2017) described similar phenomena in which this addictive, self-perpetuating cycle is personified by a hungry ghost. A hungry ghost is an aberration with a thin, spindly neck and bloated belly, driven by emotional needs and powerful desires. It tries to fill itself with all of the things that will never satisfy. It is not the desires that torture the ghost but the empty ways it tries to fill the desires that lead to suffering. You can see the metaphor of the hungry ghost in the stories and memoirs of those who have EDs. The ED symptoms leave those who struggle in an empty, self-perpetuating cycle:

You knew it was a mistake to eat the toast, says the voice in my head. Now that toast is rotting in there. And the thought of my full, hard, bloated stomach full of rotting food makes me shake, until I have to run to the bathroom and vomit again. But the high of purging boosts me, and the dreamy haze of restriction wafts me along. I crawl back beneath the covers, feeling pure and holy. No worries now. Nothing. Nothing at all. (Dunkle & Dunkle, 2016, p. 11)

Brach (2017) wrote that what is practiced is strengthened. Those who struggle see their bodies as challenges, as entities to control or suppress or, worse, as enemies (Brach, 2017; Cook-Cottone, 2015b). As they practice this way of being, it is strengthened. To recover, clients must begin to live in and from their bodies, experience their bodies as resources, and see a meaningful pathway forward (Brach, 2017; Cook-Cottone, 2015b). The shift from disorder to positive embodiment is substantial and integrates not only how clients experience their body but also how they experience their world. As they come to understand their body as an integrated aspect of self and not an object to fill or control, clients also come to realize that the world is not something to be consumed or controlled. It is the place in which they are embodied, something they coconstruct. As they grow into their being, so too their world expands. As my daughter Chloe says, "We do not need to consume or control the world to be part of it." As embodied entities, we are our bodies, and our bodies are intimately connected with the world around us.

Embodiment reflects a developing, evolving experience of self that unfolds within the context of attunement with internal needs, a personal sense of purpose and meaning, and the external experience of self in the world (Cook-Cottone, 2015b). This text explores embodiment in many forms. The first part of this book describes the evolution of the understanding of embodiment, through the lens of the practical, philosophical, and ultimately, the psychological. Specific to EDs, Part I reviews recent models of embodiment and the embodied-self model. Using this model, it explicates the diagnostic and clinical experience of disordered embodiment as it manifests in eating and body struggles. Next, disordered eating is viewed through the lens of the embodied self, setting the stage for consideration of the body as a resource in recovery and as a source for finding purpose and meaning in life.

Building on history and best practices, Part II lays out the clinical path to positive embodiment. To safely integrate an embodied approach to treatment, it is critical that we fully understand how clients got to where they are and to help them move forward. Embodied approaches are seen not as a replacement for state-of-the-art clinical practice regarding EDs but as adjunctive tools to enhance the pathway to a fulfilling and purpose-driven recovery that is about more than the absence of symptoms.

The Embodied Approach to Treating Eating Disorders (EAT-ED) framework has two axes integrating practices that serve both the present moment and forward momentum. These axes reflect both the *being* of embodiment and the *existential movement* of embodiment. Embodiment is not still—it moves, works, and engages. I have heard this phrase many times: We are not human *doings*; we are human *beings*. I argue that we are both. The embodiment approach holds that the two-winged bird of recovery has both present-moment practices and a forward momentum in time (Cook-Cottone, 2015b; Cook-Cottone & Boys, 2019), which become actionable through the four pillars of embodied practice: (a) mindful self-care and (b) being-with and working-with what is present in the current moment, and forward momentum from (c) honoring effort and struggle (i.e., self-compassion) and (d) cultivating a mission and purpose in life (see Figure I.1).

When recovery gets difficult, it is not a sense of grit that gets us through but a sense of personal worth and knowing where we are headed and why (Cook-Cottone & Guyker, 2018). This forward momentum gives us a rudder, a structure for our efforts, dreams, and work. It is also an ability to hold compassion for our failures, setbacks, and the effort we applied (Cook-Cottone & Guyker, 2018). These are tools for the challenges that are inherent in having a sense of mission, goals, and dreams. Momentum gives the ability to persist in recovery, supported by having present-moment skills for being-with and working-with the overwhelm that presents, and self-care practices that add structure to the day. Scheduled pleasant events create a direction and predictability.

In Part II, the Embodied Approach to Treating Eating Disorders (EAT-ED) begins with active mindful self-care practices and cultivating

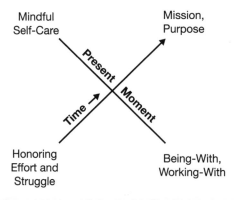

Figure I.1. Axes of the Embodiment Approach

mission and purpose. The text then focuses on each aspect of embodiment. Countering objectification and externalization, this process begins from the inside out. The primary work begins with experiencing sensations, the sensational components of emotions, and the embodied practice of self-regulating. Part II also includes physical and mental practices of embodiment that serve both recovery and relapse prevention and have shown efficacy in prevention and treatment interventions, such as yoga, mindful meditations, relaxation, gratitude practices, and body appreciation. Embodiment through mindful and intuitive eating is addressed within the context of treatment and recovery. Next, the process moves from the personal practices to the interpersonal as embodiment is explored within the context of relationships. The capacity for positive embodiment grows as clients continue to build trust in their own body, increase embodiment skills and tolerances, and begin to live in and from the body as a source of wisdom, enjoyment, and being.

PART I

Positive Embodiment

A New Understanding of Eating Disorders

———————

CHAPTER 1

Psychological Models of Embodiment

The body is our general medium for having a world.

—Maurice Merleau-Ponty

Embodiment reflects a developing, evolving experience of self. It is an unfolding within the context of attunement to internal needs. Embodiment thrives within the context a personal sense of purpose and meaning and the self-determined and attuned external experience of self as we interact with the world (Cook-Cottone, 2015b). In essence, it is the difference between having a body and being embodied. When embodied, we are living in and from the body. I see it when I teach yoga: There are those who move from their bodies, sensing their bodies in space and in relationship—the postures are an expression of self rather than an idea or form they are pursuing. There are others who frenetically move through poses, trying to burn calories, presenting postures for approval, lost in pursuit of handstands and the perfect triangle pose. And there are others who are in a heated battle of self-hatred as they spend the yoga session judging their bodies from posture to posture, afraid, somehow, that they don't belong.

You can see differences in embodiment everywhere. It is the difference between the pure, embodied joy of an ice cream cone and the overwhelm of a self-loathing-filled dieting transgression representing a loss of control over the desires of the body. It lies in the difference between a spontaneous run, feeling the wind on your skin and heart beating, and the run that serves as an obligatory exercise, a punishment for that extra glass of wine or the chocolate-covered strawberries. There is the embodied, deep-belly breath to recenter that is in stark contrast to the objectifying pause to stop and make sure the hip bones are protruding enough to feel okay. There is being in and from the body as a home versus having a body, judging the body, fighting the body, and leaving the body.

This book is about helping clients work toward the possibility of experiencing the body as a home and as a resource. It is about defining embodiment and exploring the practices that can facilitate it. In yoga it is often said that the way out is *through*. It is a reminder that waves of difficult sensations, emotions, and thoughts move through us every day. It is our work to anchor ourselves in our bodies and breathe through the waves, being-with and working-with it all. I think it is even more accurate to say that the way out is *in* (Cook-Cottone, 2016). That is, to effectively move through and learn from the experiences of life, we must live from the very center of ourselves, deep within our own embodiment. In this way, we approach every moment with bare awareness and presence, experiencing it fully. Thich Nhat Hanh (2007, p. 15) wrote, "When you touch a flower, you can touch it with your fingers, but better yet, you can touch it mindfully with your full awareness." It is from this mindfully embodied place that we grow. There are some for whom embodiment is second nature. However, for many embodiment isn't a given but an active choice—it is hard work and well worth the effort.

As a young mother, I became very aware of this choice. I was raised in a military family. My father was in the navy, and we moved often for his career. From town to town and school to school we moved, and I made and lost friends. Back then, there was no social media—unless you had the support, resources, and will to have a pen pal after a move, your friends were long gone. There was a lot of good in our lives growing up, but still, it was difficult. At a certain point, I am not sure when, I began to keep a little distance from my own feelings and from friends. I made connections as superficially as I could to protect myself from the unavoidable heartache of our eventual and certain separation. None of this was conscious or intentional—it was how I coped.

Years later, one Saturday morning I was lazily and happily lying in bed with my two daughters while my husband went running. We were quietly talking—I don't recall the topic. I gazed into their bright eyes and saw their hope that we might do something fun that day. I could smell their baby and toddler hair and feel their soft skin as we cuddled. Suddenly, I became very overwhelmed by the experience of loving them. I began to think of my inability to handle the experience of possibly losing them—what if they were in an accident, or hurt or killed at school? My heart began to beat loudly and rapidly. Suddenly, I wanted out of the experience! I wanted to get out of bed, maybe clear my mind, make some pancakes, put on the radio. I wanted anything but the feeling of overwhelm I was experiencing at that moment.

What did I do? I chose to stay, to turn in, lean in and embody all that was there to feel, know, and experience. I don't think the girls knew the gravity of that moment for me (or for them). Tears ran down my cheeks as I felt my love for them, completely, along with the terror of loving anyone that much. I breathed in and out and felt my heartbeat. I cuddled them in toward me even more, smelled their hair and vulnerable soft skin, and loved them. There was no answer or true escape in the kitchen, in pancakes, or in the words or songs that might have come from the radio if I had abandoned the moment. I found the way out of overwhelm by digging directly into the moment and the sensations, emotions, and cognitions of it all, saying softly to myself, *Everything I need is right here, within me.* When I think back to the moment, I believe it was a key defining moment of my life.

THE DISEMBODIED: HUNGRY GHOSTS

To turn toward embodiment is a powerful practice. For someone who is at risk for disordered eating or struggling with an eating disorder (ED), this is a radical, perhaps even terrifying notion. Often, these individuals experience an empty sense of self and describe feeling lost and feeling eternally hungry (Chernin, 1985). Like an abandoned neighborhood, the body is disinhabited and targeted as a trouble spot—they leave, because it is too hard to be there. It is a place where bad things can happen. They build a fence or wall around this troublesome place. Then, from a distance, they view this place with judgment. They sort out how they can control it going forward so it does not threaten the illusion of safety and being okay. Sheila M. Reindl (2001, p. 2) described the experience of Isabelle, who feared that if she stopped her frenetic activity and her bingeing and purging that she would have to face an unbearable emptiness:

ISABELLE: I would never allow myself to be alone. I couldn't be alone, had to be constantly with people or doing things. I never sat down. Myself.

REINDL: *Do you have a sense of why you didn't?*

ISABELLE: I was running

REINDL: *And why were you running?*

ISABELLE: 'Cause I was afraid to deal, or face anything, face myself. I didn't want to face myself.

REINDL: *For fear—?*

ISABELLE: 'Cause I didn't think anything was there. There was nothing worth working for.

For clients with ED there is a driving force to the perception of emptiness within that complicates their understanding of self. EDs illustrate the tragedy of the hungry self, first articulated by Kim Chernin (1994), who detailed the struggle of women as they searched to self-identify, longing to know who they truly are and the corresponding epidemic of ED arising in our culture (see also Cook-Cottone, 2015a, 2015b). She theorized that the struggle with consumption had something to do with a struggle with identity, or finding and defining inner experience. Chernin examined how external influences integral to our consumer culture facilitated a shift toward the development of who we are from the outside in, rather than a natural unfolding from our internal experiences outward (Chernin, 1994; Cook-Cottone, 2015b). Even today, we are inundated with messages extolling the simplest algorithm for happiness based on the assumption that the resources we need to survive, be well, and be happy are external. These messages hold that we must consume to feel whole, regulated, and complete (Cook-Cottone, 2015b).

In Buddhist image of the hungry ghost represents the futility of consumption (Kabatznick, 1998). The hungry ghost is forever hungry; nothing it consumes will satisfy. The hungry ghost desires blindly. It is sometimes experienced as a belief or inner voice that says, "This will make you feel better. Buy this fancy thing. Drink this drink. Eat these foods and all will be well" (Cook-Cottone, 2015b, p. 51). This concept can be expanded into current culture: adopt this identity, lose those ten pounds, get these likes and shares on social media, add a few inches to your breasts, train your waist—and you will be happy. As long as you look good on the outside, you must feel good, be good on the inside. The hungry ghost abounds in consumer culture.

What if we thought about EDs this way? EDs are, in their essence, a set of physical acts to negotiate what are perceived as overwhelming internal and external experiences. ED symptoms are often employed in a misguided effort to make everything okay (Cook-Cottone, 2016). More, as an effort to be and feel effective and connected in life, they offer the illusion of embodiment. The persistence of EDs seems to relate to how the symptoms give clients the illusion of being deeply connected to their bodies within the context of the challenging inner experiences they seem to be trying to avoid (e.g., overwhelming feelings, cognitive challenges, and physical sensations; Cook-Cottone, 2016). Further, clients are doing this within the context of an ostensibly invalidating and objectifying external world (Cook-Cottone, 2016; Fredrickson & Roberts, 1997).

Psychologically, those who struggle are working very hard to leave themselves, thereby avoiding the authentic, lived experiences of their bodies, thoughts, and feelings (Cook-Cottone, 2016). Yet, ironically, ED symptoms actively employ clients in an intense, unremitting, cognitive, emotional, and pathological engagement with their bodies (Cook-Cottone, 2016). I assert that these experiences illustrate the truth that humans have an innate need to be embodied. No matter how hard we might try to leave ourselves and our experiences, the truth remains that we are our bodies. As Maurice Merleau-Ponty (2012, p. 4) explained: "I am not in front of my body, I am in my body or rather *I am my body.*" It seems that, no matter how much the world, trauma, culture, or overwhelm triggers a drive for disembodiment, the body-oriented symptoms evidence a longing to stay connected to the body and the impossibility of any form of prolonged, lived disconnection.

I have worked with clients that were initially threatened by treatment because they feared that recovery meant abandoning any sense of embodiment in which they felt a sense of agency and self-determination or, in their words, control. For example, when I met Alex, a 21-year-old woman initially diagnosed with anorexia nervosa (AN) at age 14, she had been to three inpatient treatment centers and explained that she was terrified of getting better. Each day Alex engaged in food restriction, compulsive exercise for weight loss, and ritualistic body checking, assessing her waist, wrists, hips, and collar bones before going to bed each night. All day, every day, her body ached for food and water. It hurt her to sit on chairs that did not have cushions. She experienced headaches and muscle aches. She feared that she would die of sudden cardiac arrest because she had been restricting food for so long. Alex detailed every bit of food she ingested, recorded each mile she ran, and counted each sit-up she completed. Her thoughts and experiences revolved completely around her body, yet in therapy sessions she was unable to identify or recognize basic emotions or to describe the sensations within her body associated with feelings or the feelings and sensations that drove her decision making. She quickly became overwhelmed with the emotional content of sessions and preferred to focus on her thoughts and understanding why she was struggling and who might be to blame for her struggles. She believed that securing this understanding would be sufficient for recovery. Alex felt safer in her thoughts—in adding, subtracting, measuring, assessing, and judging. Her disordered relationship with her body revealed an attempt to bring logic and reason to her sensing, feeling, remembering, and moving body. In a sense, she was, in the short term, able to bypass her somatic experiences of memories and emotions by trying to intellectualize everything. In this way, Alex was both escaping from and connecting to her own body, creating an illusion of authentic somatic connection through her symptoms (see Figure 1.1).

Over time, Alex processed and understood the circumstances that led to her disorder and helped maintain it. Still, she struggled. Self-perpetuating in their failure to truly meet her needs, Alex's symptoms and her attempts to understand them manifested like the hungry ghost. The more she engaged in either, the less satisfied she was. Metaphorically, the concept of the hungry ghost represents the disembodiment experienced. The hungry ghost keeps seeking what it needs outside of the embodied self in the external world. What is needed, in contrast, is to be with and work with all that is happening within. I often reflect on how recovery from an ED includes many aspects of the archetypal

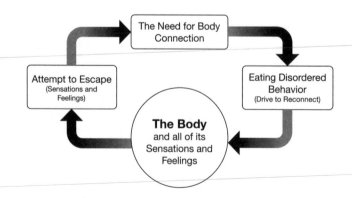

Figure 1.1. The Need for Body Connection

human voyage that has trended across time and traditions, from the travels and enlightenment of the Buddha to the journey of Dorothy, the scarecrow, tin man, and the cowardly lion to the Emerald City: what we seek can be found only by turning inward.

THE PRACTICAL AND PHILOSOPHICAL ROOTS OF EMBODIMENT

Psychological theories often have their roots in both the practical and the philosophical. To ask what it means to live in and from this human body is to contemplate the exemplar philosophical dialectic, the core logical debate on mind and matter (i.e., the body). This question lives in the minds of philosophers, psychologists, humanitarians, and, sometimes quite implicitly, in all of us every day. Stankovskaya (2014) wrote that fundamental intersection of constructivist, humanistic, and existential attempts to conceptualize the embodied self ultimately lies in their attempts to understand the embodiment of human experience—humanity.

Humanity: Embodiment as a Human Right

As part of my mindfulness and yoga work, I serve as a consultant with the United Nations Foundation (Cook-Cottone & Boys, 2019), which has brought me to an intimate relationship with the concept of human rights and the humanitarian workers who live and protect them. I contend that embodiment is the most basic human right from which all other human rights extend. That is, each of the human rights listed in the Universal Declaration of Human Rights (e.g., rights to live, think, speak, work, rest, and learn; see http://www.un.org/en/universal-declaration-human-rights/) begins with the undeclared assumption that we are born embodied and remain so. As humanitarian workers know well, humans encounter many obstacles to embodiment, including trauma, war, poverty, food scarcity, and gender-based violence, which often push us to the disembodied experiences of dissociation, depersonalization, reaction, addiction, and disorder. It is in these extremes that our loss of embodiment, and perhaps our humanity, can become very clear.

Embodiment, the basic human right, can be threatened by both external and internal forces and is perhaps threatened most profoundly when the external and internal forces merge. As I assessed the outcomes of our intervention (Cook-Cottone & Boys, 2019), I found that the very people working to protect the right to embodiment in others often abandoned their own in the midst of their extremely demanding and often traumatic work. I also found that, when given the tools and practices for connecting to the body as a resource, their access to embodiment and well-being increased.

I ask those I work with to recognize embodiment as a human right, and to recognize that we cannot effectively defend it in others if we do not defend it in ourselves.

The Philosophical Roots of Embodiment

It is in times of societal and personal unrest that ideology and lived-experience collide, and this collision can both end old and begin new ways of thinking. Embodiment lies in the nexus of the practical, psychological, philosophical, and sociopolitical (Cook-Cottone, 2015a, 2015b; Foucault, 1986; Launeanu & Kwee, 2018; Piran, 2019). I find it interesting that in current times we hold the products of the mind (e.g., ideologies) in such high regard as we ignore, discount, and disparage the experiences of the body. Ideologies can inspire humans as well as place us at tremendous risk. While writing this book, I have contemplated the notion that positive embodiment is a pathway to our humanity and can be a powerful antidote to malignant ideologies. For example, within the psychology of EDs, the idealized body and perfectionistic ideals that can drive behaviors in AN offer an illusion of ease and happiness but, when applied to the lived experience, can kill you. But this embodied truth, or interface of a destructive set of ideologies with lived experience, can also serve recovery. Embodied, lived experience can be the undoing of malignant ideals and the birthplace of work toward authentic happiness, meaning, and purpose.

One of the most inspiring philosophical developments related to embodiment came from the horrors of World War II. In 1946 neurologist, psychologist, and existentialist Viktor Frankl detailed his experiences in the Auschwitz concentration camp in his book *Man's Search for Meaning*. He defines love and a sense of meaning and purpose as key to resilience in the face of horror, as well as within the context of a normal life. Frankl distinguishes between thinking and acting, alluding to the embodiment of values above the mere idea of them. His concept of dimensional ontology emphasizes a oneness of being, an anthropological unity and wholeness comprising the somatic (i.e., body), psychic (i.e., mental), and noetic (i.e., spiritual) aspects of self (Stankovskaya, 2014). Frankl (2006) wrote that life questions each of us and that our answers must not come in talk or meditation but in right action. Here, it is through the body that the acts of the heart and mind (e.g., our passions, beliefs, and values) are articulated.

The philosophical study of embodiment evolved throughout the twentieth century. Philosophers began to question the traditional Platonic notion that the body was inferior to the mind (Smith, 2017). In 1945 the existential phenomenologist Maurice Merleau-Ponty rose up as a powerful critic of this philosophical tradition (Reynolds, 2017). Merleau-Ponty (2002) confronts the philosophical "problem of the body" and brings to the forefront the neglected and discounted dimension of experience: the lived body. For him the body occurred as a problem when "I consider my body, which is my point of view upon the world, as one of the objects of that world" (p. 73), pointing to the error of identifying the self as only the thinking part of us and of the transcendent thinking part of us perceiving our body as an object, a thing, and something that is not self. In this conceptualization the thinking aspect of self is not just separate or distinct from the body but superior to it. This way of seeing the self has deep historical roots. Historically, philosophers and theologians have held that embodiment is the consequence of a fall from an originally superior state of pure mental or ethereal existence—many speak of embodiment in terms of subject/entity being coextensive with, captaining, or even imprisoned in a body (Smith, 2017). In this line of conceptualizing the self, humans long to be free of the body and its burdens, limitations, and mortality. This way of regarding the body can also ring true in the conceptual patterns evidenced by clients with EDs.

What if we viewed our body not as something that limits and binds us but as inexorably integrated into who we are? The philosophy of existential phenomenology offers this way of understanding the body as subject and agent with no separation between bodily and intelligent conduct (Moya, 2015). From this perspective, to be embodied transcends the physiological and psychological and rests in the essence of being. The philosopher Justin Smith, in *Embodiment: A History* (2017, p. 1), defines embodiment as "having, being in, or being associated with a body . . . a feature of the existence of many entities, perhaps even of all entities." This materialist point of view contends that the subject/entity—who we think we are—may in fact be identical to or an emergent product of the body. In this way, our awareness and consciousness arise from our whole being, inclusive of our body and our thoughts. Thus, our thoughts are also part of our embodied experience. We are an embodied, integrated, and whole being that lives, senses, perceives, feels, and thinks. When we begin to think *from* body rather than *of* the body, things shift.

Citing the work of Max van Manen (2014), Hillary McBride (2018) holds that embodiment is also viewed as a broader form of knowing. This line of thinking is consistent with developmental theorists such as Jean Piaget, who asserted that the origins of thinking and intelligence are embodied (Piaget & Cook, 1952). Developmentally speaking, it has been long understood that the words and ideas that we know and speak are sourced from our lived experience. An 18-month-old first says the word *ball* not spontaneously but from hour after hour of bouncing, rolling, playing, and the lived experience of the acoustic phonemes of the letters b-a-l-l entering her ears as she sees the sphere move through space and from her hands to those of her parents. Neurologically, perhaps on the hundredth or the thousandth repetition, the connections from her sensory system, her motor systems, her articulatory systems, and her social and linguistic systems integrate—and she says "ball." She knows, from an embodied and experienced knowing, that this is a ball. Van Manen (2014) and McBride (2018) hold that the body remains our way of knowing. It is through our bodies that we can know ourselves, others, and the world. McBride (2018) explained that we know how to safely pour hot water from a kettle as we talk to a friend, as a noncognitive, embodied experience. It is how I know exactly how to press the brake pedal in my car to stop at the stop sign, to draw my foot forward and contract my belly as I move into warrior one in a yoga practice, and to press into the saddle and lift through my core to move my horse to trot. All these acts involve physics, mechanical engineering, and an understanding of energy and matter far beyond what I can articulate—and yet *I know.*

To be positively embodied, therefore, is something that may not be in the forefront of our minds (Cook-Cottone, 2018). Perhaps the embodied character of our experience stays in the subconscious background, unknown to us (Cook-Cottone, 2018). Martin Heidegger (1926) called this "being-in-the-world-normally" (see also Svenaeus, 2013, p. 83), which can be understood by considering the experience of a young child, in a safe, supportive, nourishing environment, spontaneously playing, eating, and interacting with others with and from the body, with embodied expressions of the self through laughter, crying, hugging, and moving, all extemporaneous (Cook-Cottone, 2018). In this way, there is no thinking about the body, judging how it might look or perform. The body is as the being is: here.

PSYCHOLOGICAL THEORIES OF EMBODIMENT AND EDs

In the place between the pragmatic realm of human rights and the philosophical conceptualization of the existential phenomenologists lies the psychology of embodiment. Some would argue that this is an oxymoron, juxtaposing the contradictory notions of psychology (i.e., the study of the mind and behavior) and embodiment (i.e., the realization of being). Having taught the history of psychology for years, I assert that this relatively young field has yet to find its true form. In my view, psychology is ultimately the study of the interface of body and mind, the study of being. I believe that embracing embodiment is critical to the future of effective psychological treatment and prevention as articulated in this text.

That said, embodiment has not been easy to define or operationalize, and it uniquely manifests for each individual. Over the past three decades, an aggregation of research has explored related constructs, including self-objectification (Calogero, Tantleff-Dunn, & Thompson, 2011; Fredrickson & Roberts, 1997; Tylka & Augustus-Horvath, 2011), internal orientation (Daubenmier, 2005; Cook-Cottone, 2015a, 2015b), empowerment (Parsons & Betz, 2001), instrumentality (Impett, Schooler, & Tolman, 2006), mindfulness and yoga (Cook-Cottone, 2015a, 2015b; Mahlo & Tiggemann, 2016), self-regulation and agency (Cook-Cottone, 2016), body appreciation (Avalos, Tylka, & Wood-Barcalow, 2005), physical and mental freedom (Piran & Teall, 2012), and functionality (Piran & Teall, 2012). Generally, it is believed that many of these constructs may be facets or positive correlates of embodiment, or both, with the exception of self-objectification—I include self-objectification here because I believe its emergence as a construct of study in the 1990s helped fuel interest in embodiment, as an antidote, within the field of psychology and ED research (see Impett, Daubenmier, & Hirschman, 2006). Attempts to define embodiment as a psychological and measurable construct have yielded multifaceted theories that integrate the internal and external experiences as self, well as the relational, developmental, and existential aspects of the self. Further, embodiment theories often reference context and cultural influences (Cook-Cottone, 2015b).

In one of the earlier references to embodiment in a psychological context, Emily Impett, Jennifer Daubenmier, and Allegra Hirschman (2006), coming from a feminist perspective and referencing Barbara Fredrickson and Tomi-Ann Roberts's (1997) self-objectification theory, studied a small sample of women engaged in a yoga program, citing embodiment as the key mechanism for change. They defined embodiment relatively narrowly, as "an awareness of a responsiveness to bodily sensations" (p. 41). Referencing Oliver Cameron (2001) on interoception, they emphasized internal awareness of bodily signals as a critical aspect of both self-knowledge and emotional experience. They hypothesized that greater awareness of feelings, sensations, and bodily desires might increase self-confidence, supporting effective decision making and increasing both positive emotions and well-being.

Jessie Menzel and Michael Levine (2007) took an empirical, theoretical, and quantitative approach:

> *Embodiment* refers to an integrated set of connections in which a person experiences her or his body as comfortable, trustworthy, and deserving of respect and care because the person experiences his or her body as a key aspect of—and expresses through her physicality—competence, interpersonal relatedness, power, self-expression, and well-being. (p. 1)

Critically, they defined embodiment as more than *not* disembodiment. Menzel and Levine (2011) contrasted embodiment, an uplifting, empowering, and beneficial state of being, with disembodiment. Within this context, disembodiment is viewed as a state that includes self-objectification and creates risk for disordered eating, self-injury, substance abuse, depression, and risky sexual behavior (Levine & Piran, 2004; Menzel & Levine, 2011). They hold that, as an embodied person, we do not conceptualize our body as a separate, vulnerable object that will be a source of betrayal, making us feel fat, ugly, unde-sirable, or lonely (Menzel, Thompson, & Levine, in press). More, as an embodied person, we do not monitor, measure, or assess our body in terms of its sexual currency or attractiveness to others (Menzel et al., in press).

Citing the work of Salvatore Maddi (1996) and Niva Piran (2002), Menzel and Levine (2011) conceptualized embodiment as a form of vital integration in which we accept and respect our body as an inextricable aspect of being, or existing, in the physical, social, and psychological realms. Their model holds that the combination of instrumentality and expressiveness, present within a harmonious body-self integration, allows the development of interpersonal con-nections, social competencies, and an aggregated sense of efficacy needed to support the embodiment of self and others through a fos-tering of individual and social change (Menzel & Levine, 2011). Our body is a source, a subject, and an expression of our being (Menzel et al., in 2019). As such, our embodied vitality extends to our abil-ity to be instrumental (i.e., full of agency and self-determination) as well as expressive (Menzel & Levine, 2011). Their work extends to defining experiences and activities that encourage embodiment, such as hiking, scuba diving, and yoga (Mahlo & Tiggemann, 2016). Embodying activities are believed to lead to embodiment by offering protection against self-objectification, or an externalized perspec-tive of self (Mahlo & Tiggemann, 2016; Menzel & Levine, 2011).

Taking a quantitative approach, Menzel et al. (in press) developed the Physical Activity Body Experiences Questionnaire to explore their conceptualization of embodiment more narrowly as related to body experiences and physical activity. Their two-study series of 606 female undergraduate students and a smaller test-retest sample supported a 2-factor scale: Mind-Body Connection and Body Acceptance. The questionnaire also effectively predicted body awareness, body respon-siveness, positive body image, body satisfaction, self-objection, and disordered eating (Menzel et al., in press).

Taking a theoretical and clinical approach, Mihaela Launeanu and Janelle Kwee (2018) presented an existential view of the body. They grounded their work in Frankl's (1969) tridimensional anthropological model to describe embodiment and the fundamental existential moti-vations. For them, the body represents the constitutive dimensions of a human being. The human being resides at the center of an existential paradox in which life is experienced through the body, in the body, and with the body. The body can serve as a source of groundedness, sensuality, communication, relatedness, and even a source of meaning. Across each of the dimensions, those with EDs have difficulty experiencing "I am a body" and overcompensate with an excessive focus on "I have a body" (Launeanu & Kwee, 2018, p. 41). Lost in an ED, they experience their body as an object, estranged by their suffering. This estrangement fractures the anthropological somato-psycho-spiritual unity of the human being.

Niva Piran's work can be traced to the paradigm-shifting and controversial Simone de Beauvoir (1908–1986), a philosopher of the feminine body. De Beauvoir emerged as one of leaders of the existentialist movement after World War II and is celebrated for her groundbreaking text *The Second Sex* (1940), in which she details the formative years of female development and the loss of embodiment in adolescence. For de Beauvoir, embodiment is an organic expression of individuality as well as preconscious vehicle through which a person explores her world. She asserts that the body gets away from the female adolescent. Developmentally, perhaps due to social constructs and pressures, there is a shift away from implicit ownership (de Beauvoir, 1940; Piran, 2016). "Oppressed and submerged, she becomes a stranger to herself because she is a stranger to the rest of the world" (de Beauvoir, 1940, p. 379). For the adolescent female, a conflict breaks out between her experience as a lived subject and the social pressure to assume herself as a passive object: "If I can accomplish myself only as *Other*, how will I renounce my *Self*?" (p. 397). Ultimately, embodiment shifts: the body, no longer an expression of who she is, becomes a shared expression of the girl and her culture.

Grounded in Merleau-Ponty (1962), Michel Foucault (1986), and de Beauvoir's (1940) conceptualizations of embodiment, Piran (2016) argued that it was time to move beyond the dominant yet limiting negative body image construct used to understand risk and disorder among girls and women. When a broader understanding of the body (i.e., embodiment) is explored, important lived-in experiences of the body are integrated, such as attunement to inner states of the body, experiential breath, and relationships to social structures (Piran, 2016). Studying embodiment is more relevant to the range of behavioral disruptions that can occur, such as reduced engagement in physical activities, sexual involvement without desire, self-injury, substance use, and other disruptions that may co-occur with disordered eating (Piran, 2016). The study of embodiment includes such constructs as pleasure, comfort, connection, disconnection, and self-mutilation, as well as positive behavioral constructs such as intuitive eating. Embodiment is deeply situated in culture and social structures (Piran, 2016). That is, there is no way to study the experience of the body without also studying culture and power structures (Foucault, 1986; Piran, 2016).

Piran conducted a large-scale mixed-method study of 69 girls and women, conducting 171 qualitative interviews asking about their experiences living in their bodies as they engaged in the world (Piran, 2019). Using a grounded theory approach, a multidimensional core construct emerged that reflects the quality of embodied lives, which she named *experience of embodiment* (EE). This construct ranges from positively embodied, defined as the "positive body connection and comfort, embodied agency and passion, and attuned self-care," to negative embodiment, described as "disrupted body connection and discomfort, restricted agency and passion, and self-neglect or harm" (Piran, 2016, p. 47). A girl's or woman's quality of EE reflects her experiences on each of five dimensions: body connection and comfort, agency and functionality, experience and expression of desire, attuned self-care, and inhabiting the body as a subjective site (see Piran, 2019, p. 108).

In her research, Piran (2019) found developmental trends, with early childhood associated with the most positive EE, adolescence showing a disruption in EE among all participants, and some participants showing a recapturing of positive EE during adulthood. Piran theorized that all the dimensions must be considered concurrently for a deeper understanding of embodied lives. Her theory also suggests an actionable quality to the maintenance of EE: a girl or woman can foster positive EE through engaging in positive behaviors and fostering positive attitudes, for example, positive self-talk, exercising agency, appreciating the functionality of the body, and practicing attuned self-care (Piran, 2019). It is a protective and positive approach to well-being, unlike many approaches to prevent and treat EDs that focus on reducing negative risk factors such as body dissatisfaction (Piran, in 2019). Piran and Teall (2006, 2012) developed the Experience of Embodiment Scale, a 34-item measure created from Piran's qualitative work. An exploratory factor analysis of the scale revealed a 6-factor solution, adding an additional factor reflecting the experience of the body as a site that encumbers social adjustment. Piran (2019) suggests that a broader conceptualization of embodiment may be important. For example, in a study of women, the scale correlated with life satisfaction among women, whereas body esteem did not (Piran, 2017).

Piran and Teall (2012) identified three protective factors: physical freedom, mental freedom, and social power. Physical freedom includes experience the body as a place of safety, care, and respectful ownership; a sense of freedom and feelings of competence in movement; and comfort with physical feelings and desires (Jacobson & Hall, 2018; Piran & Teall, 2012). Reflecting the possible influence of de Beauvoir, the theory emphasizes mental freedom, including freedom of voice, self-determined action, and engagement in activities that have nothing to do with appearance (Jacobson & Hall, 2018; Piran & Teall, 2012). Social power involves freedom from prejudicial treatment and discrimination related to social location, including gender, race, weight, age, and health (Jacobson & Hall, 2018; Piran & Teall, 2012). Social power also addresses context: those with social power experience a social environment that allows for social power and equity not related to appearance, as well as empowering relational connection that offer acceptance, validation, and role modeling (Jacobson & Hall, 2018; Piran & Teall, 2012).

Piran's work creates a bridge from the physiological to the lived and voiced lives of women and their experiences of their bodies. Her team's work amplifies the voices of women as they articulate what it means to be embodied and what forces affect their embodiment. This impressive body of work has produced the developmental model of embodiment (see Piran, 2019).

EMBODIMENT: BRINGING IT ALL TOGETHER

Embodiment as a construct is the subject of substantial philosophical inquiry. When we think about what it means to be human, what it means to *be*, we must also ask what it means to be embodied. Bringing together the work of embodiment philosophers and thinking through the psychological context of preventing and treating EDs (see Figure 1.2), this brings us to the experience of embodiment as nondualistic: there is no mind *and* body—the experiences are one and the same; being, sensing, feeling, knowing, and acting all occur in and from the body.

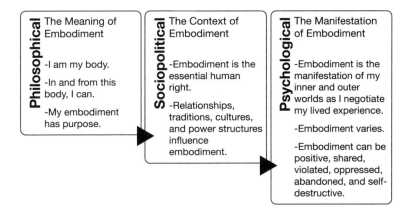

Figure 1.2. The Meaning, Context, and Manifestation of Embodiment

Embodiment occurs in relational, cultural, and sociopolitical context. *Embodiment,* as the essential, most basic human right, should be defended with great intensity in this world and in our own bodies. Fixations on appearance have developed in consumption-oriented and objectifying contexts in which the social value of the human body, and perhaps more specifically the female human body, is limited to how closely its appearance resembles the sociocultural ideal and its utility in reproduction, sexual arousal, and social status (McBride, 2018). Accordingly, clients fight, attempt to control, starve, and abuse the body in service of internalized cultural values they don't stop to question. The battle is both within them and in their world. In terms of gender, race, social class, politics, and social structures, the body is the central battleground. As you read through this book and work with your clients, remember that to study and work from embodiment is to also study context—one does not exist without the other.

The psychology of embodiment, and its utility in the prevention and treatment of disorders, is a relatively new field. Theorists and researchers generally agree that embodiment is the manifestation of our inner and outer worlds as we negotiate our lived experience. Overall, the psychological theories of embodiment share several core features:

- There is no distinction between mind and body (nondualism).
- The body is experienced as a subjective site (we are our body).
- The body is the source of lived experience.
- The body is the home of sensing and sensuality.

- The body is essential in the feeling and experiencing of and response to emotions.
- The personal experience of connection with the body, attunement to the body, and embodiment varies.
- The body can be a source of pain, limitation, and discomfort, as well as a source of sanctuary, pleasure, and resources for coping and decision making.
- It is in and from the body that we can act and have a voice in the world (functionality, agency, and vocation).
- The body is situated in relational, familial, cultural, social, power, and political contexts.
- There is purpose and/or meaning in embodiment.

From this framework, Chapter 2 presents the embodied-self model, which serves as the theoretical framework for the embodied approach to the treatment of EDs. This approach offers the pathway to positive embodiment, our most basic and essential human right.

The Embodied-Self Model

When we contemplate the miracle of embodied life, we begin to partner with our bodies in a kinder way.
—Sharon Salzberg, *Real Love: The Art of Mindful Connection*

This chapter lays out the basic theoretical framework for the embodied-self model and the Embodied Approach to Treating Eating Disorders (EAT-ED). It has evolved from my work as a clinician, researcher, and editor in the fields of eating disorders (EDs), self-regulation, and mindfulness. In my research and clinical practice, I became aware of the profound lack of positive embodiment experienced by those who were struggling. I worked to create a model or construct that could illustrate what I was seeing. To better share the concept with clinicians and researchers in academic journals and books, I adapted my attuned representational model of self (Cook-Cottone, 2006, 2015b) to develop the embodied-self model (see Figure 2.1). The attuned representation of self is embodiment (Allen & Friston, 2018; Lakoff & Johnson, 1999; Miller & Clark, 2018), in which being is understood as nondualistic, as residing in and manifesting from the body as we experience the internal (physiological, emotional, cognitive), external (interpersonal, social, and cultural), and existential dimensions of life. The self is viewed as a dynamic set of experiences and competencies that are embodied, shaped, and formed through practice. Although highly conceptual and the topic of philosophical study (e.g., Khoury et al., 2017; Lakoff & Johnson, 1999; Svenaeus, 2013), embodiment can be developed and experienced through actionable practices (Cook-Cottone, 2015b).

The nature of embodiment, as positive or negative, fully embodied or disembodied, lies in the level of attunement among the inner and outer aspects of self. Positive and full embodiment requires the development of insight, mindfulness, and the ability to utilize internal resources and external supports effectively, negotiate the challenges

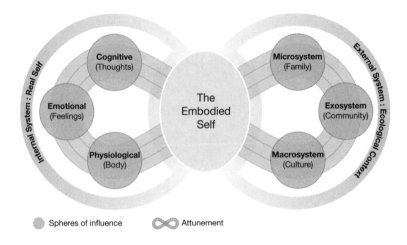

Figure 2.1. Embodied Self Model

and pressures experienced both internally and externally, and attune to the internal and external aspects within the context of our existential journey. Fundamentally, embodied being manifests from and through the body. Emotions are embraced as a felt sense. Cognitions are aligned with the sensing and feeling body. Further, in an attuned experience of self, positive embodiment is maintained by a set of internally focused tools, such as mindful awareness, an ability to listen to and connect with internal experiences of self, and corresponding self-care practices that support physiological health, emotional well-being, and effective cognitive functioning.

Externally, positive embodiment manifests via an attuned balance of engagement with family, friends, community, and culture that is experienced without losing our internal sense of self—without abandoning or harming the connection to our own body, emotions, and thoughts. Sociopolitical, community, and familial issues, such as cultural pressures, sexual orientation, and other self-in-relation experiences, are integrated into the understanding and embodiment of self. Healthy external attunement is maintained by skills that support developing interpersonal boundaries, engaging in nourishing and supportive relationships and social groups, and discerning wellness-promoting from the risk-heightening aspects of community and culture. Fortunately, for many the knowledge and skill base required for attunement and positive embodiment are passed down through family and community, modeled and taught by parents and other adults; for others it is not.

In a culture that idealizes achievement, financial success, and largely unattainable beauty ideals, attunement, well-being, and an embodied sense of self are sometimes lost. In some cases positive embodiment is completely abandoned, and engagement with external aspects of self is guided by an achievement focus and ideals that offer little long-term satiety. Cognitions are distorted and healthy embodiment is betrayed in the belief that all will be okay once some aspect of perfection is manifested. Starvation for some form of integrated embodiment and attunement sets up the risk for EDs. For some the compulsive and disordered involvement with self that accompanies an ED may be a protective reaction to their inability to balance unrealistic and unhealthy pressures while maintaining a semblance of an awareness and nurturance of their own needs (discussed further in Chapter 3).

Figure 2.2 illustrates how each of the three main EDs, anorexia nervosa, bulimia nervosa, and binge eating disorder, as well as eating in the absence of hunger and a lack of response to hunger cues that can be part of other physical and mental illnesses, all reflect a movement away from the experience of positive embodiment. In the center, there is no food restriction or binge eating. Rather, eating is determined by

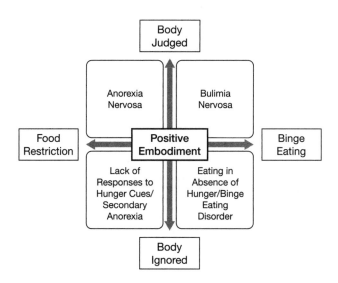

Figure 2.2. Disordered Eating Reflects a Movement
Away From Positive Embodiment

Reprinted from *Body Image*, 14, Catherine P. Cook-Cottone, Incorporating positive body image into the treatment of eating disorders: A model for attunement and mindful self-care, 158–167, 2015, with permission from Elsevier.

the needs and desires of the body, such as with intuitive eating (Tribole & Resch, 2017; see Chapter 12). In the center, the body is not judged or ignored; it is experienced and felt.

Simply ceasing maladaptive or disordered behavioral and cognitive patterns does not promote resilience and recovery; rather, these are achieved by engaging in practices that promote positive embodiment, such as yoga, mindfulness, self-care, and a sense of mission and purpose in life firmly anchored in a felt sense of personal values. These embodied practices are centripetal, pulling the client back to center, such that not only resilience and recovery but also flourishing is within reach. Moreover, those who struggle or are at risk can orient their efforts toward an integrated, embodied path for a full life of experience and contribution.

Consider Lara, a 20-year-old junior in college. She is on scholarship for cross-country and track. Her grade point average in high school was 3.8, and she achieved nearly perfect scores on the SAT. Her mother is the vice president of an accounting firm, and her father is a financial adviser. She is the oldest of three siblings. Her two brothers are still in high school. Both of her parents are marathoners; her father struggles with his left knee but continues to run despite medical advice to do yoga and swim for fitness. Her mother has recently started doing ultra-marathons. In this third-generation family of European immigrants, achievement is highly valued—it is an ethic.

Lara is underweight. She has not had her menstrual cycle in three years, eats only food she can measure and weigh, and logs her food and workouts in a journal. She sometimes feels as if she overeats and compensates by running an extra 10 miles the next day, in addition to her scheduled workouts. She has been having substantial leg aches and knows she is at risk for bone density issues, given her running, low weight, and likely malnutrition. She works hard to ignore any thoughts about that and the pain associated with it. She takes way too much ibuprofen. Lara has not dated since high school. She believes she has no time. She studies and runs and runs and studies. Her friends are her fellow teammates, although they don't talk much. She views herself as an introvert.

Lara wants to be the first medical doctor in the family. The struggle lies in the fact that, given her undiagnosed ED and compulsive exercise, she does not have sufficient time to study. She has tried listening to streamed tutorials on her headphones as she runs, but this just isn't enough. She blames her body for not having the stamina. Her performance in running is also suffering. She has been trying to take the same 10 seconds off of her event time for the past two years. She thinks that if maybe she loses just a few more pounds she can get faster. She thinks she would probably look better too. Something about her feels too big, too much.

Lara has no sense of her appearance as it is seen by others. She is so thin that people immediately assume she has been diagnosed with anorexia nervosa or that she is not well. Her coach has referred her to counseling services on multiple occasions, and the team nutritionist is working with her. Aligned with high levels of denial that the family has practiced for years, Lara's parents are annoyed with the school. They explain the family is genetically underweight, using their disordered physicality as a rationale. This is a busy, successful family that has no time for counseling, feelings, or struggles, and Lara knows this. She can't remember the last time she laughed or cried, although she could easily detail her last 10 runs and the grades she needs to get for the rest of the semester to get her GPA up to a 3.68.

Lara is a good example of a nontextbook presentation of disordered eating. To place her in the model in Figure 2.2, we consider her food restriction, her self-judgment, and her attempts to ignore her body. We look at her compulsive exercise: is it to avoid feelings or to compensate for overeating, or is it a real-life honorable goal to run and run well? She certainly falls on the left side of the food restriction axis in Figure 2.2, but it is a little tricky: she restricts while also losing control at times and compensating with her extra running. However, since her primary modality is food restriction, the left side of the model remains a good fit. Lara's situation is also not quite so clear in terms of the vertical distinction of ignoring and judging her body. She spends time judging herself and her body, yet she also works to ignore it (e.g., her feelings, her injuries). However, her primary effort is to control and judge her body and herself.

Like Lara, life rarely fits neatly into any model. However, models give us a way to think about and talk about what is happening in the lives of our clients. I often sketch the models out for clients, allowing them time and space to consider the larger context and role of their behaviors. This also gives them an opportunity to consider positive embodiment as a possibility, to explore how their efforts and goals do not serve positive embodiment, and to consider that there might be another way of being in and living from their body that might help them achieve their valid and valued goals—for Lara, begin more effective in running and in school. To do this clients need to gain competency in sensing, feeling, and caring for their body, and they need to begin to explore their relational world—all challenging tasks.

EMBODIMENT AS A SOURCE OF INNER STRENGTH AND CONNECTION

How do we get our clients to the possibility of positive embodiment? How do any of us get to the experience of our body as our home and a resource? Is it something that our clients have lost? Is it something that we are all at risk of losing? The latter has been suggested by some psychological theories of embodiment. Do babies begin life feeling completely at home in their bodies? If yes, is it something that gets lost? If no, is it part of development? Is it that throughout our years of development we eventually learn to come home to our bodies? Do we begin in partnership with others within the bellies of our mothers and then through some process of attachment and separation we learn that our body, and not our caregivers' arms, is our home and resource? Moreover, what happens for those at risk for and struggling with ED? At what point did the body become the battleground and why? Like most inquiries into the human condition, the answers are complicated.

The EAT-ED framework for recovery holds that a set of practices, or behaviors, can be learned that create the conditions necessary for healing and well-being. While babies are apparently embodied in a physical, emotional, and cognitive sense, it is well established that the processes of physical and emotion regulation and cognitive development are cultivated within the context of infants and their caregivers and, later, within children's larger environment (see Schore, 2015). Research on EDs has moved past the early theories blaming the mother-child relationship. As we seek to create the conditions necessary for solid prevention and healing through treatment, it is critical to consider the range of interpersonal and intrapersonal factors related to development, healing, and flourishing (Cook-Cottone, 2015a, 2015b).

Gabor Maté (2010) describes three environmental conditions essential to optimal human brain development: nutrition, physical security, and consistent emotional nurturing. With the exception of cases of poverty and neglect, nutrition and shelter needs are addressed within most developed countries (Maté, 2010). What is frequently disrupted is the emotional nurturing within which we feel seen, heard, connected, and as if we belong (Cook-Cottone, 2015b; Maté, 2010; Miller, 2015). It is within the context of emotional nurturing that we can best grow, develop, heal, and internalize the skills needed to self-nurture and regulate (Cook-Cottone, 2015b; Maté, 2010; Miller, 2015). Attachment theorists define this as a series of interactions between infants and caregivers in which infants are seen, heard, and responded to in an attuned and nurturing manner. Over time, infants are able to internalize the more self-regulated functions of adults as they develop into self-regulated children, adolescents, and adults (Siegel, 2015). Daniel Siegel (1999) coined the term *earned attachment* and asserted that, through the context of nurturing, attuned, and responsive relationships, at any age we can develop the qualities of a securely attached person, such as self-agency and emotion regulation (Siegel, 2015). Kim Chernin (1998) posits a model for female adult development in which adults, through attachment relationships and their own work, learn and practice acts of self-care, ultimately soothing the eternal hunger inside and becoming their own nurturer.

I am not suggesting that attachment is the central core of all EDs. Rather, this line of thinking is intended to highlight the power of internalized nurturance and self-care and the importance of developing and recruiting the client's own ability to self-nurture through awareness, self-care, and engagement in a sense of personal value that will be critical to recovery. Through certain practices a client can begin to experience embodiment. This process is actionable. Aristotle is believed to have said, "We are what we repeatedly do." Neuroscientists posit that practice helps us become the architect of our own brains, as first stated in Hebb's law: neurons that fire together wire together (Hebb, 1949; Hanson & Hanson, 2018; Siegel, 2010). Siegel (2010) reminds us that, in the context of validating, lovingly kind, and supportive relationships, we heal and grow: human connections create neural connections. Building on and aligned with the embodied-self model, Part II of this book offers a set of practices that can help clients practice their way toward positive embodiment.

THE PRACTICES FOR THE EMBODIED SELF

According to the embodied-self model, three categories of practices comprise positive embodiment: mindful awareness and presence, mindful self-care, and purpose and mission (Figure 2.3). Mindful awareness and presence are at the center of the model. They can be understood as a bare awareness in the present moment, a seeing and feeling of what is present. This presence occurs free of judgement and with an attitude of loving kindness and curiosity. For loving kindness, I often tell my clients to consider treating themselves as they might be treated by a really kind parent or coach. Curiosity means coming from a place of wonder, to have a wonderful (i.e., wonder-full) experience by bringing a sense of inquiry into their practice. Together, awareness and presence, an attitude of kindness, and a sense of wonder create the essence of positive embodiment. In this way, mindful awareness and presence provide the framework through which we experience each aspect of the self (e.g., body, emotions, thoughts, relationships, community, and culture). Rather than judging or ignoring the body, what we seek is a settling into the body, a sensing of and living though the body (Reindl, 2001).

Mindful self-care is an iterative, two-step process: mindful awareness

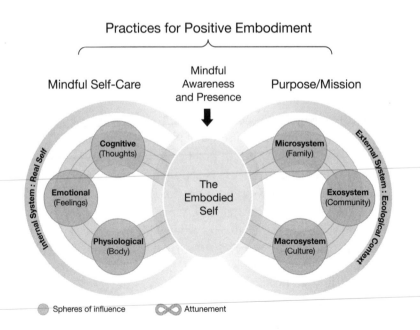

Figure 2.3. Practices for the Embodied Self

(See insert for color.)

and assessment of one's internal needs and external demands, and intentional engagement in specific self-care practices to address needs and demands that serve our well-being and effectiveness (Cook-Cottone, 2015a, 2015b; Cook-Cottone & Guyker, 2018)—that is, *being-with* what is present and *working-with* what you notice. There is so much power in knowing how to be with an experience before working with what is there. Mindful self-care exacts the most influence on our ability to positively embody our internal, physical, emotional, and thoughtful experience of self (Figure 2.3). At the most basic level, mindful self-care includes hydrating, resting, exercising, and eating sufficient amounts of nutritional foods. It also includes integrating a mindful awareness of our thoughts and feelings into daily life, as well as a set of relaxation and self-soothing strategies. It can include subtle changes to our physical environment that support our well-being and effectiveness, such as maintaining a manageable schedule, an organized work space, and a balance between the needs of others and what is important to ourselves. Mindful self-care, as measured by the Mindful Self-Care Scale, is positively associated with body esteem and negatively associated with many aspects of ED behavior (Cook-Cottone & Guyker, 2018).

Aligning with existential theorists (e.g., Frankl, 1969), positive embodiment also includes a sense of meaning, purpose, or both (Figure 2.3). A sense of meaning and purpose in life, in work, or in both is positively associated with body esteem and negatively associated with ED risk (Cook-Cottone & Guyker, 2018). A sense of purpose in life is negatively associated with hopelessness, overweight preoccupation, and body investment, suggesting a potential protective function (García-Alandete, Ros, Salvador, & Rodríguez, 2018).

Figure 2.4 shows how the practices for the embodied approach are integrated, allowing for a dynamic and flexible approach. Within the present moment, practices incorporate structure and predictability while building competency for managing challenges as they arise. On the time axis practices are associated with more formally discerning what we want to do with our life in the long term and how we want to structure goals in the shorter term. This set of embodied practices provides a sense of direction, serving as a rudder. It involves self-compassion, heartfulness, and the ability to honor the previous efforts, setbacks, and struggles, to keep moving forward, and to learn from the past mistakes.

Let's return to Lara. As she enters treatment, reluctant and likely

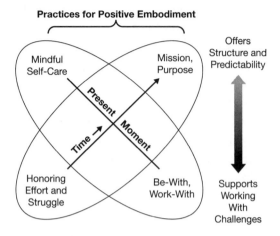

Figure 2.4. Practices for the Embodied Approach

resistant, she may feel as though she has everything to lose. Her current patterns of behavior are experienced as getting her to her goals (e.g., getting her event time down 10 seconds) and her sense of mission (e.g., being the first in her family to go to medical school). She is aligned with distorted family values, as well as family dysfunction, and has no sense of emotion literacy, emotion regulation, distress tolerance, boundary setting, voice, personal power, or internal attunement. Her embodiment is experienced in a self-destructive fashion. She often sees her body as a limitation, or something holding her back. Her solution to that is more running, more studying, and more work.

As detailed in Part II of this text, work with Lara can begin with assessment and establishing a set of mindful self-care practices to address some of her challenges and complaints. Then, aligning with her sense of mission and her goals, she can begin to explore her motivations for her behaviors and, moving through the layers of embodiment, begin to explore and align with her personal goals and need for a more effective and healthier way of being with her body. She can start the work of exploring sensations, feelings, and the being-with and working-with skills of self-regulation. As her competency with the present moment and with her challenges increases, she may be ready to consider a broader range of embodied practices and may begin to see her love of running in a new way. Setbacks and frustrations can become opportunities to learn the heartfulness practices of self-compassion, gratitude, and body appreciation. When she is ready, in partnership with her medical doctor and nutritionist, her therapist can work with instruction in mindful eating that, for some, can lead to intuitive eating practices and learning to trust and respond to internal signals of hunger and fullness.

As Lara grows in these skills and competencies, she begins to see her body as a home and a resource. Like other clients with whom I have worked, she may bring forward earlier traumas that need to be processed. With preparation, she may be ready to work with her relationship with her parents and may be ready to think (or rethink) the role of partnerships, friendships, and community in her life. I love this part of therapy because my clients begin to have an interest in the real stuff of life. They are no longer lost in measuring, weighing, counting, doing, and undoing. They want to know if this is the right person to date, wonder about their major, graduate school, and career goals, ask questions and have thoughts and feelings about politics and their role in the world, and think about social activism and personal power. It is an unfolding into the actual, embodied *now* of life—not an easy thing to face but so beautiful to watch: the gift of seeing someone who had no sense of any of it as they rally the courage to feel and be in it all. This is the hope for Lara. This is the hope of this book.

CHAPTER 3

Disordered Eating as Disordered Embodiment

I seem to myself, as in a dream,
An accidental guest in the dreadful body.

—Anna Akhmatova

I remember the first time I decided that my body was not okay. My first-grade teacher, Mrs. Story, had put together a bit of a show for our class to perform for our parents. We were able to create our own segments. I had an admiration for ballerinas and aspired to grow up to be one. My friend and I pitched a short ballet segment for the class performance, and Mrs. Story agreed it would be a wonderful addition to the show. My mother made me and my friend beautiful tutus with netting and generous satin bands around the waist that tied in the back in big floppy, lustrous bows. I recall the day I tried my tutu on. My mother positioned me in front of the mirror so that I could see how pretty I looked. I was heartbroken. Unlike my naturally thin friend, who looked just like the ballerinas in the pictures and movies, my satin waistband pressed against my belly, which seemed broader than my chest and hips. I did not look like the images I idealized, and I did not look like my friend. Noticing my proud mother, I rallied a smile. At the show we danced, the parents clapped, and the whole time I wished I had a different, better body—I was six years old.

I have spent much of my adult life studying the factors that add up to a six-year-old, in the best ballerina outfit ever, not able to be present in her body exactly as it is. I long to sit down with that six-year-old and tell her how beautiful she is, how it is so fun to watch her practice her dance and create with her friend, and how inspiring it is to see a kid with such a big heart trying something new. A six-year-old should be embodied—dancing and twirling with a big satin bow swirling behind her. She should feel the floor beneath her feet, meet the gaze of her friend, and know the surge of pride in her chest as her parents watch her actualizing her aspirations. What got in the way?

Like embodiment, disordered embodiment is a way of being. It involves attempts at living life, but life as a mind that has a body. The degree to which the body is inhabited can vary from an almost complete dissociation, as if there is no body to be present in, to a sense of being trapped in a body. The nature of how one inhabits the body can also present as neglectful disinterest, obsessive self-hatred, chronic agitation, and extreme effort to control and regulate. In disordered embodiment, the mind, with its goal and aspirations, is held as more valuable, important, and superior than the body, which is viewed as less valuable, a problem, or an obstacle. Disordered embodiment can be tethered to the expectations and demands of media, culturally assigned gender roles, and social ideals. It reduces the body to an object to be controlled, used, and suppressed and is associated with behaviors that hurt, weaken, and even destroy the body itself.

Disordered embodiment is a normative experience as well as something that is associated with high risk and severe disorders, such as eating disorders (EDs) and addiction. It can be an accidental or, perhaps more insidious, a collateral effect of daily microdecisions, such as picking up a phone, clicking on social media, having the second or third glass of wine, or scanning the body for what is too big, too much, and wrong. While some are pushed, exploited, and violated into disembodied lives, others living in privileged or safer circumstances readily give up embodiment, our most basic human right, on a daily basis. Whether due to circumstances outside of our control or our own choices and habits, there is an epidemic of loss of embodied, lived experience.

Yet with this loss of embodied experience, something ironic occurs: life seems simplified. Pathologically, a distorted form of attunement with the inner experience of self and a disordered form of embodiment are achieved (Figure 3.1). Within this context, many of the real pressures of the outside world and relationships are more easily ignored, as are the authentic needs of the physiological, emotional, and cognitive self (Cook-Cottone, 2015a, 2015b). As a result, the body, emotional growth, effective cognitive function, relationships, and genuine and successful functioning within the community are at risk or impaired. The disorder takes over the body and masquerades as meaningful. Attunement is

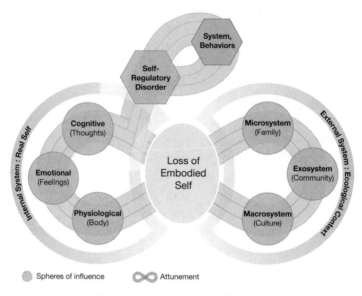

Figure 3.1. Loss of Embodied Self

Reprinted from *Body Image*, 14, Catherine P. Cook-Cottone, Incorporating positive body image into the treatment of eating disorders: A model for attunement and mindful self-care, 158–167, 2015, with permission from Elsevier.

experienced with the disorder, not with life, with a sense of purpose, or with loved ones.

In cases where there is extreme weight loss or clinical-level symptoms, the world begins to respond to the individual who is struggling with ED (Cook-Cottone, 2015b). Communication centers on the symptoms, the lack of effective functioning, and physical risk. I recall in ninth grade missing 45 days of school. My weight was the first thing that others noticed—not my gender, my smile, or my interests. People wondered to if I was sick or anorexic. I was both. I knew they wondered this because some asked me outright. My parents were entangled in doctor visits, their own shame and embarrassment related to the disorder, and trying to get me to eat and go to school. Their child who got straight As for the first eight years of school was struggling. This was not their only worry—the family was in overwhelm: my father was frequently deployed on military missions, and my brother was born with Down syndrome the same year I became clinically ill. I remember thinking I was fine, that they misunderstood, and that I did not need anything—not even food. I recall that at that point I wanted my body and my needs to vanish; short of that, I wanted both to be smaller and smaller until I didn't feel either anymore.

As I think back now, the symptoms were much easier to negotiate than trying to understand what it meant to have a brother with Down syndrome, a father who had to be away often, and to support a mom who was in over her head, all while figuring out algebra, English literature, how to stay in marching band, and run track while on a competitive year-round swim team. I was lost in overwhelm, but to me this so-called disorder made everything so crystal clear. To be successful, I simply needed the numbers on the scale to drop down, lower and lower. I had no sense of an end game or where I was headed. True embodiment was something I sought to escape at all costs.

I recall one morning I was ready to eat my breakfast, a cup of puffed rice with half cup of skim milk. I placed the puffed rice in a bowl and then went to the refrigerator to get the skim milk, but there wasn't any. My mother walked into the room. I was desperate and told her how I needed the skim milk to eat my breakfast. She suggested I try the 2% milk, of which we had plenty. But at that point in my illness I could not emotionally tolerate the thought of ingesting the additional grams of fat. A long argument ensued, which resulted in me in tears, unable to eat breakfast at all and feeling like I could not go to school without eating. My mother refused to get the skim milk. She had my brother with Down syndrome, as well as my three other siblings to help get ready for school. I was too young to drive. I was stuck. This inflexibility and obsession are characteristic of the life experience of someone with anorexia. As embodiment and a central integrating presence of self is lost, there is also an increased tendency to judge rather than experience, to ignore or dissociate rather than remain present, and to either deprive and withhold or overindulge and binge (Cook-Cottone, 2015a, 2015b).

As an aside, my brother, Stephen, is a joy in our lives and perhaps the best thing that ever happened to my family. We did not know that then. We only knew how to aspire to what we thought was perfect—yet another obstacle to embodiment (Cook-Cottone, 2015b).

EATING DISORDERS DEFINED

This text focuses on the three primary EDs: anorexia nervosa (AN), bulimia nervosa (BN), and binge eating disorders (BED; American Psychiatric Association, 2013). Other EDs, such as avoidant/restrictive food intake disorder, pica (repeated ingestion of nonfood substances), and rumination disorders (repeated regurgitation of food that has been swallowed), are beyond the scope of this text due to substantial differences in etiology, manifestation, and treatment (for more on these disorders, see Brownell & Walsh, 2017). Behaviorally, the three primary EDs are traditionally defined as a dysfunction in eating: actively restricting food (AN), bingeing (BN and BED), and purging or compensating for binge eating through intentional vomiting, use of laxatives, or exercise (AN/BN) (American Psychiatric Association, 2013). The three primary EDs also involve distinct experiences of behavior, the body, emotions, and cognitions (see Figure 2.2 in Chapter 2).

Etiological factors for EDs are not completely distinct; in fact, it is more likely that a complex interplay among risk factors is the norm (Culbert, Racine, & Klump, 2015). According to Culbert et al. (2015), transactional processes that underlie the risk for ED and ED symptoms may emerge through interactions of biological, psychological, and sociological influences. For example, biological vulnerabilities may influence reactivity to environmental events as seen in gene-environment correlations, environmental factors may interact with biological vulnerability as in gene-environment interactions, and environment or biological processes may have epigenetic effects, modifying gene expression. Below I summarize the criteria and etiological factors related to the three primary EDs (for a detailed analysis of ED etiology, see Culbert et al., 2015).

Anorexia Nervosa

AN is a complex, multifaceted disorder that affects every aspect of an individual's being. It is traditionally characterized by a drive for thinness and a corresponding fear of gaining weight, within the context of a significantly low body weight, that do not shift in intensity as weight decreases (American Psychiatric Association, 2013; Attia, 2017; Zipfel et al., 2015; see Table 3.1). Individuals diagnosed with AN restrict food and energy intake and engage in other weight loss activities, such as purging food and exercising excessively (Zipfel et al., 2015). Clients with AN judge, assess, and measure their bodies more than experience and feel them. Sensory and interoceptive experiences are often ignored as the evaluative cognitive experiences of self are primary. Exercise and movement are methods for weight loss rather than embodied experiences (Cook-Cottone, 2015a, 2015b).

AN has two subtypes, diagnosed at the time of their assessment: restricting type and binge-eating/purging type (Walsh, 2017). Those diagnosed with restricting type have not engaged in binge eating within three months and pursue thinness with restriction of food intake and exercise (American Psychiatric Association, 2013; Attia, 2017). Those diagnosed with binge-eating/purging type have engaged in binge eating or purging behavior (American Psychiatric Association, 2013; Attia, 2017) and, distinct from restricting type, are more at risk for other impulsive behaviors, such as substance use and suicide (Walsh, 2017).

The pathological pursuit of thinness can be relentless, resulting in a relatively high mortality rate compared to other mental illnesses (American Psychiatric Association, 2013; Walsh, 2017). AN can affect individuals of any age, sex, sexual orientation, race, and ethnicity, with adolescent and adult females at highest risk. Among older adolescents and adults the course can be protracted and relapsing and

Table 3.1: Signs and Symptoms of Anorexia Nervosa

| Eating and Compensatory Behavior | • Restriction of food/energy intake as the overarching approach to food.
• Persistent and relentless behavior that interferes with weight maintenance or gain.
• Excessive exercise and/or movement designed to burn calories.
• Secretly exercising and moving.
• Over time, clients may begin to lack the energy to overexercise.
• Binge eating and purging in binge-eating/purging type (correlates with increased risk for drug abuse and suicidality).
• Refusing certain foods or whole categories of food (eliminates fats or sweets).
• Food rituals such as eating foods in a certain way or order, overchewing food, and reorganizing food on the plate rather than eating it.
• Cooks meals for others and does not eat.
• Making excuses to skip meals, avoid meals, or avoid situations that involve eating.
• Dressing in layers and large clothes for warmth and to hide weight loss. |

Experience of the Body	• Dramatic weight loss.
	• Significantly low body weight (<18.5 kg/m^2).
	• Those with larger bodies can also have AN—watch for weight loss as much as low weight.
	• Feeling larger than actual size (distorted body image).
	• Tendency to judge and evaluate the body rather than engage in sensations, emotions, and bodily experiences.
	• Body dissatisfaction.
	• Body checking and measuring.
	• Difficulty feeling and responding to internal cues.
	• Altered interoceptive awareness and difficulty body mapping interoceptive sensations.
	• Reports constipation, stomach pain, difficulty tolerating the cold, and lethargy.
	• Serious medical complications such as amenorrhea (no menstruation), syncope/fainting, anemia, reduced bone density, and immune system suppression.
	• Other medical conditions: dry skin, hair loss, brittle nails, sleep problems, dental problems, fine hair on the body, muscle weakness, mottled hands, swelling in feet, poor wound healing.
Emotional Symptoms	• Intense fear of gaining weight or becoming fat (can be demonstrated via behavior).
	• Drive to ignore and avoid emotions (emotional avoidance).
	• Tendency toward anxiety, depression, shame, and defectiveness.
	• Difficulty regulating emotions.
	• Broader difficulties experiencing and expressing emotions.
	• Alexithymia (inability to identify and describe emotions in the self).
	• Overall difficulty identifying and communicating emotions.
	• Feels ineffective.
	• A strong need for control.

Cognitive Symptoms	• Lack of recognition (denial) of the seriousness of illness and low weight.
	• Preoccupation and rumination on food, exercise, size, and weight.
	• Tendency to judge and assess the size and shape of the body.
	• Tendency to avoid/ignore somatic sensations and emotions.
	• Overvaluation of body shape/weight.
	• Undue influence of body weight and shape on the evaluation of self.
	• Weight concerns.
	• Rigidity, obsessionality, and perfectionism in thinking.
	• Remaining cognitively intact until more severe malnutrition develops—the cognitive deficits are associated with malnutrition.
	• Neurocognitive deficits and challenges with theory of mind.
	• Difficulty concentrating and paying attention.

Sources: American Psychiatric Association (2013), Cook-Cottone (2015a, 2015b), Culbert et al. (2015), Lock et al. (2015), Walsh (2017), Zipfel, Giel, Bulik, Hay, and Schmidt (2015), and National Eating Disorders Association (2019). What are eating disorders? Anorexia Nervosa. Retrieved July, 2019. https://www.nationaleatingdisorders.org/learn/by-eating-disorder/anorexia.

often correlates with a high levels of disability and mortality (Zipfel et al., 2015).

Often additional AN-specific eating and exercise behaviors are present, such as long periods of fasting or set rules for periods of fasting (e.g., no eating after 6:00 P.M.; Attia, 2017). They may present as exceptionally picky, eating only certain types of foods, or demonstrate slow rates of chewing or sipping of foods. Other restriction-supportive behaviors include compulsively leaving food on their plates, using small plates and utensils, and eating only in isolation. Beyond higher engagement in formal exercise activities (e.g., running, exercise classes), those with AN may engage in ongoing, excessive physical activities in an effort to burn calories, such as shaking their legs, fidgeting, or standing or walking for long periods of time (e.g., intentionally park a car far from a building to add walking time).

AN also manifests in how individuals experience their body. Those with AN maintain a significantly low body weight within the context of what is expected for their age, sex, developmental stage, and physical health (American Psychiatric Association, 2013; Zipfel et al., 2015). They have a sense of feeling larger than they are, a distortion that does not generalize to how they see others. Many individuals with AN engage in excessive weight monitoring and body checking—touching, pinching, and examining their body to check for thinness (Attia, 2017). Medically, sequelae related to starvation in AN can affect every organ system, resulting in changes in vital signs (e.g., blood pressure, heart rate), physical features (e.g., hair loss, fine hair growth on skin), laboratory assessments (e.g., anemia, electrolyte imbalances and disturbance, and indicators associated with the immune system), and physical functions (e.g., sleep, loss of menstrual cycle, and osteoporosis; Attia, 2017; Zipfel et al., 2015).

Emotionally, many of those with AN experience anxiety and fear related to gaining weight or becoming fat (Attia, 2017). In some cases, individuals do not link food restriction to fear of weight gain or fatness (Attia, 2017; Cook-Cottone, 2015a, 2015b). Research, as well as my clinical experience, shows that a subset of clients relate their experience of anxiety to eating, rather than a fear of gaining weight, and reportedly feel less anxiety when they are not eating (Lloyd, Frampton, Verplanken, & Haase, 2017). Accordingly, the fifth edition of the *Diagnostic and Statistical Manual of Mental Disorders* (*DSM-5*) allows for diagnosis with AN for those who deny a fear of gaining weight or being bigger yet otherwise meet AN criteria (American Psychiatric Association, 2013; Attia, 2017)

Research suggests that struggles with emotions may be broader than the anxiety and fear referred to in the diagnostic criteria (Zipfel et al., 2015). Clients often experience generalized depression and anxiety, which may be premorbid as well as related to starvation (Attia, 2017; Zipfel et al., 2015). A systematic review examining the generation and regulation of emotion found that those with AN reported more feelings around defectiveness and shame than did healthy controls; had the poorest awareness and clarity of emotions generated, as well as elevated emotionality, primarily with feelings of disgust and shame; and reported less use of adaptive strategies and greater use of maladaptive strategies for dealing with emotions (Oldershaw, Lavender, Sallis, Stahl, & Schmidt, 2015).

Cognitively, those with AN present a unique set of characteristics. Neurocognitive markers include difficulties shifting between different tasks or task demands, a preference for details over global or bigger-picture processing, and attentional biases (Zipfel et al., 2015). Many individuals with AN refer to themselves as perfectionists in an attempt to rationalize or romanticize their rigidity (Cook-Cottone, 2015b). A body of research suggests that, distinct from those with BN, individuals with AN may have deficits in theory of mind, or the ability to infer the mental states of others, which may play a role in apparent unawareness of illness and illness severity and contribute to interpersonal difficulties (Bora & Köse, 2016). Conversely, individuals with AN think about and are excessively concerned with calories, food nutrients, and concern over the shape and weight of their bodies (Attia, 2017). Cognitions are often rigidly rule governed around the type and amount of foods they can eat. Individuals with AN may obsess and ruminate about food, calories, meal preparation, and their bodies from the time they wake up until they go to sleep at night—obsessionality may be related to starvation and has been documented in studies of starvation without AN. Another cognitive phenomenon is distortion of the perceived experience of the body: those with AN may experience their body as bigger or disturbing in some way (American Psychiatric Association, 2013; Attia, 2017; Cook-Cottone, 2015a, 2015b).

AN can be chronic, lasting more than five years in 7–15% of clients, and has a mortality rate of 5–18%, depending on the study and population (Lock, La Via, & AACAP Community on Quality Issues, 2015). Death is often due to complications related to starvation or suicide (Lock et al., 2015). The prevalence of AN is about 1–2% among females, with an estimated one male case for every 10 female cases (Lock et al., 2015). Limited data on ethnicity and race suggest that the disorder may be less common in those of African origin (Lock et al., 2015).

AN is considered to have a multifaceted etiology influenced by both biological and environmental factors (Attia, 2017). Risk factors for AN include a sizable genetic risk that includes a predisposition to leanness as well as personality traits such as perfectionism, obsessiveness, a tendency to negatively self-evaluate, avoidant personality features, and compliance at extreme levels (Allen & Schmidt, 2017; Culbert et al., 2015; Lock et al., 2015). Negative emotionality and neuroticism (i.e., increased likelihood of moodiness and experiencing unpleasant emotions such as anxiety and anger) are also risk factors for AN (Culbert et al., 2015). Deficits in cognitive flexibility (difficulty shifting between tasks, operations, or mental sets) may be related to starvation during the clinical manifestation of AN (Culbert et al., 2015). Developmental challenges with autonomy, self-efficacy, and intimacy have also been noted in those with AN (Lock et al., 2015).

Specific environmental risk factors include perfectionism and obsessive-compulsive symptoms (Allen & Schmidt, 2017). Impulsivity (i.e., a tendency to act without for thought) and negative urgency (i.e., a tendency to act rashly when distressed) are associated with the binge-eating/purging type (Culbert et al., 2015). Body dissatisfaction and dieting may play a role (Allen & Schmidt, 2017). Participation in activities such as ballet, gymnastic, wrestling, and modeling may increase risk (Lock et al., 2015). Generally, AN is not considered culture bound; cases of AN have been identified across time and in both Western and non-Western regions (Culbert et al., 2015). Nevertheless, increased rates of AN as been associated with cultural idealization of thinness (Culbert et al., 2015). A family culture of dieting may mask initial food-restricting behaviors because they seem normal within the family. Other factors include subtle perinatal complications that can result in brain damage, early feeding difficulties, poor infant attachment, and an altered stress response in the hypothalamic-pituitary-adrenal axis (Allen & Schmidt, 2017). Interactions between perinatal complications and childhood abuse may play a role in AN (Allen & Schmidt, 2017).

As I think through my own background, I check all of the boxes. When I my mother went into labor with me, my father was deployed. She was alone and her water broke. She was afraid to call the doctors and postponed going to the hospital for 24–36 hours, depending on the version of the story. Attachment? My sister was born 11 months and 2 weeks after I was—we are the same age for 2 weeks every year. My mother had to manage two infants on her own as my dad was deployed. My father also had meningitis during this time, coming close to death. Personality traits? The great, great grandchild of Irish, Welch, and German immigrants, I was raised under the frame of hard work and excellence and the avoidance of any stigma or shadow reflected on the family. Perfectionism was an ethic. Obsessive and compulsive tendencies run in the family, with office supplies being a favorite gift. An equal drive for disorder and overcontrol is prevalent across our generations. My heritable factors also include a fair amount of substance abuse and addiction.

My mom was on a diet for as long as I can remember—cabbage soup diets, calorie restriction diets, cottage cheese and tuna, protein diets, all of it. When I was in seventh grade we went on a diet together. My nervous system? I consider it a gift nowadays. However, truth be told, I am sensitive emotionally and physically and work hard to manage stress and take care of my nervous system. If I don't, well-being is more elusive.

Bulimia Nervosa

BN is characterized by recurrent episodes of binge eating combined with extreme compensatory behaviors to prevent the ingested food from affecting weight or shape (Keel, 2017; Slade et al., 2018; Table 3.2). The body is often experienced as something that is difficult to control (Cook-Cottone, 2015a, 2015b). There is a tendency to judge and assess the body rather than experience sensations and emotions (Cook-Cottone, 2015a, 2015b). Exercise and movement are used as compensatory strategies to undo overweight and bingeing or to lose weight (Cook-Cottone, 2015b). The nosological distinction between BN and AN–binge-eating/purging type begins with a primary focus on food restriction as seen in AN. To meet clinical criteria as indicated in the *DSM-5*, the binge-purge episodes must average once per week over three months (American Psychiatric Association, 2013). As in AN, BN is also characterized by the undue influence of weight and shape on the individual's self-evaluation (American Psychiatric Association, 2013). The onset is typically adolescence or early adulthood, beginning with a strict diet, some weight loss, and then food restriction interrupted by period of binges and weight gain (Slade et al., 2018).

Specific behavioral manifestations of BN include binge eating. Bingeing episodes are operationalized as consuming an extremely large amount of food within a limited period of time—up to two days of calories (e.g., 3,600) within a two-hour period (Keel, 2017). During the binge, clients have a sense of loss of control over eating that is experienced as an inability to prevent binge eating, lack of control what or how much is eaten, an inability to stop eating, and a sense that the binge episode is something that is happening to them rather than as a behavioral choice (American Psychiatric Association, 2013; Keel, 2017). For some, there is a planned and more ritualized binge episode absent of loss of control (Keel, 2017).

Table 3.2: Signs and Symptoms of Bulimia Nervosa

Eating Behavior and Compensatory Behavior	• Loss of control bingeing, bingeing, and compensatory behavior to offset effects of the binge (at least once per week). • Emotional eating may be present. • Inability to prevent a binge-eating episode, stop an episode, or control what and how much is eaten during an episode. • Purging (self-induced vomiting, use of diuretics and laxatives) and nonpurging (fasting, excessive/obligatory exercise, omission of insulin in diabetes) behaviors to offset effects of the binge. • Males with BN are more likely to present with overexercise and use steroids. • Disappearance of large amounts of food, empty wrappers, and containers. • Trips to the bathroom after meals, signs of vomiting, boxes for laxatives and diuretics. • Eating alone, not eating around others, fear of eating in public, avoidance of eating around others. • Skipping meals or taking extremely small portions at regular meals. • Stealing or hoarding food. • Drinking excessive amounts of noncaloric liquids. • Withdrawing from usual friends and routines and making time for binge and purge sessions. • Self-injury, substance abuse, and other impulsive risk-taking behaviors among older teens and adults seeking treatment for BN.
Experience of the Body	• May experience cravings, as in addictive disorders. • May have increased reward sensitivity. • Feeling larger than actual size (distorted body image). • Experiencing body is as something to judge, control, and assess. • A tendency to avoid or ignore physical sensations and emotions. • Body dissatisfaction.

	• Feelings/perceptions of fatness. • Unusual swelling of the cheeks or jaw area (salivary glands). • Calluses on the backs of hands or knuckles from inducing vomiting. • Discolored or stained teeth. • Bloating from fluid retention. • Weight fluctuations. • Clients are often within the normal weight range or overweight for age, gender, and height. • Medical complications such as fainting/syncope, impaired immune function, poor wound healing, menstrual irregularities, muscle weakness, thinning and brittle hair and nails, cold-mottled hands and feet, and swelling of feet. • Abnormal laboratory results anemia, low thyroid levels, low hormone levels, low potassium, low blood cell counts, and slow heart rate. • Stomach cramps and nonspecific gastrointestinal complaints, such as being constipated or experiencing acid reflux.
Emotional Symptoms	• Intense fear of gaining weight or becoming fat (can be demonstrated via behavior as well as self-report). • During binge, a feeling of loss of control over eating. • Feelings of loss of control over the body. • Desire to lose weight. • Secrecy, shame, and guilt among adolescents, which can interfere with their social and interpersonal processing. • Increased negative affect and negative urgency. • Mood dysregulation and anxiety—may present as extreme mood swings. • Difficulty with unpleasant emotions such as anger, anxiety, and sadness. • Interoceptive awareness deficits. • Alexithymia (inability to identify and describe emotions in the self). • Broader difficulties experiencing and expressing emotions.

Cognitive Symptoms	<ul><li>Tendency to assess and judge the body as a way of engaging the body.</li><li>Undue influence of body weight and shape on the evaluation of self.</li><li>Overvaluation of body shape and weight.</li><li>A perception that a binge episode is happening to the self, rather than the episode being experienced as a behavioral choice.</li><li>Weight concerns.</li></ul>

Sources: American Psychiatric Association (2013), Cook-Cottone (2015a, 2015b), Culbert et al. (2015), Keel (2017), Levinson et al. (2017), Lock et al. (2015), and National Eating Disorder Assocation (2019). What are eating disorders? Bulimia Nervosa. Retrieved June 10, 2019. https://www.nationaleatingdisorders.org/learn/by-eating-disorder/bulimia.

Compensation for binge eating is done in both purging and non-purging methods. Purging methods forcefully evacuate food and include self-induced vomiting and use of laxatives (Keel, 2017). Non-purging methods work with the body's metabolism to compensate for the binge eating (Keel, 2017), such as fasting and excessive exercise. Use of multiple methods of purging has been associated with comorbidity and suicide risk (Keel, 2017). Individuals diagnosed with BN often report feeling fat, which has both emotional and somatic components (Levinson et al., 2017). Cognitive symptoms include the undue influence of weight and shape on self-evaluation above school performance, friendships, or other aspects of self (American Psychiatric Association, 2013; Keel, 2017; Levinson et al., 2017). Body dissatisfaction may or may not play a role, depending on presence of a discrepancy between current and ideal weight and shape (Keel, 2017). Emotional symptoms include mood dysregulation, anxiety, fear of gaining weight, desires to lose weight, and feelings of loss of control (Keel, 2017; Levinson et al., 2017).

BN is believed to be increasing in urbanized areas and countries experiencing westernization (Lock et al., 2015). Overall estimates suggest that 1–2% of adolescent females and 0.5% of adolescent males meet criteria for BN (Lock et al., 2015). Risk factors of BN are believed to be both genetic and environmental, although the genetics and their integration with environmental risk factors are unknown (Allen & Schmidt, 2017). Genetic risk factors may include a predisposition to obesity and personality traits such as impulsivity, emotion dysregulation, negative affect, negative emotionality, neuroticism, and negative urgency (Allen & Schmidt, 2017; Culbert et al., 2015). Problems with inhibitory control (suppressing, inactivating, or overriding an automatic response) have been associated with binge eating and purging behaviors (Culbert et al., 2015).

Environmental risk factors for BN have found in both case-control and cohort studies. Converging evidence implicates exposure to dieting and other factors that might increase the risk of dieting, such as premorbid and parental obesity, exposure to critical comments from others about weight and shape, and body dissatisfaction (Allen & Schmidt, 2017). Additionally, general risk factors for psychiatric disorders, especially alcohol and substance misuse, adverse childhood events, and family conflict, add independently to risk. Environmental risk factors may interact to predict onset. For example, body dissatisfaction has been found to interact with depressive symptoms and negative weight-related comments from others in the prediction of the AN–binge-purge type and BN in females. Other interesting risk factor interactions include dieting when body dissatisfaction was moderate rather than high. No cases of BN have been detected in the absence of Western influences (i.e., exposure to idealization of thinness; Culbert et al., 2015). Accordingly, BN is considered a culture-bound disorder, with genetic influences contributing to risk (Culbert et al., 2015).

My path was like many. I began with a few years of AN, followed by BN in college—restriction and starvation were not sustainable for me. Some other big shifts included a family move my senior year in high school, big family stressors, romantic heartache, and a whole new set of stressors as a young woman in college. These events were associated with feelings of loss, hurt, and overwhelm (i.e., negative affect)—all feelings that I had no tools to address (i.e., deficient emotion regulation skills). I longed to be like everyone else, socializing with food at college. I was hungry, yet I was terrified of weight gain (i.e., dieting culture and dieting). I was steeped in a culture of thinness, peer fat talk, and diets. It was the late 1980s, and fitness was about thinness, and the empowerment of women was about professional possibilities and sex. Risk for body dissatisfaction was exacerbated by the media culture (see Culbert et al., 2015). Many of the businesswomen in media images were unattainably thin, wearing high heels, shoulder pads, and thin-waisted suits. My friends and I thought the sexualized and objectified images of women presented in *Cosmopolitan* and *Vogue* were our guideposts.

In the midst of complicated romantic relationships, peer relationships, partying (i.e., alcohol misuse), and my own struggle to figure out my life path and reasons for going to college, I was dysregulated and lost and felt very out of control. My eating was, too. I would lose control and then get back into control, compensating, working out, and trying to make it right, swearing to never be in this place again, only to find myself struggling the next day. Weight was a concern, a worry. But now it fell into the background behind my desperate attempts to both escape and control my body. My body moved from being a thing to control and avoid to becoming my official battle ground. When I think back, I am so grateful I survived.

Binge Eating Disorder

In 2013, BED was first included in the *DSM-5*. More research is needed exploring how it relates to the experience of the body, emotions, and cognitions. Its core feature is the occurrence of eating binges (Devlin, 2017; see Table 3.3). As in BN, an eating binge is the consumption of an objectively large amount of food in a discrete period of time along with the sense of feeling out of control (American Psychiatric Association, 2013; Devlin, 2017). A binge episode is associated with eating more rapidly, eating until uncomfortably full, eating in the absence of hunger, and eating alone to avoid embarrassment about the amount of food consumed (Lock et al., 2015). Those with BED experience a loss of control over eating and eat far past the point of fullness (American Psychiatric Association, 2013; Devlin, 2017). After the binge they may feel disgusted, depressed, and very guilty (American Psychiatric Association, 2013; Devlin, 2017; Lock et al., 2015). Distinct from BN, BED does not involve attempts to compensate (American Psychiatric Association, 2013; Devlin, 2017). The *DSM-5* has no diagnostic criteria that require overweight or obesity as part of the diagnosis, nor overconcern with shape or weight (Devlin, 2017). Those with BED experience marked distress over the binge eating (American Psychiatric Association, 2013; Devlin, 2017).

Many believe that BED may be the most common ED. Overall, BED affects 3.5% of adult females and 2% of adult males (Lock et al., 2015). Among adolescents rates are a bit lower, with BED affecting 2.3% of females and 0.8% of males. Risk factors for BED are considered less well established than those for AN and BN (Allen & Schmidt, 2017; Lock

Table 3.3: Signs and Symptoms of Binge Eating Disorder

Eating Behavior and Compensatory Behavior	• Recurrent episodes of binge eating (at least once a week for 3 months). • Inability to prevent a binge-eating episode, stop an episode, or control what and how much is eaten during an episode. • Loss of control over eating. • Eating past the point of fullness. • Eating large amounts of food when not feeling physically hungry. • Emotional eating (sometimes present). • Binge eating within the context of overall chaotic and unregulated eating patterns. • Disruption of normal eating behaviors, skipping meals, eating small portions, and engaging in periods of fasting and repetitive dieting. • Eating alone due to embarrassment about how much is being consumed. • No attempts to compensate for the amount of food eaten. • Dietary restriction and frequent diets. • Evidence of binge eating, such as disappearance of large amounts of food in a short period of time, and wrappers and boxes in the garbage suggesting large amount of food eaten. • Engaging in fad diets, cutting food groups.
Experience of the Body	• Tendency to avoid sensations and emotions as experienced in the body. • Experiencing the body as out of control internally and externally. • May experience cravings as in addictive disorders. • May have increased reward sensitivity. • Caloric intake tends to exceed those of same-weight controls on binge-eating days only. • May experience noticeable fluctuations with weight following periods of bingeing and stricter control. • Often occurs in overweight and obese individuals. • Body dissatisfaction. • Stomach cramps and nonspecific gastrointestinal complaints such as constipation and acid reflux.

Emotional Symptoms	• Marked distress regarding binge eating. • Tendency to avoid or ignore sensations and emotions. • Feelings of disgust, depression, and guilt following binge eating. • May have more depression and other psychopathology (anxiety and substance misuse) than those at same weight without BED. • Negative affect and negative urgency. • Alexithymia (inability to identify and describe emotions in the self) • Broader difficulties experiencing and expressing emotions. • Feelings of low self-esteem.
Cognitive Symptoms	• Clinical samples have shown overconcern with shape and weight, although it is not required for diagnosis. • Adolescents with BED may be limited in their abstract thinking and ability to express themselves. • Overvaluation of body shape/weight. • Extreme concern about shape and weight. • Difficulty concentrating.

Sources: American Psychiatric Association (2013), Cook-Cottone (2015a, 2015b), Devlin (2017), and Lock et al. (2015).

et al., 2015). There is clear support for a genetic component to BED, which includes a predisposition to obesity (Allen & Schmidt, 2017). Individuals with BED, compared to those at the same weight without BED, have higher rates of current and lifetime psychopathology, more depression, and more frequent dieting and weight variability (Devlin, 2017). Impulsivity, negative urgency, and problems with inhibitory control may also be associated with BED (Culbert et al., 2015). Similar to BN, two classes of environmental risks have been identified: dieting, with factors that increase the risk of dieting increasing risk, and general risk factors of psychiatric disorders (Allen & Schmidt, 2017). The same pathways to disorder seem to apply in BN and BED, but there is some evidence that the degree of exposure may be less in BED than in BN (Allen & Schmidt, 2017).

CONCLUSION

What exactly causes EDs? As the saying goes, genes load the gun, but environment pulls the trigger. This metaphor represents an important step in understanding the etiology of EDs, moving us away from older models placing the blame entirely on parenting and, more specifically, mothers. My parents most certainly did not want me to struggle as I did, and my mom was doing her best. This metaphor also helps frame our understanding of the media's role, answering the oft-asked question, "If everyone is exposed to the media and all the cultural pressures, why do only some struggle with EDs?"

But what happens when we think of the body as who we are and not as a gun that can be loaded? The body, inclusive of our genetics, holds all of our potentialities, all of our possible selves. The field of epigenetics posits that it is the interface of environment and genetics that yields our ultimate expression of self. Our own presence, behaviors, and practices are most certainly part of the conditions under which our genetics are expressed, or not—there is no gun per se; there is a creating of our own being. In this way, each of us plays a powerful role in our own genetic expression. More, we have a responsibility to work toward creating an environment and culture that support the healthy genetic expression of those around us. As human beings, we become our own embodiment as a history, a culture, a community, a family, a peer group, and as individuals.

What if my mom lived in a culture of body acceptance and love in which dieting was considered a waste of her energy and time? What if her beauty was valued in her work as an English teacher and her love of the holidays and old movies? What if, back in the day, my mother had support while my father was deployed? What if my immigrant ancestors were accepted into the culture as fellow human beings free of a need to be perfect and achieve simply to be tolerated in their new country? What if beauty ideals were not unattainable and unrealistic; placing pressure on males and females to sculpt, starve, and re-shape their bodies for acceptance? What if I had mental health education in school and learned about anxiety, obsessive compulsive tendencies, and substance use risk? What if I learned emotion regulation skills, mindfulness, and yoga in school, practicing ways to be in and live from my body? Philosophically speaking, what if our bodies were considered *who we are* and *all we may become* instead of a holder of risk, or worse, a weapon of death?

CHAPTER 4

The Body as a Resource

The body always leads us home . . . if we can simply learn to trust
sensation and stay with it long enough for it to reveal appropriate
action, movement, insight, or feeling.

—Pat Ogden

Anita Johnston (2000) describes behaviors associated with eating disorders (EDs) as a much-needed protective mechanism acquired to
help deal with emotional distress, unaccepted feelings or experiences,
or a sense of overwhelm, which happens something like this: You are
standing in an unbearable, pouring rain at the edge of a raging river.
Suddenly, the riverbank gives way and you fall into the raging river.
You are tossed about and fearful that you might drown. You grab hold
a log and hold on for dear life. It works—the log keeps you above water.
You believe it is the log saves you, not your body or your skills. The
storm passes, and you are eventually carried downstream to calm
water. But you have a dilemma: you don't trust your swimming skills or
your endurance to get you to shore—you do not trust your own body.
So there you stay, in the water, holding on to the log. You see your loved
ones at the shore, waving to you, saying: "Come to shore! Let go of the
log and come to shore!" But you can't—the log is cumbersome, too big
to drag to shore. In fact, it is as big an obstacle as the water itself.

Johnston (2000) suggests that the way forward is to honor the log and
the role it played in your life, as well as your reluctance to let it go, all
while you practice swimming, a little at a time, so that one day you can
competently and effectively let go of the log and swim on your own. Over
time you build trust in yourself and trust in your own body and develop
your swimming skills, in order to let the log go. As Johnston (2000) puts it,

Recovery from disordered eating requires honoring rather than
condemning the resistance encountered. It insists upon recognition

that any behavior that slows, stalls or creates obstacles in the pathway to recovery has meaning and purpose that can be valuable, even essential. (p. 20)

In this metaphor, the log is the ED, the holder of the log and the one who will learn to swim is embodied consciousness, and the water is experience. In Johnston's story, she refers to the swimmer as eventually making it to shore. However, consider that in life there is often no "shore," no place where there is complete and reliable security and groundedness. Metaphorically speaking, to recover clients must learn to trust their own body and to develop their competencies (e.g., learning to swim). To completely rely on the calmness of the river, the sunshine in the sky, or some sort of log to rescue them is to relegate access to their own well-being to outside of themselves. There will always be days when the river waters will be low and calm, they will be able to walk on the floor of the river, and life will be easy. There will also be days when it will storm, the waters will rage, and clients can easily lose their footing. Our clients need to learn to swim. Like Pema Chodron (2013) writes, it's not about getting out of the water but about getting competent in the middle of it all—in the middle of this river of life.

FROM OBJECT TO RESOURCE

Over time clients might begin to identify with their ED, saying things like: "I am an anorexic" or "I am a bulimic." I have worked with clients who had no sense of their identity beyond their disorders. In the model of the embodied self, between the internal and external experiences of self lies the possibility of the embodiment of self. However, once the disorder becomes a way of being, a sense of identity, clients experience a misrepresentation of self (Figure 4.1). The ED becomes the experience of self upon which all else is organized. And the disordered self, or the misrepresentation of self, is what the world responds to as well. Within this context, the authentic, real, and embodied self is lost. The constructed and disordered self is experienced as an object (e.g., "I am an anorexic"), not as an authentic representation of the person's experience, needs, and desires. It leads individuals in the person's life to see their loved one through the lens of anorexia, bulimia, or client. Instead

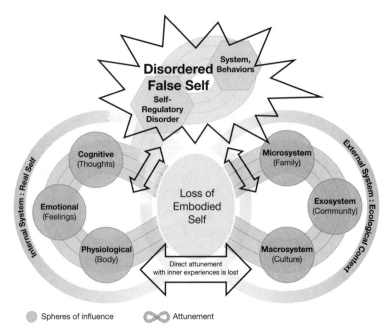

Figure 4.1. Misrepresentation of Self

(See insert for color.)

Adapted from *Mindfulness and Yoga for Self-Regulation: A Primer for Mental Health Professionals*, by C. P. Cook-Cottone, 2015, New York, NY: Springer. Adapted with permission.

of seeing the person, it can be easy to begin to interact with a loved one as a set of things that are wrong, disordered, and problematic. Ultimately, in the depths of the disorder, a person is objectified both on the inside and from the outside, by themselves and by others.

Self-Objectification Theory

I remember when Fredrickson and Roberts (1997) published their article on self-objectification. I was just finishing up my doctoral program, and I wanted to begin my dissertation all over again to include their construct. This was more than physical self-esteem, body dissatisfaction, or an external locus of control. Self-objectification theory holds that the objectifying gaze that values individuals only for their sexualized and idealized appearance can be internalized by women. These women in turn self-objectify, losing a sense of their inherent value and the true beauty of their passions and practices. In self-objectification, people see themselves as valuable only when they are close to the distorted, sexualized, beauty ideal. Media images give the same message over and over: *This is what beautiful is. This is what is valued.* And the shadow message: *You need to look like this to be of value.*

Within the process of internalizing the sociocultural objectification, the body is separated from the person, reduced to the status of an instrument or tool, and simultaneously regarded as if it represents the whole of the person (Fredrickson & Roberts, 1997; Cook-Cottone, 2019a). The girl, boy, man, or woman sees their own body as an object, holding themselves as valuable only if they are deemed outwardly attractive, wanted, or accepted by others. They might restrict food, excessively exercise, or enage in aesthetic medical procedures to look more like societal ideals. True embodiment is abandoned. The empty, self-perpetuating cycle ensues, as the drive to be valued moves the person away from an genuine and responsive relationship with their body and into an ineffective misrepresentation of self, which even if valued can never satisfy the needs of the authentic embodied self to be truly and deeply valued. The hungry ghost prevails, seeking that which will never satisfy. Christine Caldwell (2018) explains:

> When we are addicted, we can never get enough of the thing we crave and our concept of nourishment can contract into a survival-based longing for *more* coupled with a primal experience of *not enough*. When we inhabit our bodies and reclaim self-regulation, we find that nourishment consists of having just enough of the right thing. (p. 4)

When people struggling with an ED and those who interact with them treat the symptoms and the ED as the central focus of their lives, it creates a self-perpetuating cycle in which physical, psychological, and cognitive needs remain unfulfilled and the disordered self is reinforced. Without an intra- and interpersonal experience of attunement, a longing remains. This longing can further perpetuate the disorder. Essential to recovery is shifting intra- and interpersonal attunement away from the disorder and toward the authentic experience of self. This means getting to interoceptive and mindful awareness of sensation, truly sensing with and through the body. It also means becoming aware of, feeling, and working with stress reponses and emotions as they are experienced in and through the body. More, it entails shifting and reframing cognitions in a manner that integrates the experiences of the body and emotions.

Mistrust of the Body

As posited by both philosophers and psychologists, the body can be perceived as other-than-self, an object or a distinct entity. Caldwell (2018) asserts that most addicted people will tell you that they either hate their body, mistrust it, or have very little sense of it. She believes this is because their bodies are a storage space for cast-off pain related to early trauma and abuse or a dumping space of disowned aspects of their lives. Individuals who feel betrayed by, fearful of, or angry with their body often find explanations for why they might experience their body this way (Ogden & Fisher, 2015). Sensorimotor reactions and symptoms can tell the story of the self without using words, such as "I am never safe," or "I am worthless or unlovable" (Ogden, Minton, & Pain 2006, p. 3).

THE BODY AS A RESOURCE

Dictionary.com defines *resource* as a source of supply or a means afforded by one's personal capabilities. It can even refer to one's capability in dealing with a situation or meeting difficulties. Viewed as a resource, the body is not an object but a source of strength, a means afforded by capabilities. When we shift to the body as an expression of being, consciousness is no longer an "I think that" but, rather, becomes an "I can" (Merleau-Ponty, 2012, p. 139).

There is a big difference between *I know* and *I can*. Most of my clients know all there is to know about nutrition, eating, exercise, and the physiology of the body. Some of them have majored in exercise science or have a master's degree in nutrition and thus might even surpass my knowledge in some of these areas. In many cases, understanding has been their main tool for coping. They believe that, if they can understand something, then they can overcome it. I sometimes wish this were true. I think therapy could be more like a podcast or lecture: we would simply fill our clients with knowledge, and they would have insights and then recover. It is well accepted that psychoeducation is an important step in therapy. Understanding a disorder, its causes, and our own personal risk and protective factors can be an essential part of treatment. However, for most it is not sufficient. We can get caught up in therapy, meeting session after session, over-understanding the *whats* and the *whys*, and not digging into the *doing* of recovery, where the work involves getting the client from "I *know* about recovery" to "I *can* recover."

I find the word *can* fascinating. When taken as a noun, a can is a container. Ogden et al. (2006) refer to the container of the body. Dictionary.com defines the verb *can* as to be able to; to have the ability, power, or skill to; to know how to; to have the power or means to; and to have permission to. The word reflects what I hope for my clients: for them to be the container of competency, ability, skills, and power and to be the giver of permissions as they are filled with a sense of agency, purpose, and self-determination. *I can* is a powerful sentence. It involves far more than knowing. To be true it requires lived action and embodiment. It is at the heart of the efficacy of cognitive behavioral therapy, exposure and response prevention, sensorimotor psychotherapy, and the host of embodied practices like meditation and yoga. When clients say "I can recover," they know this because they have lived through a present-moment experience in which they were overwhelmed by feelings and have wanted with all of their being to restrict food or to binge uncontrollably and did not. Rather, they sat with, experienced, felt, and lived through the peak of activation and the passing of the urge. They felt it all and chose the actions that were in the best interest of their long-term health and well-being.

Each moment of competency creates a stronger platform for the next "I can" moment of aptitude. The body is the place where "I can" happens. In essence, embodiment is the source of "I can." When the body has been objectified, the sense of authentic self has been lost. Seeing the body as a resource in daily coping is the first step toward embodiment (see Figure 4.2).

How we care for and treat our body connects directly with how much we are aware of and value its role in our life. Researcher Jessica Alleva (2017) has found a connection between appreciating the functions of the body and relief from negative body image, for example, a client might counteract societal pressures to objectify the body by focusing not on how the body looks but on what it can do. Below I outline all functions of the body that are critical to well-being. It can be

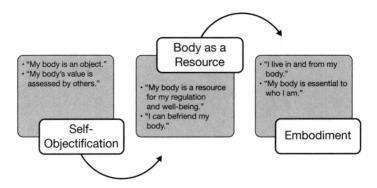

Figure 4.2. The Body as a Resource

helpful to review with clients the sophistication and complexity of the body. I remind them of the systems that make up the body as a practice in value and worth.

The Physical Body

The body comprises biological systems that make the functions of daily life possible:

- Circulatory system moving nutrients and hormones around the body
- Digestive system absorbing food, fueling the body, and removing waste
- Endocrine system secreting hormones to regulate bodily functions
- Immune system defending against bacteria, viruses, and other pathogens
- Lymphatic system helping fight infection and regulate fluids
- Nervous system controlling voluntary action and involuntary processes like breathing
- Muscular system aiding in movement, blood flow, and bodily functions
- Reproductive system allowing us to reproduce
- Skeletal system helping us move, producing blood cells, and storing calcium
- Urinary system eliminating waste
- Integumentary system (i.e., the skin) protecting us, regulating body temperature, and eliminating waste

I often link this to a review of how ED symptoms can affect each of the systems. Many online resources help with this (e.g., Shaw, 2019; National Eating Disorder Association, 2019; Abril, 2014).

The Sensational Body

Physical sensations are another important part of the human experience. I often remind my students in yoga class that tuning in to sensations is the only way to make life sensational. The body is the home of the sensational self, and the source of the five basic sensations: sight (vision), hearing (audition), taste (gustation), smell (olfaction), and touch (somatosensation). These five senses are both a way to engage in and appreciate the world around us and a warning system for when things aren't safe. They help facilitate such functions as mobility and reproduction and play a role in motivations and avoidances. The five basic senses are at the core of mindfulness and yoga, with sensing being the most basic form of awareness.

The Insightful Body (Interoception and Other Senses)

I like to think of insight as that part of us that is able to be aware of, be with, and work with what is going on inside of us. Other, more formal terms describe the awareness and knowing of our internal experiences. For example, interoception is the sense of the internal state of the body and includes information about hunger, satiety, and even what emotions feel like in the body (Jenkinson, Taylor, & Laws, 2018). The body is also the source of information coming from such senses as thermoception (temperature), proprioception (the body in space), nociception (pain reception), mechanoreception (vibration), equilibrioception (balance), and cardiovascular interoception (feeling the heartbeat), among others. I found in private practice that helping clients build interoceptive awareness is one of the greatest challenges and has shifted my therapeutic orientation toward more somatic approaches. Research aligns with my clinical experience: in a meta-analysis of 41 samples comparing people with EDs to controls, Jenkinson et al. (2018) found that large interoceptive deficits occur in a variety of EDs, as well as in those who have been deemed recovered. In their review, they cite references to this problem as early as 1962.

It is theorized that this lack of ability to accurately perceive internal sensations may result in confusion between body signals and emotions, leading to mood instability, impulsivity, recklessness, anger, and self-destructiveness. Jenkinson et al. (2018) suggested that impaired interoception should be considered a transdiagnostic characteristic of EDs. Research also suggests that approaches to develop interoceptive awareness may improve treatment outcomes. For example, a study exploring the relationship between emotion regulation, interoceptive deficits, and treatment outcomes among individuals who had attended an ED treatment program found that positive change in emotion regulation and interoceptive skills during treatment predicted reduced risk of ED at discharge (Preyde, Watson, Remeers, & Stuart, 2016).

The Emotional Body

Emotions play an important role in the etiology and maintenance of eating and ED behaviors (Cook-Cottone, 2015b; Devonport, Nicholls, & Fullerton, 2019; Lavender et al. 2015; Leehr et al. 2015). Emotions help coordinate behavior and physical states during both survival-salient events and pleasurable interaction (Nummenmaa, Glerean, Hari, & Hietanen, 2014). Ralph Adolphs and David Anderson (2019) have documented the broad range of human experiences that occur when we have an emotion. Beyond the subjective state of the emotion and even beyond the cognitive components of affect are embodied aspects of emotion: visceral changes in the body, integral somatosensory experiences and information, and motor movements (e.g., freezing, attacking). Nummenmaa et al. (2014) used a topographical self-report tool to identify how different emotional states are associated with topographically distinct and culturally universal body sensations. In a series of five experiments, they exposed participants to emotional words, stories, movies, or facial expressions and asked them to use a body outline to color bodily regions where they felt increasing or decreasing activity. Their results confirmed the independence of body-based topographies across emotions (see Figure 4.3). Further analysis found that both East Asian and European samples were concordant. The authors theorized that perceptions of the body-based and emotion-triggered changes may play a key role in generating consciously felt emotions.

Despite much evidence to the contrary, for many years emotions were treated both as a problem to be avoided or managed and as if they were solely a problem of the mind or brain. In therapy we'd talk about them,

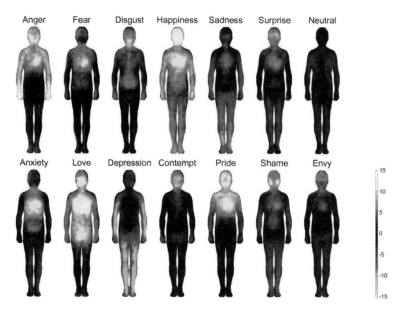

Figure 4.3 Bodily Topography of Emotions Associated With Words
The body maps show regions whose activation increased (warm colors)
or decreased (cool colors) when participants felt basic (upper)
and nonbasic (lower) emotions associated with words.

(See insert for color.)

Reprinted from "Bodily Maps of Emotions," by L. Nummenmaa, E. Glerean, R. Hari, and J. K. Hietanen, 2014, *Proceedings of the National Academy of Sciences of the United States of America*, *111*. Reprinted with permission.

work to manage them, explore triggers and associated cognitions, and then work to regulate them as a cognitive task (Cook-Cottone, 2015b; Ogden & Fisher, 2015). Over the years, embodied approaches, such as breath work, have been integrated into emotion regulation treatment. I remember in grade school learning to count to 10 while breathing to help calm down when angry or frustrated. I remember later my therapist suggesting I go for a walk when feeling triggered to have symptoms. Yet, it wasn't until the groundbreaking work of Marsha Linehan (1993) that embodied approaches became a substantial component of emotion regulation work, as demonstrated best in her modules on emotion regulation and distress tolerance. Another substantial influence in the movement toward embodied approaches to emotion regulation has been the development of the field of trauma interventions (e.g., van der Kolk, 2015; Ogden et al, 2006; Levine, 2008; Miller, 2015; Shapiro, 2017). This includes Richard Miller's (2015) Inegrative Restoration program (iRest), a restful, yoga-based program that is used to increase connection to the body as a source for coping and relaxation and help alleviate trauma sympoms.

The critical shift that includes the important work of Nummenmaa et al. (2014) and their body maps of emotion, and Miller's (2015) work with iRest, is that the sensations of emotions in the body and the experience of emotions in general are part of the body's communication system (Cook-Cottone, 2015b). That is, our emotions can be conceptualized, in part, as messengers (Cook-Cottone, 2015b; Miller, 2015). To focus entirely on managing them or distracting ourselves from them is to lose the message they seek to convey. Emotions are deeply involved in telling us what matters. They are conveyors of the past and the protectors of our emotional well-being. They help take care of us and protect us. If we silence them, it is likely they will manifest some other way. Simply being with emotions and listening to them has a tremendous power and capacity to heal (see Chapter 9).

The Stressed and Traumatized Body

As well illustrated by the title of Bessel van der Kolk's text on treating trauma, *The Body Keeps the Score* (2015), when we work with the body we are also working with clients' histories of stress and trauma well remembered in the body even if not in the conscious mind. EDs are disorders deeply rooted in our clients' relationship with their body. These disorders are uniquely entangled in their ability to nurture, feed, and care for their bodies. To treat an ED is to explore and likely rework how clients relate to their body, and that includes the history stored there. For some struggling with ED behavior, working through trauma history will be critical to successful recovery.

In their review of the literature on psychological trauma, other severe adverse experiences, and EDs, Kathryn Trottier and Danielle MacDonald (2017) found that trauma appears to be common to a significant subgroup of individuals with EDs. A small set of studies in their review found that psychological trauma history can be a negative prognostic indicator of treatment retention and outcomes. Guillaume et al. (2016) studied 192 female clients with anorexia nervosa, bulimia nervosa, and binge eating disorder in an outpatient setting. Overall, they found that childhood abuse was associated with greater severity of the key symptoms of EDs, such as food restriction, shape

Table 4.1: Rates of Reported Abuse Among Those With EDs

Form of Abuse	Percent Reporting Moderate to Severe Abuse		
	AN	BN	BED
Emotional abuse	26%	50%	31%
Physical abuse	8%	20%	4%
Sexual abuse	17%	30%	19%
Emotional neglect	28%	50%	35%
Physical neglect	25%	31%	31%

Source: Guillaume et al. (2016).

and food concerns, and daily functioning. Among those studied, many reported abuse (see Table 4.1).

Stress and trauma are risk factors in the development and maintenance of EDs. It is likely that those already at risk due to known factors such as genetic predisposition, various personality and developmental factors, and environment are especially vulnerable to the effects of stress and trauma. Given the added challenges to their physiological and emotional response systems, for some the aggregate risk added by stress or trauma can lead to ED pathology (Costarelli & Patsai, 2012; Favaro, Tenconi, & Santonastaso, 2010; Hilbert, Vögele, Tuschen-Caffier, & Hartmann, 2011). Stress and trauma can also be viewed positively and within the framework of prevention and recovery in the context of developing resilience. Not an immunity from distress or trauma, resilience is the ability to recuperate, or return to typical functioning quickly (Buckley, Punkanen, & Ogden, 2018). Effective resilience interventions provide practices that help clients capitalize on innate embodied resilience, embody somatic resources, and build deeper capacity (Buckley et al., 2018).

Together, polyvagal theory (Porges, 2018), sensorimotor psychotherapy (Ogden et al., 2006), and somatic experiencing techniques (Levine, 2008) provide a good roadmap for understanding the role of stress and trauma on the nervous system and self-regulation. These interventions help clients develop the level of conscious awareness and capacity to be present with the body's internal states as it responds to stressors, memories, and challenges (Grabbe & Miller-Karas, 2017). Informed by the polyvagal theory, these somatically based interventions uniquely focus on the sensations that underlie emotions, actively acknowledge negative affect and the associated unpleasant physical sensations, and instruct clients on how to intentionally shift toward neutral or pleasant sensations and ultimately alter their emotional state (Grabbe & Miller-Karas, 2018).

The polyvagal theory details the functioning of the autonomic nervous system and its response to stress and trauma (Porges, 2018). Specifically, it emphasizes the roles and interactions of the sympathetic and parasympathetic arms of the autonomic nervous system. The theory explains how the sympathetic, fight-and-flight system and the parasympathetic, rest-and-digest and defensive freeze system work together, allowing for social engagement during feelings of safety and calm, and self-preservation when we believe we are unsafe (fight or flight) or in grave danger (freeze). Stephen Porges (2018) explains that the evolutionary integration of the myelinated cardiac vagal pathways (via the vagus nerve, a.k.a. tenth cranial nerve) with the neural regulation of the face and head gave rise to the mammalian social engagement system. This parasympathetic, rest-and-digest system is also, in essence, a face-heart connection and serves social bonding and human connections (Porges, 2018). As humans interact, these face-heart connections communicate to others through voice (e.g., tone, volume, prosody) and facial expression and receive communications from others through the eyes and ears. The parasympathetic, system also helps slow the heart rate, inhibits the flight-or-fight mechanism of the sympathetic nervous system, and dampens the stress response.

This face-heart connection plays a critical role in embodied action. Neuroception involves a system of detectors sensitive to the intentionality of biological movements in the environment and to the body's ability to respond to these movements (Porges, 2018). In this way, the face-heart system enables us to detect the state of the nervous system in those around us as it detects signals of safety or facial expressions and vocal intonations that reflect agitation or dangers (Porges, 2018). When safety is perceived, the social engagement system is employed and engaged, and mobilization occurs without fear and often serves the drives and interests of the individual within the context of social interactions. When danger is perceived and is instantaneously assessed as potentially overriding an individual's capacity to respond effectively,

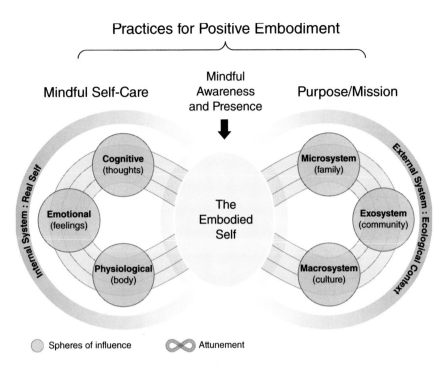

Figure 2.3. Practices for the Embodied Self

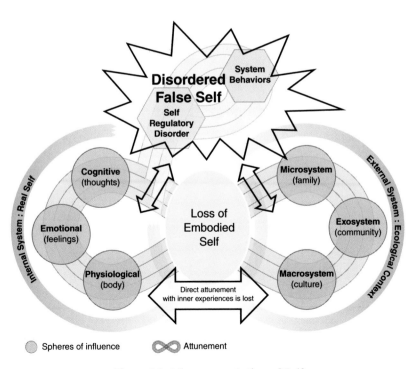

Figure 4.1. Misrepresentation of Self

Adapted from *Mindfulness and Yoga for Self-Regulation: A Primer for Mental Health Professionals,* by C. P. Cook-Cottone, 2015, New York, NY: Springer. Adapted with permission.

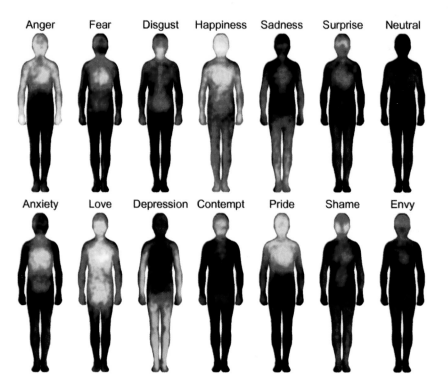

Figure 4.3 Bodily Topography of Emotions Associated With Words
The body maps show regions whose activation increased (warm colors)
or decreased (cool colors) when participants felt basic (upper)
and nonbasic (lower) emotions associated with words.

Reprinted from "Bodily Maps of Emotions," by L. Nummenmaa, E. Glerean, R. Hari, and J. K. Hietanen, 2014, *Proceedings of the National Academy of Sciences of the United States of America*, 111. Reprinted with permission.

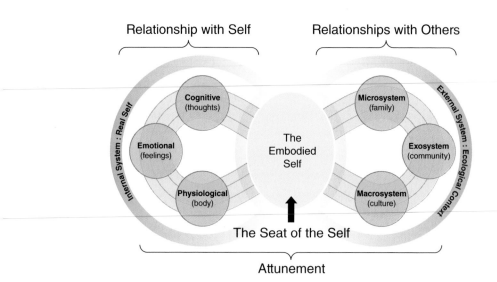

Figure 13.1. Embodied Relationships

the social engagement system is rendered functionless, the more primitive systems take over, and there is mobilization (e.g., fight or flight) or
immobilization (i.e., freeze; Porges, 2018).

An important aspect of the polyvagal theory that is central to the
practices described in Part II of this book is that the body's autonomic
state is viewed as an intervening variable—physiological state is a fundamental part of emotions and mood, biasing detection and evaluation of environmental cues (Porges, 2018). Depending on physical state,
the same environmental cues could be reflexively evaluated as neutral,
positive, or threatening. Further, a change in state can shift access to
different neural pathways and brain structures and direct actions to
either social communications and engagement or defensive behaviors.
In cases of unresolved trauma, high stress, or developmental injury,
neuroception can interfere with the ability to see things as they are
(i.e., misperception; Buckley et al., 2018). Rather than perceiving the
input and accurately predicting and anticipating in a manner that promotes resilience, there can be a shift toward seeing things as dangerous, perhaps even chronically dangerous, becoming stuck in a defense
mode or posture (Buckley et al., 2018).

Depressed heart rate variability is a biomarker of a maladaptive
stress response system. It is associated with emotion dysregulation
and implicated in specific disorders such as irritable bowel syndrome,
fibromyalgia, and mood disorders, and likely EDs as well (Porges, 2018;
Godfrey et al., 2019; Giovinazzo et al., 2019; Schiweck, Piette, Berckmans, Claes, & Vrieze, 2019; Walter, Gathright, Redle, Gunstad, &
Hughes, 2019). Porges (2018) views depressed heart rate variability as
a neurophysiological marker that indicates a withdrawal of the ventral
vagal circuit (i.e., the social engagement system) after a complex autonomic reaction to threat. That is, after feeling threatened, individuals
with depressed heart rate variability have difficulty reconnecting to the
present moment and to others. More, they do not readily return to a
state of autonomic balance between the sympathetic and parasympathetic systems—they are postured, or optimized, to support defense
and not health (Porges, 2018).

The polyvagal theory posits that working with the body to support optimal regulation is key to addressing stress and trauma. Porges
(2018) asserts that three conditions are necessary to create a sense of
safety within the response system of the body. First, safe conditions
should be set so that the autonomic nervous system is not in a defensive

state. Deb Dana (2018) calls this step creating a welcoming environment. Second, to promote health, growth, and restoration, the social engagement system should be activated by helping down-regulate sympathetic activation and help functionally contain the sympathetic and parasympathetic nervous systems within homeostasis (i.e., optimal functional range). This can be promoted via physical exercises such as gounding the feet, sitting bones, and taking three deep breaths with an extended exhale, as well as taking a yoga class or other activities detailed in Part II of this text. Third, cues of safety are needed, such as calming vocalizations and positive and engaging facial expressions and gestures, so that they can be detected by the neuroception system, putting the body at ease (Porges, 2018). This is a reciprocal process involving your behaviors (e.g., gentle eye contact, a soft smile, calming pace and prosody in voice) and your client's behaviors (e.g., working on eye contact and physical presence, putting words to their experience, labelling physical sensations and feeling states). For an easy-to-understand review of the polyvagal theory and its use in therapy, see Dana (2018).

Ultimately, to work with clients who are struggling with an ED means you must work with their body. Porges (2018) and Pat Ogden and Janina Fisher (2015) call the functional range of the body's autonomic state the "window of tolerance" within which our therapeutic work can be effectively conducted. This is the window in which your clients can stay socially engaged, responsive, and work with challenges without going into fight, flight, freeze. And to work with the body in many cases this means you will be working with clients' trauma history, working within their window of tolerance as together you also work to expand that window. Even clients who have not experienced trauma may have few effective skills for being with and managing their emotions and the stress in their lives, skills you can help them build, as addressed in Part II of this book.

CHAPTER 5

The Embodied *Why*

*Live the questions now. Perhaps you will then
gradually, without noticing it, live along some distant
day into the answer.*

—Rainer Maria Rilke

Pursuing the existential *why* means actively seeking a sense of meaning in our lives. I have found that clients often make two strategic errors in approaching this fundamental question. First, rather than living the inquiry of their existential *why*, they focus on such questions as, "Why am I sick?" "What is wrong with me?" "What is wrong with my life?" Second, if they are involved in a search for meaning, they displace meaning to existentially meaningless things like calories, steps, weight, waist circumference, clothing size, and social media likes and affirmations. To provide structure for clients in addressing both of these strategic errors, the embodied approach to treating ED behaviors emphasizes meaning making and purpose, one the four main EAT-ED intervention pillars, along with mindful self-care, honoring effort and struggle, and skills for being-with and working-with. This chapter provides the background for helping clients develop a sense of mission, purpose, and meaning.

THE VALUE OF EXISTENTIAL INSIGHT

There is therapeutic value in helping clients develop a sense of meaning and purpose in their lives. Research indicates that having a global sense of meaning in life promotes well-being, including stress reduction and better coping, and has been proposed as a basic human psychological need (Hadden & Smith, 2019). Furthermore, researchers have found meaning in life to be a unique and consistent predictor of well-being even in the absence of other basic psychological needs, such as autonomy, competence, and relatedness (Hadden & Smith, 2019). As clients work toward a future without an eating disorder (ED), arriving at an understanding of the existential *why* adds a centering rudder for their journey toward recovery.

There is good reason for clients to get caught up in such questions as, "Why do I struggle?" "Why do I have an ED?" "Why is it so hard to stop having symptoms?" Wanting to know why they struggle is a compelling human question. Furthermore, understanding the past and how it informs the current moment, choices, and behaviors can be an important part of getting better. Thus, understanding the past is integrated into many treatment protocols. However, despite being a helpful component of intervention, such understanding is often insufficient for clients with EDs. Like many others struggling with an ED, I once believed that if I could truly understand something, I would have mastery over it. I thought that if I could understand why I had my ED, I could experience a lifetime of recovery. Over the years, this evolved into a bigger question in service of all who struggled with EDs: if I could help others understand why they were struggling, then they could get better and stay better too. Dedicating years to this worthy inquiry, I was sure it was the way to mental health and well-being. Isn't that what Freud promised (Lasswell, 1939)?

After decades of contemplation, private practice, and research, I concluded that some things can never be understood, no matter how hard we try. Those things that can be understood often take time to understand, and even when we do, they are complex, multifaceted, context dependent, and subjective. And probably the most difficult for me to internalize was that understanding a thing, no matter how thorough the insight, is not equal to healing or recovering from a thing, whether it is the untimely death of a loved one or an ED (Salamon, 2019).

Nevertheless, we all love spontaneous insights and aha moments. Often, big insights are accompanied by a shift in the recovery process. Most can agree that it can be helpful to better understand the histories that continue to affect our present emotional experiences. Yet, does development of such insights help clients cultivate the skills, capacities, and contextual sense, meaning, or purpose they need to recover? No. In a moment of overwhelm, their response system shuts down—lost in a depth of insight, without tools or a larger context, they again fall to their symptoms for relief and a sense of agency.

For others, traditional insight into the past doesn't really go any-where—it is something else that the person seeks. To illustrate, Michelle Lelwica (2010) describes her experience this way:

> My parents, though not perfect, were responsible and loving. I didn't experience psychological, physical, or sexual trauma. I was successful at school and had plenty of friends. Still, there was a significant part of me that was hopelessly unsatisfied, a part that felt empty, anxious, insatiable. While I projected this dissatisfaction onto my body (with more than a little help from the media images I uncritically devoured), I sought to escape the internal void through food and the quest for a body that would somehow make me com-plete. (n.p.)

For Michelle, the insight work would be misdirected and could poten-tially foster inappropriate guilt, if it focused solely on her past. Her insight work would be most effectively focused on understanding the influence of media in the development of her self-concept, her experi-ences of hopelessness and anxiety, and the role of her symptoms in her attempts at well-being. Further, her pursuit of the thin ideal was a mis-directed search for a sense of purpose in her life. Beyond the traditional insight work, what Michelle needed was existential insight:

> I became aware of society's injustices towards women and other "others," and I learned to question some of the religious beliefs I had accepted without question. In the process, I started to envi-sion my life as having a purpose larger than the size of my body. I wasn't sure what that purpose was, but I knew, in the idealism of my college youth, that I wanted to help make the world a better place. The sense of emptiness wasn't gone, but through my edu-cation, particularly my study of philosophy, history, literature, and religion, I was beginning to understand that it was something to be explored, rather than avoided. This insight has opened up new possibilities for self-knowledge and self-definition. (n.p.)

ED symptoms are hypothesized to give clients a sense of structure, consistency, and identity (Marco, Cañabate, & Pérez, 2019). The ED can help confirm a sense of identity and give a sense of global mean-ing (Marco et al., 2019). For those in transition during the late teens and early twenties, adoption of an ED identity might distract from the age-typical developmental questions directly related to finding a meaningful life path and sense of personal identity (e.g., What should I do with my life? Should I go to college or trade school? How will I create meaning in my life?). The trouble is that the meaning and short-term reprieve offered via ED symptoms does not translate to medium- or long-term positive outcomes (Marco, Cañabate, Pérez, & Llorca, 2017).

Mia, a client who was at a very low weight, found her sense of purpose and meaning in getting to a lower and lower weight. Each pound of weight lost was a meaningful step toward self-mastery, agency, and self-determination. As per my typical inquiry in cases like this, I asked, "How many pounds do you have left to lose before you are placed in the hospital or become at risk for death? Is it 10 or 15 pounds?" She said that it was about that. I replied, "If this is the case, then you only have 10 or 15 pounds of agency or joy left." We sat with that, and she began to cry. After this pause, I asked, "Could we, perhaps, work toward developing some additional sources of existential agency and joy, so that you might have some more time?" She agreed to do this. She followed through with the work of exploring other ways of finding her path and is doing well today.

As Michelle and Mia demonstrate, the therapeutic landscape is much larger than traditional insight. Accordingly, the embodied approach integrates both traditional insight and existential insight along with honoring of the effort and struggles of the past (see Chapter 2, Figure 2.4). Existential insight is about figuring out a reason for being, which translates readily into a reason to work to get better (Salamon, 2019). Even more, having a sense of meaning in life is an essential part of self-worth, a core psychological construct that is central to clients believing that they are worth the effort it takes for them to fight for their recovery.

SPIRITUALITY:
PURPOSE, MEANING, AND RELIGIOSITY

When exploring the existential *why*, clients will source culture, religion, poetry, music, relationships, and more. For some the answers will be in the pursuit of a talent, skill, or achievement. For others it will be in service to family or others. One of my clients pursued sign language to enhance her skills engaging with clients at work, while another engaged to service work with adolescents at her church. Figuring out the existential why often overlaps with the larger concept of spirituality, as well as related constructs such as religion, meaning, and purpose. It can be helpful to have an understanding of these related terms, as well as the importance of coming from a perspective of secularity as you work through the process with your clients.

Spirituality, purpose, meaning, and religiosity have all been defined in a variety of ways over the years. One way these terms can vary regards secularity and religiosity (Cook-Cottone, Childress, & Harper, 2018). According to Merriam-Webster.com, *secularity* generally means not pertaining to or connecting with religion. Note that *secularity* refers to an absence of religiosity, not an absence of spirituality (Cook-Cottone, Anderson, & Kane, 2019). To be spiritual is to relate to spirit, which can be understood in many ways, including both secular and religious perspectives. According to Merriam-Webster.com, *spirit* can be thought of as a life-giving or animating property; a supernatural being; the immaterial, intelligent, or sentient part of a person; or a quality of mind. Spirituality is often more broadly considered a quest to find answers to the "big" questions, such as the meaning of life and relationships with transcendence (see also Akrawi, Bartrop, Potter, & Touyz, 2015). More specifically, *religion* refers to the worship of or service to the supernatural (e.g., God or gods); commitment or devotion to a religious faith practice, cause, or faith; a personal set or system of beliefs, attitudes, practices, and beliefs; or a cause, a set of beliefs of principle held to with faith (Cook-Cottone et al., 2019). Finding a sense of mission, purpose, or meaning in life is often considered a spiritual journey that can be secular, religious, or both (Cook-Cottone et al., 2019).

There is a growing body of work on spirituality, religion, and ED behavior. In a review of 22 studies, Akrawi et al. (2015) critically examined the literature addressing links among aspects of religiosity, spirituality, ED and related psychopathology, and body image. These studies did not explore the role of meaning in life specifically; rather, they took a broader look at religion and spirituality. Overall, findings were mixed and revealed some important and subtle differences in how religiosity and spirituality are experienced. Of the 15 studies that explored ED, psychopathology, religiosity, and spirituality, 6 reported positive relationships: as religiosity/spirituality increased, so did ED and psychopathology; 4 demonstrated negative relationships: as religiosity/

spirituality increased, ED behaviors and psychopathology decreased; 2 yielded both positive and negative relationships; and 3 revealed no relationship at all. Among studies exploring body image and religiosity/spirituality, 80% reported positive associations with body image, religiosity, and spirituality: as religiosity and spirituality increased, so did positive body image.

When Akrawi et al. (2015) took a closer look at the studies to help them understand the broader findings, they discovered that the quality of religiosity and spirituality mattered. For example, those with strong and internalized religious beliefs along with a secure and satisfying relationship with God had lower levels of ED, psychopathology, and body image concerns. For these protected participants, religious beliefs were often demonstrated through strong religious observance and commitment. Further, their beliefs were body positive, included seeing the body as sacred and as a manifestation of God. The authors also found evidence that for those protected by religiosity and spirituality, their beliefs and practices (e.g., prayer, reading religious materials) may have served as coping strategies. They had a positive relationship with God that was characterized by closeness, warmth, and security, with low levels of anxiety and angst. Conversely, for those had problematic relationships between religiosity, spirituality, and ED behavior and psychopathology, their faith was described as superficial and extrinsic. They reported that they pursued religion or spirituality for social reasons and viewed it as a way of achieving status, acceptance, and security. Further, their relationships with God were described as doubtful and anxious.

Interestingly, this study suggests that religion and spirituality appear to be protective when there is a deep internalization of the experience that comes from within or is embodied through active and dedicated practices. Conversely, when religion and spirituality are pursued for external reasons (e.g., status, social connections), it is associated with higher rates of ED psychopathology and poor body image. The protective influences of religion and spirituality came from within. Although more high-quality research is needed, we might hypothesize that religion and spirituality are protective if they tend to the internal experience of self.

In her essay, Michelle Lelwica (2010) refers to thinness as the holy grail that is pursued with a religious-like fervor by those who are struggling with ED. The thin body is seen is a good body, a measure of success and self-worth. In this way, the pursuit of the thin or ideal body can become a sense of purpose or meaning for some. When serving recovery, a client's mission, purpose, and meaning are personal, are specific to them, and come from within. Like an internalized sense of religion or spirituality, they may be protective.

In each of these ways, meaning can present as a critical aspect of treatment. To illustrate, I once worked with Jared, a young man whose mother and father had always dreamed of having a lawyer in the family. Taking on their dream, he worked hard in high school and college and was accepted into a top law school. During the first year, Jared became depressed. He did not love what he was doing, and he was afraid he did not even like it. He felt guilty for not loving the thing his parents had dreamed for him. As the hours of studying and coursework passed, his fears and anxieties became intermingled with resentment toward his parents and his own inability to embrace this path. He began to struggle to accept and appreciate his body as part of the larger issue he had with loving himself. He was embarrassed to go to the gym and quit eating sufficient amounts of food to maintain a healthy weight. Through our work together, he realized that he really wanted to be a mental health counselor and not a lawyer. He was able to come to terms with what he wanted for himself, tell his parents, and quit law school. This shift was an essential part of his recovery, for then he was able to get back to who he felt he was, to pursue what he wanted for his life, and to establish his own sense of well-being.

Despite the relative scarcity of research on the association between meaning in life and ED psychopathology (Marco et al., 2019), research on meaning in life and health outcomes is compelling. In their systematic review of the research, Czekierda, Banik, Park, and Luszczynska (2017) found small to moderate effects across experimental, longitudinal, and correlational studies indicating a significant relationship between meaning in life and objective indicators of better health and lower mortality. Overall, their meta-analysis suggests that meaning in life is a relevant determinant or correlate in a number of outcomes, with the strongest effects found in self-reported health indicators. This finding was similar across studies where meaning was conceptualized as having a sense of order or purpose in life. Interestingly, meaning in life may be associated with adherence to treatment, health behaviors, and coping with illness via goal formations and attitudes toward self, the world, and others.

Beginning to fill the gap in research in the field of EDs, Marco et al. (2019) built on the previous research that found that meaning in life was inversely associated with ED behaviors and a negative attitude toward food and the presence of body dissociation. They were inspired to do this research by findings among clinical samples without ED diagnosis that meaning in life was negatively associated with a variety of emotional and behavioral symptoms and some mental health outcomes that share a comorbidity or that correlate with EDs: anxiety, depression, hopelessness, emotion dysregulation, high-risk behaviors, drug overdose, aggressive behaviors, risk of suicide, and suicide threats and attempts (e.g., Abeyta, Routledge, Juhl, & Robinson, 2015; Marco, Pérez, & García-Alandete, 2016; Marco, Pérez, Garcia-Alandete, & Moliner, 2017; Park, 2010; Park & Baumeister, 2017; Sinclair, Bryan & Bryan, 2016).

Among those with EDs, overall Marco et al. (2019) found that meaning in life was inversely associated with psychopathology across all ED subtypes: anorexia nervosa, bulimia nervosa, binge eating disorder, and other specified feeding or eating disorders as a group. Further, meaning in life was associated differently with EDs, depending on the type. For participants with the restrictive subtype of anorexia nervosa, meaning in life explained a higher percentage of the variance in ED psychopathology (30%), body satisfaction (47%), and borderline personality disorder symptoms (59%) relative to other participants. For this group, the percentage of variance explained by helplessness was also high (63%), as it was for those with a purging type (63%), binge eating disorder (70%), bulimia nervosa (53%), and other specified feeding or eating disorders (68%). Overall, findings indicate that having a stronger sense of meaning in life may be protective for those with EDs, especially for those with anorexia nervosa. These findings highlight the relevance and importance of addressing meaning in life with ED clients in treatment.

LIVING THE QUESTION OF THE EXISTENTIAL *WHY*

As the emerging body of research suggests, there is potential efficacy in exploring a client's existential *why* as a component of a broader approach to ED prevention and intervention. This may take time and patience. It can mean the possibility of *living with questions* rather than knowing the answers. I have noticed that my clients often find great relief in knowing the facts—they want to know the answers *right now*, to feel a sense of groundedness and security. I believe this is in part why it feels so good for them to measure self-worth with tangibles like pounds, inches, and calories. These are things they can assess, record, and know outright.

I work with my clients on the skill of living the questions. Like the quote from Rainer Maria Rilke that began this chapter, advise clients to "live the questions now." They might, for weeks, months, or years, live such questions as, "Why am I here?" "What might be the meaning in my life?" "What is my purpose?" Often, they have not considered these questions, or when they did it was overwhelming because they did not know the answers. Teaching them how to live the questions, and working with them in developing skills to tolerate the journey of coming to know the answers and themselves, is a powerful path filled with agency, self-determination, and growth.

Going Beyond Traditional Treatment

A Clinical Pathway to Positive Embodiment

———————

Part II addresses the actionable steps to help clients achieve positive embodiment. The process is intended to work with other best-practice modalities as a set of supplemental practices to help your clients build the self that they will grow into as they shed their ED symptoms and identities. The steps in the process are as follows:

1. **Effective treatment** (Chapter 6): Create a foundational treatment strategy that is informed by empirically supported treatments and your work with a specialized treatment team.
2. **Mindful self-care** (Chapter 7): Complete a mindful self-care assessment, set mindful self-care goals, and integrate mindful self-care goals into weekly treatment.
3. **Embodied meaning** (Chapter 8): Begin exploring meaning with your clients and help them develop a mission as related to symptoms and recovery.
4. **Embodied wisdom** (Chapter 9): Work on sensations, emotions, and states of being with your clients while building their physical coping strategies, inner resources, and distress tolerance skills.
5. **Embodied doing** (Chapter 10): Work with clients to engage in activities that practice and develop positive embodiment, such as exercise, yoga, and equestrian therapy.

6. **Embodied mindfulness and heartfulness** (Chapter 11): Help clients build skills in mindfulness, loving kindness, compassion, gratitude, body appreciation, and integrity.
7. **Embodied eating** (Chapter 12): Working with the nutritionist and aligned with medical recommendations, work with your clients to explore mindful and intuitive eating.
8. **Embodied connection** (Chapter 13): Embracing a positive embodiment approach, help your clients explore relationships, with their body as a resource for information, connections, and pleasure.

Each step in the process is supported by a wide range of practice guides and scripts, as well as the The Mindful Self-Care Scale, all available at the end of each chapter that you can use to help you direct your clients' progress.

CHAPTER 6

Effective Treatment

Building on Tradition and Best Practices

If I have seen further, it is by standing on the shoulders of giants.

—Isaac Newton

As we help our clients move toward an embodied understanding of healing and recovery, we should not abandon what we know to be safe and effective treatment interventions. Each of the three major eating disorders (EDs), anorexia nervosa (AN), bulimia nervosa (BN), and binge eating disorder (BED), is potentially debilitating, with risk for serious long-term physiological and psychological outcomes, insidious courses, and increased mortality. This chapter reviews the history of the treatment of EDs and best practices for each of these disorders, with an eye toward embodiment and embodied practices.

EDs are inexorably entwined within the context of culture and how the body and the notion of embodiment are held within culture, as are approaches to ED treatment (Gordon, 2017). Joan Jacobs Brumberg (2000) wrote an exploration of EDs within the context of social change: "Today's Anorexic is one of a long line of women and girls throughout history who have used control of appetite, food, and the body as a focus of their symbolic language" (p. 5). The documented history of what is now known as EDs goes back as far as medieval Europe. Centuries passed before EDs were officially recognized as diagnosable disorders by the *DSM* in 1980 (American Psychiatric Association, 1980).

In the early 1980s, Christopher Fairburn worked with a team of psychologists at the Centre for Research on Eating Disorders at Oxford to develop a cognitive behavioral therapy (CBT) treatment specific to those with EDs (CBT-ED). Over the next 20-plus years his team studied and refined their adaptations to CBT and accumulated a large body of research on what is considered by many to be the treatment of choice for EDs. This approach is designed to be transdiagnostic, addressing ED psychopathology whatever the ED diagnosis (Fairburn et al., 2015). In clinical practice, CBT-ED is a personalized psychological treatment with versions for younger and older clients, as well as versions for outpatient, day-client, and inpatient settings (Fairburn et al., 2015; National Institute for Health and Care Excellence [NICE], 2017; Zipfel et al., 2015). Several ED-specific CBT approaches described below are based on this approach.

ANOREXIA NERVOSA

AN has a long recorded history, receiving its name over a century ago (Walsh, 2017). In the medieval times, fasting or food restriction was viewed through the lens of spiritual practice, and binge eating was considered sinful or gluttonous (Brumberg, 2000; Gordon, 2017). Although the term *embodiment* was not used explicitly, food restriction and eating were believed to be manifestations of the embodiment of good or evil. The dichotomy reflected a contrast between the goodness of the spiritual world and the evil inherent in the material world (Miller & Pumariega, 2001; Osso et al., 2016).

The first evidence of AN was recorded in the life stories of the fasting female saints in late medieval Europe, labeled "holy anorexia" (Gordon, 2017, p. 163). In the thirteenth and fourteenth centuries extreme restriction and ED behavior were reported among such religious individuals as St. Catherine of Siena, Mary of Oignes, and Beatrice of Nazareth (Brumberg, 2000). In the seventeenth century St. Veronica is said to have eaten nothing at all for three days at a time and allowed herself to chew on five orange seeds on Friday to represent the five wounds of Jesus (Brumberg, 2000). In the seventeenth and eighteenth centuries physicians began referring to these behaviors as *inedia prodigiosa* (great starvation) and *anorexia mirabilis* (miraculously inspired loss of appetite; Brumberg, 2000). During this time attitudes about the behavior gradually transformed: during the Reformation some fasting women were considered possessed, and others were seen as frauds (Miller & Pumariega, 2001). In the eighteenth and nineteenth centuries self-imposed starvation was described in a young woman called the "miraculous maiden" (Brumberg, 2000; Gordon, 2017). Although different from the AN diagnosed today, these forms of self-starvation may be psychological analogues, given the context of culture and time (Brumberg, 2000).

A somewhat famous case marked a key turning point from the romanticization of starving girls as the embodiment of miracles toward a more medical and psychiatric approach to understanding AN. Sarah Jacob, from rural Wales, was believed to live without eating (Brumberg, 2000). Many visitors came to witness this miracle and leave her gifts and money. Her case came to the attention of the medical establishment, wanting to discredit the existence of *anorexia mirabilis*, citing research indicating that a human being cannot live more than a few weeks without food and water. In response to the growing tensions between science and the folk belief in miraculous starvation, they decided that four reliable nurses would watch over Sarah to confirm that she was not eating. Ultimately, Sarah died of starvation, her parents refusing to end the observation or to force her to eat steadfastly. They insisted that God would take care of their daughter.

Across much of the last three centuries food restriction, as seen in AN, has been distanced from religious motivations and miracles and has been connected to more secular experiences of body image and representations of self, along with medical or psychiatric approaches to treatment (Osso et al., 2016). AN was first described in the medical literature in two brief case histories published in 1692 by the English physician Richard Morton, and it appeared sporadically in the literature for the next two centuries (Attia, 2017; Bruch, 1962; Brumberg, 2000; Gordon, 2017; Osso et al., 2016). AN was and remains viewed as a manifestation of potential pathology in both the patient and family members. Formal medical descriptions first appeared in 1873, in separate writings by both French neurologist Charles Lasegue and British physician Sir William Gull (Bruch, 1962; Gordon, 2017; Le Grange & Eisler, 2017). Gall gave AN its name and described food refusal and excessive activity as psychiatric symptoms (Gordon, 2017). Lasegue described behavioral and attitudinal symptoms and added notes on problematic familial patterns (Gordon, 2017). In fact, accounts from these and other clinicians at the time described parents as "particularly pernicious," recommending that patients be separated from families to ensure successful treatment (Le Grange and Eisler, 2017, p. 296). Throughout the nineteenth century AN was similarly described in Italy, Russia, and Germany (Gordon, 2017). Those who struggled were identified as patients embodying illness sometimes within a family that was viewed as disordered or difficult. Patients were objectified as medical case studies and analyzed, and we know nothing of their perceptions of needs, wants, challenges, or aspirations.

From 1915 to the early 1930s reports of AN decreased due to the identification of Simmond's pituitary cachexia, an endocrine disease seen as the source of AN symptoms (Gordon, 2017; Miller & Pumariega, 2001). Once a distinction was made between Simmond's and AN in the 1930s, interest in AN was revived. During the 1950s, reflecting the influences of the times, causes and treatments fell into either psychoanalytic theory or medical categories (Miller & Pumariega, 2001). Psychoanalytic approaches saw AN as a fear of oral impregnation, suggesting a fear of loss of agency or embodiment, as a result of unconscious conflicts about sexuality, or as a possible regression to oral stages of development (Gordon, 2017; Miller & Pumariega, 2001). The field conceptualized AN as the embodiment of psychosomatic illness with potential contribution of endocrine factors (Gordon, 2017, p. 164).

Building on theories emphasizing a need for autonomy and differentiation from attachment figures, Hilde Bruch was instrumental in shifting our understanding of AN during the 1960s and 1970s (Gordon, 2017; Miller & Pumariega, 2001). In a groundbreaking 1962 paper, she described 12 clients (three males and nine females) who had been referred for treatment due to progressive loss of weight with an absence of organic cause. Bruch's (1962) observations included a disturbance of body image in which clients showed an absence of concern about emaciation, a denial of thinness, and a dread of becoming fat. She noted an ironic fear of "ugliness" and concern regarding appearance in the face of "skeleton-like" emaciation (p. 189). She also noted inaccurate perception and cognitive interpretation of stimuli arising from the body, resulting in a failure to recognize signs of nutritional need, leading to a drastic curtailment of caloric intake. As indicated in today's diagnostic criteria, she noted both the failure of motivation to eat and the uncontrollable impulse to "gorge oneself" (p. 190).

Sometimes ignored by historical writers, Bruch's (1962) observations included a description of a paralyzing sense of ineffectiveness that she believed to pervade all thinking and behavior. Seeing the whole client and the client's need for agency, she argued that the sense of ineffectiveness was perhaps subordinate to the other symptoms. In her description of her clients, Bruch (1962) detailed what she saw as a developmental pattern:

> The need for self-reliant independence, which confronts every adolescent, seems to cause an insoluble conflict, which their childhoods of robot-like obedience and with their lack of awareness of their own resources and initiative, and of their thoughts and feelings, not to speak of their own bodily sensations. (p. 192)

Bruch (1962) also described a host of family dynamics and characteristics, including a focus on outward appearance, demands for perfectionistic performance, and a denial of any family issues, with families self-describing as normal and happy. Bruch's explanatory model of the disorder included biological, social, and emotional factors and emphasized a lack of interpersonal boundaries and the functional role of the ED in the client's attempts at self-definition and agency. Her approach included helping clients evolve an awareness of their feelings and impulses as originating from themselves. She then helped them recognize and then effectively evaluate personal drives and impulses as choices are made. Her approach, in essence, offered the clients voice and provided what she described as "the first consistent experience that someone listened to what they had to say and did not tell them how to feel" (p. 194).

Also in the 1960s, family approaches promoted by Salvador Minuchin and Mara Selvini-Palazzoli entered the field of ED treatment (Le Grange & Eisler, 2017). These clinicians identified dysfunctional family systems as primary etiological factors that, when paired with the vulnerability of children, resulted in the development of ED behavior. Families were seen as key in treatment, and normalization of the family system was a primary treatment target: once the family was normalized, the ED behaviors would lose their role in the family system and the child could recover (Le Grange & Eisler, 2017). This was an important shift away from the medicalization of EDs and toward a more system-oriented approach. Later approaches, starting in the 1980s, would integrate the family into treatment not as the cause of the disorder but as partners in recovery (Le Grange & Eisler, 2017).

During the 1960s and 1970s cognitive and cognitive behavioral approaches began to take hold. In the ED field the medical and psychiatric approach was led by psychiatrists Arthur Crisp and Gerald

Russell, who were overseeing inpatient units in London that treated patients with AN (Gordon, 2017). Disorder-specific cognitive distortions and anxieties were highlighted as critical. Drive for thinness and fear of fatness were identified as playing a central role in the disorder. The 1980s were marked by the popularization of CBT, accompanied by a wave of research supporting its use with EDs. Aligned with CBT approaches, drive for thinness and fear of fatness have prevailed as key mechanisms in AN, as indicated in their diagnostic centrality and placement as primary targets for nearly all treatment interventions (Gordon, 2017).

Despite its long history, AN remains challenging to treat, and few options show efficacy in research (Attia, 2017; Zeeck et al., 2018). Clinicians and researchers continue to explore and debate the causal factors and associated cultural and historical contexts that lead to anxieties focused on body image and the body (i.e., the home of the embodied self), as well as the persistent and sometimes fatal drive for thinness.

Current best practices include a treatment team trained to work with individuals with AN at all levels of care, including a mental health professional (e.g., psychologist, mental health counselor), a medical doctor, and a nutritionist. Guidelines from the American Psychiatric Association (2000) indicate that most individuals with AN can be treated in an outpatient setting. According to Zipfel et al. (2015), day-treatment and inpatient services are needed for those with more severe illness and who are not responding to outpatient care. Inpatient treatment is recommended for adults with extremely low weight (BMI < 14 kg/m^2) or rapid weight loss and for adolescents at $<75\%$ of the expected weight or who demonstrate rapid weight loss. Other medical status indicators for inpatient treatment include low heart rate, cardiac symptoms, low blood pressure, postural hypotension, low body temperature, and electrolyte imbalances. Additional indicators include bingeing and purging several times a day, failure to respond to other levels of treatment, severe psychiatric comorbidity, and suicidality. Depending on weight loss, refeeding for weight restoration may be a priority.

Currently accepted treatments include cognitive behavioral approaches for acute AN with the need for weight restoration (Attia, 2017) and, more broadly, family-based approaches, CBT, and individual psychotherapy (NICE, 2017; Zeeck et al., 2018; Zipfel et al., 2015). Overall, these interventions focus on weight and eating behaviors, as well as specific, identified psychological problems such as affect regulation, dysfunctional cognitions, and interpersonal difficulties (Hirsch & Deliberto, 2019; Zeeck et al., 2018). The specific research-based approaches are briefly reviewed here.

Behavioral Approaches for Refeeding and Weight Restoration

Behavioral approaches are typically used for refeeding and weight restoration for those in intensive outpatient, day treatment, and inpatient settings (Attia, 2017). To gain two pounds a week, dietary intake must be around 3,000–4,000 calories per day (Guarda & Redgrave, 2017). Supervision is provided for meals and snacks. Depending on the setting, there may be a more complex behavioral protocol with explicit behavioral guidelines and expectations that allow a client to earn increasing levels of independence with food intake and exercise; some programs include shopping, meal preparation, eating in social settings, and practicing eating normally (Guarda & Redgrave, 2017).

Noting a paucity of short- and long-term outcome data on weight restoration, Guarda and Redgrave (2017) reported that most clients reach their target weights with weight gains of about 3–4 pounds a week. It is important to avoid refeeding syndrome, a potentially life-threatening complication that includes electrolyte imbalances, edema, hypoglycemia, cardiac symptoms, and neurocognitive symptoms. Note, access to specialty behavioral programs for AN is often limited by income level, insurance, and geography. In some cases, tube feeding (i.e., supplemental nocturnal nasogastric feeds or delivery of nutrients directly into the stomach or small intestine) is used when behavioral or other approaches are not working.

Family-Based Treatments

Family-based treatments (FBTs) are structured in three phases and are typically utilized with adolescent clients (Attia, 2017; NICE, 2017; Zipfel et al., 2015). Clients with AN and their families attend 18–20 one-hour sessions over a 9- to 12-month period (NICE, 2017; Zipfel et al., 2015). In the first phase, families are empowered to release any sense of responsibility for causing the disorder and encouraged to acknowledge the positive aspects of their parenting (NICE, 2017; Smith & Cook-Cottone, 2011; Zipfel et al., 2015). The clients and their families work together formulating and following a plan to help the clients restore weight (Smith & Cook-Cottone, 2011; Zipfel et al., 2015). The second phase involves a gradual transition of the age-appropriate responsibility for eating and weight maintenance back to the adolescent (Smith & Cook-Cottone, 2011; Zipfel et al., 2015). The final phase focuses on establishing a healthy, more normative relationship between the adolescent and parents. A review by Zipfel et al. (2015) concluded that FBT and the specific Maudsley FBT are empirically supported for adolescents with AN. There is some evidence that, although it works more quickly in terms of weight recovery, FBT may not be more effective long term than more generic family therapy or individual interventions (Le Grange & Eisler, 2017; Zeeck et al., 2018).

Maudsley Model of Anorexia Treatment for Adults

The Maudsley model of anorexia treatment for adults (MANTRA) is a cognitive-interpersonal treatment based on four factors underlying obsessional, anxious, and avoidant personality traits that are believed to support the disorder: an inflexible cognitive style characterized by a focus on details and a fear of making mistakes, social-emotional impairments, positive beliefs about AN enhancing life, and unhelpful responses of close others in their lives (e.g., overinvolvement, critical feedback, and accommodating symptoms; NICE, 2017; Zipfel et al., 2015). This motivational-style treatment targets identified factors to help the client improve weight, reduce symptoms, and increase psychosocial adjustment (NICE, 2017; Zipfel et al., 2015). The treatment modules include building a nonanorexic identity and nutrition and symptom management. A review by Zipfel et al. (2015) rated the modified MANTRA as having moderate empirical support. Zeeck et al. (2018) reported that MANTRA may be especially effective for more severely affected clients.

Psychotherapy

Focal psychodynamic psychotherapy is an outpatient psychodynamic-oriented psychotherapy for clients with AN who are moderately ill (BMI > 15 kg/m^2; Zipfel et al., 2015). Following a diagnostic interview, the therapist identifies the relevant foci for therapy and then begins the three-phase treatment. The therapist works from a client-centered focal hypothesis that addresses what the symptoms mean to the client, how the symptoms affect the client and the client's relationships with others, including the therapist (NICE, 2017). Phase 1 focuses on the therapeutic alliance, AN behaviors, and ego-syntonic attitudes and beliefs that support symptoms and are viewed as acceptable by the client (Zipfel et al., 2015). Phase 2 targets the association between interpersonal relationships and the AN behaviors. Phase 3 focuses on the transition to everyday life and negotiating treatment termination (Zipfel et al., 2015).

Pharmacological Treatments

The body of research and reviews indicates that antidepressants do not show effects for weight gain or ED symptoms during the refeeding phase, and their utility for relapse prevention and post-weight-restoration phase of treatment is uncertain (NICE, 2017; Zeeck et al., 2018; Zipfel et al., 2015). Other medications are being researched for a variety of symptoms, such as illness-related thoughts, anxiety, appetite promotion, and hyperactivity reduction, without sufficient evidence to support a recommendation (Zipfel et al., 2015).

BULIMIA NERVOSA

Overeating and self-induced vomiting in ancient times are well documented (Miller & Pumariega, 2001). In ancient Rome, vomitoriums were used by the wealthy for purging foods after heavy feasting (Miller & Pumariega, 2001). Miller and Pumariega (2001) suggested that this might reflect a historical variant of BN that was also promoted by social forces. Bulimic-type behavior was first reported in a number of case reports of AN in the 1940s (Gordon, 2017). In fact, the term *bulimia* was common in AN case reports. Early psychodynamic theories viewed binge-purging as part of the symptomatology observed in AN and focused on the symbolic significance of such behaviors as a search for oral comfort, rejection of oral impregnation, or an ejection of the internalized maternal image (Miller & Pumariega, 2001).

Normal-weight BN was first described in the 1960s by French psychiatrists who detailed binge eating followed by purging among 15 women who had used diet pills (Gordon, 2017). In 1978, Marlene

Boskind-Lodahl and William White described *bulimiarexia* as a unique ED in which the person engages in a cyclic behavior of uncontrollable desire for food, consuming large amounts of food, and vomiting and laxative use to get rid of the food. The cyclic behaviors were described as being accompanied by unhappiness with the behavior, concerns about health, low self-esteem, isolation, guilt, shame, and a feeling of helplessness in controlling impulses and tensions. Beahan (1982) describes an overwhelming increase in the reports of BN on campuses following the publication of Boskind-Lodahl and White's 1978 paper.

Credit for the current term *bulimia nervosa* was given to Gerald Russell in 1979 following the publication of his article detailing the increased number of cases in the 1970s and explicating the symptoms (Gordon, 2017). In the early 1980s BN became known as the hidden epidemic when Craig Johnson and Christopher Fairburn's inquiries resulted in responses from thousands of people who reportedly kept their struggle a secret for years (Gordon, 2017). In 1980, when the term *bulimia* was first included in the *DSM*, it was characterized by binge-eating episodes and not necessarily defined by engagement in compensatory behaviors such as vomiting or exercise, so it could include those diagnosed with AN who also binged and purged (Keel, 2017). Later revisions of the *DSM* defined BN much like it is today, with criteria related to compensatory behaviors, concern with weight and body image, and distinctions between AN with bingeing and purging (Keel, 2017).

Early interventions were behavioral, attempting to eliminate bingeing and purging. Expanding on behavioral interventions, Fairburn et al. (2015) developed an effective cognitive behavioral intervention that integrated self-monitoring, normalization of eating, and cognitive restructuring to address body image distortions. According to NICE (2017) guidelines, current treatment for BN includes physical health assessment and monitoring, as well as treatment with both a nutritionist and a mental health professional. Heart monitoring is recommended for anyone presenting with rapid weight loss, excessive exercise, severe purging behaviors, cardiac-related symptoms (i.e., bradycardia, hypotension), excessive use of caffeine or other prescribed or nonprescribed medications, muscular weakness, and electrolyte anomalies. In addition to acute medical care to address needs (e.g., electrolyte supplements), clients should have regular medical and dental reviews. If physical health is compromised, or there is a need for psychological stabilization, day treatment should be considered. If the client continues to be at increased risk or the client's caregivers cannot provide support and keep the client safe from significant harm, inpatient treatment should be considered. No medications are recommended for the sole treatment for BN. For all levels of care, a variety of approaches have been developed, as briefly described below.

Cognitive Behavioral Therapy With a Focus on BN

According to Fairburn (2017), CBT for EDs has its origins in the late 1970s with a focus on CBT for BN (CBT-BN), because it had been described as "intractable" (Fairburn, 2017, p. 284). Between 1981 and 2000 CBT-BN was developed and studied through a series of randomized controlled trials comparing CBT-BN to wait-list controls, other psychological treatments, dismantled versions of CBT-BN, and various medications (Fairburn, 2017). According to Fairburn (2017), the results were consistent across studies, with 40% of clients who entered treatment ceasing bingeing and purging behaviors for up to a year (for a detailed description of CBT-BN, see Fairburn 2008).

Interpersonal Psychotherapy

Interpersonal psychotherapy (IPT) is a short-term psychological treatment that addresses current interpersonal problems. While it was originally designed for depression, it has been adapted for BN (Fairburn et al., 2015). The theory holds that problems with interpersonal functioning lead to negative affect and low self-esteem, which in turn lead to engagement in ED symptoms as a coping mechanism (Wilfey & Eichen, 2017). Clients end up in self-perpetuating cycles as the ED symptoms are thought to exacerbate interpersonal problems (Wilfey & Eichen, 2017). Briefly, with IPT mental health professionals aim to identify problematic interpersonal patterns associated with the onset and maintenance of EDs. Clinicians then help clients develop goals and strategies to change maladaptive interpersonal functioning in order to reduce experiences of negative affect and improve symptoms (Wilfey & Eichen, 2017).

IPT is typically delivered across 15–20 sessions over four to five months in three phases (Wilfey & Eichen, 2017). Connections are made between interpersonal functioning and ED behavior, setting up the framework for IPT that addresses such problem areas as grief, interpersonal role disputes, role transitions, and interpersonal deficits (Wilfey & Eichen, 2017). Typically, the therapist is active but not directive, allowing clients to generate their own solutions in problem areas (Wilfey & Eichen, 2017). Overall research indicates that IPT can achieve results similar to those of CBT, though at a slower pace (Slade et al., 2018; Wilfey & Eichen, 2017).

Guided Cognitive Behavioral Self-Help Programs

Self-help programs for BN arose to broaden access to treatment for those with limited access to experienced mental health care providers (Sysko, 2017). Self-help interventions are based on the standard outpatient CBT-BN, which has been translated into accessible formats to be used at home (Sysko, 2017). Interventions are delivered in either book or electronic format and include didactic information about EDs and specific strategies to reduce symptoms (Sysko, 2017). These programs can be delivered as pure self-help or guided self-help, which combines the self-help program with a few brief visits with a therapist (Sysko, 2017). Evidence supports the use of guided behavioral self-help (Slade et al., 2018; Sysko, 2017). For a sample self-help program, see Fairburn (2013).

Family-Focused Therapy for Bulimia Nervosa

Family-focused therapy for bulimia nervosa is recommended for children and young people with BN. NICE (2017) describes this intervention as comprising 18–20 sessions administered over six months that involve a mix of family and individual sessions with clients. Time is spent supporting and encouraging the family to assist in the client's recovery through provision of information regarding body weight, dieting, and the adverse effects of purging behaviors. A collaborative approach is utilized, enabling the family to work with the client to establish regular eating patterns, reduce compensatory behaviors, and increase self-monitoring of eating and bulimic behaviors. Later phases of treatment focus on clients establishing independence with self-monitoring of eating and BN behaviors appropriate for their level of development, plans for treatment termination, and relapse prevention. A well-designed study comparing a CBT program designed specifically for adolescents with BN and FBT for BN showed that there were no differences between the two interventions at the end of treatment (Poulsen et al., 2014).

BINGE EATING DISORDER

Binge eating can be documented throughout history in literature and historical records. According to Gordon (2017), historical reviews suggest that BED may have a more extensive history than AN or BN. Ironically BED, the most common ED, was the last to be identified by the modern diagnostic systems. Albert Stunkard introduced the term *binge* in 1959 and helped formulate criteria for bulimia in the *DSM* in 1980. The focus on bingeing and purging among middle- and upper-class college students has led to a transformation of "bulimia" to BN, ignoring what we now know as BED until the early 1990s. A group led by Robert Spitzer, including Stunkard, proposed the inclusion of BED as a distinct diagnosis in the *DSM*, resulting in its adoption as a provisional diagnosis in need of further study (American Psychiatric Association, 1994; Gordon, 2017). The *DSM-5* included BED as one of the EDs (American Psychiatric Association, 2013).

Food addiction and the ongoing debate about its validity as a mental disorder or an ED have complicated the evolution of BED as a diagnostic category. According to Meule (2015), food addiction is the idea that highly processed, palatable, and caloric foods may have addictive potential (i.e., addiction to the substance) and that certain forms of overeating may be addictive in nature (i.e., addiction to the behavior). The twenty-first century has seen an exponential increase in scientific publications on the topic, but the idea of food addiction can be documented as far back as 1890 in reference to chocolate. Theron Randolph coined the term *food addiction* in 1956, defining it as a combination of sensitivity and adaptation to regularly consumed foods and a pattern of symptoms similar to addiction. In 1960 Overeaters Anonymous, a self-help organization based on the 12-step program of Alcoholics Anonymous, was founded, following an addiction framework supporting abstinence from certain foods. ED specialists such as Stunkard reportedly believe that the term *food addiction* was not justified as a parallel to the processes seen in addiction to alcohol and drugs. Some argue that the phenomenon should be described as *eating addiction*, reflecting the behavioral addiction qualities that may be stronger influences than the addictive qualities of certain foods. Treatment protocols described here are designed to treat BED. According to NICE (2017), those seeking treatment for BED should be told that psychological treatments aimed at BED have a limited effect on body weight and that weight loss is not the target of therapy.

BED-Focused Guided Self-Help Programs

Similar to self-help approaches for BN, self-help approaches to BED are based on CBT-ED models (Sysko, 2017). BED-focused self-help programs use cognitive behavioral self-help materials (NICE, 2017). Mental health professionals can support clients' adherence to the program through brief supported sessions (e.g., four to nine 20-minute sessions over 16 weeks). If this approach is unacceptable, contraindicated, or ineffective after four weeks, group CBT-ED is recommended (NICE, 2017).

CBT-ED Programs for BED

According to NICE (2017) guidelines, group CBT-ED programs for adults with BED typically consist of 16 weekly 90-minute group sessions administered over four months. The focus is on psychoeducation, self-monitoring of eating behaviors, and helping group members analyze their problems and goals. Sessions also include developing a daily food intake plan and identifying triggers associated with binge-eating episodes, as well as body exposure training to help clients identify negative beliefs about their bodies. In later stages of group help members work on avoiding ED responses and coping with current and future challenges and triggers. If this format is not available or the individual rejects it, individual CBT-ED for adults with BED is recommended.

NICE (2017) guidelines describe individual CBT for BED as typically consisting of 16–20 sessions to help clients develop a formulation of their psychological issues to determine how nutrition and emotional factors may contribute to binge-eating episodes. Based on the initial formulations, mental health professionals may advise clients to eat regular meals and snack in order to avoid feeling hungry. In addition, sessions address emotional triggers using cognitive restructuring, behavioral experiences, and exposure. Sessions often include weekly monitoring of binge-eating episodes, nutrition, and weight. Body image issues, if present, are addressed. NICE (2017) guidelines do not recommend that the client attempt to lose weight during treatment, as that is believed to trigger binge eating.

FROM TRADITIONAL TREATMENTS TO EMBODIED APPROACHES

Overall, treatments for EDs have improved, with a growing empirical base indicating, at best, moderate efficacy (Linardon & Wade, 2018; Zeeck et al., 2018). For AN, no one treatment appears to have superiority over another (Zeeck et al., 2018). Even with the most robust outcomes, FBT for adolescents has resulted in only 30% of clients remaining weight restored at the 4-year follow-up (Zeeck et al., 2018). In a study comparing specialist supportive clinical management, MANTRA, and CBT-ED, Byrne et al. (2017) found that, of those with AN who began the study, 60% completed the program and 52% completed the 12-month follow-up, with no difference across treatments for treatment rates, BMI, ED psychopathology, general psychopathology and psychological impairment. Across all conditions, an average of 50% of participants achieved a healthy weight, and only 28.3% achieved remission at 12-month follow-up, a finding consistent with other reports. Thus, despite progress, more effective interventions are needed.

As with AN, the efficacy of the current treatments for BN and BED is worrisome. A meta-analytic review of 45 randomized clinical trials with 78 psychotherapy conditions found that, although many BN clients show some improvements during therapy, over 60% fail to fully abstain from bingeing and purging, even after receiving the most empirically supported treatments (e.g., CBT-BN), and findings are moderate for treatment of BED (Linardon and Wade, 2018). A meta-analysis of 45 studies found moderate support for the efficacy of CBT and guided self-help for the treatment of BED; only modest support was found for IPT and medication (Ghaderi et al., 2018). Overall, findings reinforce the contention that treatment interventions have yet to address the full scope of variables driving ED behavior (for a guide to practice, see Dilberto & Hirsch, 2019).

The treatment recommendations described here help decrease the core symptoms expressed in EDs and key mechanisms underlying core symptoms with only modest success. The approaches to date

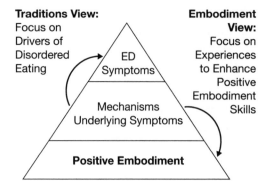

Figure 6.1. Traditional and Embodiment Views of Eating Disorders

hold symptoms and underlying mechanisms as abnormal, disordered, and targets for reduction or eradication. This approach has the potential for cognitive alignment with the symptoms, leaving clients at risk for relapse and long-term insecurity regarding their genuine capacity for wellness (see Figure 6.1). In contrast, the positive embodiment perspective, informed by mindfulness, yoga, and positive psychology approaches, sees these experiences as opportunities to practice skills and develop increased capacity for positive embodiment. Within this shift in perspective, clients still learn useful behavioral and cognitive behavioral tools for symptom management, all while honoring of the body as a resource for experiencing, coping, decision making, and finding meaning and purpose.

There is a difference between managing symptoms and embodying a positive relation to oneself. Through the lens of embodiment and personal power, this text provides a rationale for this new approach that integrates an embodied pathway into treatment and recovery. Mindfulness-based and embodied approaches begin with acceptance and allowing and make space and give tools for embodiment. Combined with what we already know in the cognitive and medical fields, perhaps we have a pathway forward that embraces our common humanity and capitalizes on the core capacities of those who struggle.

CHAPTER 7

Embodying Mindful Self-Care

No matter the challenges we confront . . . there is no escaping this
reality, no matter what others, or we, try to say about it.
If we don't care for ourselves, we'll be limited in how we can care for
others. It is that simple. And it is that important—
for you, for others, and for our planet.

—Daniel Siegel, *The Mindful Therapist*

At their core, mindful self-care practices are pathways to embodiment
(Cook-Cottone, 2015b, 2017; Cook-Cottone & Guyker, 2018; Jennings,
2015). Positive embodiment can be thought of as a living and breathing
process, and mindful self-care is the breath and heartbeat of that process (Cook-Cottone, 2019a). Mindful self-care gives life to the part of
us that loves and nurtures. However, unlike the breath and heartbeat
that continue to support us, whether or not we pay attention to them,
mindful self-care does not always unfold so naturally.

When I think of the natural way self-care unfolds for some people, I think of Kim Chernin's work related to the internalization of the
caring we receive from others in our lives. Chernin (1998) details the
success and, in some cases, the failure of human development related
to self-regulation and care. For some, the process of learning how to
care for the self is developed through years of effective and loving
parenting. But sometimes a healthy set of self-care practices does not
develop, for reasons occurring across both the internal (i.e., physiology,
emotions, and cognitions) and external (i.e., family, community, and
culture) domains of the self (Cook-Cottone & Guyker, 2018; Dolan &
Metcalfe, 2012; Fleche, Smith, & Sorsa, 2012).

Our own set of vulnerabilities and inclinations can impair the development and practice of self-care skills. For those who are "other-ori-
ented," focusing on the self can seem foreign and feel uncomfortable.

For some, it might not even come to mind. For others, there may have been interruptions and/or failures in the parenting or mentoring process. Further, cultural beliefs can get in the way. In some cultures, self-care can be seen as an indulgence, while achieving and striving are held as the only true valuable pursuits. Work and school cultures can exacerbate this mindset; focusing on worker and student achievement above well-being. Within the larger context of national priorities, a citizen's engagement in self-care suffers under the influence of entire economies focused on increasing gross national product and favorable trade balances without a metric for measuring national well-being (Dolan & Metcalfe, 2012; Fleche, Smith, & Sorsa, 2012).

My hope is for a worldwide recognition that positive embodiment is the most basic and fundamental human right. More, a critical aspect of realizing this human right is accessing the ecological support to engage in embodying practices. A shift is occurring, as seen within the World Health Organization, the United Nations, and standards of practice across a variety of helping professions: well-being is now being integrated in how we assess the state of human condition (World Health Organization, 2014; United Nations Mental Health Strategy Steering Group, 2018). To illustrate, in 2014 the World Health Organization redefined mental health as "a state of wellbeing in which every individual realizes his or her own potential, can cope with the normal stresses of life, can work productively and fruitfully, and is able to make a contribution in her or his own community" (WHO, 2014). Embodying practices like self-care not only are a powerful part of recovery but also are relevant and necessary to successful engagement in the world as a recovered person.

THE MINDFUL SELF-CARE PROCESS

Mindful self-care has been defined as the daily process of being aware of and attending to our basic physiological and emotional needs, including the shaping of our daily routine, relationships, and environment as needed to promote self-care (Cook-Cottone, 2015b, 2017, 2019a; Norcross & Guy, 2007). In essence, self-care is a salutogenic practice. Integrating self-care with treatment for EDs aligns with both research on flourishing (Seligman, 2011) and the growing field of positive body image (Cook-Cottone & Guyker, 2018; Tylka & Piran, 2019).

Also at its essence, self-care is the foundation of physical and emotional well-being (Cook-Cottone, 2015b, 2017). Without self-care, we become susceptible to exhaustion, emotional and physical burnout, fatigue, and depletion and unable to give of ourselves (Cook-Cottone, 2017; Jennings, 2015; Sutterfield, 2013). Lack of self-care shows up in the body, in emotion regulation, and in thoughts. A pathway back to a better experience of self, self-care is associated with positive physical health, emotional well-being, and mental health. Overall, the steady and intentional practice of self-care is seen as protective, by preventing the onset of mental health symptoms and burnout, as well as increasing body image and decreasing ED symptoms (Cook-Cottone, 2015b, 2017, 2019a; Cook-Cottone & Guyker, 2018).

Mindful self-care is one of the four pillars of embodied practice (EAT-ED), along with skills of being-with and working-with, meaning making and purpose, and honoring effort and struggle. It is one of the ways in which we can manage both the internal and external experiences of self. It serves the larger goal of attunement among all aspects of self and provides the foundation for self-regulation (Cook-Cottone & Guyker, 2018; Cook-Cottone, Tribole, & Tylka, 2013). Ironically, many people say that they will take better care of themselves and do healthy things once they feel better emotionally, yet self-care is the foundational practice for feeling better (Cook-Cottone, 2015b; Cook-Cottone et al., 2013). Self-care is the thing to do now to feel better later. Emotional regulation is inextricably linked to physiological stability, homeostasis, and cessation of symptoms, and daily self-care practices can enhance these (Cook-Cottone et al., 2013; Cook-Cottone, 2015b; Linehan, 1993).

Mindful self-care may play a uniquely powerful role in the prevention and treatment of EDs (Cook-Cottone, 2016). In my experience working as a psychologist with individuals struggling with ED behavior, I have noticed the irony that symptoms allow clients to be deeply connected to their own bodies, the challenging internal experiences while trying to avoid an ostensibly invalidating and objectifying external world (Cook-Cottone, 2016). To effectively prevent and treat EDs, those at risk and struggling must learn how to navigate life without leaving themselves or turning against their bodies (Cook-Cottone, 2016). Mindful self-care shifts behaviors at the ED pathology—the client's relationship with the body (Cook-Cottone, 2016; Cook-Cottone & Guyker, 2018).

As shown in Figure 7.1, the mindful self-care process I describe here

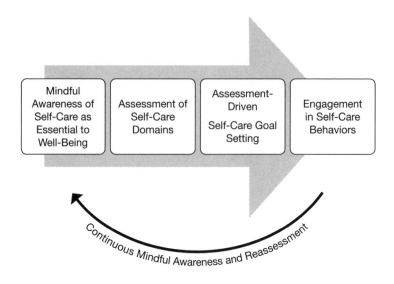

Figure 7.1. The Mindful Self-Care Process

Reprinted / Adapted from Cook-Cottone, *Mindfulness and Yoga for Self-Regulation: A Primer for Mental Health Professionals*, New York: Springer Publishing Company; 2015. Reproduced with the permission of Springer Publishing Company, LLC.

involves four steps (Cook-Cottone, 2015b; Cook-Cottone & Guyker, 2018), as discrete phases of an ongoing process, a continuous mindful awareness of one's own self-care behaviors, continual assessment, goal setting, and goal-directed engagement in self-care behaviors (Cook-Cottone, 2015b; Cook-Cottone & Guyker, 2018).

THE MINDFUL SELF-CARE SCALE

To help individuals identify areas of strength and weakness in self-care behavior, my colleague and I developed the Mindful Self-Care Scale, which I describe in detail below and provide in full at the end of the chapter. I initially developed a general self-care scale for use with a yoga-based ED prevention program to help girls both assess and engage in self-care practices (Cook-Cottone & Guyker, 2018; Cook-Cottone et al., 2013). This earlier version of the scale addressed nutrition, hydration, exercise, soothing, rest, and medication and supplements and was appropriate for use with children middle school age and above. Building on the original work, the Mindful Self-Care Scale (Cook-Cottone

& Guyker, 2018) goes beyond traditional self-care, integrating cultivation of mindful awareness and responsiveness to internal and external experiences (i.e., attunement; Cook-Cottone & Guyker, 2018), incorporating both formal practices (i.e., scheduled intentional practices that require dedicated time) and informal practices (i.e., practices that you weave into your day or alter the manner in which you engage in a daily acivtity). Mindful Self-Care also adds a layer of mindful awareness through ongoing monitoring and reflection on the sufficiency and quality of one's overall self-care (Cook-Cottone & Guyker, 2018).

The Mindful Self-Care Scale has a long form intended for clinical use a short form that resulted from extensive psychometric development to be used for research, and a brief form to research mindful self-care among populations for whom lengthier surveys are not feasible (e.g., medical personnel, hospice workers). They are all based on the set of questions in the long form presented here. (See catherinecookcottone.com for free access to all three versions of the scale, with updates on research outcomes.)

The Mindful Self-Care Scale-Long (MSCS-L) is an 84-item scale that measures the self-reported frequency of self-care behaviors (Cook-Cottone, 2015b; Cook-Cottone & Guyker, 2018). The scale addresses 10 domains of self-care: six target primarily the internal aspects of self (i.e., physiological, emotional, and cognitive), three address the external experience of self (i.e., family, community, and cultural), and one addresses awareness and attunement within the center of self, with orientation toward both the internal (self-awareness) and and external (mindfulness) experiences of self (see Figure 7.2). The scale also includes three general items assessing general or more global practices of self-care.

When using the Mindful Self-Care Scale, read the definition and information on the domain, and then have your client carefully answer the questions in the related subscale. Then using the blanks at the end of each subscale, add the scores and average them across the subscale. (Note that some questions are *reversed scored*, as indicated in the subscales.) Averages of 0 to 2 suggest that this area of self-care can be targeted for improvement (Cook-Cottone, 2015b).

Once you and your client have gone through and assessed each of the domains of self-care and identified both the average scores and the two items with the lowest scores for each domain, it is time to set some self-care goals. Using Practice Guide 7.1, you and your client can

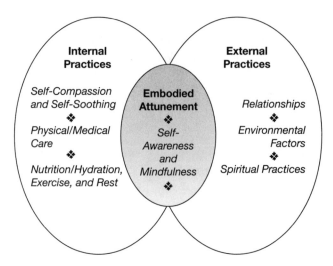

Figure 7.2. Mindful Self-Care Scale Domains

summarize these scores and begin to identity actionable self-care practices. I recommend you review these goals with you clients at each session and reassess mindful self-care every three to six months, charting changes and growth.

SUBSCALE 1: Nutrition and Hydration

Nutrition is an essential component of the treatment of EDs (Hart, 2016). This subscale is not intended to replace the crucial role of the nutritionist in ED treatment. Rather, it provides a longer-term view of nutrition as a self-care practice through the recovery process and beyond. Addressing nutritional needs includes both eating a healthy amount of healthy foods and engaging in the planning needed to make that happen (Cook-Cottone, 2015b).

Addressing basic nutritional needs can deeply affect self-regulation, and more specifically emotion regulation, as well as the body's response to stress overall (Cook-Cottone, 2015b; Hart, 2016). Research confirms that a healthy body responds to the unavoidable stress in life better than an unhealthy body (Davis, Eshelman, & McKay, 2008; Harper, 2013). Good nutrition supports attention, mood regulation, efficient cognition, sleep, and exercise performance (Hart, 2016). For example, drops in sugar levels, insufficient or excessive energy intake, and nutrient deficiencies (i.e., low iron intake, low vitamin D and B12 levels) have all been identified as affecting mood and sense of well-being and can be dysregulating (Cook-Cottone, 2015b; Duyff, 2011; Hart, 2016). Because of its support of self-regulation, nutrition is part of foundational practices in both anxiety and emotion regulation protocols (Davis et al., 2008; Linehan, 1993; for nutritional guidelines and tools for enhancing nutrition, see Davis et al., 2008).

Water is also essential for life, and maintaining recommended levels of hydration is critical to healthy functioning (i.e., 1.2 liters per day, or about 6–8 glasses; Benelam & Wyness, 2010; Cook-Cottone, 2015b; Cook-Cottone & Guyker, 2018; Liska et al., 2019). Adequate hydration is essential for skin health, neurological function, gastrointestinal and renal function, and maintenance of body weight and composition (Liska et al., 2019). While extreme dehydration is very serious and can be fatal, symptoms can be associated even with mild dehydration (i.e., 2% loss of body weight), such as headaches, fatigue, and reduced physical and mental performance (Benelam & Wyness, 2010; Liska et al., 2019). Too much water can also be a problem, resulting in hyponatremia (low sodium levels; Benelam & Wyness, 2010). The focus on nutrition and hydration as self-care practices is on the nutritional value of food, variety, planning, regularity (not skipping meals) and paying attention to the body for hunger, thirst, and satiety cues (Cook-Cottone & Guyker, 2018). Your clients with EDs will be able to see their eating behaviors within the context of an overall self-care plan and as key to self-regulation. Unique to the ED client, be sure their plans in this domain are aligned with the treatment team's goals and plans. Sample questions include, "I drank at least 6 to 8 cups of water" and "I planned my meals and snacks."

SUBSCALE 2: Exercise

The association between exercise and well-being has been well documented, with emerging research suggesting it may help in developing positive body image and preventing and treating EDs (Calogero, Tylka, McGilly, & Pedrotty-Stump, 2019; Cook-Cottone, 2015b; Cook-Cottone & Guyker, 2018; Norcross & Guy, 2007). In 2017, the Centers for Disease Control and Prevention released a research-based statement advocating for focus on physical activity, for all of us, and away from a focus on weight, size, and shape as a path to physical health (Dollar, Berman, & Adachi-Mejia, 2017).

Exercise reduces stress by releasing endorphins into the bloodstream, decreasing muscle tension, increasing alpha-wave activity, improving strength and flexibility, lessening fatigue, increasing resting metabolism, ridding the body of toxins, improving blood flow to the brain, and reducing risk for those with stress-related medical conditions (Cook-Cottone, 2015b; Davis et al., 2008). The beneficial effects of regular exercise include improvements on measures of cognition and psychological well-being in healthy individuals (Cook-Cottone, 2015b; Hopkins, Davis, VanTieghem, Whalen, & Bucci, 2012).

Exercise has been a controversial topic in ED treatment, as some clients may take part in physical exercise as a way to engage in ED symptoms, and others might present with medical risk and have been given medical advice not to exercise until after substantial weight gain, physiological stability, and nutritional gains have been achieved. In a synthesis of the literature on exercise and the treatment of EDs, Cook et al. (2016) recommended that appropriate exercise programs be designed for clients' physiological condition, and screening for exercise-related psychopathology (more on this in Chapter 10). Sample questions include, "I did fun physical activities (e.g., danced, played active games, jumped in leaves" and "I planned/scheduled my exercise for the day."

SUBSCALE 3: Rest

The rest domain of self-care includes getting enough sleep, taking restful breaks, and scheduling time to rest and restore (Cook-Cottone, 2015b; Cook-Cottone & Guyker, 2018; Harper, 2013). Sleep is a critical aspect of self-care for those in ED recovery (Allison, Spaeth, & Hopkins, 2016). Insomnia is related to an increased risk of EDs, and EDs are related to disrupted sleep (Allison et al., 2016). The National Sleep Foundation recommends 7–9 hours of sleep per night for adults and between 8 and 10 hours for teenagers (Hirshkowitz et al., 2015). Lack of sleep and too much sleep are associated with negative outcomes (Irwin, Olmstead, & Carroll, 2016). Both short and long duration of sleep are predictors, or markers, of negative cardiovascular outcomes (Cappuccio, Cooper, D'Elia, Strazzullo, & Miller, 2011; Cook-Cottone,

2015b; Irwin et al., 2016). Researchers have noted cognitive effects of sleep deprivation (i.e., speed and accuracy; Lim & Dinges, 2010). In a review of the research, Irwin et al. (2016) found that sleep disturbances, as well as extremes of sleep duration, were associated with inflammation, which increases risk for a variety of inflammatory diseases and all-cause mortality. A review of the literature also suggests that insomnia impacts diverse areas of health-related quality of life (Kyle, Morgan, & Espie, 2010).

Rest involves taking breaks from current activity or sustained attention (Cook-Cottone, 2015b; Cook-Cottone & Guyker, 2018; Harper, 2013; Norcross & Guy, 2007). Planned breaks, rest, and relaxation are vital to health and well-being (Bottaccioli, Bottaccioli, & Minelli, 2019; Cook-Cottone, 2015b; Norcross & Guy, 2007). Seemingly counterproductive, breaks can also help us experience more goal-directed energy during work time (Cook-Cottone, 2015a, 2015b; Cook-Cottone & Guyker, 2018; Norcross & Guy, 2007). Breaks and relaxation can be days off, week-long vacations, or short, 5- to 10-minute breaks away from work, the computer, or interpersonal interactions (Cook-Cottone, 2015b; Norcross & Guy, 2007).

Rest can vary from client to client. For example, if your client is going to school and has been sitting all day, rest might be a brief walk or a yoga class (Cook-Cottone, 2015b, 2017). Rest for someone who is teaching yoga or fitness classes all day might be taking time to meditate or have a cup of chamomile tea (Cook-Cottone, 2017). For some activities everyone may benefit from taking a break. For example, research suggests that electronic screen time increases stress overall, and those who depend on screens for entertainment and social networking experience substantially more stress (Khalili-Mahani, Smyrnova, & Kakinami, 2019). Sample questions include, "I got enough sleep to feel rested and restored when I woke up," and "I planned restful/rejuvenating breaks throughout the day."

SUBSCALE 4: Physical and Medical Care

The physical and medical domain of self-care addresses the maintenance of medical and dental care, practicing daily hygiene, adherence to medical advice (e.g., taking prescribed medicines or supplements, and brushing teeth), and avoiding substance abuse (Cook-Cottone,

2015a, 2015b; Cook-Cottone & Guyker, 2018). As indicated in Chapter 6, medical care is critical in the management of EDs (Golden et al., 2015). During treatment there should be ongoing assessment of the degree of malnutrition and management of the other physiological symptoms such as dehydration, neuroendocrine instability, arrested growth and development, and acute medical problems (Golden et al., 2015). An extensive review of the literature concluded that the comorbidity for EDs and substance use is over 20% and that individuals with EDs should be regularly screened for substance use and offered treatment for substance use disorder during treatment for their EDs (Bahji et al., 2019).

Including physical and medical self-care items and goals is an important part of clients taking a personal responsibility for their health outcomes, health care, and substance use (Cook-Cottone 2015a, 2015b). It is an important shift toward health and well-being metrics and away from reducing calories, weight, shape, and size. The effects of this shift can help move clients more quickly toward recovery. Interestingly, the more we take care of our body in positive ways, the more likely we are to have positive feelings about our body such as body appreciation (see Cook-Cottone, 2015a). To illustrate, questions include, "I accessed the medical/dental care I needed."

SUBSCALE 5: Self-Soothing

Self-soothing is the capacity to calm the self while in a state of emotional distress with psychological, autonomic arousal (Beck et al., 2017). The development of self-soothing skills is believed to be influenced by the internalization of calming and soothing experiences during childhood (Beck et al., 2017). Self-soothing is a positive, healthy response to feeling stressed or distressed or experiencing an intense emotional reaction (Cook-Cottone, 2015b; Cook-Cottone & Guyker, 2018). The regulation of strong emotions is an essential skill for recovery and well-being (Beck et al., 2017). Specifically, self-soothing practices are believed to play a critical role in psychological and neurobiological regulators of affective states and prepare us to deal with future stressful experiences (Beck et al., 2017). Self-soothing can be both a response to a trigger and a prevention tool, helping keep the nervous system calm and soothed (Cook-Cottone & Guyker, 2018; Davis et al., 2008). Accordingly, self-soothing is an effective tool in emotional regulation and distress tolerance (Cook-Cottone, 2015b; Cook-Cottone & Guyker, 2018; Linehan, 1993).

Self-soothing includes relaxation techniques (e.g., progressive muscle relaxation), deep breathing, and pursuit of stimuli or activities that are calming and relaxing (Cook-Cottone, 2015b; Cook-Cottone & Guyker, 2018). The primary function is to connect with the present moment and to calm the nervous system. There are many ways to self-soothe, such as reading, writing, and cultivating sensory awareness (Cook-Cottone, 2015b; Davis et al., 2008; Norcross & Guy, 2007). Clients can learn to use self-soothing in response to a trigger and as a planned preventive tool (Cook-Cottone, 2015b; Cook-Cottone & Guyker, 2018; Davis et al., 2008; Norcross & Guy, 2007). Questions include, "I used deep breathing to relax," and "I prioritized activities that help me relax."

SUBSCALE 6: Self-Compassion

Self-compassion entails "treating oneself with kindness, recognizing one's shared humanity, and being mindful when considering negative aspects of oneself" (Neff, 2011, p. 1). Research indicates that self-compassion decreases the effects of stress, increases social connectedness, and elicits kindness toward ourselves and others (Sutterfield, 2013). It is the antidote to rigid cognitive stances such as perfectionism, which is sometimes held as achievable and honorable. In private practice, I actively discourage perfectionism by defining it as "romanticized rigidity" (Cook-Cottone, 2015b, 2017)—my clients pause to think about it, laugh, and then get it. By dropping perfectionism and labeling it as just another way to be rigid, clients can more easily move toward self-compassionate ways of thinking about behaviors, goals, and the self (Cook-Cottone, 2015b, 2017). In their review of the literature Braun, Park, and Gorin (2016) found that self-compassion was a protective factor against poor body image and eating pathology. Questions on this subscale include, "I kindly acknowledged my own challenges and difficulties," and "I reminded myself that failure and challenge are part of the human experience."

SUBSCALE 7: Relationships

Supportive relationships enhance well-being (Cook-Cottone, 2015b; Cook-Cottone & Guyker, 2018; Norcross & Guy, 2007; Shin et al., 2014).

Being mindful of the nature of our relationships is a critical aspect of mindful self-care (Cook-Cottone, 2015b; Cook-Cottone & Guyker, 2018). In a review of the literature, Jones, Lindekilde, Lübeck, and Clausen (2015) found an association between interpersonal problems and EDs, and most of the studies reviewed found that interpersonal problems at the start of therapy were associated with detrimental outcomes. Building relationship awareness and working it into the intervention can help clients develop the support network they need to recover. An important aspect of healthy relationships is appropriate boundaries (Cook-Cottone, 2015b; Norcross & Guy, 2007; Sayrs, 2012). In relationships, a boundary "denotes maintenance of a distinction between self and other—what is within bounds and what is out of bounds" (Norcross & Guy, 2007, p. 93). Norcross and Guy (2007) recommend that relationship boundaries be clear and flexible. This scale includes questions such as, "I spent time with people who are good to me (e.g., support, encourage, belive in me)" and "I knew if I needed to, I could stand up for myself in my relationships."

SUBSCALE 8: Environmental Factors

Most approaches to self-care focus on changing the behavior of the individual without adequately addressing environmental factors (Cook-Cottone & Guyker, 2018; Norcross & Guy, 2007), such as work space, life space, schedule, and even choices in clothing or gear (Clements-Croome, Turner, & Pallaris, 2019; Cook-Cottone & Guyker, 2018). Research suggests that physical environment can affect well-being—the comfort and appeal of lighting, furniture, decorations, flooring, and windows can make a difference in the overall tone of a space (Clements-Croome et al., 2019; Cook-Cottone, 2015b; Norcross & Guy, 2007). Barriers to daily functioning can play a large role in stress. Similar to the concept of microaggressions that can accumulate over time, microstressors can aggregate, chipping away at resiliency and the ability to cope (Cook-Cottone, 2017). Is there a door that needs fixing? Would it help to take some time to clean the closet, study, or work area? Self-care involves noticing and addressing these types of environmental issues (Cook-Cottone, 2015b; Cook-Cottone & Guyker, 2018), as well as maintaining an organized work space, balancing work for others and our own initiatives, wearing suitable clothes, and doing small things to make each day a little bit better (Cook-Cottone

& Guyker, 2018). Questions on this subtest include, "I maintained a manageable schedule," and "I avoided taking on too many requests or demands."

SUBSCALE 9: Spiritual Practice

As detailed in Chapter 5, having a sense of mission, purpose, and meaning can play an important part in ED recovery. The spiritual practice subscale helps clients incorporate spirituality in their lives, bringing meaning or purpose into work or school life, as well as into personal life, and cultivating spiritual experiences and connections (Cook-Cottone, 2015b; Cook-Cottone & Guyker, 2018). Questions in this subscale include, "I experienced meaning and/or a larger purpose in my work/school life," and "I spent time in a spiritual place (e.g., church, meditation room, nature). (More on this in Chapter 8.)

SUBSCALE 10: Self-Awareness/Mindfulness

Self-awareness and mindfulness are fundamental and unique features of mindful self-care (Cook-Cottone, 2015b; Cook-Cottone & Guyker, 2018). Well reviewed and detailed throughout this text (see also Cook-Cottone, 2015b, 2017), self-awareness, one-mindedness, and active mindfulness practices such as meditation and yoga are increasingly acknowledged for their effectiveness as self-care practices (Cook-Cottone, 2015b; Cook-Cottone & Guyker, 2018; Linehan, 1993; Norcross & Guy, 2007; Sayrs, 2012; Shapiro & Carlson, 2009). Question prompts in the subscale include: "I had a calm awareness of my thoughts."

General Subscale

The general self-care items were designed to provide a broad sense of variety of self-care strategies utilized, planning of self-care, and creativity and exploration of self-care. These questions are included to help clients consider these core aspects to a continually evolving relationship with mindful self-care. There is no single self-care strategy that alone can help us manifest well-being (Cook-Cottone & Guyker, 2018; Norcross & Guy, 2007). For some, one beloved hobby or leisure pursuit can be more effective than engaging in a variety of self-care strategies (Cook-Cottone, 2015b; Cook-Cottone & Guyker, 2018; Norcross & Guy, 2007). Using Practice Guide 7.1, you can help your clients set goals based on their answers to each question. For example, if the score on "I explored new ways to bring self-care into my life" is a 1 or 2, you may want to consider adding as a goal, "I will explore new ways to bring self-care into my life."

MINDFUL SELF-CARE PROCESS

The Mindful Self-Care process involves four steps: (a) mindful awareness of self-care as essential to wellbeing, (b) assessment of self-care domains, (c) assessment-driven self-care goal setting, and (d) engagement in self-care behaviors (See Figure 8.3: The Mindful Self-Care Process; Cook-Cottone, 2015a; Cook-Cottone & Guyker, 2018). The four steps are discrete phases of an ongoing process, a continuous mindful awareness of one's own self-care behaviors, continual assessment, and goal setting (Cook-Cottone, 2015a; Cook-Cottone & Guyker, 2018). Mindful self-care is a process of constant remembering to connect with and nurture the self (Cook-Cottone, 2015a; Cook-Cottone & Guyker, 2018). Once you and your patient have gone through and assessed each of the domains of self-care and identified the average score for each domain and the items with relatively lower scores for each domain, it is time to set some self-care goals (use the Mindful Self-Care Scale at the end of this chapter). Summarize your patient's scores and begin to identity actionable self-care practices using Practice Guide 7.1 at the end of the chapter. Complete a review of goals each session. It can be helpful to reassess mindful self-care every 3 to 6 months charting changes and growth.

CONCLUSION

Flourishing and well-being should be considered possibilities for those who are in the midst of an eating disorder diagnosis (Cook-Cottone, 2015b). Cultivating mental health goes beyond the process of decreasing symptoms, and it asks for more than the absence of symptoms (Cook-Cottone, 2015b). Mindful self-care is a foundational self-regulating practice and the first supplemental step in integrating embodiment practices into eating disorder treatment (Cook-Cottone, 2015a; Cook-Cottone & Guyker, 2018). It is a constant practice of bringing awareness to self-care, assessing self-care practices, setting self-care goals, and actively engaging in self-care practices (Cook-Cottone, 2015a; Cook-Cottone & Guyker, 2018). It is recommended that mindful self-care be assessed at preset intervals so that progress can be reviewed and new goals and plans can be set. For the latest research on the Mindful Self-Care Scale and mindful self-care please see catherinecookcottone.com. You will find a link to all three versions of the scale as well as PDFs of all of the research associated with the scale and the practice.

MINDFUL SELF-CARE SCALE

Have your client carefully answer the seven questions in each of the 10 subscales and the general self-care assessment below. Practice Guide 7.1 can then help you and your client summarize these scores and begin to identity actionable self-care practices

For each item, mark the following scores. Please note, some questions are *reversed scored*:

Items Not Reverse Scored

0 = never (0 days)

1 = rarely (1 day)

2 = sometimes (2–3 days)

3 = often (4–5 days)

4 = regularly (6–7 days)

Items *Reverse Scored*

4 = never (0 days)

3 = rarely (1 day)

2 = sometimes (2–3 days)

1 = often (4–5 days)

0 = regularly (6–7 days)

Add up responses for the questions for each subscale. This is the subscale raw score. Then divide the subscale raw score by the number of questions to get the average score for the subscale, which will be between 0 and 4.

Averages of 0 to 2 suggest that this area of self-care can be targeted for improvement (Cook-Cottone, 2015b).

SUBSCALE 1: Nutrition and Hydration Assessment

This past week how many days did I do the following?

I drank at least 6–8 cups of water.

   0 = never   1 = rarely   2 = sometimes   3 = often   4 = regularly

Even though my stomach felt full enough, I kept eating.

   4 = never   3 = rarely   2 = sometimes   1 = often   0 = regularly

   (reversed scored)

I adjusted my water intake when I needed to (e.g., for exercise, hot weather).

   0 = never   1 = rarely   2 = sometimes   3 = often   4 = regularly

I skipped a meal.

   0 = never   1 = rarely   2 = sometimes   3 = often   4 = regularly

   (reversed scored)

I ate breakfast, lunch, dinner, and, when needed, snacks.
    0 = never   1 = rarely   2 = sometimes   3 = often   4 = regularly

I ate a variety of nutritious foods (e.g., vegetables, protein, fruits, and grains).
    0 = never   1 = rarely   2 = sometimes   3 = often   4 = regularly

I planned my meals and snacks.
    0 = never   1 = rarely   2 = sometimes   3 = often   4 = regularly

Average score for Nutrition and Hydration subscale
(total score divided by 7 questions): _____
    The two lowest items:
    1. _____
    2. _____

SUBSCALE 2: Exercise Assessment

This past week how many days did I do the following?

I exercised at least 30–60 minutes.
    0 = never   1 = rarely   2 = sometimes   3 = often   4 = regularly

I took part in sports, dance, or other scheduled physical activities (e.g., sports teams, dance classes).
    0 = never   1 = rarely   2 = sometimes   3 = often   4 = regularly

I did sedentary activities instead of exercising (e.g., watched TV, worked on the computer).
    4 = never   3 = rarely   2 = sometimes   1 = often   0 = regularly (reversed scored)

I sat for periods of longer than 60 minutes at a time.
    4 = never   3 = rarely   2 = sometimes   1 = often   0 = regularly (reversed scored)

I did fun physical activities (e.g., danced, played active games, jumped in leaves).
    0 = never   1 = rarely   2 = sometimes   3 = often   4 = regularly

I exercised in excess (e.g., when I was tired, sleep deprived, or risking stress/injury).

    4 = never   3 = rarely 2 = sometimes 1 = often 0 = regularly

    (reversed scored)

I planned/scheduled my exercise for the day.

    0 = never 1 = rarely 2 = sometimes 3 = often 4 = regularly

Average score for Exercise subscale

(total score divided by 7 questions): _____

    The two lowest items:

    1. _____

    2. _____

SUBSCALE 3: Rest Assessment

This past week how many days did I do the following?

I got enough sleep to feel rested and restored when I woke up.

    0 = never 1 = rarely 2 = sometimes 3 = often 4 = regularly

I planned restful/rejuvenating breaks throughout the day.

    0 = never 1 = rarely 2 = sometimes 3 = often 4 = regularly

I rested when I needed to (e.g., when not feeling well, after a long work out or effort).

    0 = never 1 = rarely 2 = sometimes 3 = often 4 = regularly

I took planned breaks from school or work.

    0 = never 1 = rarely 2 = sometimes 3 = often 4 = regularly

I planned/scheduled pleasant activities that were not related to work or school.

    0 = never 1 = rarely 2 = sometimes 3 = often 4 = regularly

I took time away from electronics (e.g., turned off phone and other devices).

    0 = never 1 = rarely 2 = sometimes 3 = often 4 = regularly

I made time in my schedule for enough sleep.
0 = never   1 = rarely   2 = sometimes   3 = often   4 = regularly

Average score for Rest subscale
(total score divided by 7 questions): _____
    The two lowest items:
    1. _____
    2. _____

SUBSCALE 4: Physical and Medical Care Assessment

This past week how many days did I do the following?

I engaged in medical care to prevent/treat illness and disease (e.g., attended doctor visits, took prescribed medications/vitamins, was up to date on screenings/immunizations, followed doctor recommendations).
0 = never   1 = rarely   2 = sometimes   3 = often   4 = regularly

I engaged in dental care to prevent/treat illness and disease (e.g., dental visits, tooth brushing, flossing).
0 = never   1 = rarely   2 = sometimes   3 = often   4 = regularly

I took/did recreational drugs.
*4 = never   3 = rarely   2 = sometimes   1 = often   0 = regularly
(reversed scored)*

I did *not* drink alcohol.
0 = never   1 = rarely   2 = sometimes   3 = often   4 = regularly

I practiced overall cleanliness and hygiene.
0 = never   1 = rarely   2 = sometimes   3 = often   4 = regularly

I accessed the medical/dental care I needed.
0 = never   1 = rarely   2 = sometimes   3 = often   4 = regularly

I did not smoke.
0 = never   1 = rarely   2 = sometimes   3 = often   4 = regularly

I did not drink alcohol in excess (i.e., more than   1 to   2 drinks [1 drink = 12 ounces beer, 5 ounces wine, or 1.5 ounces liquor]).
     0 = never   1 = rarely   2 = sometimes   3 = often   4 = regularly

Average score for Physical and Medical Care subscale
(total score divided by 8 questions): _____
     The two lowest items:
          1. _____
          2. _____

SUBSCALE 5: Self-Soothing Assessment

This past week how many days did I do the following?

I used deep breathing to relax
     0 = never   1 = rarely   2 = sometimes   3 = often   4 = regularly

I did *not* know how to relax.
     4 = never   3 = rarely   2 = sometimes   1 = often   0 = regularly
     (reversed scored)

I thought about calming things (e.g., nature, happy memories).
     0 = never   1 = rarely   2 = sometimes   3 = often   4 = regularly

When I got stressed, I stayed stressed for hours (i.e., I couldn't calm down).
     4 = never   3 = rarely   2 = sometimes   1 = often   0 = regularly
     (reversed scored)

I did something physical to help me relax (e.g., taking a bath, yoga, going for a walk).
     0 = never   1 = rarely   2 = sometimes   3 = often   4 = regularly

I did something intellectual (using my mind) to help me relax (e.g., read a book, wrote).
     0 = never   1 = rarely   2 = sometimes   3 = often   4 = regularly

I did something interpersonal to relax (e.g., connected with friends).
     0 = never   1 = rarely   2 = sometimes   3 = often   4 = regularly

I did something creative to relax (e.g., drew, played instrument, wrote creatively, sang, organized).

   0 = never   1 = rarely   2 = sometimes   3 = often   4 = regularly

I listened to relax (e.g., to music, a podcast, radio show, rainforest sounds).

   0 = never   1 = rarely   2 = sometimes   3 = often   4 = regularly

I sought out images to relax (e.g., art, film, window shopping, nature).

   0 = never   1 = rarely   2 = sometimes   3 = often   4 = regularly

I sought out smells to relax (lotions, nature, candles/incense, smells of baking).

   0 = never   1 = rarely   2 = sometimes   3 = often   4 = regularly

I sought out tactile or touch-based experiences to relax (e.g., petting an animal, cuddling a soft blanket, floated in a pool, put on comfy clothes).

   0 = never   1 = rarely   2 = sometimes   3 = often   4 = regularly

I prioritized activities that help me relax.

   0 = never   1 = rarely   2 = sometimes   3 = often   4 = regularly

Average score for Self-Soothing subscale
(total score divided by 13 questions): _____

   The two lowest items:

   1. _____

   2. _____

SUBSCALE 6: Self-Compassion Assessment

This past week how many days did I do the following?

I noticed, without judgment, when I was struggling (e.g., feeling resistance, falling short of my goals, not completing as much as I'd like).

   0 = never   1 = rarely   2 = sometimes   3 = often   4 = regularly

I punitively/harshly judged my progress and effort.

   4 = never   3 = rarely   2 = sometimes   1 = often   0 = regularly
   (reversed scored)

I kindly acknowledged my own challenges and difficulties.
    0 = never   1 = rarely   2 = sometimes   3 = often   4 = regularly

I engaged in critical or harsh self-talk.
    4 = never   3 = rarely   2 = sometimes   1 = often   0 = regularly
    (reversed scored)

I engaged in supportive and comforting self-talk (e.g., "My effort is valuable and meaningful").
    0 = never   1 = rarely   2 = sometimes   3 = often   4 = regularly

I reminded myself that failure and challenge are part of the human experience.
    0 = never   1 = rarely   2 = sometimes   3 = often   4 = regularly

I gave myself permission to feel my feelings (e.g., allowed myself to cry).
    0 = never   1 = rarely   2 = sometimes   3 = often   4 = regularly

Average score for Self-Compassion subscale
(total score divided by 7 questions): _____
    The two lowest items:
        1. _____
        2. _____

SUBSCALE 7: Relationship Assessment

This past week how many days did I do the following?

I spent time with people who are good to me (e.g., support, encourage, and believe in me).
    0 = never   1 = rarely   2 = sometimes   3 = often   4 = regularly

I scheduled/planned time to be with people who are special to me.
    0 = never   1 = rarely   2 = sometimes   3 = often   4 = regularly

I felt supported by people in my life.
    0 = never   1 = rarely   2 = sometimes   3 = often   4 = regularly

I felt confident that people in my life would respect my choice if I said "no."
    0 = never   1 = rarely   2 = sometimes   3 = often   4 = regularly

I knew that, if I needed to, I could stand up for myself in my relationships.
    0 = never   1 = rarely   2 = sometimes   3 = often   4 = regularly

I made time for people who sustain and support me.
    0 = never   1 = rarely   2 = sometimes   3 = often   4 = regularly

I felt that I had someone who would listen to me if I became upset (e.g., friend, counselor, group).
    0 = never   1 = rarely   2 = sometimes   3 = often   4 = regularly

Average score for Relationships subscale
(total score divided by 7 questions): _____
    The two lowest items:
    1. _____
    2. _____

SUBSCALE 8: Environmental Factors Assessment

This past week how many days did I do the following?

I maintained a manageable schedule.
    0 = never   1 = rarely   2 = sometimes   3 = often   4 = regularly

I avoided taking on too many requests or demands.
    0 = never   1 = rarely   2 = sometimes   3 = often   4 = regularly

I maintained a comforting and pleasing living environment.
    0 = never   1 = rarely   2 = sometimes   3 = often   4 = regularly

I kept my work/school work area organized to support my work/school tasks.
    0 = never   1 = rarely   2 = sometimes   3 = often   4 = regularly

I maintained balance between the demands of others and what is important to me.
    0 = never   1 = rarely   2 = sometimes   3 = often   4 = regularly

Physical barriers to daily functioning were addressed (e.g., needed supplies for home and work were secured, light bulbs were replaced and functioning).

    0 = never   1 = rarely   2 = sometimes   3 = often   4 = regularly

I made sure I wore suitable clothing for the weather (e.g., umbrella in the rain, boots in the snow, warm coat in winter).

    0 = never   1 = rarely   2 = sometimes   3 = often   4 = regularly

I did things to make my everyday environment more pleasant (e.g., put a support on my chair, placed a meaningful photo on my desk).

    0 = never   1 = rarely   2 = sometimes   3 = often   4 = regularly

I did things to make my work setting more enjoyable (e.g., planned fun Fridays, partnered with a coworker on an assignment).

    0 = never   1 = rarely   2 = sometimes   3 = often   4 = regularly

Average score for Environmental Factors subscale
(total score divided by 9 questions): _____

    The two lowest items:

       1. _____

       2. _____

SUBSCALE 9: Spiritual Practice Assessment

This past week how many days did I do the following?

I experienced meaning and/or a larger purpose in my *work/school* life (e.g., for a cause).

    0 = never   1 = rarely   2 = sometimes   3 = often   4 = regularly

I experienced meaning and/or larger purpose in my *private/personal* life (e.g., for a cause).

    0 = never   1 = rarely   2 = sometimes   3 = often   4 = regularly

I spent time in a spiritual place (e.g., church, meditation room, nature).

    0 = never   1 = rarely   2 = sometimes   3 = often   4 = regularly

I read, watched, or listened to something inspirational (e.g., watched a video that gives me hope, read inspirational material, listened to spiritual music).

    0 = never   1 = rarely   2 = sometimes   3 = often   4 = regularly

I spent time with others who share my spiritual worldview (e.g., church community, volunteer group).

    0 = never   1 = rarely   2 = sometimes   3 = often   4 = regularly

I spent time doing something that I hope will make a positive difference in the world (e.g., volunteered at a soup kitchen, took time out for someone else).

    0 = never   1 = rarely   2 = sometimes   3 = often   4 = regularly

Average score for Spiritual Practice subscale
(total score divided by 6 questions): _____

    The two lowest items:

    1. _____

    2. _____

SUBSCALE 10: Self-Care Self-Awareness/ Mindfulness Assessment

This past week how many days did I do the following?

I had a calm awareness of my thoughts.

    0 = never   1 = rarely   2 = sometimes   3 = often   4 = regularly

I had a calm awareness of my feelings.

    0 = never   1 = rarely   2 = sometimes   3 = often   4 = regularly

I had a calm awareness of my body.

    0 = never   1 = rarely   2 = sometimes   3 = often   4 = regularly

I carefully selected which of my thoughts and feelings I used to guide my actions.

    0 = never   1 = rarely   2 = sometimes   3 = often   4 = regularly

I meditated in some form (e.g., sitting, meditation, walking meditation, prayer).

    0 = never   1 = rarely   2 = sometimes   3 = often   4 = regularly

I practiced mindful eating (i.e., paid attention to the taste and texture of the food, ate without distraction).

    0 = never   1 = rarely   2 = sometimes   3 = often   4 = regularly

I practiced yoga or another mind/body practice (e.g., tae kwon do, tai chi).

    0 = never   1 = rarely   2 = sometimes   3 = often   4 = regularly

I tracked/recorded my self-care practices (e.g., journaling, used an app, kept a calendar).

    0 = never   1 = rarely   2 = sometimes   3 = often   4 = regularly

I planned/scheduled meditation and/or a mindful practice for the day (e.g., yoga, walking meditation, prayer).

    0 = never   1 = rarely   2 = sometimes   3 = often   4 = regularly

I took time to acknowledge the things for which I am grateful.

    0 = never   1 = rarely   2 = sometimes   3 = often   4 = regularly

Average score for Self-Awareness and Mindfulness subscale (total score divided by 10 questions): _____

    The two lowest items:

      1. _____

      2. _____

General Self-Care Assessment

This past week how many days did I do the following?

I engaged in a variety of self-care strategies (e.g., mindfulness, support, exercise, nutrition, spiritual practice).

    0 = never   1 = rarely   2 = sometimes   3 = often   4 = regularly

I planned my self-care.

    0 = never   1 = rarely   2 = sometimes   3 = often   4 = regularly

I explored new ways to bring self-care into my life.

    0 = never   1 = rarely   2 = sometimes   3 = often   4 = regularly

For the general questions there is no need to sum or average your score.

Practice Guide 7.1 : Identifying Actionable Self-Care Practices

The answers to the Mindful Self-Care Scale can help create mindful self-care goals. First, place average scores for each subscale in the Mindful Self-Care Scale below:

Subscale	Score	Actionable (Below 3)?
1. Nutrition and Hydration	_____	Yes / No
2. Exercise	_____	Yes / No
3. Rest	_____	Yes / No
4. Physical and Medical Care	_____	Yes / No
5. Self-Soothing	_____	Yes / No
6. Self-Compassion	_____	Yes / No
7. Relationships	_____	Yes / No
8. Environmental Factors	_____	Yes / No
9. Spiritual Practice	_____	Yes / No
10. Self-Awareness and Mindfulness	_____	Yes / No

List your strengths (domains with scores that are 4 or above):

_____

_____

_____

_____

List your growth areas (domains with scores less than 3; if no score is ≤3, list the lowest scores). You might also list any low scoring item, across domains:

_____

_____

_____

_____

_____

_____

Now circle or star the two domains you would like to work on (if you already have goals in nutrition, consider work in another self-care area). Review the questions and your responses in each of these domains. Are there items that look like a good place to start?

Choose one or two items from each identified domain and rework them into goals. For example, if you choose the item "I maintained a manageable schedule" to work on, you could reword it as a goal: "Each day I will maintain a manageable schedule." You can then develop a few plans to do that, such as creating a to-do list that includes tasks to complete, time for exercise, and time for at least two nutritious meals.

Goal 1 (with plans):

_____
_____
_____
_____

Goal 2 (with plans):

_____
_____
_____
_____

Goal 3 (with plans):

_____
_____
_____
_____

CHAPTER 8

Embodied Meaning

Purpose and Mission

Tell me, what is it you plan to do
with your one wild and precious life?

—Mary Oliver, "The Summer Day"

What is your embodied *why*? The answer can be a sense of mission that you have known since you were little, or it can be something that you contemplate for years. It can be one thing, or many. It integrates the heart, the belly, and the soles of our feet. Living and embodying our why is all about orienting our mind toward considering that there is reason for doing what we do, thinking what we think, and creating what we create. It is bigger than we are, bigger than this moment, and most certainly bigger than any ED symptom. I have found, through my own experience and through working with clients with EDs, that figuring out the value, meaning, and purpose of life after recovery can make a substantial difference in treatment outcomes (see Chapter 5 for review of research and theory).

Part of the ED psychopathology is giving meaning to things that don't really mean that much in the big picture (e.g., calories, carbohydrates, inches, pounds). It leads to a self-perpetuating, insidious migration or displacement of meaning that becomes increasingly validated the more entrenched the disorder becomes. Suddenly everyone is talking about calories and macronutrients like it is life or death—because for some patients it is. Viktor Frankl (1978) describe it this way:

> It turned out that, if a neurosis was removed, more often than not when it was removed a vacuum was left. The patient was beautifully adjusted and functioning, but the meaning was missing. The patient had not been taken as a human being, that is to say, a being

in steady search for meaning; and this search for meaning, which is so distinctive of [humans], had not been taken seriously. (p. 20)

GETTING TO THE *WHY*: MISSION AND REASON FOR BEING

Cultivating a mission and purpose is one of the four pillars of the embodiment approach to the treatment of EDs (EAT-ED), along with mindful self-care, being-with and working-with skills, and honoring effort and struggle. It involves clients both looking more deeply into their reason for being and developing a personal mission statement— they can do both or either. Some clients prefer to explore a broad sense of meaning in their lives (e.g., love and connection), whereas others prefer a more linear approach, such as developing a mission statement and a set of goals and plans to achieve them. Offer both as possibilities, and consider that, at any given stage of recovery, one or the other might be a better fit. When working on existential being from an embodied perspective, allow agency and self-determination to be primary drivers. In this way, questions of meaning, value, and purpose are based on what clients want their life to be about (Hayes, 2006; Manlick, Cochran, & Koon, 2013; Sandoz, Wilson, & Dufrene, 2010; Scritchfield, 2016).

The components of an individual's reason for being or mission vary substantially, but the literature suggests that they involve three essential components: values, meaning, and purpose (Astrachan-Fletcher & Maslar, 2009; Harris, 2009; Hayes, Luoma, Bond, Masuda, & Lillis, 2006; Hayes, Strosahl, & Wilson, 2012; Scritchfield, 2016; Vos et al., 2019; Wong, 2012). *Values* help identify desired qualities of action (Harris, 2009; Sandoz et al., 2010; Scritchfield, 2016). They are broader and give a sense of what types of things matter, such as education, family, balance, independence, and risk. *Meaning* grants and conveys the reasons for the value and its merit and significance (Scritchfield, 2016; Vos et al., 2019). It explains why something is important. For example, education is a strong value of mine because I believe that education empowers. *Purpose* fulfills meaning and gives aim or direction. For example, for me, the purpose of education is to increase knowledge for both students and teachers. Once these three components are understood, they facilitate a clearer vision of both mission and reason for being. From there, clients can choose their actions more purposefully and live with intention (see Figure 8.1).

Figure 8.1 Components of Mission and Reason for Being Help Define Purposeful Actions

Clarifying Values

Clarifying values is the first step in identifying a reason for being and/ or mission. It is essential for creating a life of meaning (Harris, 2009; Hayes et al, 2006; Sandoz et al., 2010). Values can be defined generally as what matters to us (Harris, 2009; Hayes et al., 2006; Sandoz et al., 2010). They help identify the desired qualities of the actions we take:

> Deep in your heart, what do you want your life to be about? What do you stand for? What do you want to do with this brief time on the planet? What truly matters to you in the big picture? (Harris, 2009, p. 11)

In acceptance and commitment therapy (ACT), defining values is one of the six core therapeutic processes (Harris, 2009; Hayes et al., 2006; Sandoz et al., 2010; Wilson, Sandoz, Kitchens, & Roberts, 2010). Values help us do what matters. In ACT values are often compared to a compass, because both offer direction. Values also help us be more attuned and congruent in our everyday life—a way of being that decreases stress and increases our sense of coherence and well-being. Values help us align our inner world with our actions in our external experiences of self (recall Figure 2.3 in Chapter 2).

Hayes et al. (2006) define values as the "chosen qualities of purposive actions that can never be obtained as an object, but can be instantiated moment by moment" (p. 8). They are not considered an end in themselves; rather, they help create a clearer path toward a values-consistent life (Hayes et al., 2006). Values have a global quality and are always present in the here and now, rather than a specific nature that is forward looking, like a goal (Harris, 2009). According to the ACT framework, values never need to be justified, are freely chosen, and can vary from person to person (Harris, 2009; Sandoz et al., 2010; Wilson et al., 2010). They are self-determined.

When working with clients, you can offer a list of values as examples (see Table 8.1). You might also use the Valued Living Questionnaire, which helps individuals assess value domains such as family, empowerment, education and training, and physical well-being (Wilson et al., 2010). The assessment can be found easily online. In the workbook *ACT Made Simple*, Harris (2009, p. 201) offers 17 different value-clarifying

Table 8.1: List of Values to Use as Examples

Achievement	Fun	Recognition
Acknowledgment	Generosity	Reliability
Adventure	Gratitude	Resourcefulness
Affluence	Growth	Respect
Agency	Healing	Risk
Balance	Health	Safety
Beauty	Helping	Security
Belonging	Independence	Self-determination
Benevolence	Influence	Self-expression
Creating	Inquiry	Service to others
Compassion	Integrity	Social equity
Competition	Improvement	Spirituality
Connection	Justice	Sportsmanship
Conservation	Kindness	Stability
Devotion	Knowledge	Strength
Discipline	Learning	Teamwork
Education	Love	Thoughtfulness
Equality	Loyalty	Trust
Equanimity	Mindfulness	Truth
Fairness	Nonviolence	Understanding
Family	Patience	Validation
Financial security	Personal character	Vision
Freedom	Personal development	Wisdom
Friendship	Physical challenge	Other: _____

activities, such as imagining what you would do if you had all the money in the world, and writing a speech for your birthday or retirement party.

As an embodied practice, it will be important to check in on the physical experience of considering values. Values that ring true might be accompanied by an exciting feeling in the stomach or a sensation around the heart. Sometimes people report feeling a restlessness throughout their bodies, or a call to action, when they think about a value that means something to them. Further, clients may notice different physical sensations and feelings associated with considering values that make someone else happy and values that come from the heart. It can be helpful to do a body scan (see Script 8.1) and then consider several values, noticing accompanying body sensations.

Once your clients identify several values that feel aligned with who they are, have them choose one to three of the values to work with. They can write them down in a journal or use Step 1 in Practice Guide 8.1. Now they are ready to move to meaning.

Conveying Meaning

Meaning grants and conveys merit and significance to a value. Some therapists believe that meaning is so important to recovery that it is the basis of their entire approach. For example, meaning therapy is based on the premise that psychological difficulties are more likely to occur when actions and direction addressing clients' basic needs for meaning, purpose, and significance are missing from their life (Vos et al., 2019). Informed by logotherapy, Viktor Frankl's methodology based on finding meaning in one's life, meaning therapy posits that life is inherently meaningful and that meaning can be discovered in every situation, no matter how challenging (Vos et al., 2019).

When working with clients on clarifying meaning, start with the value they selected:

1. It can be helpful to prepare for this process doing a seated meditation and body scan (see Script 8.1). As they consider the chosen value, guide them through a meditation and body scan, noticing the sensations and feelings that are connected to the value.
2. Ask clients to explore the meaning that the value brings to their life. Allow time at the end of the meditation and body scan to simply allow them to be and breathe as they consider the question.

3. It can be helpful for clients to freewrite for 10–15 minutes on the topic, letting their thoughts flow (see Script 8.2). Ask them to explain to you why the value is significant to them and the world. From that narrative, work to edit their meaning into a sentence or phrase.

Clients may need to do the meditations, body scans, and freewriting a few times before they get to a coherent sense of meaning. When this work is new to clients, it is important to move through the process slowly. Consider doing this work for 15–20 minutes of a session over a period of weeks or months as clients work on symptom reduction and self-regulation. Give them time and permission to live some of these questions, rather than feeling as if they should know the answers right away. For some of our clients, these questions are part of the etiology. Once your clients are ready, they can record their meaning in Step 2 in Practice Guide 8.1.

Identifying Purpose

Purpose can be defined as the eventual outcome, the aim that fulfills meaning (Marrero, 2013). It has a more functional nuance to it. For example, a *value* of health promotion might be *meaningful* because health promotion can save lives. Its *purpose* might be to reduce illness. Note that this purpose is not an action, like developing prevention programs or running health clinics. The purpose is the outcome that is hoped for, not the action to achieve that outcome.

Ask your clients to list one to three aims related to the value they chose and the meaning they detailed (you can use Step 3 in the practice guide in Practice Guide 8.1). Review it with them to be sure it is not an action—detailing actions will follow the consideration of a reason for being and/or mission, below. Once your clients have identified one to three aims, they are ready to clarify their reason for being and mission.

Developing a Personal Reason for Being and Mission

Your clients now have the components to develop a reason for being and a personal mission statement. The process of developing reasons for being, mission, and related goals and plans begins with broad and general ideas and moves toward the more specific. Some clients feel at home in the broad and general, and some prefer the specific and sequential. Because reasons for being are broader than mission statements, it can be helpful to explore them first with your clients. Then, if clients desire, they can refine their reasons for being into a mission statement with specific plans and goals.

Developing a Reason for Being. A reason for being is a broad statement that encompasses values, meaning, and purpose. It moves us and helps us want to experience life. We often feel compelled to be in action and to share it with others. It is what we love, our passion. Some believe that a reason for being is a universal need. For example, the Japanese word *ikigai* is defined as the realization of hopes, dreams, and purpose. It entails actions of devotion to the pursuits one enjoys, issues feelings of accomplishment and fulfillment, and involves an awareness of values, purpose in life, and the meaning of existence (Kumano, 2018).

We can have one or many reasons for being. They change as we age and as our world shifts, sometimes present simultaneously and sometimes sequentially. For example, for many toddlers, their reasons for being are to love, play, and learn. For adults, they may be a vocation (e.g., I am here to be a teacher, a researcher, and mentor) or a set of actions (e.g., I am an explorer, world traveler, and seeker of relationships across the world). A reason for being can be about work and honor (e.g., I am here to document the lives of those who were lost in war). It can be very focused (e.g., I am here to support the animal rescue in my town) or broad (e.g., I am here to be a good friend). A reason for being that is well lived might outlive its purpose and evolve (e.g., I am here to support my children as they find their way in the professional and familial worlds).

With your clients, review their values, meaning, and purpose. It might be helpful to begin by looking to their pasts and giving examples from your own life and/or this book. By starting with younger versions of themselves, or a time before they had symptoms, their reasons for being and the longer-term patterns of their values, meaning, and purpose can be clearer. Then, ask them to let go of the need to find the right answer and consider, "What is my reason for being?" Remind them that it is okay to live the question for a time.

Vision board work is a popular trend among personal coaches and self-help workshops and has been implemented to explore careers, vocations, and future orientation in a culturally sensitive manner among youth (Waalkes, Gonzalez, & Brunson, 2019). Vision boards are multipurpose, flexible, and creative tools that can integrate expressive arts and work related to reasons for being (Waalkes et al., 2019), and they are fun and easy to create. The vision board process can tap into imagination and creative, nonlinear thinking (Waalkes et al., 2019). It promotes self-reflection without overly relying on verbal expression (Waalkes et al., 2019). Vision boards can also help clients move away from the need to get the answer right and toward an exploration of the self (Waalkes et al., 2019). They may also be a tool for freeing clients to include wishes or dreams that might be below their consciousness (Waalkes et al., 2019).

Materials for vision board work include a large piece of paper or a poster board; colored markers, crayons, or colored pencils; magazines and other print media; colored paper; stencils and other scrapbooking materials; and any other materials you think would be fun and inspiring. Next, have clients ask the question, "What is my reason for being?" or "If I lived my life in accordance with a heart-felt reason for being, what would be present in five years?" Allow your client to be in creation for the next hour or so, or to take the project home.

Visualization is another useful approach, involving freewriting to the same questions. Before freewriting, it might be helpful to use the meditation and body scan (see Script 8.1) to help clients develop the visualization. As they are building their visualization with the meditation and body scan, you can add prompts, such as asking them to detail where they are, who is with them, what they are doing, even what they are wearing. You can ask them to visualize how they are feeling and any physical sensations they might have, such as what they see, hear, smell, taste, and feel internally. After the body scan and mediation, allow 15–20 minutes for the freewriting (see Script 8.2). For both the vision board and visualization activities, end with clients developing their broad reason-for-being statement. It can be helpful to work with the ideas for reasons for being on a large piece of paper, in a journal, or on a white board. Once your clients are ready, they can record their reason for being in Step 4 in Practice Guide 8.1.

Developing a Personal Mission Statement. Once a broader reason for being is established, your client might be ready to work on a personal mission statement. This work is based on the effectiveness of value-driven actions used in ACT (Sandoz et al., 2010). Working with undergraduates, Searight and Searright (2011) developed a process for working with mission statements. First, aligned with the work related to reasons for being, have your clients reflect on what they might want to experience and/or accomplish in 5, 10, or more years, or what they would like to accomplish by the end or their lives (Searight & Searight, 2011). The mission statement is intended to work like an internal compass, building off of the values, meaning, and purposes the client has already identified. This is the step in which the reason for being is more actionable.

Begin with visualization. Have your clients imagine that they are looking back over the past several years or over their entire life (whichever is the best fit). In the visualization, address all the components of a mission statement, as outlined in Table 8.2. For example, ask your clients to imagine what a dear friend or loved one might say your clients have *accomplished*, including educational accomplishments, business ventures, and creative work. Once the visualization is complete, your clients can work on developing their personal mission statements in writing. When your clients are ready, they can record their mission statement in Step 5 in Practice Guide 8.1.

Table 8.2: Components of a Mission Statement

Accomplishments	What you want to do and accomplish? (education, business, creative, travel, etc.)
Location	Where do you want to be? (continental United States, Africa, in the tropics, on a mountainside, etc.)
Skills and strengths	What personal skills and strengths will you use? (creativity, curiosity, passion for helping others, etc.)
Character	How do you want to act or behave? (truthful, trustworthy, brave, sober, recovered, reliable, etc.)
Priorities	Which values will be more important? (truth over compromise, family over career, tenure before travel, etc.)

Developing Goals and Plans: Actions

Once your clients have worked through their reason for being and/or their personal mission statement, they are ready to create goals and plans to get them there. These are best broken down into 6- or 12-month segments that will eventually lead your clients to their reasons for being or missions. Clients who are very forward thinking can lay out a more general 5-year plan and then break things down for the next 6–12 months.

A goal is what your clients would like to accomplish that will help them reach their mission. For example, for someone who wants to be a research professor, the first step is often securing an undergraduate education at a research university. The goal could be articulated as, "I will get accepted into a research university for next fall."

A plan is the set of actions that will help them accomplish the goal. The plan should include a specific action and a date for accomplishment of that action. Further, many goals require multiple plans. For example,

1. I will write a general college interest essay identifying my long-term mission and shorter-term goals and review it with my school counselor by September 15th.
2. I will research and identify the research universities most aligned with my interests, travel limitations, and budget by October 1st.
3. I will create a list of all of the universities to which I would like to apply and their requirements by November 1st.
4. I will write all required essays using my general essay as a framework by December 15th.
5. I will save money from my job each week to pay for my college applications for a total of $1,500, which breaks down to $50.00 a week for the next 30 weeks.
6. I will apply to 10 research universities by February 1st.

Goals and plans help your clients engage in the embodiment, the doing of their dreams. They can use their journals to do this, or you can help them use a white board or sketch it out on a large piece of paper. Once their goals and plans are set, they can record their action plans in Step 6 in the practice guide at the end of this chapter. It can also be helpful for clients to add their action plans to their electronic calendar, possibly even adding shorter-term steps and reminders. Build in time during therapy sessions to review progress and support your client's work on some of the goals.

THE MORITA TABLE: CLIENTS' *WHY* AND ED SYMPTOMS

For clients, getting to know their *why* is a big step toward achieving a groundedness that serves as a tool to address triggers and symptoms. When the present moment is difficult and overwhelming and it feels like having a symptom is the only option, it can be helpful for clients to remember two things: (a) their reason for being and/or mission—their *why*; and (b) that they and their *why* are worth the effort. Accurately referencing self-worth may be at the core of both EDs and a sense of mission or meaning in life (Manlick et al., 2013). Essentially, mission and a reason for being are about being human and being inherently worthy: your clients being worthy of a mission in life and worthy of being in a way that only they can be.

The Morita table helps clients recall their reason for being and/or personal mission when triggers are present, helping them make choices in the present moment and decide what to be with and work with (Astrachan-Fletcher & Maslar, 2009). This process was developed by Japanese psychiatrist Shoma Morita, who used acceptance as the main frame for his therapy. Over the years, I have used the concepts in the Morita table and modified it substantially to support clients as they struggle with triggers, symptoms, and choices. The Morita-based action model (Table 8.3) helps clients work within the context of an overarching sense of meaning and mission in life to help choose intentional actions. I use this to help clients consider what might be the right thing to do next when they are triggered, considering what is and is not under their personal control. It reminds clients to simply be with what is present in the moment, outside of their control, and to consider accepting and allowing it to be as it is, and then to shift toward what can be controlled. Once aware, grounded, and breathing, clients are better able to engage in intentional thoughts and actions.

The Morita-based action model can be written on a 3-by-5 card that your clients can hold in their wallet or purse. Some of my clients use

Table 8.3: Morita-Based Action Model: Being-With and Working-With the Present Moment

Things I Cannot Control	Things I Can Control
• The natural unfolding of life events • Sensations and physiological reactions • Feelings • Automatic thoughts	• My awareness and attention • Physical grounding and breath • Intentional thoughts • Purposeful actions
Be With the natural unfolding of life, sensations, psychological reactions, feelings, and automatic thoughts. Consider that you can simply accept and allow them as they arise.	**Work With** being fully aware and attentive to what is occurring, ground your feet and breathe. As your body and mind settle, consider your reason for being or your mission. Bring your thoughts and actions in line with what matters to you and what you are working on. Act with purpose (this may mean doing nothing).
My Reason for Being or Mission *(fill in)*: (Ask: Do my thoughts and actions align here?)	

Source: Informed by the modified Morita Table from Astrachan-Fletcher and Maslar (2009, p. 23).

sticky notes that they keep in their journals or post in their rooms. They can also take a photo of it and keep it handy on their smartphones.

CONCLUSION

Consider you client is overwhelmed with life and feels like they are drowning. They are holding on to the log of their ED and wanting to swim to shore. They do the work, learn the skills, and are able to swim to shore. But now what? They have learned to not drown and are now able to stand on the shore without falling back into the depths with each stressor. Is this what is left, standing on the shore, hoping nothing pushes them back into the struggle? Figuring out the "Why?" serves our clients like a rescue line, pulling them up toward recovery. If you bring a client's awareness to what is possible and help them develop realistic, intentional plans that are based on their heartfelt values, personal meaning, and a sense of purpose, you give them something to work toward that is bigger than a life of simply trying not to have symptoms. Even better, when the mission work is deeply embodied, the person throwing the lifeline is the future self; the one who knows where they are headed, the one who has a good sense of how wonderful realizing life's purpose will feel. As Pat Ogden has written:

> In our bodies, in this moment, there lives the seeds of impulses of the change and spiritual growth we seek, and to awaken them we must bring our awareness into the body, into the here and now."

Practice Guide 8.1: What Are Your Reason for Being and Mission?

Use this practice guide to clarify your mission or reason for being by working from your values, meaning, and purpose. Note that you may not come to conclusions that feel settled as you work through the process. The hope for this process is to support your work in getting to a closer understanding of what matters to you and how to use that to guide your actions. Complete this process as many times as you'd like for as long as you'd like and enjoy living the questions.

The steps you will take follow this trajectory:

Values → Meaning → Purpose → Reason for Being → Mission → Actions

STEP 1: Clarify Your Core Values

Your core values are your internal compass. They help you find valued direction in your actions. They include values like love, family, education, connection, and achievement. You might work with your therapist or take an assessment to help you identify your top values. When you are ready, list your top three values here:

1. _____
2. _____
3. _____

Now circle the value you'd like to work on first.

STEP 2: Convey Meaning

Meaning grants and conveys the merit and significance of your values. Using your circled value above, write here about why this value is important to you and/or the world. Use as much space as you need (use additional sheets or your journal if needed). It might be helpful to take some time to consider, or to discuss this with your therapist or someone you trust, and to take 10 or more minutes to freewrite, before writing down your narrative.

This value is important to me and/or the world because

_____
_____
_____

_____

_____

Next, taking some time to edit, boil down the essence of your meaning to one or two sentences. It might be helpful to take some time to consider, or to discuss this with your therapist or someone you trust, before editing down your narrative.

This value is important to me and/or the world because

_____

_____

_____

STEP 3: Identify the Purpose

Purpose fulfills meaning and can be framed as an aim: what is to be accomplished (e.g., my actions will be kind and compassionate, fewer people will have lung cancer). Write one, two, or three aims here:

These things will be accomplished when I live into my values and meaning:

_____

_____

_____

_____

_____

_____

STEP 4: Write Your Reason for Being

Your reason for being is a broad statement that explains what you are here to be in this life. It is is informed by your values, meaning, and purpose. You might have more than one, and they may have changed over the years. You can do visualization or vision board work and work with your therapist to help you develop some ideas. Then, document your ideas here:

I am here to

_____

_____

_____

_____

_____

_____

_____

_____

_____

STEP 5: Develop Your Mission Statement

Your mission statement is intended to work like an internal compass, building from the reasons for being you have already identified. This is the step in which the reason for being is more actionable. You use visualization work, looking back at your life from the future, and work with your therapist to construct your personal mission statement. Try using the structure below:

I will _____ (accomplishments)

in _____ (describe the setting or location),

using _____ (list strengths and skills)

and integrating _____ (list character traits),

prioritizing _____ (values) over _____ (values/challenges).

Here are a couple of examples of mission statements:

"I will graduate from my high school free of symptoms, using my inherent gift of persistence and my newly developed distress tolerance skills to manage my symptoms, integrating my commitment to health and friendships over giving in to drama and body shaming."

"I will be a blog writer sharing the pathway to recovery internationally, using my natural writing abilities and skills learned during my undergraduate training as an English major, integrating my commitment to empirically supported treatments and prioritizing healing over sensationalizing symptoms."

Write your full mission statement here:

_____

_____

_____

_____

_____

_____

_____

_____

STEP 6: Define Your Actions Through Goals and Plans

Goals are the things you need to accomplish to realize your mission statement. You can look at the larger five-year picture so you have a sense of the larger process of realizing your mission. Next, focus on the next 6–12 months to develop specific goals and plans you will accomplish to keep you on track and on mission. Your goals are the things you would like to accomplish (e.g., get accepted into a research university, write a play, start a blog):

In the next 6–12 months I would like to

_____

_____

_____

_____

_____

_____

_____

_____

Next, using your journal or some scrap paper, begin to break down your goals into small, accomplishable steps. You can work with your therapist for guidance. These are the specific actions with completion dates that you will need to do to accomplish your goals in the next 6–12 months. Write your plans and dates below:

I will

_____

_____

_____

by (date) _____

I will

_____

_____

_____

by (date) _____

I will

_____

_____

_____

by (date) _____

I will

_____

_____

_____

by (date) _____

I will

_____

_____

_____

by (date) _____

I will

_____

_____

_____

by (date) _____

Script 8.1: Simple Meditation and Body Scan

Begin by finding a comfortable seated position. Be sure your feet are grounded on the floor and your sitting bones are connected to your chair. From grounded feet and a connected seat, extend through your spine, reaching through the crown of your head, keeping your chin neutral. If you'd like, soften your gaze or close your eyes.

Bring your awareness to your breath, noticing each inhale and exhale. Breathe here for several breaths. Consider adding a narrative, "Breathing in, I know I am breathing in. Breathing out, I know I am breathing out." If you notice that your mind is thinking, simply label it thinking, and return to your breath. "Breathing in, I know I am breathing in. Breathing out, I know I am breathing out." (*long pause*)

Allowing your breath to continue, bring your awareness to your feet. Simply notice your feet and their connection to the floor. There is nothing to fix or change. Simply breathe and notice your feet. Next, notice your ankles (*pause*) your lower legs (*pause*) your knees (*pause*) and your upper legs. (*pause*) Breathe here for several breaths, noticing your feet, ankles, and legs. (*long pause*)

Now, move your awareness to your sitting bones, the connection to the chair, your core and extended spine, all the way through the crown of your head. There is nothing to fix or change and everything to simply be with. (*pause*) Breathe and notice your sitting bones, (*pause*) the connection to the chair, (*pause*) your core and your extended spine (*pause*), and the crown of your head. (*pause*)

Gently move your awareness to your shoulders, upper arms, lower arms, and hands. Breathe here, noticing your shoulders, (*pause*) your upper arms, (*pause*) your lower arms, (*pause*) and your hands. (*pause*) You might notice each of your fingers on your hands, the first, second, third, fourth, and your thumbs. Breathe and notice your fingers. (*pause*) Now, bring your awareness to the palms of your hands. Breathe here and notice the palms of your hands. (*pause*)

Gently take one hand and then the other, and place them over your heart. Bring your awareness to your hands and your heart.

You may notice your heart beating. You may notice your breath. Rest your awareness here, (*pause*) noticing your heartbeat, your breath. (*pause*)

Now, consider your work on [*add the topic here*]. As you consider this work, do you notice any shifts in your body? Do you notice a change in where you are feeling sensations or emotions, in your breath or your heartbeat, a lightness, heaviness, contraction, or expansion? Allow for whatever you notice to be present and okay just as it is. It might be a decrease or an increase in sensation. You might feel substantial shifts and changes. Whatever you notice, allow it to be. (*long pause*)

Now, bring your awareness back to your breath. You might add the narrative, saying to yourself, "Breathing in, I know I am breathing in. Breathing out, I know I am breathing out." Take several breaths here to connect back with this present moment and your breath. (*long pause*) When you are ready, slowly bring your awareness back to this room, finding one thing on which to anchor your awareness. (*pause*) As you are ready, slowly broaden your awareness to the whole room and to this moment. (*pause*) Thank you for practicing.

Script 8.2: Freewriting Instructions

Find a pen and open your journal to a blank page. When you are ready, review the prompt, [*add the prompt here for your client*]. When I say begin, place your pen on the paper and begin writing. The goal is to keep writing on the topic, about the topic, or about the process of writing about the topic until I tell you the time is up. There is no perfect or right way to do this. Work toward allowing what is and let go of trying to get it right or not get it wrong. You might ask yourself, "How might my heart answer this question if my mind was quiet?" As you write, breathe. If you are not sure what to write, you can write, "I am not sure what to write." You have about 10 minutes. [*You can vary this time, depending on the task and the client.*] If you need my support, let me know. Otherwise, keep writing and allow your thoughts, feelings, and ideas to flow from your pen. [*Repeat the prompt here.*] Begin.

CHAPTER 9

Embodied Wisdom

Sensing, Feeling, and Self-Regulating

The body speaks clearly to those who know how to listen.
—Pat Ogden, *Sensorimotor Psychotherapy*

I first heard the African proverb "Never leave yourself" while doing research with the Africa Yoga Project in Kenya. When I hear something this compelling, I allow the phrase to stir in my mind for a time—this one has stuck with me for years. I asked myself over and over: "Why not leave yourself? What is the cost?" After years of contemplation, I realized that whenever I had hurt myself or someone else, I had left myself in some way or another. It seems that there is something inherently unsafe about the disembodied self. They say that the monsters that are popular in media during certain periods of history tell us about our collective fears during that time. Right now, zombies and the walking dead are the monsters of the day. Maybe subconsciously we know that we are checked out, lost in technology, and too far away from our embodied selves to be fully human. Disembodied, our material selves wander disinhabited, hurting one another without full consciousness or remorse. The walking dead scare us because they should—they are today's version of hungry ghosts.

As I consider what happens when I leave myself, I begin to see the patterns. How did I get injured while running or working out? I was not fully present. How did I lose my temper and say or communicate something that did not serve me or another? In these cases, I had fallen into the experience, abandoning my sense of self as witness. As I contemplated disembodiment, I came to realize that there were many ways we leave ourselves. We can drink alcohol or skip meals. We can get lost in anger, anxiety, or fear. We can be so busy that we are no longer fully conscious. We can check out, experience symptoms, or dissociate.

When we leave ourselves we leave our main source of wisdom, connection, calming, and self-soothing—our bodies. This can be seen very clearly in the pathology of an ED. Conscious awareness is no longer partnered with the body as an ally. There is no physical guide to help us move effectively through the world and within relationships. In some cases, if we treated others like we treat our own bodies, we would be arrested for abuse, neglect, and in some cases assault.

For a decade, my team created and studied the Girls Growing in Wellness and Balance yoga-based prevention program for early adolescent females (Cook-Cottone et al., 2013; Scime & Cook-Cottone, 2008). This intervention included a letter to the self that was a long-withheld apology based on a letter to self in Kimberly Kirberger's *No Body's Perfect* (2003). In the process, a sample letter is read aloud before everyone writes their own letter. You can use Script 9.1 to help your clients to write a letter to their own body. When I do this in a class, I often keep the letters and mail them to students months later so that they can be reminded of the promises they made to themselves. It is a powerful practice to help clients get back to a relationship with their body.

Writing this letter is a great way for clients to engage in the content of this chapter. The goal is to shift their efforts and intentions toward embodiment—living in, of, and through the body. The hope is that their body becomes not just a resource but a source of being and wisdom for them. In an embodied way of being, clients are no longer an outside observer judging their body. Rather, clients live with an experience of internal awareness and intuitive and embodied wisdom with which to engage in the world. Living this way grants access to the embodied wisdom available in our interceptive experiences, sensations, emotions, and states of being as the whole body works to keep them both safe and connected.

This chapter focuses on the being-with and working-with pillar of the Embodied Approach to Treating Eating Disorders (EAT-ED), which gives clients tools to address whatever might show up in the moment, whether it is a trigger, feeling, or a life event. Along with the other three pillars that offer structure and direction—mindful self-care, honoring past effort and struggle, and cultivating mission and purpose—it helps clients develop an effective and reliable experience of embodiment. This chapter covers embodied wisdom as it manifests in interoceptive awareness, sensations, feelings, and states of being, and how the body can be a source of calming and self-regulation. This chapter prepares you and your client for the content in Chapter 10, which covers embodied practices such as yoga and working with horses to help clients connect to the self and to other sentient and sensitive beings.

EMBODIED WISDOM

There is an illusion perpetrated by insight-oriented therapies that all we need to do is think differently or understand more (Cook-Cottone, 2016). Seane Corn, an internationally acclaimed yoga teacher and activist, talks about the phenomenon on over-understanding (Corn, 2013). Of course it can be good to understand something; *over*-understanding occurs when understanding is an attempt to avoid experiencing feelings or memories. When there is nothing more to understand and everything to feel, over-understanding is a way to avoid somatic and emotional experience. Some call it a flight to reason; others refer to it as *intellectualization*, a psychodynamic term for a defense mechanism (Perry & Bond, 2017). Jane Goldberg (2017) posits that acknowledging so-called negative feelings can ultimately increase our capacity to feel everything, including love, to create what she calls a healthy psychological immune system. Neuroscientists agree: memories and feelings must be felt and experienced for them to be processed or integrated and to move us toward well-being (Hanson & Hanson, 2018; Siegel, 2010).

Embodied wisdom comprises the four cornerstones of being-with and working-with: states of being, interoceptive awareness, physical sensations, and feelings. Each is a way that our body communicates with us about our internal and external experiences. They tell us a bit about our past, concerns about our well-being, and the state of the present moment. They give us cues as to when we might be overreacting or biased because of our wounds and hurts. They can help us figure out the safety or lack of safety inherent in a situation or person. They can tell us what we need and what we do not. Like Pat Ogden said, "The body speaks clearly to those who know how to listen" (Ogden & Fisher, 2015, p. 25). I have found that the two steps to embodied wisdom, learning to listen to the wisdom of the body, are (1) learning that the wisdom of the body exists (a monumental task in a culture that thrives on thinking and judging), and (2) learning how to listen it.

States of Being and the Growth Zone

The first cornerstone of embodied wisdom is awareness of states of being: the body's response to stress and triggering events, as well as openness for growth and learning. When overwhelmed or in a state of extreme stress, the body can go into survival mode, and it can feel like we have little choice over our actions. Recovering from an ED means facing some challenges that have been avoided, difficult physical sensations, incredibly strong urges, intense and complicated feelings, and sorting through big life issues and questions. Further, recovery for some clients feels like a dismantling of their identity. If having an ED has become a big part of who your clients are, their brain may respond to treatment as a personal threat. For others in treatment, their system may be sensitized by traumatic or chronically stressful life experiences, and they are chronically defensive and alert to potential danger and threat. Despite our good intentions and hope for our clients, treatment can exacerbate an already stressed-out nervous system. To approach treatment well, we must support our clients' progress in therapy without pushing them into overwhelm. This requires creating an attuned cycling between effort and rest/restoration. When clients push recovery too hard and go too fast without a deep connection with their body's arousal system, the result is often relapse or the uptake of a new struggle (e.g., substance use, cutting). I have seen this happen to some of the most motivated clients. Paying attention to this cornerstone of embodied wisdom can help clients manage the stress of recovery along with the stress of life. They can learn how to move forward in a very sustainable way.

It can be useful to begin by helping clients honor and understand the protective aspects of their nervous system and how the parts of the brain work together to make daily lives possible. The part of the nervous system that deals with perceived threat is very primitive. This aspect of our being is regulated by the involuntary, autonomic nervous system (ANS; Bhat & Carleton, 2015; Ogden & Fisher, 2015). The ANS is housed in what some researchers refer to as the reptilian brain, comprising the brainstem, medulla, and pons. The reptilian brain is believed to be the first to evolve among living beings and concerns itself with survival-related functions of the body (Bhat & Carleton, 2015; Ogden & Fisher, 2015). It is located at the back of the head and runs such life-sustaining functions as heart rate, respiration, digestion, and regulating body temperature (Ogden & Fisher, 2015). It is also responsible for reflexes and instinctive responses to danger and threats, such as the startle response, defensive cries for help, fighting, fleeing, freezing, and feigning death (Ogden & Fisher, 2015).

In humans, the ANS has many neurological interconnections that help it coordinate with other regions of the brain—the mammalian brain and the neocortex. The mammalian brain is concerned with emotions and relationships. It is less primitive and is believed to have evolved along with the first mammals. Unlike most reptiles, mammals depend on being fed and cared for at birth, making relationships critical. This mammalian middle brain area helps us know the effects of the actions of others and the impact of their actions on us through emotion networks. This area is also believed to be the seat of attachment and social engagement systems. With connections to both the involuntary and voluntary aspects of the brain, this system is associated with intentional, reactive, and instinctual behaviors.

The ANS also interconnects with the neocortex, which is responsible for much of our planning, reasoning, abstract thinking, and self-awareness (Bhat & Carleton, 2015; Ogden & Fisher, 2015). The outermost layer of the brain, the neocortex is believed to be one of the last areas to evolve, and many think its functions are what make humans unique. The neocortex is the home of many of the functions we call self-regulating. It is believed to be the seat of our intention and purposeful behavior. It helps us intentionally regulate the rest of our brain and act with agency and self-determination. To work well, all three regions of the brain, ANS, mammalian brain, and neocortex, should share the processing load in an integrated manner so that our instincts, feelings, and thoughts can all work together as we make choices and engage in daily activities.

Our states of being are deeply influenced by the ANS and can shift quickly and automatically in response to perceived threat, danger, overwhelm, and stress. As described in Chapter 4, this system has two branches that have distinct and reciprocal functions: the sympathetic nervous system (SNS) and the parasympathetic nervous system (PNS; Bhat & Carleton, 2015). The SNS is associated with fear and arousal and initiates both instinctive emergency responses and conscious effort. In an emergency, the fight-or-flight mobilizing response is associated with the SNS. The PNS supports gentle activities, digestion, deep relaxation, and sleep—the rest-and-digest functions. When there is extreme and overwhelming stress, the PNS can be activated immediately before or after the SNS, causing an immobilizing freeze response, or shutdown. This involuntary immobilization can be associated with debilitating somatic symptoms such as psychological and emotional shutdown, dissociation, and feelings of entrapment and helplessness.

Pat Ogden, in her work with sensorimotor psychotherapy for attachment and trauma, has done the most extensive and detailed exploration of integrating the body in therapy (Ogden & Fisher, 2015). In her work, she uses Siegel's (1999) window of tolerance to help clients understand how their states of arousal affect the experience of self. When we are working within our window of tolerance (i.e., not too aroused and not in shutdown), we can perform optimally and live most effectively. However, when we move outside the window of tolerance, the nervous system is focused on survival and defense and we are too stressed to respond or engage effectively. For clients who have been through trauma, repeated treatment placements, familial discord and abuse, community violence, or extreme stress, their window of tolerance may be very small, and the therapeutic process is designed, in part, to expand it. From an embodied perspective, it means that we increase the capacity to remain present in the body with full awareness and agency.

Our curriculum for trauma-informed yoga, Yogis in Service, integrates two additional conceptualizations within the window of tolerance, the growth zone and the comfort zone, which I have found to be very helpful in working with clients in treatment for ED (Cook-Cottone et al., 2017). As summarized in Practice Guide 9.1, the growth zone is the state within which we can engage in optimal psychological and interpersonal growth (Cook-Cottone et al., 2017; Ogden & Fisher, 2015. Siegel, 1999). It is inherently uncomfortable in the growth zone because it exists outside of our comfort zone. In our comfort zone, we are comfortable—we are doing things over which we have 100% mastery and are functioning with the familiar and predictable. If we remain in our comfort zone, we might not grow (Cook-Cottone et al., 2017). As therapists, we want to move our clients out of their pathological and comfortable routines and into their growth edges without moving them beyond the boundary of effective coping and/or outside of what they can effectively tolerate. In essence, we want them to practice being uncomfortable without moving directly to overwhelm and reaction.

When outside of the window of tolerance and overwhelmed, clients are at risk for two things. First, they may move into fight-or-flight mode as their SNS system becomes highly activated (Ogden & Fisher, 2015; Siegel, 1999). In this state, fight or flight is experienced as a drive to aggressively engage or escape as they feel a strong urge toward mobilization within the context of their fear or stress. Second, for some under extreme stress, the PNS places them in acute shutdown (Ogden & Fisher, 2015): they are immobilized within the context of fear or stress. If your clients move into escape, fight, or shutdown, the best action is to help them self-regulate first and then engage. If the client is pushed further when in any of these states, the result is a fight, an attempt to escape, or shutdown—not therapeutic progress.

Both the reptilian and mammalian brain can move us into reaction. The reptilian response can be very physical, as described above. Because we, like other mammals, depend on others for survival, our emotional system also functions as a threat detector. An argument with someone we love very much can be experienced by the mammalian brain as a threat. The ANS is activated, and before we know it, we are saying and doing hurtful things that we would never do or say if the three parts of our brain were working together to make choices. This is often called an *emotional hijack* of the brain. This can happen at meal times, when ED clients perceive a particular food as a threat. They may move into fight or flight in a way that makes no sense to family members or themselves. A client once told me that she physically hit a family member because that person was trying to stop her from purging her meal. In another case, a parent almost came to blows with a child who was refusing to eat. To do this work, clients and (when possible) their family can benefit greatly from learning about the activation of the nervous system under stress and threat.

The sweet spot for recovery work is outside of the comfort zone and solidly within the growth zone, where the client is not overwhelmed yet highly engaged, learning new things, and tolerating new ranges of experiences (Cook-Cottone, 2015; Cook-Cottone et al., 2017). In our growth zone we are safe yet a bit uncomfortable. We are in a learning state in which not everything is known or mastered and we do not have 100% assurance for how everything will work out. In the growth zone we are in a state Ogden and Fisher (2015) call "regulated arousal" (p. 227), where we can mobilize or immobilize in the service of what we are doing, learning, and/or experiencing (Ogden & Fisher, 2015). In this state, our SNS and PNS are working in harmony to keep us balanced and engaged.

For clients to work within the growth zone, we need to effectively and gradually increase their window of tolerance, which involves communication and coping strategies. Help your clients become aware of their state of being and to know what each state of being feels like in their bodies, so that they can recognize them and take the right action. You can use Practice Guide 9.1 to help them detail their own experiences in each state of being and develop action plans and signals for when they are outside their window of tolerance.

Arousal Scale and Grounding and Breathing Practice. It is important that your clients learn and practice two simple and fundamental embodiment tools for coping and down-regulating their nervous systems: the Arousal Scale, and grounding and breathing. For some clients, reengaging with the body can feel triggering. It is often said that we should move at the speed of trust—this trust must exist between you and your clients, and between your clients and their nervous system. The goal is to work toward insight and growth, which is often accompanied by nervous system arousal as clients work outside of their comfort zones. This effort should be balanced with rest and intentional down-regulating of the nervous system back to baseline. These tools are adapted from my text on mindfulness and yoga for self-regulation (Cook-Cottone, 2015) and the work I have done with Kelly Boys, a mindful expert, in our work as consultants for the United Nations Foundation.

The Arousal Scale is a quick way for your clients to communicate where they are in terms of physical and emotional arousal. Introduce your clients to the scale in Table 9.1—it is fairly simple to use. The first step is to figure out a baseline state of being, what it is, and what it feels like. For the most part, most of us are rarely at a 1, which is completely calm, or a 10, which is completely distressed. Note: it can also be productive to work with your clients to create their own self-awareness scales with physiological, emotional, and cognitive indicators of their own.

The next step is to teach and practice grounding and breathing (see Script 9.2). Keep this practice very simple and short. It is simple guidance to ground the feet and sitting bones and stabilize the core, and then to take four extended exhalation breaths—that's it. As a short and simple practice, it can be woven into sessions as needed. Once this practice is part of your routine, it can be very helpful to practice along with your client any time there is a sense that arousal, agitation, or overwhelm is approaching an intolerable level, say, above a 6 or 7 on the Arousal Scale and moving toward a 10. As you get to know your

Table 9.1: Arousal Scale

Relaxed, Calm (1 to 2)	Engaged (3 to 6)	Distressed (7 to 10)
I am aligned with my *Comfort Zone*. My body, emotions, and thoughts are clear. I feel safe and competent. I can rest here.	I am aligned with my *Growth Zone*. My body, emotions, and thoughts are active and manageable. I can grow and be effective here.	I am aligned with the edge and/or outside of my *Window of Tolerance*. My body, emotions, and thoughts are not manageable. I am overwhelmed, lost in reaction, or shutdown.

Source: Adapted from Cook-Cottone (2015b) and work I have done with Kelly Boys, a mindful expert, in our work as consultants for the United Nations Foundation.

client, you can develop a bit of a shorthand for engaging in the grounding and breathing practice. For example, a client might say: "I am feeling at about a 7 and moving toward an 8; can we ground and breathe right now?" You can then lead the client through the practice, followed by another Arousal Scale assessment. The client might then report: "I am at a 5 now and can continue." As you go through the body wisdom work that follows, you can check in and down-regulate as needed.

    Distress Tolerance: The Five Senses. As you work with your clients across the additional cornerstones of embodied wisdom, they will be working to feel and become aware of internal and external body sensations, as well as a wide range of emotions. Often this work can move clients to the edge of their window of tolerance, where they are feeling triggered and aroused, or distressed. Distress tolerance skills comprise one of the four modules of dialectical behavioral therapy (DBT) because they help clients cope with the present moment rather than engaging in symptoms or acting out (Linehan, 1993). The manifestation of symptoms is considered a way that some clients avoid distress and uncomfortable experiences (Astrachan-Fletcher & Maslar, 2009; Cook-Cottone, 2015b). Having alternative strategies can help clients remain embodied and able to avoid symptoms. If you are using the Arousal Scale (Table 9.1) with clients, you might use distress tolerance tools if they are feeling anything from a 6 or above.

In developing distress tolerance, strategies help clients shift their physiological state, either drastically, by holding an ice cube, splashing their face with water, or taking a cold shower, or gently, by using exercise, paced breathing, progressive muscle relaxation, distracting activities, and self-soothing tasks (Astrachan-Fletcher & Maslar, 2009; Cook-Cottone, 2015b; Linehan, 1993). Many of these approaches are all included in this text throughout the various chapters. Another approach involves focusing on sensations (see Script 9.3). Clients can use this tool in situations where they are distressed but are physically and emotionally safe, when they cannot change circumstances in the moment and need to simply be with what is. The grounding process moves from the feet on the floor, to the breath in the body, and then dials into each of the five senses and away from an escalating narrative in the mind.

Riding the Wave of Arousal. Learning to ride the wave of arousal can be another powerful tool for doing embodied wisdom work and avoiding symptoms. In relapse prevention work, this is called urge surfing. Learning how to ride the waves of distress, arousal, feelings, urges, and senses is critical to recovery. Riding the wave of arousal, or urge surfing, is a mindfulness and acceptance-based technique (Cook-Cottone, 2015b; Juarascio, Manasse, Schumacher, Espel, & Forman, 2017). The arousal or urge is noticed and observed (Bowen, Chala, & Marlatt, 2010; Juarascio et al., 2017); they have a pattern, and they pass like waves (Cook-Cottone, 2015b). The client's awareness, grounded feet, and breath can stay steady as the wave of arousal or urge arises and passes. I encourage some clients to actually time the length of the wave and estimate its intensity, documenting it in a journal.

So often we focus on symptoms, with clients saying, "I binged and purged five times last week." However, we also want to know how many times they were deeply challenged and yet did not engage in symptoms, and how they did it. The client may report,

I binged and purged five times last week. It was a very stressful and challenging week. I was able to ride the wave of arousal 7 times and have no symptoms. The longest one lasted 15 solid minutes and I swear it was a 10 out of 10. It is the strongest urge I have felt in a while. I watched it. As it got stronger, I pulled my dog up onto my lap and held him and kept breathing as it peaked and then passed. I think that is the strongest I have ever been.

These are two very different perspectives: a focus on the symptoms, and a focus on when the client was able to powerfully negotiate the urge and not experience symptoms. For more specific instructions, see Script 9.4, which you can teach to clients so that, when they first notice they are getting close to the edge of their window of tolerance, they can practice it as soon as they are able, to help them ride the wave of arousal.

Interoceptive Awareness

Interoception, the second foundational cornerstone of embodied wisdom, is the sense of the internal state of the body and includes information about our hunger, satiety, and even to some degree what emotions feel like in our body (Jenkinson et al., 2018). Specifically, it is afferent (moving toward) information arising from within the body and moving toward the brain that influences the thinking and behavior of an organism, whether or not the organism is aware (Ainley, Maister, Brokfeld, Farmer, & Tsakiris, 2013). The interoceptive senses are also considered aspects of the self (Ainley et al., 2013). Some believe that our basic feelings of existence are maintained by the continuous mapping of information about the interoceptive state of the body—we know we are here because we can feel ourselves deeply from within (Ainley et al., 2013; Biasetti, 2018). Interoception may also be connected to exteroception, or sensitivity to what is outside of the body (Ainley et al., 2013). In fact, it is theorized that those with low interoceptive awareness might have more malleable mental representations of the self in response to exteroceptive signals (Ainley et al., 2013).

In their review, Jenkinson et al. (2018) noted that in 1962 Hilde Bruch warned that clients with EDs were less accurate in their perceptions and cognitive interpretations of stimuli arising from the body (Bruch, 1962). To give you a sense of the scope of the challenge, in their meta-analysis Jenkinson et al. (2018) identified 41 samples comprising 4,308 people with various types of EDs and compared these with 3,459 people without EDs. They found that if you were to choose, at random, a person from the group with an ED, there would be an 87% chance that the person would have a greater interoceptive deficit than a person picked at random from the control group. The effect size of this difference was very large (1.62). Moreover, they found that clients with anorexia nervosa (AN) or bulimia nervosa (BN) had more pronounced deficits than those with binge eating disorder (BED). Among a small sample of recovered individuals, there was some evidence that the deficit in interoceptive awareness may persist for those with AN and BN.

For many years, interoceptive awareness has been considered difficult to change, and some even believe it is a trait—a stable characteristic (Ainley et al., 2013). Ainley et al. (2013) were able to increase interoceptive awareness in an experimental condition, asking participants to look at photographs of their own faces and in another condition to gaze at self-generated sets of autobiographical words (e.g., their first name or their hometown). Using a heartbeat perception task, the researchers demonstrated that in both of the self-awareness conditions the self-awareness participants increased their ability to accurately perceive their heartbeats compared to controls.

The insula, a brain structure buried deeply inside the lateral sulcus, is believed to play a role in self-awareness, perception, and cognition and is considered to be the region through which interoception occurs. Recently, researchers identified the insular cortex to be a key component of the neural correlates with meditation (Calì, Ambrosini, Picconi, Mehling, & Committeri, 2015). Pat Ogden and Janina Fisher (2015) hold in their text on sensorimotor psychotherapy that techniques used for trauma and attachment to conceptualize internal body sensations (interoceptive experiences) are the main building blocks of the present-moment experience.

To help clients develop a sense of internal awareness, it can be useful to repeatedly direct them to notice these experiences, engage in in embodied mindfulness practices that strengthen the awareness of and sensitivity to cues coming from within the body (see Chapter 10), and build in intuitive eating exercises to help develop awareness of satiety and fullness cues (see Chapter 12). You can begin with two simple exercises: awareness of breath and heartbeat (Script 9.5) and self-awareness journaling (Script 9.6).

Script 9.5 will help you guide clients through the breath and heartbeat meditation. After the exercise, you can ask questions to help your client process the experience, in a way that is experiential and free of judgment, releasing the need to achieve anything. Create a dialogue around what your client noticed, felt, and experienced, as well as the client's observations, asking "What did you notice?" and "How was the experience was for you—can you describe it?" Clients can also record the meditation session on their smartphones so they can use it to practice at home—it can be helpful to do the same meditation many times.

Self-awareness journaling (see Script 9.6) can be done directly after the breath and heartbeat exercise, or they can be done in separate sessions to allow more time for processing. After the journaling session, you can use questions to help clients process the experience. The process is intended to be experiential and free of judgment, releasing the need to achieve anything. Create a dialogue around what clients noticed, felt, and experienced, asking "What did you notice?" and "How did it feel to spend time thinking and writing about, or with, yourself?"

Once your clients complete this first introduction, suggest they take time each day to write in their journal about how their day went, the sensations they experienced (e.g., smells, sights, sounds, textures, tastes), how they felt about the things they experienced during the day, and what they think about it. Remind them that, as they write, it is better not write about their disorder or symptoms. Encourage them to highlight details about their sensations and feelings—this is the good stuff.

Physical Sensation

Physical sensation, the third foundational cornerstone of embodied wisdom, is critical to embodiment. Physical sensation has a tremendous capacity to bring us back to the here and now. It is the present-moment experience of our sensory receptors making contact with the world— noticing the sound of a bird's song as you sit in your backyard, the feel of an old hardwood floor under your feet as you walk, the smell and touch of freshly laundered sheets as you slip into bed, the smell, the look, and the taste of homemade apple pie as you enjoy the artistry that created it. A true sensory experience is not a memory about the past or a plan for the future—it is in the now.

Sensory experience is not a concept, idea, or thought; it is the raw, unprocessed experience. It is sensory and, for most of us, a bit perceptual, but it is not cognitive. In a sensory experience there is *sensation* as the physical stimuli and its physical properties are detected and registered with our sensory neurons and sensory organs. This information is immediately filtered and organized by the brain and linked to memories, emotions, and more. Mindfulness is the work of getting back to the raw, sensational experience, in the here and now, and staying with it, working to slow down the quick movement to interpretations, judgment, and knowing.

Integrating sensory awareness into treatment may help shift clients out of their rigid ED narratives. Neuropsychological practitioner and theorist Daniel Seigel explains that sensory experiences are primarily processed in the inner layers of the neocortex, considered the perceptual and thinking part of the brain (Siegel, 2010). Conversely, the conceptual aspects of knowing, consciousness, thought, and language are primarily processed in the outer layers of the cortex (Siegel, 2010). It is within the middle layers of the cortex that sensory information and thinking meet (Siegel, 2010). Consider this: How do you change your mind about something? Sometimes, someone appeals to your reasoning (i.e., the outer layers of your cortex) and you change your mind. However, many times, it is because you experience something that is in conflict with what you thought you knew. Getting to the embodied and sensory aspects of the self can help literally change the mind from the inside out.

By focusing on their sensory experiences, your clients can move their experiences out of the crystallized thought patterns aligned with their disorder and activate brain areas deeply connected with the present moment—*the only time when changes in behavior can ever take place*. Clients locked in the cortical pattern will see the here and now differently, in a disorder-aligned way, unless they engage the sensational experience of the present moment and do something different.

Due to the neuropsychological role they play in shifting awareness and breaking behavioral patterns, physical sensations are a key part of mindfulness and yoga, DBT, and other mindfulness-based interventions for EDs (Cook-Cottone, 2019a). As discussed earlier in this chapter, focusing on sensations is a key part of distress tolerance skills in DBT for EDs (Astrachan-Fletcher & Masar, 2009). The same is true for emotion acceptance behavior therapy for AN (Wildes & Marcus, 2016), in which clients are taught to remain in contact with the present moment by focusing their attention on the physical sensations that accompany nonmental tasks such as walking, doing the dishes, and cleaning (Wildes & Marcus, 2016). Subscale 5 of the Mindful Self-Care Scale (see Chapter 7) examines self-soothing and relaxation using sensations and other techniques.

I ask clients to consider the word *sensational*. It is often taken to mean a very good, even great, experience. But the word's origins relate to the senses and sensations—to make our life sensational, we need to get back to the sensory experiences in our life. Two practices that can increase awareness of, and connection to, the sensory experience are setting up a sensory-based self-soothing center (Script 9.7) and sensory-based mindful walking (Script 9.8).

Taking time in a sensory-based self-soothing center and taking a sensory-based mindful walk are both considered formal practices (Cook-Cottone, 2015b). That is, clients have set aside a specific time to practice sensory focus. They can also engage in informal practices. Informal practices are ways to weave the practices into everyday life, such as paying attention to the sensory experiences while washing dishes, attending to the smell of the soap, the feeling of the water and the soap, the sound of the dishes in the water. Other ideas might involve using body lotion with a pleasing scent or wearing a soft and silky pair of socks.

For mindful walks, advise clients to choose their spaces carefully. Recent research suggests that spending time in nature may improve body esteem. Swami, Barron, Weis, and Furnham (2016) found that nature exposure and feelings of connectedness to nature were associated with body appreciation in women and men. Advise clients to consider how and where they might spend their sensory time, and encourage them to spend some time identifying both outdoor and indoor options for exposure to nature.

Feeling (Emotions)

Feelings, or emotions, are the fourth cornerstone of embodied wisdom. At their core, emotions exist to serve motivational functions and control the basic behavioral systems (Frederickson, 1998; Ogden & Fisher, 2015; Macht, 2008). According to Ogden and Fischer (2015), "Our emotional brain steers our attention toward certain cues, people, and situations that have meaning and value for us on a feeling level, and then the emotions we experience motivate our actions in response to these stimuli" (p. 639). Emotions coordinate our behavior and physiological states during both survival-salient events and pleasurable interactions (Nummenmaa et al., 2014). Our body moves us, drives us, and tells us what is important and what feels good. It is a tremendous messenger and can be our ally if we learn to listen to it. For many with EDs, this communication pathway between the emotional system and decision making is complicated with a disordered relationship with emotions, a tendency to avoid or suppress unwanted emotions, and few skills for coping effectively with emotions.

Most accept that mood, emotion dysregulation, and reduced ability to cope with and manage emotions contribute to the cause and maintenance of ED behavior across diagnostic categories (Dingemans, Danner, & Parks, 2017; Lavender et al., 2015). For example, in a review of the research, Dingemans et al. (2017) concluded that negative emotions and maladaptive emotion regulation strategies play a part in the onset and maintenance of binge eating in BED: poor mood precedes binge-eating episodes and binge eating may be an attempt to down-regulate emotional distress. In their review, Lavender et al. (2015) concluded that those with AN and BN struggled with global difficulties in regulating affective states and possessed a limited repertoire of adaptive emotion regulation skills and an increased tendency to use maladaptive coping strategies (Lavender et al., 2015). Accordingly, learning to be-with and work-with emotions is a critical aspect EAT-ED.

Feelings Are Embodied. I like referring to emotions interchangeably as feelings. It reminds us how physical they are: we feel them. The way we speak of them highlights their embodied essence. In sadness we have heartache, are heavy hearted, feel blue, see darkness, and feel lost and empty. In happiness we jump for joy, feel light as a feather, and move as if we had wings on our feet. In anxiety and fear we are shaken and wrought.

Individuals with EDs often struggle to identify and describe feelings in their bodies (Westwood, Kerr-Gaffney, Stahl, & Tchanturia, 2017). In a systematic review and meta-analysis of alexithymia in EDs, Westwood et al. (2017) found that alexithymia, literally having no word for mood, is characterized by particular difficulties identifying and describing emotions. This difficulty was transdiagnostic across the spectrum of EDs. Their review and analysis of 44 studies found that individuals with AN, BN, and BED consistently had higher alexithymia than healthy controls. Overall, the results validated the recognition and management of emotions as important treatment targets across the EDs (Westwood et al., 2017).

There is a saying in the psychology of emotions: name it to tame it (Cook-Cottone, 2015b). By naming an emotion, we activate the linguistic and emotional parts of the brain simultaneously, creating a neurologically integrative experience that can enhance emotion regulation (Cook-Cottone, 2015b). The problem is that clients cannot name what they do not feel. Helping clients notice, feel, and identify feelings in the body is a large part of my clinical work. If clients are not able to talk about or locate emotions their body, I begin with a blank sheet of paper and a basket of hundreds of crayons to start the process of identifying their emotional landscape on paper. I simply ask clients to represent, in any way what they would like, what they are feeling in the present moment (see Script 9.9). When they are finished, I ask them to tell me about the patterns, placement, and colors used, and which feelings they represent. I write their responses on their paper using arrows to connect their verbal responses to their art. I also date each piece so that we can review the images over time and consider shifts and changes in the emotional landscapes. I have found that clients who are not able to talk about their emotions, or to locate the associated sensations in their bodies, are often able to produce something on paper. Once they do that, they are then able to talk about what they have done. In this way, we create a bridge to their emotional experience. I use this as a stepping stone to somatic body maps (see below). After some work on the paper, I ask them to notice if they feel anything in their bodies as they tell me about the emotion. If they are, or are not, able to notice something, I jot it down on their paper as well.

I also use body maps to help clients increase their ability to notice, identify, feel, and describe their emotions (see Script 9.11), based on research that has identified universal body maps of emotions (see Figure 4.3 in Chapter 4). If you find this work compelling, there are additional studies with more complex maps: see Nummenmaa, Hari, Heitanen, and Glerean (2018) for maps of subjective feelings and Hietanen, Glerean, Hari, and Nummenmaa (2016) for bodily maps of emotions across child development. I use the more basic map in private practice because I find it gets the point across without being overly distracting or complex.

In practice, I use Figure 4.3 almost weekly—I print it out and have color copies in case a client wants to take it home. A colleague has had it printed and laminated poster size because she uses it so often. I explain to clients that these images are averages or aggregates of the self-reports of hundreds of people and do not reflect the right way to feel anything. Rather, these images help us see that emotions can be identified via body sensations and that this may be one way to connect with our emotional selves and to begin identifying emotions in the body. You can use the being-with emotions body scan (Script 9.10) to begin this process, which helps clients welcome and be with emotions

(Miller, 2015); then you can help clients process the experience using body maps (Script 9.11).

For some clients, it can be a challenging and even overwhelming experience to begin to explore emotions, as they have engaged in months and sometimes years of avoiding and suppressing them. You can weave in grounding and breathing practices (e.g., Script 9.2) or any of the self-soothing activities to help practice self-regulation as you do this work. It can also be initially a bit confusing to work on interoceptive awareness, body sensations, and feelings, as these body signals can get confused or mistaken for one another (Lattimore et al., 2017). Working very specifically with noticing, identifying, feeling, and describing emotions as they are experienced in the body is the first step in regulating emotions.

Managing Difficult Emotions. As your clients learn to identify and feel emotions in their body, they will likely want additional tools to negotiate difficult emotions. Kristen Neff and Christopher Germer's *Mindful Self-Compassion Workbook* (2018) includes methods for negotiating difficult emotions. Acknowledging that emotions have physical, emotional, and cognitive components, the soften-allow-soothe technique helps clients locate and anchor emotions in their body and gives them a narrative for being-with and working-with emotions (Germer & Neff, 2013). I have adapted the process slightly to integrate a stronger sense of being-with, to align more closely with the EAT-ED process (see Script 9.12).

Supporting and Listening to Emotions. Our emotions are our friends, our allies. They help us know the state of things inside and out and compel us to act. Richard Miller, the psychologist who created iRest, a yoga-based program for the treatment of posttraumatic stress disorder among military veterans, emphasizes the importance of seeing emotions as messengers. In his text on iRest, Miller (2015) writes,

> At their core, feelings and emotions are feedback mechanisms. I call these feedback mechanisms messengers. These messengers are designed by nature to provide you with the information necessary to help you survive and thrive. . . . In and of themselves, feelings and emotions are neither good nor bad. They're neither right nor wrong. They are simply providing information. Avoiding or reacting to your feelings and emotions blocks your ability to accurately respond to the world around and within you. (p. 97)

Ogden and Fisher (2015) remind us that emotions can be confusing, as they are in constant flux, moving with changes in our internal and external landscapes. Emotions can be related to our most primitive animal defenses and our attachment histories, challenges, and experiences. In this way, there is a past, future, and present orientation in many emotional experiences as our system works to protect us and to get us what we need.

Emotions not only help our bodies and psychological systems communicate to us what we need but also motivate us to communicate our needs to others. Those whose expressions were ignored or reacted to with anger or punishment might self-silence (Ogden & Fisher, 2015). Those who could elicit attention and connection only when they were upset or hurting may believe that emotional intensity is the only state through which needs are met (Ogden & Fisher, 2015). Through these being-with practices we can teach our emotional systems that they are seen and heard in all of their subtleties and intensities. Through practice we can remind our emotional selves that we are worth attention and effort and that our emotional experiences are seen and heard.

We can care for our emotional systems by supporting the houses within which they live: our bodies. EDs symptoms often complicate the emotional communications system as food restriction, bingeing, and compensatory behaviors further dysregulate the nervous and emotional systems. When standing on a physiological foundation dysregulated by symptoms, the psychological and emotional landscape can feel treacherous, dangerous, and unpredictable. One way to support and befriend your emotions is through the cessation of symptoms that destabilize their physiological foundation. Encourage your clients to see their work with their nutritionist and their work on symptom reduction as a way to create a steady, strong physiological home for their emotions.

Like any friendship, it can be helpful for those in the relationship to spend time together. Miller (2015) suggests that "inviting an emotion to tea" can be a good way to create a structured time to have a dialogue with emotions. Script 9.13 is for introducing your clients to a practice based on this concept.

Emotions and Eating. Emotions can influence our eating, including what we eat or don't eat, when we eat, and how we eat. Our eating may also, in turn, regulate emotions (Macht, 2008). It can be helpful for your clients to understand these connections as a pathway to better understanding and having compassion for their body, cravings, and behaviors. Taking into account individual characteristics and emotion features, Macht (2008) proposed five classes of emotion-induced changes in eating among typical, non-ED individuals, which suggest reflective questions about a range of food-emotion interactions that clients can use to pause before engaging in symptomatic behaviors, discussed below and summarized in Table 9.2.

Macht (2008) provides research evidence suggesting that food-induced emotions are powerful determinants of food choice. For example, tasting energy-dense food such as sugar and fat can evoke positive

Table 9.2: Reflective Questions for Food-Emotion Connections

Food-Emotion Connection	Reflective Questions
Emotional control of food choice	Am I wanting this food because I am wanting the emotion that I believe is paired with it?
	Might there be other ways, outside of ingestion of food right now, that I can use to regulate my emotions?
Intense emotion suppressing food intake	Am I considering the effect of the emotions I am having right now on my urge to restrict food intake?
	Might there be an emotion-based reason for not feeling hungry?
	Could I engage in a relaxation practice right now to allow my system to down-regulate and prepare me to nourish my body as I should?
Negative and positive emotions impairing cognitive eating controls	Am I eating enough food frequently enough to nourish my body?
	Am I following my meal plan, including the calorie and macronutrient requirements?
	Could I be overestimating food portions so that I am undernourished?
	Knowing I have only one stress-response system, am I adding extra stress to my system by overly restraining my food intake?
	What is my emotional landscape right now?
	How can I manage my emotions without eating or restricting eating?
	What resources and supports do I have?

Negative emotions eliciting eating to regulate emotions	Am I trying to avoid a difficult feeling or emotion right now?
	Does it make sense, within the context of what I have eaten today and my activity levels, that my craving levels are this high?
	Could this craving be an effort to avoid the present moment?
	What tools and resources could I use right now to help me lean into what I am feeling?
	If I am not feeling ready to do that, are there other ways I can distract myself, like a walk, a self-soothing practice, a hot shower, or connecting with a dear friend?
Emotions modulating eating in congruence with emotion features	How is my current mood affecting my eating?
	What might happen if I engaged in an activity to shift my mood before I engage in eating?
	What activities could help lift my mood and prepare me to make more effective eating choices? Could I attend a yoga class? Go for a walk?
	Could I engage in something that brings me joy, like playing with my dog or watching a funny video with a friend?

Source: Informed by Macht (2008).

affective responses that promote ingestion. A bitter compound, a taste correlated with toxins, can evoke a negative affective responses. Food-related stimuli can elicit a strong desire to eat, or a craving, and can trigger binge eating. For example, cakes and pies, ice cream, and chocolate bars are often paired with celebrations and/or coping, such as birthday cake or the breakup pint of ice cream.

Intense emotions can suppress food intake. This has been found to be true among animals and humans, as intense emotions are linked with physiological responses and behaviors that interfere with eating. Macht (2008) provides examples, such as intense sadness being associated with deactivation and withdrawal from the environment, and intense fear motivating flight and avoidance. When our ANS is in stress response mode, there is an overall inhibition for eating, and physiological changes are activated that can interfere with digestion as the system shuts down and/or as energy is allocated to other systems (Cook-Cottone, 2015b; Macht, 2008). This can be especially challenging for clients with AN or BN who have been restricting. Eating itself can cause an emotional reaction that suppresses eating.

Negative and positive emotions can impair cognitive eating controls. In this case, the focus is on individuals working to restrain or inhibit their eating in some way. Macht (2008) calls overeating in this case an ironic process, in that the more people exert cognitive control over their eating, the higher their vulnerability to overeat will be. Among the list of studies Macht (2008) provided for evidence, he cited Boon, Stroebe, Schut, and Jansen's (1998) limited capacity hypothesis, in which, for restrained eaters, intake is increased if their cognitive capacity to maintain restricted food intake is limited by distraction (emotional or otherwise). This can be especially salient for clients who are subclinical chronic dieters or those who have approached their recovery from BN or BED via attempts to overly restrain or restrict food intake by relying on willpower. For these clients the line of inquiry should address their efforts to restrain food intake, and manage emotions and other stressors in their lives.

Negative emotions can elicit eating to regulate emotions (Macht, 2008). For some individuals, emotional eating is an attempt to cope with emotions and stress. The mechanisms of this class of food and emotion connections include eating to reduce arousal of the nervous system, to shift mood to a more positive mood state, to reduce stress, or to escape from aversive self-awareness. Further, particular foods such a carbohydrate-rich foods (or what we refer to as comfort foods) may have mood-elevating and stress-reducing effects on serotonin levels (a neurotransmitter implicated in mood regulation). Negative mood may improve immediately after eating highly palatable foods, which, due to their positive affective reactions in the body, offers a hedonistic mechanism of distraction.

Emotions can also modulate eating in congruence with emotion features (Macht, 2008). The congruency effect can be seen in cognitions. For example, during negative mood, negative verbal information is retrieved more readily than positive information, and vice versa. Research indicates that this can be true for food and emotions. For example, sadness may be associated with a decrease in experiences of food pleasantness and motivation to eat, whereas joy is related to increased food pleasantness and motivation to eat. Macht (2008) details the associations of the emotion and the eating-related response. For example, sadness is associated with a slowing of thinking processes and motor activity, reduced interest, and a lowering of attention to the outside world. Conversely, joy is associated with increased cognitive capacities and a readiness to engage in activities.

Consider reviewing with clients the categories and questions listed in Table 9.2 and having them develop their own sets of reflective questions about food-emotion interactions that they can use to pause before engaging in symptomatic behaviors.

THE BODY AS A RESOURCE

A goal of embodied wisdom is to shift from seeing the body as a source of discomfort, pain, and the battlefield of the ED to seeing it as a resource. The body has a tremendous capacity to calm, soothe, and engage. It can lead and guide us. In our body we can find the central aspects of resilience and recovery, our inner resources. Frequently used by popular mindfulness experts such as Sharon Salzberg and Rick Hanson, the term *inner resource* was first introduced by psychologist Richard Miller, who developed a yoga intervention for military service members who were experiencing posttraumatic stress disorder (Miller, 2015):

> You possess within yourself an inner resource that's designed to empower you to feel in control of and at ease with every experience you have during your life. Your inner resource is a place of refuge within you. It provides you with inner support on every step of your healing journey. (p. 53)

Miller's yoga-based treatment method prioritizes the integration of the experiences of self, as well as restoration of joy, peace, and well-being, enabling practitioners to feel more connected to themselves and their lives. Rather than seeing the body as part of the problem or a derivative of the problem (e.g., a need for body acceptance, a need to regulate and control the body), intentional embodiment practices as a pathway to connect with and cultivate of inner resources are based on the realization, or the remembering, that our own body, our own experience can be the source of well-being.

For many, especially those who are at risk for or struggling with ED behavior, this is a profoundly different way of viewing the individual self. Being with the body and of the body, there are no thoughts to shift or reframe or past histories to analyze. Rather, clients work with experiencing and being with the body sensations, emotions, and thoughts in the present moment. This approach presents as central the notion that each person has the capacity for wellness and calm. Salzberg (2017) refers to this practice as "taking a refuge inside" (p. 47). We become the unique and reliable source of our well-being: "Your inner resource is an internal felt sense that you carry with you. It is unique to you. Like drawing water from a well, you draw strength and comfort from your inner resource" (Miller, 2015; p. 57).

You can help your clients develop their inner resources and guide in layers: their internal and external senses, their feelings, and their state of being. Script 9.14 provides a step-by-step meditative script to help clients align their intuitions, emotional wisdom, and mind to develop their inner resource and guide. Spending time in a calm and relaxed state and tuning in toward the body allows the brain to integrate this state of being into the experience of self. Aristotle is believed to have said, "We are what we repeatedly do." As our clients add minutes, hours, and days being-with, for, and of their bodies and increasingly less time engaged in ED thinking and doing, it can gradually become true for a client to say, "I am at my center, calm, grounded, and filled with beauty. My body is a source of wisdom that I connect to and am guided by."

Table 9.3 summarizes practices to develop the four cornerstones of embodied wisdom, states of being, interoceptive awareness, physical sensation, and feeling, to help your clients access their embodied wisdom. These practices, along with your clients' inner *why*, provide a foundation for grounding and self-regulation as your clients work through the next steps toward full embodiment. As your clients spend positive, down-regulated, and effective time in and with their bodies, how they see and embody themselves will unfold, dismantling objectification and supporting agency and self-determination. As you prepare to move forward, remember to cycle back to the inquiry around mission and self-care. These practices are the directional and structural pillars of the embodied approach.

Table 9.3: Cornerstones of Embodied Wisdom and Associated Practices

Embodied wisdom cornerstone	Associated practice
States of being The experience of and listening to the various states of arousal of the body	States of Being and the Growth Zone (Practice Guide 9.1) Distress Tolerance—The Five Senses (Script 9.3) Riding the Wave of Arousal (Script 9.4)
Interoceptive awareness The experiencing of and listening to the body's internal state	Awareness of Breath and Heartbeat Meditation (Script 9.5) Self-Awareness Journaling (Script 9.6)
Physical sensation The experiencing of and listening to the body's sensory input	Sensory-Based Self-Soothing Center (Script 9.7) Sensory-Based Mindful Walking (Script 9.8)
Feeling (emotions) The experience of and listening to embodied emotions	Drawing My Emotional Landscape (Script 9.9) Being With Emotions Body Scan (Script 9.10) The Body Maps of My Emotions (Script 9.11) Adapted Soften-Allow-Soothe Meditation (Script 9.12) Having an Emotion Over for Tea (Script 9.13) Reflective Questions for Food-Emotion Connections (Table 9.2)
Fundamental embodiment practices	Arousal Scale (Table 9.1) Grounding and Breath Practice (Script 9.2) Developing Your Inner Resource and Guide (Script 9.14)

CONCLUSION

This chapter worked to address two simple (although not easy) aims: (1) learning that the wisdom of the body exists (a monumental task in a culture that thrives on thinking and judging), and (2) learning how to listen to this wisdom. I have found that the Self-Awareness Assessment and effective discourse around arousal and the associated tools to be a key part of my practice. As your clients spend positive, down-regulated, and effective time in and with their bodies, how they see and embody themselves will unfold, dismantling objectification and supporting agency and self-determination.

Practice Guide 9.1: States of Being and the Growth Zone

This practice guide will help you identify your comfort zone, growth zone, and window of tolerance, so that you can to learn how to be your growth zone without moving directly to overwhelm and reaction.

STEP 1: Explore States of Being and the Growth Zone

Review the table below, consider how each state feels, and see if you can recall times when you've experienced your comfort zone, growth zone, and the edge of your window of tolerance.

Comfort Zone		
(Inside of the Window of Tolerance)		
Body	**Emotions**	**Thoughts**
My body is relaxed, my breath is smooth, and my heart rate is slow. I feel calm. My body can restore here. There is no physical defensiveness most of the time. I feel open.	My emotions are pleasant and positive. I feel safe, confident, and peaceful. I am more likely to have a positive feeling toward another person. I like it here.	My thoughts are clear and reflective. My thoughts come from a sense of safety and tend to be positively oriented. I may be more likely to give people the benefit of the doubt and be open to their ideas.

In the comfort zone,
↓ **move to the growth zone when ready for challenge** ↓

In the growth zone
↑ **move to comfort zone to rest, restore, and repair** ↑

Growth Zone		
(Inside of the Window of Tolerance)		
Body	**Emotions**	**Thoughts**
My body is active and alert. My muscles can easily engage and relax. My breath is steady and aligned with the task at hand. My heart rate reflects the work I am doing, and I can slow my heart rate when I slow my breath.	My emotions are aligned with the challenge with which I am engaged. They feel manageable, and I am able to access and use the tools I need to be with and work with my emotions. I feel them without feeling overwhelmed by them. I sometimes have mixed feelings about others. I can work through these feelings.	My thoughts are rational, supportive, and compassionate. They have the essence of a good coach, seeing my strengths, efforts, and challenges clearly. I am able to be aware of myself, my body, and my mind, and I am able to make effective choices. I can think rationally about the intentions and actions of others.

In the growth zone, ↓ work to challenge and expand the edge of embodied capacity ↓		
The Edge of the Window of Tolerance		
At the edge of the window of tolerance, ↑ engage in grounding and breathing practices as you begin to show signs ↑ of escape, flight, or shutdown		
↓ Outside of the Window of Tolerance ↓		
Mobilization in Fight or Flight (Acute SNS Activation)		
Body	**Emotions**	**Thoughts**
Mobilization is the priority of the system. My body is highly activated, with muscles ready to fight or run. My breath is rapid, and my heart rate is fast. I have physical sensations indicating that the situation is not safe for me and/or others.	Emotions are big, compelling, and overwhelming. They are often aligned with anger and fear, which are the respective emotions of fight and flight. I do not feel like I can manage them. My interactions with others are clouded by anger, fear, and safety needs.	I may have no thoughts at all, or they are aligned with fighting or escape. My thoughts may be attacking and aggressive, or oriented toward getting out of here. I have difficulty seeing the intentions of others clearly. I am biased by anger, fear, and concerns for safety.
Immobilization in Shutdown and Freeze (Acute PNS Activation)		
Body	**Emotions**	**Thoughts**
My body feels immobilized. It feels numb, heavy, and difficult or impossible to move. I feel dissociated from my body.	I don't feel anything. If I feel, I feel hopelessness, apathy, overwhelm, despair. I might feel inappropriately guilty or worthless. I have trouble feeling anything toward anybody, including myself.	My thoughts are shut down. They seem foggy and confused. It is hard, if not impossible, to decide what to do next. I have no plan. I cannot connect with myself or others.

STEP 2: Identify Your Own States of Being

Complete the table below describing your experience in each of the states of being and your growth zone. Include the arousal level of each feeling you describe. Once you are done, circle one or two indicators in each area that you think will be best for you to notice when you are triggered or struggling (e.g., under *Body* in the *Escape or Fight* row, you might circle "my heart is racing"). These will help you develop awareness of your state of being. The goal is to become aware of your state and to learn to use the tools you need to shift or stay in that state.

State of Being	Body	Emotions	Thoughts
Shutdown Arousal Level			
Escape or Fight Arousal Level .			
Growth Arousal Level			
Comfort Arousal Leve			

STEP 3: Choose Your Actions

Working with your therapist, list your preferred course of action for each of the areas:

The best actions to take while I am in an *escape or fight* state of being are

_____

_____

_____

_____

The best actions to take while I am in a *shutdown* state of being are

_____

_____

_____

_____

The best actions to take while I am in my *comfort zone* to help me move into my *growth zone* are

_____

_____

_____

_____

STEP 4: Choose Your Signals

Work with your therapist to prepare a signal you can use with your therapist, family members, and friends to communicate that you need support. Consider using the Arousal Scale (Table 9.1) and Cornerstones of Embodied Wisdom and Associated Practices (Table 9.3) as you develop your plan.

The way I will signal that I am not okay and that I need support is

_____

_____

_____

_____

Script 9.1: An Apology Letter to My Body

First, provide a piece of blank paper for your client.
I will reading a sample letter of apology to the body, and then you
will have time to write your own letter. (*pause*)

Dear Body,
This letter is long overdue and for that I am very sorry. You have
been with me from the beginning, never leaving me no matter what
I did to you. I remember it all and know what I have done. In the
beginning, we were best friends, never going anywhere without
the other—laughing, playing, taking long lazy naps, and trying to
figure out my crazy family—ha ha. You always told me when to
be careful and when it was okay to run as fast as I could. I used to
listen to you. You knew the best snacks and when we should take a
break. You were the same age as me, yet somehow you were so very
wise. I remember one time when you knew a little girl at school was
not as nice as she pretended to be—way before I knew. You tried to
tell me. And then later we cried together. You were always with me
when I was hurting, even when I did not listen to you.

I know when it was—it was first grade. That is when I first
started wholeheartedly rejecting you. You weren't quite the shape
I wanted you to be. I began to discount how smart you were and
started picking you apart. You weren't perfect, small, or pretty like
the other bodies I saw. I thought even my mom wanted you to be
prettier and smaller. I started to wonder why you were always so
hungry and got mad at you for wanting me to eat all of the time,
so I would punish you by not eating, and the fights would start.
I starved and ignored you, and you yelled louder about wanting
food, and maybe, just maybe, you wanted me. I didn't care. I
wanted you to be different. By seventh grade I was done with
you and left you for a long time. Sure, when I needed you I would
check back in—on the days when I was hurting and wanted you
there while I cried. You cried with me.

I spent years doing really terrible things to you. We both know
the depth of it. I am lucky I did not kill you. Here I am today, in
tears, remembering it all, with my heart, our heart, heavy. I am so

very sorry. You did not deserve any of this. Your shape is exactly as it should be, with all of its curves and scars. You helped me create two beautiful babies, run marathons, and teach thousands of yoga classes. We have written books, loved friends, and seen the world together. In your beautiful shape, you have never left me, heart beating, lungs breathing, feet grounded even when I was not paying attention.

Okay, so here it is. I am going to make a promise: I will not leave you or hurt you anymore. It has taken me decades to get you—no, us—right. I have fallen and failed. Each time I have gotten back up for you, for us. You are worth every single try, every single time. If I have not said it clearly enough before, I love you and I am sorry. Did you hear me? I love you.

Your soul mate,

Catherine

Now, using the piece of paper I have given you, write a letter to your body. It can be a letter of apology, one of friendship, a promise, or any of these. You decide what the content should be based on your ongoing relationship with your body and the status of that relationship right now. You may want to include some of the positive and challenging history you have shared in your relationship with your body. Consider letting your body know the positive things it has done for you, even in the more difficult times. Again, you may want to apologize. You might consider making a promise of commitment to your body. You have time to work on it here, and if you'd like, you can work on this at home and share it with me at our next session. Let me know.

Script 9.2: Grounding and Breathing Practice

"Begin by pressing your feet into the floor and your sitting bones into the chair. Imagine that you can root into the floor and your chair like a tree roots into the earth. As you press into the floor and chair, extend throughout your spine, engage your core, and reach through the crown of your head. Allow your shoulders and jaw to be soft.

Bring your awareness to your breath. Place one hand over your heart and one hand over your belly. Engage in extended exhalation breaths, breathing in for 1, 2, 3, 4 (*pause*) and out for 1, 2, 3, 4, 5. (*pause*) Repeat the extended exhalation breaths for three more cycles (*you can guide these if needed or simply practice with your client*). When you are done, let your breath return to normal, and place your hands on your lap.

Script 9.3: Distress Tolerance—The Five Senses

Press your feet into the floor and, if seated, press your sitting bones into the chair, and then begin to breathe. Once you have connected to your body and breath, do the following:

5: Acknowledge five things you see around you: This can be anything, a table, a chair, a picture on the wall, the sky through the window, or the window itself. (*pause*)

4: Acknowledge four things you can touch near you: This can be your chair, the floor, your hands touching each other, or the sleeve on your shirt. (*pause*)

3: Acknowledge three things you can hear: This can be a sound coming from you, from the room you are in, or from outside of the room. (*pause*)

2: Acknowledge two things you can smell: This can be an essential oil that you have, a plant in the room, your tea or coffee, or the shirt you are wearing. (*pause*)

1: Acknowledge one thing you can taste: This can be the taste of the tea or coffee you just sipped, or of some dark chocolate or a mint in your desk or bag.

Script 9.4: Riding the Wave of Arousal

Find a comfortable seat and ground your feet on the floor and your sitting bones on the chair, and begin to breathe. If it feels okay for you, close your eyes or soften your gaze. Next, follow these steps:

1. Try to locate the sensations related to arousal or urge in your body. If they are in more than one spot, focus where they are the strongest.

2. Try to describe the feeling or sensations. Is it big or small, constricting or expansive, cool or warm? Simply notice and describe what you notice.

3. Now, bring your awareness back to your breath and notice your breath moving in and out of your body. Do this for a few breaths, and when you are ready, turn back to where you feel the arousal or urge.

4. Tune in to the feeling and imagine that it is a wave. Researchers have studied arousal and urges, and they have found that they arise and pass, just like waves rolling on the beach. If we try to fight the wave, it can crash down on us. It can be exhausting trying to outrun it over and over. Instead, imagine that you are a surfer, riding on top of the wave as it arises and passes.

5. If you need extra support, find something physical you can touch to further ground yourself in this moment, and breathe.

6. When the arousal or urge has passed, thank yourself for your hard work. You might want to record the arousal or urge in your journal. Record how long it lasts, where you felt it, and how strong the peak was (e.g., 1 = mild and 10 = the most severe).

Informed by Cook-Cottone (2015b), Bowen et al. (2010), and Juarascio et al. (2017).

Script 9.5: Awareness of Breath and Heartbeat Meditation

Find a comfortable position with your feet grounded on the floor and your sitting bones firmly grounded on a chair. Pressing down into the floor and your sitting bones, engage your core and extend through the crown of your head, allowing your shoulders to soften and to gently rest on your back. Soften your face, and if you'd like, soften your gaze or close your eyes. If you have your eyes open, find a neutral anchor and rest your eyes on it, perhaps an object on the table. (*pause*) As you practice this meditation, your awareness might turn to your thoughts or an outside noise. If this happens, simply notice and then bring your awareness back to my voice, and back to your breath and your heartbeat.

Place one hand over your heart and another hand over your belly, and bring your awareness to your breath. You might add the narrative, "Breathing in, I know I am breathing in. Breathing out, I know I am breathing out." Continuously bring your awareness to your breath and repeat your inhalation and exhalation cycle four more times. (*long pause*)

Slowly, release the words "Breathing in, I know I am breathing in. Breathing out, I know I am breathing out," and simply focus on your breathing. Begin at your nose. Closing your mouth, breathing through your nose, notice the air as it passes through your nostrils and into your body. You might notice the temperature of the air as it comes into your body and the temperature and humidity of the air as it leaves. Breathe here, noticing the sensations of the breath as it moves through our nose. (pause)

Now, follow the air as it moves into your body. You might feel it pass through your throat and into your lungs. (pause) Consider: you might feel something here, and you might not. Simply notice. (pause) Now, move your awareness to your lungs, your chest, and your belly as the air moves into them on the inhalation and leaves them on the exhalation. You might notice an expansion at your chest and across your belly on the inhalations. (pause) You might notice the sensation of air as it fills and leaves your lungs. (pause) You might notice subtle movements under your hands as your chest and belly rise and fall with the breath. Breathe here and notice the lungs, the chest, and the belly. (pause)

As you breathe, slowly bring your awareness to your heart. You can use both your internal awareness and the sensations you might notice under your hand that is on your chest. (pause) It might help to slow and quiet your breath a bit so you can really tune in to the beating of the heart. (pause) You might notice something both inside of you, deep in your chest, and through the palm of your hand. (pause) You might notice only the inside sensations or only the sense of your heart beating under your hand. You might not feel anything. Simply breathe and notice. (pause)

If you are able to feel your heartbeat, see if you can whisper to yourself slowly, counting each heartbeat all the way up to 10.

Be sure to keep breathing even as you focus. (pause, counting slowly to 10 to make sure you give the client enough time) If you aren't noticing your heartbeat, simply count your inhalations and exhalations, allowing for the possibility of feeling your heartbeat as you breathe. (pause, counting slowly to 10 to make sure you give the client enough time)

If you'd like, release your hands to your lap or the arms of the chair and allow your breath to move naturally in and out. Breathe here for five more breaths. (long pause) Slowly bring your awareness back to this room by gradually opening your eyes, if they are closed, and anchoring your awareness onto something in the room. As you breathe, slowly broaden your awareness to the room, with your feet and sitting bones grounded. Thank you for your practice.

Script 9.6: Self-Awareness Journaling

Often people who have come to treatment for an eating disorder notice that they don't really know themselves. This makes sense. It is hard to know someone with whom you have not spent quality time. This journaling activity is like taking yourself out for a cup of tea or coffee and sharing who you are, with yourself. As you write, do not write about your disorder or symptoms. This is about the rest of you, the part of you that needs to be seen and heard.

Before you begin, find or take a photo of yourself. You can have it printed or on your screen so that you can see it readily as you write. Next, make a cup of tea or coffee or get a nonalcoholic drink that feels just right for this session. Then, settle into a comfortable seat with your pen and journal. Imagine that you are telling your journal about you. When you need to pause and think, breathe and look at the photo of yourself until the next thought arises. Once a thought comes to you, about you, keep writing. Take 15–20 minutes, or more time if you'd like, to tell your journal all about yourself.

Remember, as you write, do not write about your disorder or symptoms. You might want to tell your journal about your values, the things you love. You can tell your journal about the food you like and how you take care of your body. You can tell your journal about what you like about your vocation, work, and your leisure time. Stick with who you are and not what you aspire to be. This is about getting to know you in the here and now. Other ideas are pets, places you love to visit, your bedtime routine, how you relax, your favorite people, favorite restaurants, and what makes you feel really, really safe.

Script 9.7: Sensory-Based Self-Soothing Center

Setting up a sensory-based self-soothing center can help you enhance your mindful self-care routine, as well as help you practice tuning in to your sensory experiences. This will help you rely less on your cognitive coping strategies by building up sensory experiences that are inherently relaxing and soothing.

Find a place in your room, apartment, or home in which you can keep your sensory supplies, such as a shelf space, a basket, or a box. Consider your senses as you select items to cover the range of sensations: touch, smell, hearing, sight, and taste. Some ideas are (*list some ideas from each of the columns in the following table*):

Touch	• Body/hand cream • Hand massaging tool • Worry stone • Feather • Tennis ball for foot rolling • Beads • Stress ball • Weighted blanket • Satin pillow
Smell	• Essential oils • Scented candles • Incense sticks • Scented lotion • Jars of herbs and spices, such as lavender, cloves, and mint • Small bottles of extracts, such as vanilla, anise, or lemon

Hearing	• Playlists for different moods • Singing bowls • Simple instruments like chimes or a wooden recorder • Nature sounds • Small water fountain • Open window
Sight	• Photos of your loves and loved ones • Plants • Artwork • Glitter jar • Image collage • Affirmations on 3 x 5 cards or sticky notes • Sketching supplies • Colored pencils and an adult coloring book
Taste	• Electric tea pot and water • Soothing teas, like chamomile or mint • Hot chocolate • Dark chocolate • Flavored water • Favorite coffee • Fruit, such as bananas, oranges, apples, pears, or berries

Once you have set up your center, you can schedule a time each day to spend time there, and you can use this center as a resource for when you are stressed, tired, or triggered:

1. Find a comfortable seated position.
2. Choose your sensory experience.
3. As you engage in your sensory experience, allow the sensation to become an anchor for your awareness.
4. If you notice yourself thinking, worrying, planning, or judging, simply bring your awareness back to the sensory experience and rest your awareness there.
5. You can engage in one sensory experience per session, or choose two or three to do in sequence. For example, place lotions on

your hands, smelling the scent and massaging it into your hands. Next, once your hands are soft and relaxed, light a scented candle and practice sight awareness with your hands placed on your lap, palms up. If you'd like, place a worry stone in your hands to give them weight. Sit here, noticing the scent and the candlelight for 2–10 minutes, longer if you'd like.

You want to keep your practice time manageable and positive. Make sure you stop or shift senses while you are still enjoying the sensation.

Script 9.8: Sensory-Based Mindful Walking

Sensory-based mindful walking is a formal practice that allows you to be in the movement while engaging the senses. You might find that moving while engaging in the senses works best for you some days, while sitting works best for you other days.

1. Your first step is to set aside 20–60 minutes to take a walk.
2. Next, choose a location within which to walk. Here are some ideas:
   - Find a pleasant path outside that is free from a lot of traffic and noise and is filled with as much nature as possible—a park, zoo, or garden.
   - Create your own labyrinth using a piece of rope in a large room, laid out in a spiral. Place a stone or plant in the center and follow the rope in and out as you walk.
   - Find a loop in your building, perhaps up one set of stairs and down another.
3. Begin to walk, noticing the following:
   - Feel the sensation of your feet as they touch the ground. Notice from heel to toe, step after step.
   - Feel the sensation of your breath moving as you walk and your heart beating as you breathe.
   - Feel the sensation of your clothes moving on your body, your socks or shoes on your feet, fabric on your legs, and clothes on your torso.
   - Feel wind or air on your skin.

- Smell, taste, and feel the air moving in and out of your mouth or nose as you breathe. Do you notice the mechanical scent of the building or the essence of grass, forest, or sea air? How might you describe this to someone else who could not experience it?
- Listen to the sounds of your feet, the movement of your clothes, and your breath as you move.
- Listen to the layers of sound you can hear, within 3–5 feet, then 10 feet away, and then faraway sounds. Spend time identifying each layer.
- See, really see, the path you are following on the floor, dirt, or pavement. Notice its texture, if it is dry or wet, clean or dirty.
- See what is within five feet of you on your right, then your left, then ahead of you. Are there plants, flowers, animals, walls, books, desks? What is there and what are their shapes and forms? If you did not know what they were called, how would you describe them to someone else who also did not know their names?
- See as far as you can ahead of you, the broad vision, a skyline, a horizon, the scope of a room or hallway. What is its depth, breadth, and color?

4. As you finish, still walking, bring your awareness back to your feet. Simply feel your feet as they support you as you walk. Do this for about 1–2 minutes to close your practice.
5. Thank your body and your senses for all they do and all the beauty they bring to you.

Script 9.9: Drawing My Emotional Landscape

Using the crayons in the basket and this blank piece of paper, represent your feelings right now. This paper represents your entire emotional landscape, all that is there right now in this moment. You can represent your feelings anyway you'd like. Take your time, and let me know if you have any questions.

Once your client is done, ask the following:

1. Tell me about what you have drawn on the paper.
2. *For each color,* Tell me what this color represents or means to you.

3. *For the placement on the paper, the size of the expression, the intensity of the pressure on the paper, the juxtaposition of one color or shape to another,* Tell me about [*placement, size, intensity, juxtaposition*] and what it represents or means to you.
4. *Consider asking the client at any point in the inquiry,* Tell me, do you notice sensations related to this feeling or these feelings, anywhere in your body? Can you or would you like to show me or describe where they are and what you are noticing?
5. Is there anything else you think is important for me to know about your drawing?

Place the client's name and the date on each drawing so you can align it with session notes and review changes over time as treatment moves forward.

Script 9.10: Being With Emotions Body Scan

Find a comfortable place to sit or lie down. Bring your journal and a pen/pencil with you so that you can jot down your experience after the meditation.

While lying down or sitting in a comfortable position, take a few moments to simply breathe and notice your breath, allowing your body to settle. If it feels right for you, you can close or soften your eyes. (*pause*) Notice, with a sense of welcome, the sounds around you, the sensations of your body on the chair or couch, the feeling of your clothes on your body, and the smell of the air.

Bring to mind an emotion you would like to work with. Breathe and relax as you invite the emotion into your awareness, remembering that you are working toward befriending your emotions and your emotional experience. Experience the emotion, considering your whole body, your breath, even what is going on in your mind and thoughts. Then, bring your attention to just your body.

We will begin by simply being with the emotion as it is experienced by your body. Where is the feeling present in your body? Do you notice any sensations in your feet, (*pause*) your legs, (*pause*) your core, (*pause*) your chest, (*pause*) your shoulders, (*pause*) your arms, (*pause*) your hands, (*pause*) your neck, (*pause*) your scalp, (*pause*) your face? (*pause*) Can you describe the feeling that you are noticing? (*pause*) Does it have form, shape, firm boundaries, or is it widespread with no edges or endpoints? (*pause*) Is it a big feeling or a small feeling? (*pause*) Is it a comfortable or uncomfortable feeling? Is there tension or relaxation with this feeling? (*pause*) Do you have a sense of wanting it to go away or wanting it to stay? (*pause*)

Now, we will be with this emotion as it is experienced by your breath. How is your breathing as you experience this emotion? (*pause*) Is it fast, slow, deep, shallow, smooth, or filled with pauses and stops? Does your breath come from your chest or your belly? Where do you notice it most? (*pause*)

We will now be with the emotion as it resides in your thoughts. Bringing your awareness to your thinking self, do you notice a thought pattern that goes with this feeling? (*pause*) Are there memories that kick in? (*pause*) Judgments? (*pause*) Doubts? (*pause*) Do you notice your brain trying to solve or fix something or change the feeling in some way? (*pause*) What do you notice about your thoughts? (*pause*) Breathe here.

If you'd like, before we end this practice, travel back through the layers—your body, the breath, your thoughts—noticing how the emotion resides in each layer of you. (*pause*)

When you are ready, begin to bring your awareness back to the room, the chair or the couch. You might wiggle your toes and fingers and roll your ankles and wrists. Slowly open your eyes if they were closed, and find an object in the room on which you can anchor your eyes. Slowly bring your awareness back to the room. If you'd like, pick up your journal and write down what you noticed across each layer of you—your body, breath, and mind.

Informed by Cook-Cottone (2015), Miller (2015), and Ogden and Fisher (2015).

Script 9.11: The Body Maps of My Emotions

First, give the client a copy of the blank body silhouette included below. Using this image of a human body and these crayons, reflect the emotions as you experience them in your body. You can use whatever colors, shapes, or representations you'd like. There is no right or wrong way to do this, and you may notice one or more emotions as you complete this activity. You might not notice anything, or you might feel nothing in some or all of your body. You can draw that too. Simply draw what you notice. After you are done, I will ask you a few questions about your drawing.

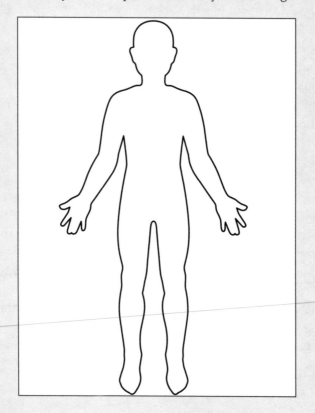

Once your client is done, ask the following:

1. Tell me about what you have drawn on the image of the body.
2. *For each color,* Tell me what this color here represents or means to you.

3. *For the placement on the paper, the size of the expression, the intensity of the pressure on the paper, the juxtaposition of one color or shape to another,* Tell me about [*placement, size, intensity, juxtaposition*] and what it represents or means to you?

4. *Consider asking your client at any point in the inquiry,* Tell me, what sensations are related to this feeling, or these feelings, that you notice in your body? If you are feeling them right now, can you or would you like to show me or describe where they are and what you are noticing? You might even notice things shifting and moving as you are aware of them and talk about them. Let me know if you notice shifts in location.

5. Is there anything else you think is important for me to know about your drawing?

Place the client's name and the date on each drawing so you can align it with session notes and review changes over time as treatment moves forward.

Script 9.12: Adapted Soften-Allow-Soothe Meditation

The following lists the steps to work through with your clients, rather than specific scripts, to allow you to tailor your instructions to individual clients' needs and responses. A recording of the full meditation in its original form, which is free to access, can be found at https://self-compassion.org/wp-content/uploads/2016/11/softensootheallow_cleaned.mp3.

1. Prepare your clients for the practice by asking them to sit in a comfortable position, with their feet and sitting bones grounded, core engaged, and spine extended. They may want to soften their gaze or close their eyes.

2. Using a calm and soothing voice, ask your clients to recall a difficult situation or thought that was associated with a challenging emotional experience. Give them time to consider this request.

3. Ask them to notice the difficult emotions associated with the situation or thought. Pause here, giving them time to process the

request. Then, ask your clients to choose one with which to work. Give them time to consider this request as well.

4. Ask your clients to locate the emotion in their body. You might add a simple body scan here, based on the script in Script 8.1, bringing their awareness to their feet, legs, hands, arms, torso, neck, and head. Ask them to notice if they sense the emotion in their body and to identify the area in which they feel it the strongest. Ask them to bring their awareness there and pause. This begins the being-with process.

5. Now, ask them to soften around the edge of the area. Mention that we are simply being with the emotion and not asking it to go away. This softening is a form of physical compassion for the embodied emotion. Take time to pause here and be with the physical sensation of the emotion. It might be helpful to guide your client in noticing the qualities of the emotion: Does it feel hard, deep, tingly, clenched, tight, or painful? Is it big, small, warm, cool? Does it radiate or contract? Is it still or is it moving? Is its size stable, or getting bigger or smaller? They might repeat the word *soften* to themselves as they breathe.

6. Next, ask your client to allow the emotion to be there. It may be helpful to ask your clients to imagine breathing around the edge of the emotion, a way of softly holding a physical space for the embodied emotion. Remind them that there is nothing to fix or change, and everything to notice. Pause here and allow the being-with experience to simply be. You might ask them to place their hands on the spot where they are noticing the emotion, and encourage them to be with that part of their body, with the hand resting on the spot or slowly massaging the spot while breathing. They might repeat the word *allow* to themselves as they breathe.

7. The next step is to help clients soothe themselves with loving kindness. Here, guide clients in acknowledging how hard it is to feel difficult emotions and to stay with them, softening and allowing. Remind them that it is difficult for all humans to feel difficult emotions and that we all struggle in this way sometimes. Encourage them to offer loving kindness to themselves in the form of gratitude for engaging in the practice and for doing the work that it takes to grow. Encourage them to thank themselves for reminding themselves that they are worth the effort. They might repeat the word *soothe* to themselves as they breathe.

8. The final step is to slowly bring them out of the meditation. You can bring their awareness to their breath and have them slowly open their eyes, anchoring their gaze on something in the room.

Informed by Germer & Neff, 2013; Neff & Germer, 2018)

Script 9.13: Having an Emotion Over for Tea

Find a comfortable seated position in which your feet and sitting bones are grounded, your core is engaged, and you are extending through the crown of your head. Allow your jaw and shoulders to soften. Breathe. (*pause*) If you'd like, you can close your eyes or soften your gaze.

Choose an emotion that you would like to work with today. It might be one that keeps coming up for you or one that you have been avoiding. You are going to invite this emotion to come over for tea. Take a moment here and select one emotion. (*pause*)

Imagine that you are sitting at home, and your emotion has come knocking on your door. You expected this—you invited this emotion over to have some tea. It was time. Either you have been avoiding this emotion, or it kept coming around wanting to be seen and heard. You walk to the door and invite the emotion in. You show the emotion to a comfortable chair and ask what type of tea it would like. You graciously prepare the tea, for yourself and for your emotion, and set the cups and saucers on the table. You offer sugar, milk, and cream. You might imagine what the emotion selects. (*pause*)

With your feet and sitting bones grounded, you take a few deep and calming breaths. You remind yourself that you can ask the emotion to leave at any point. This visit is on your terms.

You begin by asking the emotion what it would like to tell you. For example, "Hello anger, I am glad that you are here. What is it that you wanted to tell me?" (*listen, then pause*)

It is so nice to have the emotion right here because you can ask it anything you'd like. You might ask the emotion if it is concerned with things that happened from the past, things that might happen in the future, or things that are present right now. If it feels right, ask your emotion this question: "Are you concerned with the past, the future, or right now?" Then, simply listen to what you emotion has to say.

You can ask your emotion about what it needs and wants. You can ask it if it has ideas about what it might want you to do. You can say, "What do you need? What do you want? Do you have ideas about what you would like to do?" (*pause*)

Remember this is just information. Emotions often have lots of ideas about our actions. Some of them might be just the right thing, and some ideas that emotions have for us are not the best ideas. When they are big or intense or feel like they have been ignored, emotions don't consult with the other aspects of self that are more rational. Often the thinking part of ourselves and our gut intuition have not been consulted. You can ask your emotion about this: "Have you consulted the rational or the intuitive mind regarding these ideas?" Remind your emotion to be really honest. You might ask your emotion, "If you have not, why not?" Then, listen to what your emotion has to say. (*pause*)

As you finish your tea, you might ask your emotion any other questions you are thinking of. (*pause*) Then, thank your emotion for the visit. As you walk your emotion to the door, assure it that you have seen and heard your emotion and that you will deeply consider all that it had to say.

Once your emotion has left, place one hand on your heart and one on your belly and thank yourself for your courage and openness to feel. (*pause*) Bring your awareness back to your breath. Breathe a few calming breaths here. (*pause*) Slowly open your eyes, if they were closed, and bring your awareness to an object in the room, gradually expanding your awareness out to the entire room. Close the session with one more deep inhalation and exhalation.

Script 9.14: Developing Your Inner Resource and Guide

It might be helpful to have your journal and a pen with you so you can jot down your inner resource details once you have finished. Find a comfortable seat and press your feet into the floor and your sitting bones into the chair. If you'd like, close your eyes or soften your gaze. Bring your awareness to your breath. Take four calming breaths, slightly extending your exhalations. (*long pause*)

Begin by remembering or imagining a place where you feel completely safe and content. Where are you? Is it far away? Near? Is it inside or outside? Bring detail into your image. What do you see? (*pause*) Are there sounds that you notice? What are they? (*pause*) What does it smell like there? (*pause*) Do you notice the wind, a coolness, warmth, the sun? What do you feel? (*long pause*) Using your brain as a recorder, intentionally place this image in your memory. This image can be an access point to your inner resource, your internal reservoir of calm and peacefulness. Remember this image. It is uniquely and completely yours to come to whenever you'd like.

Now, bring your awareness to what your body feels like in your remembered or imagined place—this place where you can feel relaxed, calm, and at peace. There is nothing to do, nothing to fix. You need only be. (*pause*) Do you feel safe, secure, clear, grounded, open, well, flowing, stable, steady, still? (*pause*) How do you feel while you are in this place? (*pause*) Using your brain like a recorder, move these feelings into your memories. Your body has the capacity to feel all of these beautiful and positive feelings. (*pause*) It is okay if some opposite emotions come to mind. Feelings and sensations often travel in pairs. Simply notice and bring your awareness back to the comforting emotions and allow them to settle into your memories. (*pause*)

Now, notice your body. How is it, feeling this remembered or imagined place? Notice any softening, relaxation, letting go that might be there. Allow for the possibility of relaxation and calmness within your body. Using your brain like a recorder, intentionally remember what you are feeling right now. Your body has the capacity to relax, to open, and to soften. As you breathe, know that each moment you spend here in this relaxed state is helping you create a reservoir of relaxation and calm that you can resource and remember whenever you are stressed, triggered, or simply wanting to relax. This feeling is yours and yours uniquely to draw on whenever you need it. (*long pause*)

Place a hand on your belly and a hand on your heart. It is time to connect with your inner guide. Noticing your hand on your belly, know that your gut instincts and intuitions are there in your body. They reside right under your hand. They are a source of great wisdom. Breathe and notice your belly. (*pause*) Perhaps you can say to yourself, "My intuition is a source of great wisdom. I will practice being aware of and listening to my intuition." (*pause*)

Next, noticing your hand on your heart, know that your heart is connected to your emotional systems. Think of how your heart flutters when you love someone or something, and how it beats when you are passionate about something. It is a source for your passions and hurts. In this way, it is a great source of wisdom. (*pause*) You might bring you awareness to your heart and say, "I know you are the source of my emotional wisdom. I will practice being aware of and listening to my emotional wisdom." (*pause*)

Now, bring your awareness to your mind. Its work is to think. It is always trying to help you know your truth. It is the source of your intellectual wisdom. (*pause*) Bring your awareness to the very center of your forehead. You might say to your mind, "My mind is a source of intellectual wisdom. I will practice noticing its messages and patterns." (*pause*)

Whenever you have a big question to contemplate, consider tuning in to all three sources of your wisdom: first your intuition, then your emotional wisdom, and finally your intellectual wisdom. When these three are aligned, know that you are getting closer to your truth. Here you have found your inner guide. It resides in the intersection of intuition, emotion, and intellect. Breathe here. (*long pause*)

Take a final moment to recall your remembered or imagined place, the feelings associated with this place, and the sense of calm and peace that resides in your body. (pause) Now, bring to your attention your belly, your heart, and your mind as they align in your body. Breathe as if you could breathe awareness into all three, the sources of your inner guide. (pause) Your body is a resource, a growing reservoir of peace, calm, and wisdom.

As you are ready, return your awareness to your breath and take a few calming breaths, allowing your exhalations to be longer than your inhalations. (pause) Bring your awareness back to the room, slowly opening your eyes and anchoring your gaze on something in the room. Slowly broaden your gaze. If you'd like, take time to journal about your place, the feelings, and body sensations associated with your inner resources.

CHAPTER 10

Embodied Practices
for Self-Regulation

You only have to let the soft animal of your body love what it loves.

—Mary Oliver

Perhaps it was Hilde Bruch in 1973 who first began to question the sufficiency of using body image alone to describe the disrupted relationship with the body experienced by those struggling with EDs (Gaete & Fuchs, 2016). To get to embodiment, we have to go much deeper than constructs like objectification and body image. Humans are deeply materialistic beings. However, it is not the Galleria Mall version of materialism that we seek. It is a *deeper and more authentic materialism*. This deeper materialism is lived as a profound connection with our own bodies, the earth, nourishing food, water, and embodied doing and being that causes our hearts to beat, lungs to work, and minds to be filled with gratitude and awe. The words *materialism* and *matter* come from the Latin root *mater* which means *mother* (Knaster, 1990). This root, mother, means not only the source of something (a noun), it also means to love and nourish (a verb). This more profound materialism is true to its Latin root. It deeply respects, values, and nurtures matter, the earth, food, water, and our bodies. It is both a thing we source and a way we can be. When we go deeper, embodying activities offer protection against superficial self-objectification, or an externalized perspective of self (Mahlo & Tiggemann, 2016; Menzel & Levine, 2011).

To be clear, body image work is beneficial and a necessary part of treatment for many clients. It is important for clients to have tools to fight the media and to protect themselves from the constant barrage of messages suggesting they need to look and be a certain way to be enough. In fact, research suggests that body image work can increase body image, decrease objectification, and maybe even reduce ED risk and pathology

(Alleva, Sheeran, Webb, Martijn, & Miles, 2015; Cook-Cottone, 2015a, 2015b). However, fighting only at the cognitive level engages in cortical-level, top-down dialogue. Without embodied action (bottom-up activation for neurological change), cognitive resources become drained. Clients fatigue as they work to convince themselves to feel a different way. Body image experts agree that approaches need to be both top down and bottom up (see, e.g., Tylka & Piran 2019). A host of experiences and activities encourage embodiment, such as athletics, hiking, dancing, climbing, horseback riding, scuba diving, martial arts, and yoga (Mahlo & Tiggemann, 2016). To address the key issues and cover a range of embodied practices, this chapter reviews issues related to exercise and the treatment of EDs, and focuses specifically on relaxation and breathing techniques, yoga, exposure to nature, and equestrian therapy (EQT), detailing essential elements that lead to embodiment.

POSITIVELY EMBODIED PHYSICAL PRACTICES

We were made to move and engage in this world (Caldwell, 2018; Cook-Cottone, 2015a, 2015b; Scritchfield, 2016). I often have my clients simply consider how our bodies are shaped, with our arms and legs 10–25% longer than our torsos. It is easy to see that, from an anatomical standpoint, we were designed for action and doing. In fact, all human behavior requires movement, including cellular functions and system processes like digestion and respiration, as well as our postures, gestures, locomotion, and vocalization (Caldwell, 2015).

When we do what we were made to do, we are happier. Exercise and physical movement are considered core components of the "upward spiral" approach to well-being (see Korb, 2015): There are ways to move and engage in the world that are aligned with wellness. When we engage in healthy physical movement, we have increased positive affect and feel happier. Being happier increases the chance that we will engage in more positive behaviors, making us a bit happier. As we cycle upward, positive (not negative) affect predicts improvements in coping and creative responding (Fredrickson & Joiner, 2018). Over time, through aggregated periods of creative coping, we begin to increase our repertoire of coping resources, preventing the downward spiral into isolation, withdrawal, and symptoms (Fredrickson & Joiner, 2018). Integrating the cultivation of positive emotions into ED treatment may have a positive impact on prevention, treatment, and improved quality of life (Tchanturia, Dapelo, Harrison, & Hambrook, 2015). To do this, healthy physical activity and the body are key.

How embodiment through physical activity is approached matters. For those with EDs, physical activity is complicated (Calogero et al., 2019). Exercise itself does not automatically promise positive embodiment and its benefits simply by putting in the time exercising (Calogero et al., 2019). Despite our bodies being a source of comfort, calm, connection, and enjoyment, the cultural focus on healthism, body shaming, competitive outcomes, discipline, control, and appearance for some can create an externalized and detached relationship with physical activity (Calogero et al., 2019; Greenleaf & Hauff, 2019). Some clients use physical activity as part of their pathology, exercising to compensate for calories consumed, as punishment for a perceived indulgence, to pursue an extreme thin or muscular ideal, or to further objectify the body in pursuit of an achievement. They have no concept of physical activity as a pathway inward toward effective being.

For example, in his memoir Mathew Sanford (2008) wrote about how he took his self-destructive struggle to his yoga practice. He details his recovery from a traumatic car accident that killed members of his family and left him with a severe spinal cord injury. Yoga became his pathway to healing. However, for a time he used it as part of his striving and pushing. "I know the moment my yoga practice passed over into the threshold of violence" (p. 203), he wrote: he pushed and strained so hard in a pose that he broke his own leg. Being embodied means finding the window of tolerance, the range within which we can grow and rest safely. It also means adjusting this as we develop, gain skills, catch a cold, lose loved ones, maybe get married and have children or suffer an injury, and age. It is a mindfulness practice and a lifelong dedication to attunement with and loving kindness for our body. For our clients it means finding how physical activity can help them be with and work with what is present in their life.

Individual Approaches to Movement and Positive Embodiment

Research, theory, and personal accounts all suggest that it is not the physical activity per se that is beneficial or problematic when it comes to EDs, risk, or maintenance of disorder; rather, it is the approach taken by both the community and the individual that makes all of the difference (Cook-Cottone & Douglass, 2017; Greenleaf & Hauff, 2019; Sanford, 2008). Working with your clients, it is important to help them be in, of, and for their bodies in all aspects of life, finding a physical embodiment approach that lies between the extremes of being lost in the pursuit of something and being disengaged from their body.

Calogero et al. (2019) used the term *dysfunctional exercise* to capture a range of problematic exercise attitudes and behaviors that are linked to etiology, maintenance, and relapse of EDs. In a review, Calogero and Pedrotty-Stump (2010) reported that dysfunctional exercise may precede the onset of pathological eating behavior, may predict longer hospitalizations and faster relapses after discharge, and frequently persists after other ED symptoms have resolved. Dysfunctional exercise can include frequency and duration of exercise, as well as the mind-set, dysfunctional embodiment, and disembodiment in approaching exercise (Calogero et al., 2019).

At one extreme, physical embodiment is characterized by being lost in the pursuit of something (Calogero et al., 2019: Scritchfield, 2016). Here, the body is seen not as an essential aspect of your being but as a tool for, an object of, or an obstacle in the way of that pursuit. At the other extreme, physical embodiment is characterized by ignoring the body. The clients may believe that if they simply ignore their bodies or do not engage in any sort of physical practice, they won't have to deal with their sensations, feelings, or potential compulsions to exercise or ruminate about their body's shape, size, and capabilities (Cook-Cottone, 2019a).

Between these extremes, physical embodiment comprises embodied, attuned, intuitive doing. Here clients are in partnership with the body. As they engage in physical activity, they are present to their internal sensations and needs, emotions, thoughts, and the me-in-the-world aspect of being. They are connected to the body wisdom present in the belly, heart, and mind. There is a balance between effort and rest. They are sufficiently rested, nourished, supported, and skilled to engage in the activity (Calogero et al., 2019; Cook-Cottone, 2015a). Some call this intuitive exercise (Reel, Galli, Miyairi, Voelker, & Greenleaf, 2016). In this way, the approach to exercise is flexible and can vary in duration, type, and intensity (Reel et al., 2016). The emphasis is on how the body feels and what the body needs rather than relying on the external cues like calories burned or miles ran (Greenleaf & Hauff, 2019).

Working with physical activity in recovery is as important as working with eating behaviors. There are good reasons to restrict physical activities when clients are medically fragile. However, a growing body of work suggests that pairing exercise with psychoeducation and replacing dysfunctional exercise with more attuned exercise have positive implications for recovery (see Calogero et al. 2019). This can be done without interfering with overall recovery or increasing risk for relapse after recovery (Calogero et al., 2019). Once clients have medical clearance, it is important to have them practice being with and for their bodies physically. You can review the core features of embodied, attuned, and intuitive doing with your clients, helping them practice staying in the embodied being zone and noticing and self-correcting when they are at the edge of being lost in pursuit or completely ignoring their physical selves. Practice Guide 10.1 offers a step-by-step process to help clients sort through these issues and develop a plan for embodied doing and physical self-regulation.

The central approach to embodied doing has several core features: mindful attunement; sustainability; safety, process, and joy; self-determination and agency; focus on function; opportunity for flow; and competition as empowerment. Each of these is detailed below.

Mindful Attunement. Mindful attunement can be thought of as the "pulse" of the self, a continuously moving awareness, responsiveness, and coordination of the experiences of the body and the mind, including emotions and cognitions, as they work together to navigate and respond to the demands and challenges of the environment, including friends, family, community, and culture (Cook-Cottone, 2019a, p. 58). Mindful attunement involves an awareness of, attention to, and intentional regulation of each of the domains of self, mind, body, and self-in-the-world. Caldwell (1996) described a similar cycle of awareness in her work on recovering the body: awareness → owning → acceptance → action → awareness. Embodied activities have task demands that require a high level of coordination and integration of the self. This includes an intentional letting go and ignoring of everything outside of the moment, with the focus turned to exploration. This is mindful attunement.

Sustainability. Sustainability in exercise and embodied physical practice is about balancing effort and engagement with nourishment, hydration, rest, and restoration. Caldwell (1996) calls this "active rest," a state in which we are doing a relatively goalless activity, such as a meandering walk, tinkering with a puzzle, mindful coloring, or watching the leaves blowing in the wind. We all need a period in which we are simply resting, taking in all of the food and water that we need, and letting our bodies restore. Sustainability is about knowing when to rest and listening to the body wisdom that provides all of the cues. In our Yogis in Service teacher trainings, I say it this way: "Great effort should be followed by great rest. We are worth both. We are worthy of both."

Safety, Process, and Joy. Calogero et al. (2019) developed a program called Attunement with Exercise (AWE) that introduces physical activity experiences in a manner characterized by being in the body and caring for the body. This program was developed for, and has been studied with, women in residential treatment for EDs. The AWE program is built on three essential levels: safety, process, and joy. Safety focuses is on being safe with the body during exercise: fueling the body, hydrating appropriately, and carefully selecting and engaging with the external environment within which the person chooses to exercise. Process refers to mindful awareness and staying present during exercise. It involves continuous training in bringing the mind back to the body and the physical experience and away from judgements, making comparisons, and disconnecting from the body. Bringing joy into exercise emphasizes that physical activity is meant to help alleviate stress, increase pleasure, and help rejuvenate and expand the experience of self. It is incompatible with dread, suffering, and the concept of "no pain, no gain." Seeking joy can help in the selection of activities as clients look for physical experiences that are fun and uplifting rather than depressing and exhausting.

Self-Determination and Agency. Embodied self-regulation is defined as engaging in an active practice of mind and body integration that honors the process, balances sustainability and self-mastery, and emphasizes attunement within the self and among others (Cook-Cottone, 2015a). It is a process of self-determination and agency. To be self-regulating and to remain true to embodiment, movement practices must emphasize self-determination and agency. As humans, we tend to oscillate between more primitive and more complex movements and brain states (Caldwell, 2015). In embodied doing, we inhabit the moments of spontaneous, physical unfolding and being with our bodies in which we can be self-determining and filled with a sense of agency. They integrate our voluntary nervous system, muscles, and bones and access our metabolic responses, all in the service of our creative acts of movement.

Focus on Function. Body functionality includes everything the body can do and integrates the functions related to the whole range of motion, from internal processes to communicating with others (Alleva & Martijn, 2019). Body functionality is believed to foster positive embodiment through the reduction of self-objection and by increasing the experience of connection between the mind and body. First, by focusing on what the body can do, attention is diverted from what the body looks like. It is antithetical to self-objectification. Second, aligned with Piran's (2019) developmental theory of embodiment, engaging in activities that emphasize body functioning, and achieving attunement with the body leads to a sense of mind and body connection that directly promotes positive embodiment (Alleva & Martijn, 2019).

Opportunity for Flow. Flow is an intrinsically rewarding psychological state that is experienced when a person is in complete absorption in an activity, perceives control and agency, and has the subjective feeling that everything is clicking (Csikszentmihalyi, 2002). Mindfulness and flow are becoming increasingly important in competitive sports environments (Greenleaf & Hauff, 2019). In their systematic review, Jackman, Hawkins, Crust, and Swann (2019) found that flow during exercise is associated with a variety of positive outcomes, including a sense of achievement, confidence, positive energy and emotions, and intrinsic motivation. Flow is also believed to contribute to an increased likelihood of long-term engagement in an activity (Jackman et al., 2019). Greenleaf and Hauff (2019) assert that facilitating flow and mindfulness in physical activity is a realistic and attainable strategy for creating embodying experiences in traditional sports spaces. However, there has been no research on flow and its impact on ED recovery.

Competition as Empowerment. When competition becomes all there is and winning becomes more important than anything, including health and safety, perhaps clients have lost their way. This includes competition with the self or an increasingly unattainable personal best. When my clients are working out for more than an hour a day, I find this to be a good questioning point. Note: An exception may be clients on development or college teams who have coaches, nutritionists, and sports physicians working with them to monitor and support their bodies. Regardless, given the broad range of professional training experiences of athlete support professionals, I still make sure that what is being recommended makes sense. If needed, a medical doctor should be active on the ED treatment of sports development teams. I assert that anyone who is acutely ill with a clinical ED should be benched until the ED specialist releases him or her for participation.

Sports involvement has been associated with positive embodiment (Greenleaf & Hauff, 2019). Greenleaf and Hauff (2019) suggest that, when done well, competition can be an empowering opportunity. The pursuit of achievement can help clients and those at-risk have a sense of direction as they partner with their bodies physically (Greenleaf & Hauff, 2019). I have watched kids rediscover themselves by engaging in competitive team sports. Competition and team sports can also help increase appreciation for the functionality, power, and performance of the body (Greenleaf & Hauff, 2019). Rather than objectifying the body, there is a shift toward the appreciation of the power of the legs that run, the lungs that breathe, and the body that make the winning shot in basketball or can spike the winning return in volleyball.

Community Characteristics Surrounding Movement and Positive Embodiment

I have been in yoga studios that romanticize thinness and restricted eating, with group cleanses and idealized role models who are extremely underweight. I have also been in yoga spaces in which all bodies are celebrated and accepted and individuals are encouraged to explore their own pathways to nutrition and health. Communities can vary greatly in their support of positive embodiment. I have found that most people are trying to do the right thing and have good intentions. The fitness industry can be competitive, and there is a belief that focusing on weight loss or body sculpting will attract followers. The truth is, most people want to be in their bodies, experience health and well-being, and feel safe as they engage in the process.

There is little direction for how to create a safer space for embodiment. A few years ago, I sought out some literature that I could offer to a yoga studio owner to help her be more body inclusive. After searching both the academic and popular literature, I found nothing close to being complete, so I helped author a piece on how to create a safer space for all bodies (Cook-Cottone & Douglass, 2017). Table 10.1 lists specific community risk factors to watch for in each of these categories, and Table 10.2 lists specific characteristics of caring climates to look for in selecting venues for embodiment practices. It can be helpful to review these characteristics with your clients as you help them select their own venues.

Table 10.1: Risky Exercise Communities: Negative Practices for Embodiment

Idealization of body types and achievements over connection to self

- Primary purpose of exercise and physical engagement is to lose weight and change the body.
- Spaces recognize or reward a thin or ultralean physique that is unrealistic and attainable only via unhealthy body management practices, such as food restriction of excessive exercise.
- Idealized images are posted on the walls and/or unhealthy role models are employed as instructors, coaches, or leaders.
- Coaches and instructors ask for body change or shape above skill instruction (e.g., "I'd like you to gain some weight to be a stronger defender," "I'd like you to lose weight to reduce your running times," "This player is the right look/size for this position irrespective of skill level").
- Winning or achieving a goal is more important than personal embodiment and/or connecting as a team.
- The focus is on calories burned, duration of session, and intensity over tuning in to internal cues.
- An ethos propagates the "no pain, no gain" or "it doesn't count if it doesn't hurt" mind-set.

Questionable leadership (coaches, instructors, trainers)

- Role boundaries are confusing or blurred (e.g., coaches playing the role of therapist or nutritionist).
- Leaders are struggling with their own eating, body image, and idealization issues and are not ready to lead from a healthy and empowered way of being.
- Leaders undermine participants' relationship with their therapist, doctor, or nutritionist.
- Leaders do not address participants who are obviously struggling with eating and body image issues or refer them for support.
- Leaders are not willing to have forums or meetings to discuss embodiment issues within the community.

Negative body talk and communication culture

- Leaders make comments on participants' shape, weight, or eating behaviors.
- Leaders yell at and berate participants.
- Leaders use or allow bullying or chronically hurtful criticism of efforts and outcomes.

Unhealthy expectations and no opting out

- There is a culture of overexercising in which participants train for more than 60–90 minutes a day without effective cross-training, monitoring, and assessment by a sports physician, or without adequate rest and recovery times.
- There is a culture of increasing intensity, frequency, and duration of workouts without periods of recovery and rest.
- There is a culture of pushing effort and engagement to the point of injury.
- There is no discernment between athletes training for national and international titles who have adequate time and resources to rest and recover and those who are working out as full-time students or employees who do not have the resources or capacity to adequately recover from workouts.
- There are no clear ways to opt out of or accommodate specific routines, postures, or other offerings for participants or employees.
- There are no clear methods for opting out of activities, hands-on assists, and other components of class.

Nutrition or medical advice from those not trained or licensed to practice in those areas

- Coach or instructor without a license in the nutritional field attempts to prepare a meal plan, diet, or cleansing experience.
- Community members ask you to change your diet without consulting your doctor.
- The community promotes cleansing, dieting, or bulking-up practices that have not been supported by research.
- Local community members who are trained and licensed to practice are not consulted or integrated into partnerships or referral networks.

Apparel and merchandise sales

- If apparel is sold, it is offered only in small sizes or a reduced range of sizes.
- Apparel offered has only reduced coverage of the body (half-shirts, off the shoulders).
- Merchandise is oriented around appearance, weight loss, or dieting or offers products that have not been approved for the outcomes they promote.

Sources: Informed by Calogero et al. (2019), Cook-Cottone and Douglass (2017), Greenleaf and Hauff (2019), and Scritchfield (2016).

Table 10.2: Caring Exercise Communities:
Positive Practices for Embodiment

Experiential emphasis
• The primary focus is on body awareness, care for the body, and connection to the body. • Participants are encouraged to notice internal and external body sensations. • Awareness and inquiry are primary to fixing, correcting, and altering the experience of the body. • There is acknowledgment of feelings as somatic experiences that arise and pass during the session or practice. • Focus is on the journey and the process rather than the form or the outcome.
Communication and discourse
• Language used focuses on positive embodiment and the participants' experiences in the present moment. • Participants have a voice in body-oriented decision and policy making. • There are forums, workshops, and trainings on positive embodiment within the community. • Instruction includes the cultivation of awareness of inner dialogues and coaching for how to challenge and ignore the harsh inner critic and cultivate self-compassion, positive self-talk, and present-moment awareness. • Training is offered on the language used in class, helping the community use language that more deeply connects participants with the experiences within their own bodies. • There is a safe and clear way for participants to communicate a need for and seek support if they are struggling. • Referral lists are offered for professionals with expertise in eating disorders and medical care that are accessible and visible to all community members.
Studio, space, and community characteristics
• There is a board of directors or a team to consult that consists of directors of mental health facilities, eating disorders treatment providers, researchers, and civil leaders with the purpose of building more resilient communities that can effectively respond to challenges.

- The community engages in outreach that is specifically welcoming to and inclusive of a range of individuals.
- The community prioritizes diversity when hiring.
- There is an overarching practice of no negative body talk within the community.
- Community members collectively practice shutting down diet and weight talk.
- Nonjudgmentally, in private settings community members check in on participants who appear at risk (e.g., "I noticed x, y, z, and I wanted to make sure you are okay. I have been worried about you. Are you okay?").
- Advertising, marketing, and decorative images are inclusive of a range of shapes, sizes, genders, ages, ethnicities, and races.
- There are no, or limited, mirrors.
- Equipment and spacing are appropriately sized and placed for all body shapes and sizes.

Leaders (coaches, instructors, and trainers)

- Leaders embody the mindful self-care practices, body loving kindness, and awareness that is hoped for their participants.
- Leaders are of varied sizes, shapes, ethnicities, races, ages, sexual orientations, and gender identification.
- Leaders welcome challenging ideas.
- Leaders celebrate positive body image, body functionality, competence, autonomy, and resilience.
- Leaders encourage participants ways to listen to their body's internal cues (e.g., "Am I tired?" "Does that hurt?" "Does this feel good in my body?").
- Leaders teach participants ways to experience their bodies, feel what is present inside and out, and acknowledge a broad range of human sensations and emotions.
- Leaders model compassion for all emotions and experiences.
- Leaders defer to experts in nutrition that support health and well-being of participants rather than advising outside of their scope of practice.
- Leaders set and maintain clear boundaries between themselves and participants.
- Trainings on positive embodiment are offered for leaders.

Movement routines
• Routines and practices integrate mindfulness, awareness of the body, reminders to tune inward and respond to information form the body, and time for self-regulation. • Within the routines, attunement with the body and individual self-care are encouraged and celebrated. • There is opportunity for participants to develop the portions of the activities (e.g., plays, sequences, dance routines) as a form of community involvement, contribution, and agency.
Agency and opting out
• Leaders offer choice and encourage self-determination and agency. • There are clear methods for opting out of activities, hands-on assists, and other components of class. • There is ongoing permission for participants to choose alternative versions of poses or practices and to take breaks to rest as needed.
Medical and nutritional advice
• Nutritional guidance, if offered, is provided by a licensed dietician or nutritionist. • If necessary at all, weigh-ins are done only by medical personnel and only for medical and health reasons. • Warning signs for eating disorders and excessive exercise are posted, with associated referral information. • Leaders and community members collaborate with licensed professionals to provide best practices within the community and develop a network or partnerships for consultation and referral. • Information sheets are offered to provide useful referrals for expert nutritional support, eating disorder assessment and treatment, physical therapy, and medical support for injury.
Apparel
• If apparel is sold, a range of apparel is offered that varies in the degree to which the physique is revealed. • The apparel offered covers a wide range of sizes for all bodies.

Sources: Informed by Calogero et al. (2019), Cook-Cottone and Douglass (2017), Greenleaf and Hauff (2019), and Scritchfield (2016).

PHYSICAL PRACTICES AND THE CAPABLE SELF

Physical practices can help clients discover the boundaries of the capable self. Many times, clients move between two extremes: feeling unbearably fragile or indestructable. Feeling unbearably fragile, they avoid feelings, sensations, relationships, challenges, and even therapy. They are afraid of being upset or overwhelmed because it feels like they are not going to be okay. Everyone tiptoes around them. On the other extreme is patients acting as if they are indestructible. Individuals with eating disorders often have a distorted view of what their bodies can handle. It is not uncommon for patients to tell me that they take higher than recommended doses of over the counter medicine, work out without rest or hydration, or engage in physical feats that are dangerous and unhealthy because they rationalize that it is okay for them to do that to their bodies. Often, there is a wholesale denial of the physiological needs of the body. In therapy, I frequently shift the perspective to a loved one or friend, "If your sister was doing this would it be okay?" Interestingly, the answer is "No, of course not! Not for her, but for me...."

Shifting the understanding of self to a more equanimous, balanced understanding of what is okay for the body can help move the patient to the middle path. For patients who believe they are uniquely indestructible, a yoga instructor can remind them that they can use a strap, take a block, drop a knee, and take child's pose. Also, yoga instructors can remind students/patients to turn inward and use their body cues to make a choice in the pose and for the next pose. No matter what activity or sport, it is important to honor a client's medical status, working with them to slowly move toward embodied competency. For some patients, it may mean they are medically withheld from physical activity until they reach specific medical markers. For those who are released to participate, part of the work we can do through physical practices is working toward the middle way, believing "I can, and if I am not sure if I can, I can try." Between the extremes of unbearable fragility and indestructibility is the capacity for recovery, the belief that "I am capable of feeling and doing things I wasn't sure I could."

EMBODIED DOING PRACTICES

Within the context of the Embodied Approach to the Treatment of EDs (EAT-ED), embodied doing practices are being-with and working-with practices. This section reviews relaxation techniques, yoga, and equestrian therapy (EQT) as embodied doing practices commonly used as adjuncts to ED treatment. Many other practices can also enhance embodiment, such as tai chi, biking, running, massage, sports, gardening, art, and dance. Using the criteria and tables above, and the examples that follow, you can work with your clients to help them select practices specific to their needs, preferences, and stage of recovery. First, I briefly review movement-based therapies that have evolved mainly from the field of trauma recovery, as possible future directions in the field of EDs and to distinguish between embodied practices and movement-based therapies.

Movement-Based Therapies

Movement-based therapies are based on the premise that movement must be made consciously and deliberately to be therapeutic (Caldwell, 2015). There is an assumption that movement often reveals and has the potential to heal unconscious processes. Caldwell (2015) categorized movement-therapy work as (a) creative/expressive, (b) developmental/physiological, (c) sensory-motor processing, and (d) sequencing and completing.

Movement-based therapies work with clients' attention and intention as they address movements that alter consciousness and impair or block healing, such as stereotypical, chaotic, or cutoff behaviors saturated with inattention (Caldwell, 2015). It is believed that, as conscious awareness of the movement is altered, the unconscious is able to rise up into visibility. In many of these therapies, physically free associations follow, with movement serving as a reference point for navigating and integrating the emergent unconscious material. Once integrated, these experiences can serve as resources for clients as they negotiate daily life and its challenges.

Creative and expressive movement-based therapies use the healing power of creative movement (Caldwell, 2015). They include dance and movement therapy and psychodramatically based systems. Developmental and physiological methods work through developmental frameworks and through body systems. Sensory-motor processing works with the sensory motor loop from sensation to sensory processing to behavioral response, which includes Pat Ogden's sensorimotor psychotherapy and Peter Levine's somatic experiencing.

Some clients who do not respond to more traditional treatment, especially those who have trauma histories, may particularly benefit from movement-based therapies. If you decide to explore this type of referral, first clear it with the treatment team and ensure that your client continues with all other aspects of the ED treatment program.

The embodiment practices described below are distinct from therapeutic interventions, and should be used as adjuncts to the empirically supported treatments described in Chapter 6.

Relaxation

Relaxation has been used in therapy for decades as a way to help clients down-regulate their nervous systems, negotiate triggers and urges, and promote sleep (Cook-Cottone, 2015a). Cowdry and Waller (2015), in a study of how clients with EDs described their experiences of cognitive behavioral therapy, found that over 50% reported that their therapists integrated relaxation exercises. According to the National Center for Complementary and Integrative Health (2019), relaxation techniques can help manage a variety of physical and mental health conditions and are considered to be generally safe. A number of practices, including progressive muscle relaxation, guided imagery, and deep breathing exercises, are intended to induce the body's natural relaxation response (i.e., slower breathing, decreased blood pressure, and increased feelings of well-being); they require practice to produce effects, and benefit is more likely with more frequent use (National Center for Complementary and Integrative Health, 2019). These techniques are relatively easy to integrate into your practice and for clients to develop a home practice.

Progressive Muscle Relaxation. Progressive muscle relaxation involves tightening and relaxing various muscle groups and can be combined with guided imagery and breathing exercises (National Center for Complementary and Integrative Health, 2019). The technique allows the mind and body to relax with the progressive tensing and relaxing of muscle groups. It involves tensing each group with vigor and effort but not to the point of strain, holding the tension for about 5 seconds, and then releasing, bringing awareness to the changes in the physical sensation (see Script 10.1). Deep and steady breath throughout the session is encouraged. If there is an injury or pain in a certain area, it is okay to skip that area. Your clients can use this technique to help them fall asleep or reconnect to their body if they are feeling a trend toward disconnection. It can help prepare for down-regulation after a triggering event. As the body is relaxed and down-regulated through practice, this becomes part of being.

Guided Imagery. Guided imagery includes a range of techniques, such as simple visualizations, direct imagery-based suggestion, use of metaphor, and storytelling (Utay & Miller, 2006). It is believed that guided imagery helps clients connect with their own cognitive, affective, and somatic resources (Utay & Miller, 2006) and that imagery, compared to verbal representation, may be uniquely able to access emotion (Cooper, 2011). It can be used in treatment to learn and rehearse skills, to visualize and manage triggers or highly stressful situations, and to more effectively problem solve by visualizing various outcomes (Cooper, 2011; Utay & Miller, 2006). Script 10.2, for example, can be used to generate a sense of the body as a sanctuary during triggers.

Esplen, Garfinkel, Olmsted, Gallop, and Kennedy (1998) used guided imagery to support the internalization of soothing experiences among clients diagnosed with bulimia nervosa (BN). At the end of this intervention, the imagery group, compared to controls, showed a significant reduction in binge-eating and purging episodes, drive for thinness, body dissatisfaction, and ineffectiveness. These results were comparable to cognitive behavioral therapy interventions. Mountford and Waller (2006) suggest using imagery to combat the restrictive mode or mind-set among those with anorexia nervosa (AN). Tiggemann and Kemps (2005) assert that mental imagery can play a role in food craving. Cooper (2011) and Tatham (2011) suggest it can help clients with EDs rescript memories and modify core beliefs—beliefs they may have taken on early in life or those aligned with pathology in ways that can be inflexible, persistent, and applied across a variety of situations in their lives, creating a resistance to change (Cooper, 2011).

Breathing Exercises. Breathing exercises help in self-regulating the nervous system and mediating the stress response (Cook-Cottone, 2015b, 2016). Incorporating breathing exercises into therapy can give clients a way to manage their stress as they approach difficult topics and explore new ways of being. Breath work has been used to induce relaxation responses since the seminal paper of Benson, Beary, and Carol (1974). The American Institute of Stress (2019) reports that eliciting the relaxation response through breath can slow heart rate, relax muscles, and decrease blood pressure, reversing the signs of stress. It is recommended that clients engage in deep breathing work one or two times a day (Cook-Cottone, 2015b). Script 10.3 offers a script you can use with your clients; for more suggestions, see Brown and Gerbarg (2012).

Yoga

From its roots, yoga is a meditative practice meant to turn us toward our present-moment, sensational, physical embodiment and to experience the world as it is, not through the filter of our perceptions and rehearsed narratives (see Table 10.3). Because of its design, yoga can be a pathway to positive embodiment and can support the prevention and treatment of EDs (Cook-Cottone, 2015a, 2015b, 2019b; Douglass, 2011). Research generally supports integrating yoga into ED treatment and offers no indication that it does harm or increases or exacerbates symptoms (Cook-Cottone, 2006, 2015a, 2015b, 2019b; Daubenmier, 2005; Klein & Cook-Cottone, 2013; Mahlo & Tiggemann, 2016).

The yoga used as a complementary therapy for EDs treatment typically has four essential practices: asana (i.e., postures and sequences), breath work, meditation, and relaxation. Yoga gives clients a method for practicing the negotiation of life and its challenges through an embodied practice, without leaving oneself or turning against the body (Cook-Cottone, 2016, 2019b). In yoga, body awareness is increased as the physical cues guide students inward to interoceptive awareness and outward through proprioceptive awareness (Cook-Cottone, 2017, 2019b). As clients move through and hold poses, they can move from body awareness to choice, noticing the effects of their actions and breath work on the body (Cook-Cottone, 2015b, 2019b). In practice, yoga students learn tools for distress tolerance and emotion regulation as they notice and negotiate thoughts and feelings in movement and rest (Cook-Cottone, 2015b, 2019b). Those who have struggled with EDs have an opportunity to practice a cessation of thoughts related to objectifying the body (Boudette, 2006; Cook-Cottone, 2019b).

Klein and Cook-Cottone (2013) published the first review of the effects of yoga on ED symptoms and correlates, finding that yoga practitioners were reported to be at decreased risk for EDs, ED behaviors, and ED risk. Others studies identified positive results: reduced risk factors and correlates, such as body dissatisfaction, drive for thinness, media influence, and poor interoception; increased positive findings, including higher levels of such protective factors as competence, positive physical and social self-concept, and emotion regulation; and decreased ED behaviors, such as bulimic behaviors, binge eating, and food preoccupation (Cook-Cottone, 2019b; Klein & Cook-Cottone, 2013). Domingues and Carmo's (2019) review of yoga and ED behaviors and correlates found that yoga practice was usually associated with healthier eating behaviors, lower ED symptoms, and higher positive

Table 10.3: Embodying Aspects of Yoga

Being in and of the body
• Noticing the effects of awareness, breath, and movement on the body
• Turning and returning awareness inward
• Practicing new ways of being while remaining in and of the body
• Engaging in a range of awareness: interoceptive (internal sensations), proprioceptive (body position), and kinesthetic (position and movement of parts of the body)
• Caring for the body by building strength and flexibility, allowing for up- and down-regulation of the nervous system, and engaging in cycles of effort and rest
• Practicing being with and of the body as a resource for coping and down-regulating the nervous system
Embodying emotions
• Feeling and allowing all emotions as felt, embodied experiences
• Noticing the body states associated with and body locations of emotions
• Being with the rise and passing of emotions
• Practicing distress tolerance
Embodying thought
• Embodying new ways of thinking about the body, emotions, self, and life
• Embodying self-reflection (e.g., how the body, breath, heart, and mind feel right now)
• Practicing awareness, direction of attention, and intention while engaging the body and attempting poses, sequences, breath work, and meditation

Embodying choice
• Resourcing the breath as a powerful form of self-regulation and self-determination, as the window between the voluntary somatic nervous system and the involuntary autonomic nervous system, • Practicing making decisions using the body as a source of information about the state of the body (e.g., arousal and reaction), emotions, and connection • Practicing self-determination and agency: choosing classes and instructors, taking challenges and/or choosing support and accommodations, accepting or not accepting assists, and using or not using props

Embodying narrative and collective
• Moving the body and breathing in attunement with the instructor, with the instructor's words, the body and the breath aligning in one place and time • Developing an internal narrative of positive self-talk, reminders to turn inward, and remapping worlds of support, encouragement, loving kindness, and compassion onto moments of challenge, enhanced heart rate and breathing patterns, and stillness • Moving through sequences, poses, and breath with a group of people also working to be in and of their bodies (in a class environment) • Experiencing the flow of a group of people moving in synchrony, breath, body, and presence (in a class environment)

Sources: Informed by Cook-Cottone (2015b, 2019b) and Cook-Cottone and Douglass (2017).

body image and body satisfaction. Overall, research and research funding are needed to support the continued exploration of yoga in the prevention and treatment of EDs.

Nature Time

It is believed that people living in the United States typically spend about 90% of their lives within buildings and that this disconnection from nature has negative effects (Evans & McCoy, 1998; McMahan and Estes, 2015). Being in nature can range from going for a hike to having a picnic at the city park. You can intentionally exercise in nature (e.g., trail running, scuba diving, or mountain climbing), referred to as green exercise, which is associated with enhanced body esteem and increased mood, mindfulness, and psychological well-being (Greenleaf & Hauff, 2019). Exposure to nature is believed to increase enjoyment, help decrease attention to everyday worries and stressors, and enhance an inward focus and mind-body connections (Greenleaf & Hauff, 2019).

Simply spending time in nature may have positive influence on psychological well-being. Nature facilitates embodiment, bringing us to our senses—the smells, the earth or snow underfoot, access to the sun and wind on our skin, and the sounds of birds, waves, and leaves turning in the wind. In a systematic review of research exploring the effects of spending time in forests, Oh et al. (2017) found that among populations ranging from healthy young university students to elderly individuals with chronic disease, spending time in a forest can play a role in health promotion and disease prevention. Their review found positive effects in hypertension, cardiac and pulmonary function, immune function, inflammation, oxidative stress, stress hormones, anxiety, depression, and emotional response (Oh et al., 2017). McMahan and Estes (2015) conducted a meta-analysis of 32 studies with a total of 2,356 participants and found that exposure to natural elements was associated with a moderate increase in positive affect, and a smaller yet consistent decrease in negative affect, compared to control conditions.

Viren Swami has done a series of studies exploring exposure to nature and the effects on body image (see Swami, Barron, & Furnham, 2018). He and his team found that students exposed to photographs of natural environments (e.g., outdoors in nature), but not of built environments (e.g., city street or in a building), showed improved body image. Further, community participants who went on a walk in a natural environment showed significantly higher rates of body appreciation than did those who walked in a built environment. When researchers recruited individuals as they were entering a designed green space on their own, they found that spending time in the green space also led to improved body appreciation.

Equestrian Therapy

Horses have been associated with healing since the days of Hippocrates. Therapeutic work with horses is distinct from recreational horseback riding (Hayes, 2015; Kendall, Maujean, Pepping, & Wright, 2014; Kendall et al., 2015; Rudolph, 2015; Thomas & Lytle, 2016). There are many EQT programs using different styles and approaches, with different methods and goals (Hayes, 2015; Kendall et al., 2015; Thomas & Lytle, 2016). Some programs focus on education and physiological outcomes, such as increased range of motion and strength, whereas others focus on mental health outcomes (Kendall et al., 2015).

In EQT, work with horses and other equine-related activities are intended to bring about a range of positive outcomes (e.g., physical, emotional, social, behavioral, and cognitive; Kendall et al., 2015). The mechanisms of change are not well understood. Horses are animals of prey and have evolved to be highly sensitive, attuned with their environments, and have strong fight-or-flight responses. Some believe that horses can detect discrepancies between our inner experiences and the appearance we display to others (Equine Assisted Growth and Learning Association, 2019). Because horses are nonverbal, communication through nonverbal, physical movements and verbal expressions is most effective when they are aligned and clear. Horses' sensitivity and needs for safety and trust are also believed to be aspects of their therapeutic value. To work well with a horse, a client must develop a calm, centered, predictable (not impulsive), aligned, and embodied way of being.

Kendall et al. (2014) hypothesized that there are three layers of the therapeutic value of working with horses: psychological benefits of therapeutic riding, unrelated to the horse, which would occur in any similar program; the horse itself as a positive context that can facilitate psychological gains derived from other sources; and therapeutic qualities that are unique to horses, such as an opportunity for an undemanding, judgement-free relationship, and learning from the horse's sensitive nonverbal communication system. Working with horses requires the integration of the senses, emotions, and communication systems, as well as cognitions to determine actions and behavioral nuances, such as the warmth or firmness in tone of voice, hardness or softness of touch, developing and maintaining a sense of rhythm while riding, negotiating the smells and sounds, and being stable and predictable to conduct grooming activities, leading the horse, and riding (Kendall et al., 2014).

Cumella, Lutter, Smith-Osborne, and Kally (2014) reported that up to a quarter of inpatient and residential ED treatment facilities often include EQT in their programs. Preliminary research evidence suggests that animal-assisted therapies may help clients across a range of psychiatric disorders and challenges (Cumella et al., 2014). In the most comprehensive study to date on EQT and EDs, Cumella et al. (2014) found that clients who participated in EQT at least once per week, in addition to their standard therapy, had lower discharge scores for drive for thinness, ineffectiveness, interpersonal distrust, impulse regulation, depression, and anxiety compared to non-EQT controls. More research is needed to fully understand and validate the mechanisms of change related to EQT. We need to understand the unique needs of clients with EDs within the context of the benefits that EQT offers. If your clients want to explore EQT, look for a program certified by either the Professional Association of Therapeutic Horsemanship or the Equine Assisted Growth and Learning Association. Practices can be guided by the professional guidelines offered by these two associations, prioritizing partnership and coordination with the treatment team and ongoing approval of the treating physician. Three helpful books on the topic are Thomas and Lytle (2016), Hayes (2015), and Rudolph (2015).

DOSAGE: HOW MUCH AND HOW OFTEN?

The dosage of physical activity is a particularly complicated for those struggling with an ED. Treatment guidelines for ED tend to focus on mental health and nutritional interventions and do not offer specific recommendations for exercise. The treating physician often balances physiological risk with the benefits of engaging in physical activity when making individual client decisions. This assessment must also include the client's attitude when entering into physical activity. As Mathew Sanford (2008) reminded us, anything can be used as an instrument of our struggle, even the things that might otherwise help heal us.

In terms of recovery goals, the World Health Organization (2019) recommends that healthy children and adolescents 5–17 years of age practice at least 60 minutes of moderate- to vigorous-intensity physical activity daily, that physical activity longer than 60 minutes daily will provide additional health benefits, and that exercise should include activities that strengthen muscle and bone at least three times per week. For adults 18–64 years of age, the World Health Organization recommends at least 150 minutes of moderate-intensity or at least 75 minutes of vigorous-intensity physical activity throughout the week, or an equivalent combination of moderate- and vigorous-intensity activity, with muscle-strengthening activities involving major muscle groups at least twice a week. For additional health benefits, adults should increase their moderate-intensity physical activity to 300 minutes per week, or equivalent.

Gentle physical practices such as relaxation and exposure to nature can generally be done safely by nearly all clients. These can be done briefly and daily as a way to work toward positive embodiment. McMahan and Estes (2015) recommend that even incorporating brief experiences of nature into our daily routine can be a relatively easy and enjoyable way to increase subjective well-being. Yoga, with its wide range of approaches and intensities, is often considered a good choice for those slowly working back into engagement in physical activity after a medically advised leave. Although there has been no dosage study of yoga for those with EDs, research on yoga suggests that three days a week (about every other day) is a likely minimum to expect benefits, with sessions running about 60 minutes, and intervention protocols extending six weeks or more (Cook-Cottone, 2013).

CONCLUSION

With all modalities of recovery, it is important to consider physical activity a vital component of the treatment plan, with specific goals, assessment of progress and setbacks, and an eye toward healthy engagement in physical practices in recovery. Physical practices offer the ultimate low-cost learning environment for embodiment. A low-cost learning environment is one in which our patients can experiment with different ways of being and the emotional, relational, and social costs are minimal. These practices offer a way to shift from talking about what it is like to live from an embodied place and actually trying it. The reward is the embodiment, even if it is for fleeting moments at first. It is what we human beings long for in our distracted, externalized world. It is what those who struggle with an eating disorder need to fully recover—to practice being-with, in, and of their bodies. It is through this work that trust in and love for the body can be developed. With hope, our patients can find the sweet and wholly authentic way of being so beautifully expressed by Mary Oliver "You only have to let the soft animal of your body love what it loves..." (1986, p. 23).

Practice Guide 10.1: Embodied Doing

This practice guide is designed to help you create your physical embodiment plan. The first step is to identify how you know you are engaging in healthy and potentially unhealthy behaviors. Next, along with your therapist, choose the physical activities you'd like to include in your recovery plan, and detail a plan for integrating them into your weekly schedule.

STEP 1: Identify Specific Ways You Approach Physical Embodiment

Take a moment to consider what it is like for you in your body and mind when you are in each of the approaches to physical embodiment listed in the table below. Write the physical activity you have been engaged in, along with the intensity, duration, and frequency of the activity. Then document physical sensations, emotions, and thoughts that are present in each of these areas (use your journal or additional paper if you need more space).

Physical Embodiment Approach	Physical Activity
My body as an object, tool, or obstacle: lost in pursuit	List physical activity (or activities): How often per week for each activity? _____ How long are the sessions? _____ How intense are the sessions? (1 = not intense at all and 10 = extremely intense) _____ What do you notice in your body? What do you notice emotionally? Give three examples of thoughts you have.

My body as me: embodied, attuned, engaged, intuitive doing	List physical activity (or activities): How often per week for each activity? _____ How long are the sessions? _____ How intense are the sessions? (1 = not intense at all and 10 = extremely intense) _____ What do you notice in your body? What do you notice emotionally? Give three examples of thoughts you have.
My body is ignored: disconnection and dissociation	List physical activity (or activities): How often per week for each activity? _____ How long are the sessions? _____ How intense are the sessions? (1 = not intense at all and 10 = extremely intense) _____ What do you notice in your body? What do you notice emotionally? Give three examples of thoughts you have.
Other: my unique approach to physical embodiment	List physical activity (or activities): How often per week for each activity? _____ How long are the sessions? _____ How intense are the sessions? (1 = not intense at all and 10 = extremely intense) _____ What do you notice in your body? What do you notice emotionally? Give three examples of thoughts you have

Once you're done, review your responses with your therapist. What do you notice? What warning signs could you use to help you stay in an embodied, healthy, and growing zone?

STEP 2: Create Your Physical Embodiment Practice Plan

Choose the physical embodiment practices that you will engage in for the next two weeks (e.g., walking, relaxation exercises, taking time in nature, yoga, and horseback riding), and list them in the following table. Then plan your physical activity schedule for each embodiment practice. Keep in mind (a) your current stage of recovery, (b) what places you at risk for backsliding, and (c) long-term sustainability of your practice within the context of your other daily commitments. At the end of your plan, include a few notes about your body's cues for knowing your health parameters.

Day of the Week	Physical Practices	Duration (how many minutes?) Intensity (1-10)
Sunday		
Monday		
Tuesday		
Wednesday		
Thursday		
Friday		
Saturday		
My body's cues for knowing my health parameters:		

Patient Signature: _____

Therapist Signature: _____

Treating Physician Signature: _____

Script 10.1: Progressive Muscle Relaxation

Find a comfortable position while sitting or lying down in a room or location in which you know you will not be interrupted. If you'd like, you can soften your gaze or close your eyes. Take a deep breath in and a deep breath out, extending your exhalation if you'd, breathing in 1, 2, 3, 4 and breathing out 1, 2, 3, 4, 5. (*pause*)

Bring your awareness to your body. If you notice your thoughts beginning to wander or any distractions, simply bring your awareness back to your body. Breathe here, holding your whole body in your awareness.

Now, bring your awareness to just your breath, and take a deep, big belly breath, inhaling for 1, 2, 3, 4. Hold here for 1, 2, 3, and then exhale slowly. Repeat this for four cycles of breathing, noticing your belly rising and falling with your breath. If it helps, place your hands on your belly and increase your awareness of and attention to the movement of your belly as you breathe. (*long pause*)

Each time you inhale, imagine that your breath is nourishing your body, and each time you exhale, imagine that you are able to release just a little bit of tension as it flows out of your body with your breath. (*pause*)

Now, beginning with your feet, curl your toes under, engaging the muscles of your feet. Squeeze and hold. Remember to continue breathing as you engage your feet. Notice the sensation of holding, the feeling of tension in your feet for 1, 2, 3, 4, and 5. Now, on an exhale, release your feet. Notice the sensations in your feet as you breathe. (*long pause*)

Now, flex your feet, pulling your toes toward your shins and engaging your calves. Feel the tension in your lower legs. Hold for 1, 2, 3, 4, and 5. On an exhale, release. Notice the sensations in your lower legs as you release. Breathe. (*long pause*).

Engage your thighs by pressing your knees toward each other. Hold for 1, 2, 3, 4, and 5. On an exhale, release. Notice the sensations in your upper legs as you release. Breathe here. (*long pause*)

Now, tighten the area around your sitting bones, hugging the muscles in toward your bones. Hold for 1, 2, 3, 4, and 5. On an exhale, release. Notice the sensations in and around your sitting bones and the sensation of release as you breathe. (*long pause*)

Bring your awareness to your stomach and engage your core, drawing your ribs toward your hips while breathing. Hold for 1, 2, 3, 4, 5. On an exhale, release. Notice the sensations in your belly as you breathe. (*long pause*)

Now, tighten your chest by taking a big inhalation into your chest and holding for about 5 seconds, 1, 2, 3, 4, and 5. Exhale and release. Imagine you are letting tension go with your exhale. (*long pause*)

Engage your upper back by drawing your shoulder blades toward each other. See if you can make your shoulder blades touch. Hold for 5 seconds, 1, 2, 3, 4, and 5. On an exhale, release, letting all of the tension go. (*long pause*)

Now, lift your shoulders to your ears, engaging the muscles of your shoulders and neck. Hold here, breathing for 1, 2, 3, 4, and 5. On an exhalation, release, letting go of any tension. (*long pause*)

Engage your triceps by extending out through your arms and engaging your muscles to lock your elbows. Hold for 5 seconds, 1, 2, 3, 4, and 5. Release your arms and breathe. (*long pause*)

Now, engage your biceps, flexing them. Continue to breathe as you hold for 1, 2, 3, 4, and 5. On an exhale, release and allow the muscles to relax. (*long pause*)

Tightly clench your fists, drawing your hands in toward your forearms and engaging your lower arms. Hold here and breathe for 5 seconds, 1, 2, 3, 4, and 5. Notice the tension and be with it. On an exhale, release. (*long pause*)

Now, roll your head back to look up at the ceiling, engaging the muscles of the neck. If you are on the floor, you can press your head into the floor. Be sure not to strain. Simply engage and notice the tension. Hold for 1, 2, 3, 4, and 5. On an exhale, release. Allow the tensions to melt as your head and neck rest. (*long pause*)

Now, engage your face. Begin with your jaw, clenching your teeth. Add a big smile, drawing the edges of your lips to your eyes. Now, squeeze your eyes closed and tense your forward. Hold here for 1, 2, 3, 4, and 5, On an exhale, release. (*long pause*)

Now, imagine a rolling wave of relaxation moving from your head, flowing all the way down to your feet as you inhale. With your exhale, imagine the wave rolling all the way back up to your head. Breathe in relaxation to the feet, and breathe out relaxation from your feet to your head. Breathe here. (*long pause*)

As you are ready, slowly bring your awareness back to your breath for a few breath cycles. (*pause*) When you are ready, slowly return your gaze to an object in the room and anchor it there. Gradually broaden your gaze to the room. If you'd like, offer gratitude to your body and breath for the practice.

Script 10.2: Guided Imagery for the Body as a Sanctuary During Triggers

Begin by finding a comfortable seated or lying down position. You might want to journal after. If so, have your journal and a pen or pencil handy. Make sure you are able to relax and feel supported. When you are ready, you can soften your gaze or close your eyes. Begin by breathing deep relaxing breaths. If it feels right for you, you can slowly extend your exhales, breathing in 1, 2, 3, and 4 and breathing out 1, 2, 3, 4, and 5. Take some time to breathe here. Consider that you could be completely relaxed, letting your tensions go and becoming increasingly present and open. (*pause*)

Now, allow yourself to listen to my voice and free your imagination to explore. Consider saying to yourself, "I am relaxed, and my imagination is open. It can be so relaxing to imagine beautiful and empowering things." (*pause*) Breathe here and consider reminding yourself one more time, "I am relaxed and my imagination is open. It can be so relaxing to imagine beautiful and empowering things."

Now, imagine yourself walking on a path. It is a clear and beautiful day. It is not too warm, not too cool, and there is a slight breeze. You are headed to a house nestled in the trees, just up the path. This house is your sanctuary. It was built for you. It is a peaceful place, quiet, surrounded by nature, and completely safe. As you walk, you see your sanctuary. What does it look like? Imagine it. It is exactly what you'd hoped for. It was built in exactly the style you love, the type of home that helps you feel relaxed and welcomed. Imagine the shape of the house, the windows, the doors. Are there gardens or landscaping? What do they look like?

How close to the house are the trees? What kind of trees are they? Is there a pond or a pool? Breathe here and imagine all of the details of the outside of your home. (*very long pause*)

You have finally arrived at your sanctuary. You approach the front door and open it, revealing the inside of the home. What do you see? You are so happy because, as you look, you see it has been decorated exactly how you love a home to be decorated. You look and see a dining room, sitting room, kitchen, and nook. You walk upstairs and there is a beautiful room for sleeping and another room in which you can relax, meditate, exercise, or do yoga if you'd like. Take a moment and imagine all of the rooms—the dining room, (*pause*) sitting room, (*pause*) the kitchen and kitchen nook. (*pause*) What are the stairs like as you walk up them? (*pause*) What is the sleeping room like? The furniture, the decor? (*pause*) What is your practice and relaxation room like? (*pause*)

Now, in your relaxation room, you sit or lie down—you decide. You are in this sanctuary, upstairs in this lovely room in which you are completely safe. If you'd like, you can pause and open the window in your sanctuary so you can feel the air and see the trees as you relax. In this sanctuary. Your body feels completely safe and relaxed. You are loved and accepted here. This place was built for you with everything you need.

Now imagine yourself there in your room. Bring your awareness to your body. Your body, in this place, is also a sanctuary. Your body is here for you, strong, breathing, heart beating. Your body is able to relax here and be completely accepted exactly as it is. This house was made for you and your body. There is nothing you must earn or achieve. It was made for you exactly as you are. You notice how safe and loved your body feels in this place, and you allow yourself to completely drop into your body. With your body as a sanctuary, you feel your (*speak very slowly*) toes, legs, your sitting bones, belly, (*pause*) chest, shoulders, arms, hands, neck, head, breath, and heartbeat. (*pause*) You are here in this sanctuary of a house, in the sanctuary of your room, in the sanctuary of your body, completely accepted and loved exactly as you are. You let go of any thoughts of not being enough, or not being right, or somehow broken. You realize here, in your sanctuary of your beautiful home and your body, that these discouraging ideas and thoughts have no place. They do not belong here.

You are accepted, loved, and uniquely valued exactly as you are. As if you could press the record button of your memory systems, record the body sensations of love, acceptance, and worth. Record your breath and heartbeat. Record the room, the house, the setting, and your pathway there. Remember it all in case you need it when you head back to your daily life activities. (*long pause*)

As you are present here in your body and your sanctuary, consider that this is a resource for you if you are triggered or upset. You can ground your feet into the earth below you, take several deep relaxing breaths, and find your way back to this sanctuary in which you are completely safe, loved, and valued. You have this beautiful sanctuary of a home built and decorated exactly how you need and want it to be. Turn your awareness away from the trigger, the stressor, and find the body sensations, the breath and heartbeat you recorded in your sanctuary. This is your inner resource that you can take with you anywhere. You can call on your sanctuary and the feelings of safety and security in your body whenever you need them. Here in this safe place, you can simply notice the trigger, the craving, the reactions as they arise and pass, as all things do. Breathe as you watch. (*pause*)

When you are ready to come back, bring your awareness to your breath. Breathe several cycles of relaxing breaths, extending the exhale, breathing in for 1, 2, 3, and 4 and out for 1, 2, 3, 4, and 5. (*long pause*) When you are ready, you can bring your gaze to anchor on something in the room. Then, slowly broaden your gaze. Take a moment to offer gratitude to your sanctuary, body, breath, and heartbeat. If you'd like to journal, consider writing a bit about your sanctuary, your body, and your experience. You might draw as well.

Script 10.3: Diaphragmatic Breathing

Begin by getting comfortable in your seat. Place one hand on your chest and one hand on your belly. Bring your awareness to your breath. Soften your belly so that it is free to move. Rest the muscles in your torso connected to your rib cage. (*pause*) Slowly, begin to breathe deeply, extending your inhalations and your exhalations gradually as you breathe. (*pause*)

Notice your hands, your chest, and your belly. Notice your hands rise and fall with your breath. Now, notice whether your hand on your rib cage moves more or less than the hand on your belly. To bring your breath toward deep diaphragmatic breathing, inhale so deeply that the hand on your belly lifts as the belly expands. See if you can breathe so that the hand on your chest is moving only slightly as your rib cage expands, and the hand on your belly is rising and falling noticeably with each breath. (*pause*)

Be sure to keep your breath slow, deep, smooth, and even. If you notice that you are getting lightheaded, pause at the end of each inhalation and exhalation and count to four before cycling to the next part of your breath. Continue breathing with your hands on your chest and your belly, breathing deeply into the hands on your belly for 10 more breath cycles.

Adapted from Cook-Cottone (2015b).

CHAPTER 11

Embodied Practices for Mindfulness and Heartfulness

We think that the point is to pass the test or to overcome the problem, but the truth is that things don't really get solved. They come together and they fall apart. Then they come together again and they fall apart again. . . . The healing comes from letting there be room for all of this to happen: room for grief, for relief, for misery, for joy.

—Pema Chodron, *When Things Fall Apart*

Mindfulness and heartfulness approaches are a way get under the barrage of thoughts that are continuously running through our minds. These approaches slow down our thoughts and allow us to choose and create the content of our minds. Viktor Frankl (2006) describes mindfulness like this: "Between stimulus and response there is a space. In that space lies your power to choose. In your response lies your growth and your freedom." I believe who we are lies in this space, after we have been triggered, and before we react (see Figure 11.1). In this space we find our true selves. Contemplative philosopher Michael Singer (2007) says that, if you really want to know who you are, don't follow the urge to think or react; just sit with, be with what is present. It is under the layers of reactions, judgments, thoughts, and narratives that we can find ourselves.

Mindfulness begins bare awareness, simply seeing what we see and accepting and allowing what is. Mindfulness is the being-with part of the Embodied Approach to Treating EDs (EAT-ED). Heartfulness is the nature of our mindfulness. When we see someone else's struggle, compassion is our guide. In the midst of our own aches, painful memories, failures, and desperate attempts to get it right, self-compassion is our guide. When it is our bodies, nature, or any other beautiful thing, body appreciation and gratitude are our guides. Integrity is our guide as we make choices. This chapter covers mindfulness as a concept and as

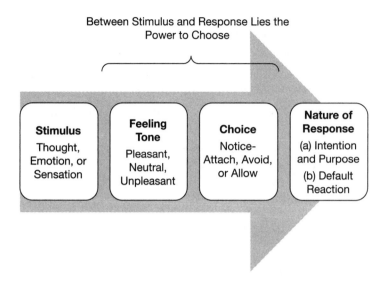

Figure 11.1. In the Space Between Stimulus and Response Lies the True Self

Reprinted / Adapted from Cook-Cottone, *Mindfulness and Yoga for Self-Regulation: A Primer for Mental Health Professionals*, New York: Springer Publishing Company; 2015. Reproduced with the permission of Springer Publishing Company, LLC.

both formal and informal practices, along with self-compassion, body appreciation, gratitude, and integrity.

MINDFULNESS

Mindfulness is a clarity in the awareness of one's inner and outer worlds (Brown, Ryan, & Creswell, 2007; Cook-Cottone, 2015b). This includes the internal experiences of thoughts, emotions, and actions and our external, moment-by-moment experiences (Brown, 2015; Brown et al., 2007; Cook-Cottone, 2015b). Mindfulness is a unique quality of consciousness, a receptive awareness of ongoing internal states, behavior, and external realities (Brown, 2015; Brown et al., 2007; Cook-Cottone, 2015b). When achieved, mindfulness is an open and distortion-free perception of what is (Brown & Kasser, 2005: Cook-Cottone, 2015b). At the practical level, mindfulness means to be aware, to notice, in the present moment, without judgment. It is distinct from both self-awareness (i.e., awareness of self-relevant thought) and self-focused attention (i.e., focus of attention on aspects of self; Brown et al., 2007).

Mindfulness can help us be more aligned with who we truly are and who we aspire to be. When we are mindful, our behaviors tend to autonomously regulate in accord with chosen interests and values rather than aligning with socially derived pressures (Brown et al., 2007; Cook-Cottone, 2015b). In this way, mindfulness is a protective mechanism, an antidote to consumerism and messages from the media (e.g., Cook-Cottone, 2015b). Research reviews indicate that mindfulness is associated with well-being and voluntary simplicity, a lifestyle shaped around intrinsically satisfying pursuits and expressions of self and away from material goals (Brown & Kasser, 2005; Cook-Cottone, 2015b).

The Attributes of Existence

Mindfulness helps us negotiate life as it is, what it means to exist in this world. Grabovac, Lau, and Willett (2011) explain the three attributes of existence, impermanence, suffering, and not-self, as well as how we respond to them and how our responses can lead to rumination and risk for psychopathology. They also demonstrate how awareness of these attributes can support well-being.

Impermanence. Impermanence represents the reality that everything changes. It is the nature of things to arise and pass away. In terms of self-regulation, all sense impressions and mental events are transient (Cook-Cottone, 2015b; Grabovac et al., 2011). As the quote by Chodron at the start of this chapter reminds us, we do not suffer because things are impermanent but because we resist or deny this fact (Bien, 2006; Cook-Cottone, 2015b; Kabat-Zinn, 2013).

Suffering. Suffering occurs when we do not practice nonattachment, the process of not attaching to and not avoiding thoughts, feelings, people, things, and so on (Cook-Cottone, 2015b). Nonattachment is difficult to master because much attachment is below consciousness. It begins with our automatic need to judge (Kabat-Zinn, 1990). We judge in order to feel safe (Linehan, 1993): Is something good or bad? Will it make us sick or nourish us? But when overgeneralized and displaced, judgment can get in the way of clear and objective thinking.

Attachment begins at the level of sensations and thoughts. In mindfulness theory, sensations and thoughts are considered two aspects of the same experience: a sensation is referred to as a *sense impression*, detected by the physiological aspects of self (Cook-Cottone, 2015b;

Grabovac et al., 2011), whereas a thought or memory is referred to as a *mental event*, detected by the thinking or cognitive aspect of the self. Each sense impression (i.e., an internal or external sensation) or mental event (i.e., thought or memory) is reflexively paired with a *feeling tone* (Cook-Cottone, 2015b; Grabovac et al., 2011), which is much more basic than emotions: a simple valence of positive (i.e., pleasurable), negative (i.e., aversive), or neutral, nothing more. Grabovac et al. (2011) explains that we are naturally drawn to the positive or pleasurable feeling tones and are compelled to avoid the negative or aversive ones. Suffering occurs when we cling to that which gives us pleasure and avoid that which we find aversive, thus the phrase "pain is inevitable, suffering is optional." Engaging in mindful practices (e.g., meditation and yoga) can bring the judgment process to awareness so that we can be with what is there, and neither attach to nor avoid it.

Not-Self. Not-self is sometimes considered one of the most difficult mindful teachings for Westerners to understand (Cook-Cottone, 2015b; Shapiro & Carlson, 2009). In Western culture, we have a strong sense of identity, as part of our way of viewing human development. Contrary to these strongly held beliefs, mindfulness teachings tell us that there is no stable, unchanging entity that can be called *self* (Cook-Cottone, 2015b; Shapiro & Carlson, 2009). It is also true that both sense impressions and mental events do not contain anything that could be called a self (Cook-Cottone, 2015b; Grabovac et al., 2011).

In private practice, I frequently meet people who identify whole-heartedly with a particular disorder: "I am anorexic" or "I can't control myself." I watch for these statements to reveal their sense of a nonchanging, permanent self that serves their disorders or struggles. When I hear statements like this, I tell them what I notice and ask them to reword the sentence in an empowering, malleable manner (Cook-Cottone, 2015b), for example, changing "I am anorexic" to "I currently struggle with food restriction when I feel overwhelmed" (Cook-Cottone, 2015b). Acceptance and commitment therapy uses the term *self-as-context*, holding that the self is a separate aspect of consciousness. In the EAT-ED model, it is the embodied self: clients are not the anorexic, bulimic, or binge eaters—these conceptualized versions of self are not flexible enough to respond to the world as it is with all its impermanence, flux, and ever evolving change (Juarascio, Manesse, & Espel, 2016).

Qualities of Mindful Practice

Engaging in mindfulness practice is a way to practice being with those attributes more effectively. Both informal and formal mindfulness practices can help slowly erode the underlying assumptions driving ED symptoms and add to a useful set of tools for self-regulation and symptom management. The qualities of mindful practice, as informed by Jon Kabat-Zinn (1990), and acceptance and commitment therapy approaches designed for clients with EDs (e.g., Juarascio et al., 2016), are as follows:

- Acceptance: accepting what is
- Defusion: cognitive distancing from or discernment of internal and external events (see Practice Guide 11.1; for more activities with fusion and defusion, see Harris 2009)
- Beginner's mind: seeing everything as if it is for the first time
- Nonjudging: witnessing experience with impartiality
- Nonstriving: not doing, achieving, or fixing
- Trust: honoring the wisdom of the mind and body
- Patience: allowing the life experiences to unfold at their own pace
- Letting go: putting aside the need to cling to some aspects of experience and reject or avoid others

Formal Mindfulness Practices

A formal mindful practice is a systematic meditation practice with the specific aim of cultivating mindfulness, practicing being with the three attributes of existence—impermanence, suffering, and not-self—and cultivating the qualities of mindfulness (Cook-Cottone, 2015b; Grabovac et al., 2011; Kabat-Zinn, 1990; Shapiro & Carlson, 2009; Stahl & Goldstein, 2010). Formal practices provide a structure or format for practice and can include seated meditation, walking meditation, mindful eating, body scans, progressive muscle relaxation, and yoga. As daily practices, they involve an intentional commitment of time and active engagement for a specific period (e.g., 5–60 minutes). They can be practiced in session and offered as homework for clients (Cook-Cottone, 2015b). Like mindful self-care, formal practices add predictable experiences of embodiment into clients' weekly routine. Several wonderful meditation apps for smartphones offer options such as interval and end timers. The Insight Timer (https://insighttimer.com) and

Simple Habit (https://www.simplehabit.com) are two of my favorites. A large set of meditations related to eating, EDs, and trauma that are aligned with the context of this text are available on Simple Habit.

One of the benefits of mindfulness is that it requires few if any supplies (Cook-Cottone, 2015b), just a space that is quiet, is free from distractions, and cultivates a sense of peacefulness (Cook-Cottone, 2015b). This should be a dedicated space for meditation that is not used for sleep, work, or entertainment (Wallace, 2011). Finding a comfortable seat is important for meditation practice (Cook-Cottone, 2015b). The head and neck should be aligned with the spine (Hanh, 1975). Eyes can be open, partially closed, or closed (Cook-Cottone, 2015b; Stahl & Goldstein, 2010). If open, eyes should be focused a few feet in front (Hanh, 1975). Script 11.1 can be read at the beginning of any seated meditation to help clients get settled and prepared for the meditation (Cook-Cottone, 2015b).

For beginners, it can be helpful to begin with short meditation practices of 2–5 minutes and no longer than 20–30 minutes (Cook-Cottone, 2015b; Hanh, 1975; Wallace, 2011). Clients should be guided to turn inward to assess the correct length of time for their practice. The just-right length for practice will be to end when clients still feel present and have a sense that they could easily continue (Cook-Cottone, 2015b; Wallace, 2011). Engaging in 2–3 minutes a day as a start is a strong base for a sustainable practice, which can lengthen as clients develop their meditation skills.

The two general forms of meditation are concentration and insight (Brown, 2015; Cook-Cottone, 2015b). Concentration meditation involves a focus on an object of meditation (Brown, 2015; Cook-Cottone, 2015b; Hanh, 1975; Kabat-Zinn, 2013; Stahl & Goldstein, 2010): a word or phrase, a concept or idea, an object, the flame of a candle, or the picture of a loved one (Cook-Cottone, 2015b). Insight meditations are practiced in a manner that brings full attention and awareness to the present moment and to both mind and body, simply observing fluctuations of the mind and experiences of the body (Cook-Cottone, 2015b; Hanh, 1975; Kabat-Zinn, 2013; Stahl & Goldstein, 2010).

Concentration Meditation. Concentration meditation is simply a practice of cultivating the qualities of meditation as you focus on an object (Cook-Cottone, 2015b). There is no further work to gain insight or to notice anything else. If the mind becomes distracted, the practitioner labels it as "distraction," "thinking," or "remembering."

Whatever comes up, it is simply labeled and awareness is brought back to the object of concentration. Script 11.2 offers a script you can use with your clients for concentration on breath.

Script 11.3 offers a script for walking meditation, another form of concentration meditation. Because it is active, it can be more accessible for those who have trouble sitting still. Walking meditation involves moment-by-moment awareness with each step, noticing each foot as it lifts, moves forward, and returns to the ground (Cook-Cottone, 2015b; Davis, Fowler, Best, & Both, 2019; Hanson & Mendius, 2009; Kabat-Zinn, 2013; Stahl & Goldstein, 2010). A practice in nonstriving, walking meditation is not about reaching a certain destination or getting somewhere (Cook-Cottone, 2015b). Rather, it is an awareness of each aspect of the act of walking. Walking meditation does not need much space, only about a 10- to 20-foot length of space (Cook-Cottone, 2015b; Shapiro & Carlson, 2009). I have effectively led walking meditations in classrooms and on small patches of grass. Gardens and labyrinths can be beautiful places for walking meditation (Cook-Cottone, 2015b). It can be helpful to set a timer to know when to stop (Cook-Cottone, 2015b).

Insight Meditation. Our mind is a construction of thoughts, reactions, and ideas about how things should be and who we are (Brown, 2015). Insight meditation is an opportunity to let go of those constructions, to simply notice them as they arise as dominant in our awareness and then pass (Brown, 2015; Cook-Cottone, 2015b). While sitting in meditation, stimuli are noticed—a thought, feeling, or sensation (Cook-Cottone, 2015b). This is not an easy practice, as the natural tendency is to attach and build on the feeling tone, cultivating concepts, emotions, and maybe even a line of thinking or ruminating (Grabovac et al., 2011). By staying present, moving awareness to the object of concentration, the stimulus is allowed to run its course (Cook-Cottone, 2015b). As clients practice, they notice the space, the choice, and the competence that comes from allowing and being present with what is (Cook-Cottone, 2015b). This can change the way clients experience their struggles.

Script 11.4 offers a script for aformal sitting meditation on the space between, to help your clients bring awareness to thoughts, emotions, and physical sensations (inside and outside), the accompanying feeling tones, the choice to notice and then attach or allow, and finally the active choice of a response (Cook-Cottone, 2015b, Grabovac et al., 2011, Wallace, 2011). You can work with your clients on their space between using the meditation along with their identified patterns.

Practice Guide 11.2 offers a practice guide to help your clients recognize and use the space between stimulus and response to increase their ability to make effective choices. Practice Guide 11.3 offers instructions for you or your clients to create your own meditation practices. Sometimes clients want you record a meditation for them using your voice, and sometimes it is helpful to have clients record their own meditations. Hearing their own voice as a guide can be a first step in internalizing qualities of mindfulness. There is no need for fancy equipment—the voice memo function on a cell phone can record and save the meditations.

Informal Mindfulness Practices

When Thich Nhat Hanh was asked, "How are we to practice mindfulness?" he answered, "Keep your attention focused on the work, be alert and ready to handle ably and intelligently any situation which may arise—this is mindfulness" (Hanh, 1975, p. 14). Informal mindful practices are defined as the bringing of mindfulness to everyday activities (Cook-Cottone, 2015b; Kabat-Zinn, 2013; Stahl & Goldstein, 2010). Creating a mindful embodiment has three steps: mindful awareness, embodied action through the formal practices, and sustained presence through informal practices to maintain lasting embodiment (Cook-Cottone, 2015b). Sustained presence is cultivated through the informal practice of awareness of the presence, thoughts, and attitudes we bring to our day and how we complete activities (Cook-Cottone, 2015b). Bien (2006) reminds us that informal mindful practices help keep the waters of awareness still and clear. Like the lake, when the water of our being settles, the surface becomes as smooth as glass, reflecting life clearly, without distortion (Bien, 2006; Cook-Cottone, 2015b).

Opportunities for informal practice of mindfulness can be found everywhere and at any time: walking in a beautiful garden or through the city, taking a bath, at home getting the children ready for school, at college angry at your roommate, or at the Department of Motor Vehicles waiting in line. For example, many of us do our chores while ruminating about the day or the fact that we have to do chores at all (Cook-Cottone, 2015b). Changing chores to informal mindfulness practices means intentionally bringing an accepting, open, and discerning awareness to whatever we are doing (Cook-Cottone, 2015b; Kabat-Zinn, 2013; Shapiro & Carlson, 2009). Each object we handle becomes an object of contemplation; each bowl, each item of clothing, each household object is sacred in its own way, filled with memories and connections to other times in the past and future (Cook-Cottone, 2015b).

HEARTFULNESS

Heartfulness is a form of mindfulness that brings in loving kindness, compassion, and integrity (Cook-Cottone & Vujnovic, 2018). Heartfulness offers a way to be with and work with what is present while honoring effort and struggle past and present (Cook-Cottone, 2017)—these are two of the four main ED intervention pillars, along with meaning making and purpose, and mindful self-care. Heartfulness reminds us that it is not the striving or the goals we achieve that matters. If we lose ourselves in the achievement, or in the pursuit of anything, even if it is a good thing, then we have lost our way. Positive embodiment requires that, as we stay fully embodied, we are able to give and receive loving kindness and compassion. Critical to positive embodiment is that we do what we do with integrity: we do not betray the truth of what our bodies need, the messages present in our emotions and thoughts, or the needs and concerns of those we care about. Heartfulness brings back the connection that starves the ED of its symptoms and feeds the client's hopes and dreams.

Loving Kindness

Loving kindness is one of the four immeasurables in yoga philosophy (along with equanimity, compassion, and joy). The four immeasurables are guidelines for the way we can effectively be in our lives and in our actions (Roach & McNally, 2005). The metta, or loving kindness meditation, brings a focus to loving kindness and helps reduce resistance and enhance presence, especially with difficult people in our lives (Cook-Cottone, 2015b). Loving kindness practice helps dissolve barriers that can build up in our minds, such as self-centeredness, resentment, bitterness, and anger (Cook-Cottone, 2015b; Stahl & Goldstein, 2010). Neurologically, the practice of metta can help activate our social and self-engagement systems, bringing compassion and kindness toward self and others into our choices and actions (Cook-Cottone, 2015b; Siegel, 2010).

Many of my clients have difficult people in their lives, and figuring out the most effective way to be with them is a part of the work we do (Cook-Cottone, 2015b). Linehan (1993) theorizes that an invalidating environment can contribute to the dysregulation seen in borderline personality disorder. Clients can be invalidated when important people in their lives neglect, ignore, or otherwise invalidate their emotional experience, talent, or sense of self (Cook-Cottone, 2015b). Valuable time and energy can be spent in reaction to people who do not behave in the ways we want (Cook-Cottone, 2015b; Wallace, 2011). The metta meditation can help shift the focus away from the unproductive or triggering feeling states associated with difficult relationships and allow a return to present-moment awareness and experience (Cook-Cottone, 2015b; Wallace, 2011). Hutcherson, Seppala, and Gross (2008) found that a brief practice using metta, compared with a closely matched control task, significantly increased feelings of social connection and positivity toward novel individuals on both explicit and implicit levels. Feliu-Soler et al. (2017) found that three weeks (three sessions a week) of loving kindness and compassion with clients diagnosed with borderline personality disorder increased acceptance of the present-moment experience and contributed to improvements in the severity of borderline symptoms, self-criticism, mindfulness, acceptance, and self-kindness. See Script 11.5 for loving kindness meditation that you can share with your clients.

Tonglen

Some consider tonglen, another heartfulness meditation practice, to be a form of loving kindness meditation. Tonglen practice is a method for connecting with our own suffering and the suffering of others (Chodron, 2019). Many of my clients are very sensitive to the experiences and emotional states around them. Tonglen practice can help manage this type of compassion stress. The practice begins by focusing on the suffering of a person known to be hurting, and then breathing in that suffering and, while exhaling, sending happiness and joy and offering them relief. The core of the practice is breathing in others' pain so that they have more space to be, and breathing out a wish for their relief. This practice works in opposition to attachment and aversion. Instead of avoiding or pushing away the suffering, we breathe it in, and instead of breathing in what we need for ourselves, we breathe out a wish for relief for others. See Script 11.6 for tonglen meditation practice that you can share with your clients.

Self-Compassion

Self-compassion "involves treating yourself the way you would treat a friend who is having a hard time even if your friend . . . is feeling inadequate, or is facing a tough life challenge" (Neff & Germer, 2018, p. 9). Self-compassion, as a construct, has three components (Neff & Germer, 2018):

Self-kindness, the practice of being as kind to yourself as you would be to a good friend or loved one

Common humanity, a sense of interconnectedness that acknowledges that everyone fails and makes mistakes and that we all experience hardships in life

Mindfulness, an awareness of moment-to-moment experiences in a clear and balanced manner

Self-compassion appears to be protective against the drive for thinness, especially for those who experience shame and/or body image dissatisfaction. In a study comparing clients diagnosed with an ED and women from the general population, Ferreira, Pinto-Gouveia, and Duarte (2013) found that, overall, self-compassion was negatively associated with external shame, general psychopathology, and ED symptomatology. For the women from the general population, increased shame predicted drive for thinness, particularly through lower self-compassion. In the client sample, increased shame and body image dissatisfaction predicted increased drive for thinness through decreased self-compassion.

Neff and Germer's (2018) *Mindful Self-Compassion Workbook* takes you step by step through their self-compassion program. I find their units on backdraft, shame, and body compassion especially helpful with clients. You can find out more about retreats, resources, and trainings on self-compassion at the Center for Mindful Self-Compassion website (https://centerformsc.org). If shame is involved in barriers to self-compassion, Table 11.1 offers a journaling exercise that can help your clients work through it, which can be done in distinct sessions or as homework and processed in session, as well as and suggested meditations.

Table 11.1: Working With Shame Through Journaling, Embodiment, and Meditation

Journal Exercises for Clients	• Entry 1: Ask your clients to detail an incident in which they experienced shame (i.e., a painful feeling of distress related to their behavior). • Entry 2: Have them locate where this experience resides as a felt sense in their body. Let them know that it is okay if that means they feel nothing—feeling nothing is something too. Ask them to write down where this feeling resides and the nature of the feeling. You can have them use figure drawings and colors to reflect this experience (see Script 9.11). • Entry 3: Ask clients write down any core beliefs that they have associated with this incident (e.g., "I am worthless," "I am stupid," "I am not enough"). • Entry 4: Have clients write about what it feels like to hold this core belief. • Entry 5: Ask clients to consider the common humanity of their experience and their core beliefs. Ask them to describe the experience they are processing and how it might show up in the lives of other people. What do they think it is like for these others? What feelings and experiences do your clients share with them? • Entry 6: Have clients write a concerned letter to one of the people they imagined or described in entry 5. Ask them to fill the letter with kindness and compassion. Perhaps they can let this person know that they understand the feeling, that they know what this person is going through. Perhaps they can tell this person what they think this person needs to hear. • Entry 7: Ask your clients to read the letter from entry 6 aloud to themselves, as if they wrote it to themselves. Then have them write about how experience the felt for them.

Embodiment and Meditation Practices for Clients	• Help clients practice using the Self-Awareness Scale at the end of Chapter 7 to monitor their body states as they process these experiences. Use the grounding and breathing practice (see Script 8.2) as needed to help them take care of their psychological self as they do this work. • Guide clients in practicing the adapted soften-allow-soothe meditation (Script 9.12) to experience and process the feelings and associated body sensations related to this experience. • Have clients practice the loving kindness meditation (Script 11.5) to offer love to themselves and to those around they as they go through this process. • Guide clients in practicing the tonglen meditation (Script 11.6) for themselves and for others who may be suffering in this way.

Sources: Informed by Cook-Cottone (2015b) and Neff and Germer (2018).

Gratitude and Body Appreciation

Gratitude and body appreciation are heartfulness approaches to embodiment. Gratitude is a broader life orientation that involves noticing and appreciating the positive in the world (Cook-Cottone, 2015b). Gratitude can help reduce ED behavior and its correlates. For example, in a randomized controlled trial, Wolfe and Patterson (2017) found that those in the gratitude-based intervention group performed better from pre- to posttest than those in the cognitive restructuring and control conditions, showing increasing body esteem, decreasing body dissatisfaction, reducing dysfunctional eating, and reducing depressive symptoms. Fritz, Armenta, Walsh, and Lyubomirsky (2019) found that teens who expressed gratitude, by writing weekly gratitude letters, reported healthier eating behaviors over time relative to controls who listed their daily activities each week. This effect was partially mediated by reductions in negative affect. Table 11.2 lists gratitude practices that can be added into your practice.

Table 11.2: Gratitude Practices to Suggest to Clients

- Write a letter of gratitude to themselves or someone to whom they are grateful.
- Write letter of gratitude to their body.
- Begin a gratitude journal, listing three things each night for which they are grateful.
- Do a what-went-well activity, writing down three things that went well each day.
- Write thank-you notes. They can buy a box of thank-you cards so that they are handy, or use sticky notes for more informal thank-you notes.
- When having trouble sleeping, they can begin to list 100 things for which they are grateful.
- Before dinner, each person at the table can one thing for which they are grateful.
- Make a grateful jar and add items to the jar each day.
- Make gratitude stones: use a permanent marker to write on stones things for which they are grateful. They can store the stones in a basket on their desk. The stones can be part of loving kindness meditation or an object focus as a gratitude meditation.
- Make a gratitude collage with photos and images of all for which they have gratitude. The can frame it and hang it in their room or by their desk.

Cultural barriers and toxic beauty ideals can inhibit engaging in gratitude for the body. Body appreciation approaches, the Health at Every Size movement, and authors, poets, and activists like Sonya Renee Taylor (2018) offer a pathway for our culture and our clients to negotiate such barriers and to move toward more embodied lives, in gratitude and love for our bodies. Table 11.3 lists practices to suggest to clients for cultivating body appreciation, and Table 11.4 summarizes the Health at Every Size and weight-inclusive principles.

Body appreciation is about knowing that the body is not an apology. In her book *The Body Is Not an Apology,* Taylor (2018) describes how this powerful phrase manifested while in a soulful conversation with a friend: "A reel of memories scrolled through my mind of all the ways I told the world I was sorry for having this wrong, bad body" (p. xi). Her book offers a deeply passionate and many times poetic journey into body appreciation. Each chapter introduces a new concept, such

Table 11.3 Practices to Suggest to Clients
for Cultivating Body Appreciation

- Engage in writing exercises in which they emphasize the appreciation or gratitude for their body. Ask them to include their appreciation for the body's functionality and focus on assets.
- Journal about how the beauty and fitness body ideals negatively affect them. Remind them to include their emotions, the way they talk to themselves and their body, and the behaviors related to these ideals.
- Write their own definition of beauty. They can experiment with a broad conceptualization that is inclusive, unconditional, and honors beauty within and the beauty in actions.
- Give their body a massage with body butter.
- Give their body nourishment, hydration, and rest. See the Mindful Self-Care Scale at the end of Chapter 7 for a wide range of ideas for taking care of the self.
- Do a mirror exercise in a safe and private location. In this exercise the clients stand naked in front of a mirror, looking at each body part, taking time to really see it, breathe deeply, and tell each body part what they appreciate about it.
- Write a list of ways they can combat beauty and fitness ideals, for example, "Do not follow beauty- or fitness-ideal-oriented social influencers." They can imagine that they have a force field around them protecting them from the media and ideals, or create a no-negative-body-talk zone that follows them everywhere.
- Practice filtering cultural information about body ideals, accepting what is positive about and supportive of their body and dismissing or refuting what is negative.
- Take care of their body through health and positive physical exercise, joyful activities such as dance, and creative activities such as music and art. Caution them to be sure the instructors emphasize body appreciation and respect.
- Find an all-bodies, all-levels, all-styles yoga studio and practice there.
- Follow body-positive social media accounts.
- Engage in the Health at Every Size movement. They can visit the Health at Every Size website at https://haescommunity.com/ or the Association for Size Diversity and Health website at https://www.sizediversityandhealth.org.
- Read and engage in the exercises in Sonya Renee Taylor's empowering book My Body Is Not an Apology (2018), or visit her website at https://thebodyisnotanapology.com.

Sources: Informed by Becker and Stice (2017), Cook-Cottone and Douglass (2017), Cohen, Fardouly, Newton-John, and Slater (2019), Cook-Cottone and Guyker (2018), Dunaev and Markey (2018), Taylor (2018), Tylka et al. (2014), and Wood-Barcalow and Augustus-Horvath (2018).

Table 11.4: The Health at Every Size and
Weight-Inclusive Principles

Health at Every Size Principles
1. Weight Inclusivity: Accept and respect the inherent diversity at body shapes and sizes.
2. Health Enhancements: Support health policies that improve access, and well-being and meet individual needs.
3. Respectful Care: Provide services from an understanding of weight bias and discrimination, intersectionality, and individual needs and support.
4. Eating for Well-being: Prompt flexible, individualized eating based on hunger, satiety, nutritional needs, and pleasure.
5. Life Enhancing Movement: Support physical activities that allow people of all sizes, abilities, and interests to engage in enjoyable movement, to the degree that they choose.

Principles for Weight Inclusive Practice
• Eradicate weight stigma.
• Target internalized weight stigma.
• Target body shame.
• Redirect focus from external critique of weight and size to a "partnership" with the body.
• Look for signs of diminished well-being.
• Look for signs of disordered, emotional, and/or binge eating.
• Respond to requests for weight loss with a holistic approach.
• Sustain health promoting practices.
• Reconnect with food and internal cues.

Source: Informed by Tylka et al. (2014, pp. 7, 10).

as radical self-love, shame, guilt, and apology. The text offers opportunities for radical reflection and unapologetic inquiry, which can be used for self-regulation and journaling. You can see the power of her words by viewing her TEDxMarin talk (https://www.tedxmarin.org/sonya-rene-taylor/), and her website offers more resources, support, and information (https://thebodyisnotanapology.com).

Integrity

Integrity is embodied truth. The root of integrity is *integer*, which means whole. *Integration* shares the same root and meaning, essentially the bringing together of all of the parts. Truth is an alignment with reality, in all of its layers, from our physiology and emotions and out into the world, in what we experience within the context of our family, community, and culture (Cook-Cottone, 2015b; Siegel, 2010). The embodied-self model considers attunement between the inner and outer aspects of self impossible without integrity, a full-on acceptance of what is, and ownership of our choices. The center of it all is integrity. Without integrity, there is no self-care or realization of mission or purpose. It is through the embodied layers of being that we learn our truth, and that truth will be the passageway to growth and recovery. "There are times when our unflinching honesty, vulnerability, and empathy will create a transformative portal, an opening up to a completely new way of living" (Taylor, 2019, n.p.).

Integrity is a mindfulness-based practice that may be related to decreases in EDs symptoms. Avoidance is one of the roots of suffering. I encourage my clients to work each week to be honest with themselves and with others. Each session, I ask clients the following questions, rating the answers on a scale from 1 to 10:

1. Generally, how hard has it been to be honest with yourself?
2. Generally, how hard has it been to be honest with others?
3. How honest have you been with yourself?
4. How honest have you been with others?

This gives clients an opportunity to express their struggle with integrity. Clinically, I have found that, as their integrity scores go up, symptom scores go down.

Without integrity, it is extremely difficult to be therapeutic. EDs are filled with shame, hidden symptoms, and a lack of integration of self (Cook-Cottone, 2015b). A substantial part of the disorder is about hiding and not telling the truth to others in subtle and not so subtle ways. Often, clients have not been truly honest with anyone in a long time. In therapy, one of the most powerful experiences your client can have is learning how to be with and work with the truth, no matter how difficult the truth may be to hold. Taylor (2018) speaks to the importance of truth:

When we hear someone's truth and it strikes to some deep part of our humanity, our own hidden shames, it can be easy to recoil into silence. We struggle to hold the truths of others because we have so rarely had the experience of having our own truths held. (p. x)

CONCLUSION

Both Pema Chodron and Viktor Frankl wisely guided us toward seeking space, space for all the things and life to unfold as they should and space for finding out who we are between stimulus and response. Mindfulness and heartfulness practices that help us be with what is present in the here and now, in this embodied moment. By digging into the space between, your clients are engaging in the practice of holding a loving and kind space for who they authentically are, a practice that makes moving forward in recovery possible.

Practice Guide 11.1: Fusion and Defusion

In embodied mindfulness, we work to notice the thoughts and feelings we are having by carefully selecting those that best serve our well-being and recovery. When you are fused with an idea, you are letting it control your behavior without questioning it. For example, you might say, "I am worthless" or "I am defined by my eating disorder." You can be fused with ideas about many things: rules (e.g., about life and about eating), reasons why you can't recover, judgments, ideas about the past or future, or ideas about yourself (e.g., "I am broken"). This practice guide will help you identify your possible areas of fusion and develop a plan for defusion.

Consider that some thoughts that you have can be helpful and some thoughts can get in the way of your recovery. In defusion, you create a distance between your observing, noticing self and your thoughts. You no longer take them as truths and question their helpfulness in your life.

STEP 1: List Recurring Thoughts

Using the form below, list three recurring thoughts that you think might be getting in the way of your recovery. Next to each thought, indicate how helpful it is in your work toward well-being and recovery by writing number between 1 (not at all helpful) and 10 (very helpful). Remember to consider all types of thoughts: rules, reasons, judgments, ideas about the past or future, and ideas about yourself.

STEP 2: Question the Thoughts

Working with your therapist, question each thought you wrote down. Does this thought help you with your recovery, mindful self-care, or your sense of purpose or mission? Is it old news, something you have been telling yourself for a long time? What happens if you believe it is true? Does it help you take an effective action in your life?

Thought 1: I notice my mind is telling me _____
_____
_____
_____
_____

When I question this thought, I realize _____

_____

_____

_____

Thought 2: I notice my mind is telling me _____

_____

_____

_____

_____

When I question this thought, I realize _____

_____

_____

_____

_____

Thought 3: I notice my mind is telling me _____

_____

_____

_____

_____

When I question this thought, I realize _____

_____

_____

_____

_____

Practice Guide 11.2 The Space Between

This guided practice will help you become more aware of the space between stimulus and response and increase your ability to make effective choices based on your intentions and sense of purpose and meaning. Complete these steps with your therapist, or process this at home and bring it to session for exploration (see Figure 11.1).

STEP 1: Identify the Stimulus

Think back to the last time you made a choice that did not serve you. Perhaps it was a symptom you engaged in, or you behaved in a way you regret. See if you can think back to when you were first feeling triggered. This is your stimulus. It can be a sensation you noticed in your body, a feeling, a thought, or an event that occurred. Write it here.

Stimulus (sensation, feeling, thought, or external event):

_____
_____
_____
_____

STEP 2: Identify the Tone of the Stimulus

Identify the feeling tone associated to the stimulus.

Was it aversive and unpleasant, neutral, or pleasant? Describe what you notice: _____
_____
_____

Do you notice any associations in the body? Where are they? Are they broad or constricted? Are they steady, moving and transient, deep or surface level? Describe what you notice: _____
_____
_____
_____
_____

Do you notice any associated emotions or thoughts? What are they? List them here: _____

_____

_____

_____

_____

STEP 3: Identify What Happened

What happened next? What was the choice process like? Were you able to notice, or did it feel like things were just happening in reaction? Did you notice yourself wanting to attach or cling, or did you notice that you were trying to push sensations or feelings away? Were you able to practice allowing sensations, feelings, and thoughts? What was that like?

Choice (notice, attach, avoid, and/or allow): _____

_____

_____

_____

_____

STEP 4: Identify Your Response

The last step is to detail both (a) the response that unfolded and (b) the response you hoped for. Responses can be driven by intention and aligned with purpose. They can also be a default reaction to the stimulus and feeling tones, and aligned with disordered eating and other symptoms. Also, (c) list the embodied practices and tools you might use to realize presence, awareness, and your preferred response. This can include grounding and calming breaths, more structured practices such as yoga sessions and meditations, enhanced self-care in any of the domains, or sensations and feelings work.

Response (intention and purpose or default reaction):

(a) **What did you do?** Include any sensations, feelings, and thoughts you have associated with your choice: _____

_____

_____

_____

_____

_____

_____

_____

_____

(b) **What would you have liked to have happened?** Include any sensations, feelings, and thoughts you notice as you consider the possibilities:

_____

_____

_____

_____

_____

_____

_____

(c) **What embodied practices and tools can you use to help you realize presence, awareness, and your preferred response?**

_____

_____

_____

_____

_____

_____

_____

_____

Practice Guide 11.3: Writing and Recording
a Mindful Meditation Script

Creating your own meditation script can be a fun and creative way to begin to develop ownership in your meditation practice. To create a script, you will want to include breath, physical presence and sensations, an object for focus, perhaps a story about the object, a section that brings awareness back to breath, and a closing, bringing yourself back to current moment awareness (see the form below; use extra sheets of paper as needed). Once you have written out your script, read it aloud and make any corrections you feel are needed. Next, using your computer or cell phone, record the script digitally. E-mail or text it to yourself so you have it wherever you need it. You may want to make several versions of various lengths (3, 5, 10, and 20 minutes) for different settings or applications (adapted from Cook-Cottone, 2015b).

_____

_____

_____

_____

Getting Seated: Describe the process of finding a comfortable seated position for your meditation. Include how to sit, placement of hands, and other details that are relevant to your setting (e.g., the type of chair or pillow, etc.).

_____

_____

_____

_____

Breath Awareness: Write about how to bring awareness to breath. Would you like to count or extend breaths? Watch inhalations shift to exhalations?

_____

_____

_____

_____

Physical Presence: Provide guidance on how to attend to the physical body and sensations. Here, you can detail awareness of body parts (as in a body scan) or you can bring awareness to the senses, noticing smells, feelings, and sounds. Be descriptive and specific.

_____

_____

_____

_____

Emotion Awareness: If you choose to explore emotions, you can add a section to notice feelings. You may want to locate feelings in the body and breathe into the feelings.

_____

_____

_____

_____

Focus Object and Thoughts: Many meditations bring focus to an object. You can choose breath, body, or feelings; a statement (e.g., "I can be present in the moment," or "I am worth the effort"); a color; or a favorite place. If it is a place, describe it in detail—what it looks like, sounds, smells, the wind, etc. Also bring notice other thoughts as they arise and pass away and to bring focus back to the object.

_____

_____

_____

_____

Centering and Closing: To bring the meditation to a close, first bring awareness back to the body and breath. Slowly guide back to the present moment, the sensations of the body, and the breathing described during the early part of the meditation. Then, guide slowly back to engagement in your current world (e.g., sitting up, slowly opening your eyes and checking in).

_____

_____

_____

_____

Adapted from Cook-Cottone (2015b).

Practice Guide 11.4: Recording Informal and
Formal Practices

Use the chart below to record your formal and informal practices. Record
how many minutes you engaged in each practice, as well as a short description of how the practice went. You might also choose to write at the bottom of the sheet, or in your journal, anything you noticed or insights that you
might have had.

Day of the Week	Duration (minutes)	Formal or Informal Practice (provide a short description of how it went)
Sunday		
Monday		
Tuesday		
Wednesday		
Thursday		
Friday		
Saturday		
Notes:		

Script 11.1: Getting Seated for Meditation

"Find a comfortable and quiet place to sit. Be sure that you are well grounded: your feet are touching the floor, and your sit bones and legs provide a stable base. Roll your shoulders back, engage your core, and extend and straighten your spine as you reach the crown of your head toward the ceiling. Make any adjustments needed to help you maintain this posture. You might roll a blanket and place it under the back edge of your sitting bones or place supports under your knees. (*pause*)

If it feels okay for you, close your eyes. If you leave your eyes open, choose a focal point a few feet in front of you and rest your eyes there. Place your hands in your lap or on your thighs, wherever they feel most comfortable. If it feels right, let a half smile come to your face. (*pause*)

Take a few moments to bring your awareness to your body, becoming present from the soles of your feet to the crown of your head. Notice what is present. Notice your breath, heart rate, and any tensions in the body. Breathe into any tensions you may feel, and exhale to release them. With each exhalation, release tension and soften your body. Let go of everything. Hold on to nothing but your breath and your half smile.

Adapted from Cook-Cottone (2015b) and informed by Hanh (1975), Kabat-Zinn (2013), and Wallace (2011).

Script 11.2: Concentration on Breath

Start with Script 11.1; then begin the following script. Bring your awareness to your body. Notice any tensions or places you might need support, and make any adjustments that you need. Breathe here. (*pause*)

Now, bring your awareness to your breath. If possible, close your mouth and breathe through your nose. Do not try to change your breathing. Notice the qualities of your breath. Is it smooth? Is your inhalation the same length as your exhalation? Can you feel your heart beating as you breathe? What is the pace of your breathing? Is it fast, slow, moderate? See if you can notice without judging. Simply notice. As you are being aware of your breathing, you may notice that other objects enter your awareness. Simply notice that they are there. You may want to label them as thinking, remembering, noticing, and so on, and then bring your attention directly back to your breath. (*pause*) Do this as often as needed as you practice breath awareness. (*pause*)

Bring your awareness to the very tip of your nose. Notice the air as it passes just underneath the tip of your nose. Breathe here. (*pause*) Now, bring your awareness to your nostrils. Notice the quality of the air, the warmth as the air leaves your body and the comparative coolness of the air as it enters. Notice if the air is dry or moist as it enters and leaves your body. As you breathe, remain aware of the focus of your mind. Continuously bring it back to your breath, your nose and your nostrils, the quality of the air, the pace of your breath.

Begin to notice how the air feels as it passes your nostrils and enters your nose. See if you can feel the air enter your body, move from your nose to your throat and into each of your lungs. (*pause*) Notice the pathway, how the breath feels as it moves from your nose to your throat and then from your throat to your lungs. Can you feel the breath divide as half enters one lung and half enters the other? (*pause*)

Now, notice how your rib cage rises and falls as you inhale and exhale. You may begin to notice that your rib cage expands from front to back and from side to side as you inhale. You may notice that the ribs and the sides of the body gently soften as you exhale. Continue breathing here. As before, notice the contents of your awareness, and as needed, bring your focus back to your breath.

Now, bring your awareness to the qualities of your breath. Notice the length of the exhalations and inhalations. Bring awareness to the fullness of your breath. Is it shallow and in your chest? Does it go deep into your body, expanding both your chest and your belly? Is your breath smooth as it moves in and out of your body? Are there pauses at the transition from inhalation to exhalation?

Slowly begin to deepen your breath. Count to four as you inhale, 1, 2, 3, 4, and then count to four as you exhale, 1, 2, 3, 4. Continue this for four breaths. (*long pause*) Now, continuing with even deeper breaths, notice the transition from inhalation to exhalation. Once you feel as if you cannot inhale any further, allow your body to move, without effort, to exhalation. As you feel you cannot exhale any further, allow your body to shift to inhalation. Continue this for four breaths. (*long pause*)

Now, allow your breath to return to normal breathing. When breathing shorter breaths, become aware. Notice the qualities of your normal breathing. Describe them to yourself as you breathe. You might think, "My breathing is smooth, even, and without pause." Breathe and notice the qualities of your breath. (*pause*)

Now, expand your awareness from your breath to your chest and head and then to your entire body. Breathe as if you could breathe into your entire body. Inhale, a big, whole-body inhale, and exhale a big, whole-body exhale. Notice your body again. Notice any shifts or changes in the experience of your body. (*pause*)

Slowly bring your palms together and rub them, palm to palm, generating a little warmth. Then, take the palms of your hands to your eyes, softly cupping them. Slowly open your eyes into the palms of your hands and spread your fingers slightly to allow light in. Slowly withdraw your hands from your eyes, breathing normally.

Adapted from Cook-Cottone (2015b) and informed by Bien (2006), Davis et al. (2019), Kabat-Zinn (2013), Stahl and Goldstein (2010), and Wallace (2011).

Script 11.3: Walking Meditation

Begin your walking meditation by standing with your feet hip distance apart, hands at your sides, shoulders soft, and tailbone neutral. With your eyes open, draw your chin to neutral, and look around. See what you see? Do you see people? Are there trees or grass? Are you inside and see the floor and furniture? Take it all in. (*pause*)

Check in on what you are experiencing inside as well. How do your feet feel on the ground? Is the surface hard or soft? Do you feel supported? Are you wearing socks, shoes, sandals? Scan your body from your feet to the crown of your head, across your shoulders, and down your arms to your fingertips. Do you feel tension? Are you relaxed? Can you breathe into any tension you are feeling and let it go? (*pause*)

Take a big breath in, hold it for a count of four, and then release your breath slowly, returning to regular breath. (*pause*)

Anchor your gaze about three feet in front of you. Noticing you're connected to the earth, lift your right foot off of the ground, bending at the knee, and then move your foot forward. Notice how your leg feels when you lift your foot. Notice how your foot lands on the ground. Do all four corners of your foot connect to the ground below at once? Or does the heel meet the ground, followed by the ball of the foot and then the toes? Place your weight on your right foot, and lift your left foot as you begin to walk. Now that you are in motion, how does the action of lifting your left foot differ from the action of initiating movement with the lifting of your right foot? How does lifting your left foot feel in your leg, your core? Place your left foot on the ground and notice the nature of the contact of your foot on the ground. (*pause*)

Begin to walk in a slow and steady pace that allows you to notice each and every step as you lift, propel, and place each foot. For a period of time, keep your awareness on the stepping aspects of walking. Be very curious about any changes in your steps. Perhaps you turn a corner or avoid a small rock. What does that feel like in your body? Does your pace change? Does your breath stop? If you are wearing shoes, notice your feet in your shoes and the sensation of the foot, to shoe, to ground. How does the wearing of shoes feel as you walk? Do you notice qualities of the shoe? If you are barefoot, what do you notice and feel?

As you walk, bring your awareness to your breath. Your body is a system. Your breath fuels your walking as oxygen is sent to the muscles in your body to propel you. Notice the rhythm of your steps, your breath, your heartbeat. Notice the synchrony of your body as it moves step by step. Expand your awareness to your whole body. Feel your body move through space as you breathe and take step after step. Feel the air on your skin as you move forward. (*pause*)

Become mindfully aware of any thoughts or feelings that may be arising as mental events. Simply notice them and bring your awareness back to your feet and to the aspects of each step, the lifting, the moving of the foot forward, and the placing to your foot on the ground. (*pause*)

Once you have reached your allotted time for walking meditation, return to your point of origin. Place your feet hip distance apart and your hands at your sides, soften your shoulders, and neutralize your chin. Take a moment to offer gratitude for your feet, your body, your breath, and your heart. Offer gratitude for your awareness during your walking meditation and the insight brought to you by your practice.

Adapted from Cook-Cottone (2015b) and informed by Davis et al. (2019), Hanson and Mendius (2009), Kabat-Zinn (2013), Shapiro and Carlson (2009), and Stahl and Goldstein (2010).

Script 11.4: Space-Between Meditation

Start with Script 11.1; then begin the following script. Take a few moments to bring your awareness to your body. How do you feel? Pause and be present here in this moment. Bring your awareness to your breath. Notice if it is even, regular, and smooth. Do not try to change your breath. Simply be present with it. Notice it. (*pause*) Now, take a deep breath in and exhale. (*pause*)

Your breath, body, emotions, and thoughts are your object of concentration for this meditation. As you breathe, you will become aware of sensations. This can be something that you see, smell, taste, hear, feel on your skin or inside of your body. You may hear children outside, birds chirping, a lawn mower or snow blower going. You may have a candle lit and notice a flicker in the flame and feel a slight breeze on your skin. Your stomach may grumble, or your muscles may tighten. These are sensations. Notice them as they arise. As they arise into your awareness, say to yourself, "I am hearing the chirping of the birds," or "I am feeling the grumbling of my stomach." Notice that these sense impressions arise and pass away and that your breath is a constant. Notice this and bring your awareness back to your breath. (*pause*)

As your sensations arise, you will also notice that they feel pleasant, neutral, or unpleasant. Notice this. Notice how your brain tends to automatically label your sensations. Perhaps you heard the birds chirping and you feel a pleasant feeling tone. Or maybe you hear a lawn mower and you feel an unpleasant feeling tone. Notice this. (*pause*)

Notice that the feeling tones arise and pass away as well. The feeling tone comes to your awareness, it peaks, and then it softens and passes away. As you notice the sensations and the feeling tones, allow them to be and bring your awareness back to your breath. (*pause*)

As you are sitting, breathing, and attending to the nature and quality of your breath, you may notice mental events: thoughts, memories, concepts, and ideas. (*pause*) These can also be feelings tied to ideas and memories. When mental events arise as feelings, you will notice that sensations come with them. You might feel sadness in your belly and heaviness as you think about the dog you loved when you were little. You notice these mental events, memories, ideas, stories, as they arise. As you notice, bring your awareness back to your breath. Your breath is your anchor. (*pause*)

Notice that the mental events arise in your consciousness, gain a stronger presence, and then pass away, getting softer as they move out of your awareness. Notice this pattern. Notice that as mental events arise and pass away, your breath is a constant cycle of inhalation and exhalation.

As you sit and breathe, you may notice that your mental events also have an associated feeling tone. You notice that your brain labels them as pleasant, neutral, or unpleasant. Notice that you think and that the feeling tone is present with the thought. As you notice these feeling tones, you notice that they arise and pass away just as your sense impressions and mental events arise and pass away. Notice this and bring your breath back to your awareness. (*pause*)

As you practice, sitting and breathing, you may notice that some sense impressions and feeling tones pull for your attention. As you sit, you may hear a sound and notice that the feeling tone that comes with it is unpleasant. You may find your thoughts dwelling on other unpleasant thoughts that come with it, one after another. Notice that, as your mind works and works, your breath and your choice are lost. (*pause*)

Your power is in your anchor, your breath. The moment that

you notice that you have left your breath, no matter how long you left it, bring yourself back to your breath. The growth is in your noticing. As you sit, you will see your habits of the mind. You will get to know them. As you see them, notice them. "Ah, there it is. I notice it, and I will bring myself to my breath." Perhaps it is different, pleasant. "Ah, there are the birds chirping, I notice them. I notice the pleasant feeling tone. I bring myself back to breathing." Breathe. (*pause*)

As you are sitting, bring your awareness wholly to your breath. Notice the qualities of your breath. Is it even, smooth, moving in and out without pause? Breathe and notice. (*long pause*) When it is your time to finish, cultivate gratitude for your practice, for your ability to sit and notice, and for your insights gained during your practice today.

Adapted from Cook-Cottone (2015b) and informed by Brown (2015), Grabovac et al. (2011), and Wallace (2011).

Script 11.5: Loving Kindness Meditation

Start with Script 11.1; then begin the following script. Grounded, bring your awareness to your breath. Breathe deeply, inhaling and exhaling. (*pause*) Cultivate a sense of awareness and simple attentiveness. Begin to expand your awareness to encompass your whole body. (*pause*)

Imagine that you are surrounded by a sphere of loving kindness and that you are at the very center. Imagine that the sphere is like a mother holding a beloved infant with care, warmth, and abounding love. This is the nature of the sphere that is around you now. (*pause*)

As you sit within the sphere of loving kindness, say these words to yourself:

"May I be happy.
May I be well.
May I be safe.
May I be peaceful and at ease."

Once you have finished, bring your awareness back to your breath, to your whole body, and then out to the sphere. Breathe. (*pause*)

Now, bring to mind a loved one or someone who has shown you great love and kindness. Imagine that the sphere of loving kindness that surrounds you now is expanding to include your friend or loved one. Breathe and visualize you, your loved one, and the sphere of loving kindness. Repeat these words:

"May you be happy.
May you be well.
May you be safe.
May you be peaceful and at ease." (*pause*)

Now bring to mind a friend or neighbor, somebody for whom you feel a warmth and kindness. This can be someone from your daily travels, the person who lives next door to you, or your yoga teacher. It can be anyone you choose. Breathe and visualize you, your loved one, and your friend or neighbor within the sphere of loving kindness. Repeat these words:

"May you be happy.
May you be well.
May you be safe.
May you be peaceful and at ease." (*pause*)

Now, think about someone about whom you feel neutral. It may be someone in your life with whom you interact yet you have no feelings, good or bad, associated with this person. Maybe it is the person who serves your coffee or tea at the shop in your town or city. Hold this person in your awareness. Breathe and visualize you, your loved one, your friend or neighbor, and the neutral person within the sphere of loving kindness. Repeat these words:

"May you be happy.
May you be well.
May you be safe.
May you be peaceful and at ease." (*pause*)

Now, bring to mind someone with whom you struggle. Perhaps it is someone close to you, in your family, or someone at work. Bring that person to mind. Breathe and visualize you, your loved one, your friend or neighbor, the neutral person, and the difficult person within the sphere of loving kindness. Repeat these words:

"May you be happy.
May you be well.
May you be safe.
May you be peaceful and at ease."

Now, it is time to expand your loving kindness to all beings everywhere. Bring to mind those who are hungry, cold, tired, and impoverished, as well as those who have great wealth and abundance. Bring to mind beings that are sick and those who have great health. Bring to mind all beings in your town, city, state, and nation. Bring to mind all beings across the world, those who are here, those yet to be born, and those who have passed. Bring to mind all beings everywhere. Breathe and visualize you, your loved one, your friend or neighbor, the neutral person, the difficult person, and all beings everywhere within the sphere of loving kindness. Repeat these words:

"May all beings be happy.
May all beings be well.
May all beings be safe.
May all beings be peaceful and at ease." (*pause*)

Feel the radiating love and kindness as you breathe. Feel the expansiveness of your sphere and the possible connections with all beings. Slowly bring your awareness back to your breath and your body. When you are ready, rub your hands together, warming them gently. Raise your hands to your eyes and slowly open your eyes into the palms of your hands. When you are ready, rest your hands on your thighs, eyes open, and breathe steady.

Adapted from Cook-Cottone (2015b) and informed by Hanson and Mendius (2009), Shapiro and Carlson (2009), Siegel (2010), Stahl and Goldstein (2010), Wallace (2011), and http://www.mettainstitute.org/mettameditation.html.

Script 11.6 Tonglen Meditation

Start with Script 11.1; then begin the following script. Once you are seated and ready, turn your focus to your breath. (*pause*) Breathe here for several breath cycles: "Breathing in, I know I am breathing in, and breathing out, I know I am breathing out." (*pause*)

Bring your whole body to your awareness, your feet on the floor, sit bones grounded, long spine, your breath, emotions, thoughts, all of you. (*pause*) Bring to mind something that has been difficult for you. (*pause*) Now, notice the emotions and body sensations associated with that experience. Notice and experience them. (*pause*)

Breathe into the feelings of pain and discomfort associated with your challenge, taking a deep breath into your belly. Then exhale, wishing relief for you and for anyone else who might be struggling this way. (*pause*) Breathe into the suffering and challenge, and breathe out a wish for relief for you and for anyone who might be suffering in this way. Repeat this for a few breath cycles. (*pause*)

Now, bring to mind someone you care about who is suffering. (*pause*) What are they experiencing? (*pause*) Now, notice the emotions and body sensations associated with that experience. Notice and experience them. (*pause*)

Breathe into the feelings of pain and discomfort associated with your loved one's suffering, taking a deep breath into your belly. Then exhale, wishing relief for your loved one and for anyone else who might be struggling this way. (*pause*) Breathe into the suffering and challenge, and breathe out a wish for relief for your loved one and for anyone who might be suffering in this way. Repeat this for a few breath cycles. (*pause*)

When you are ready, bring your awareness back to your breath. Offer gratitude to your body, breath, and heart for your practice. Slowly open your eyes, anchoring your awareness on one spot in the room, and gradually broaden your awareness out to the room.

CHAPTER 12

Embodied Eating

Mindful and Intuitive Interactions With Food

It is amazing how many hints and guides and intuitions for living come to the sensitive person who has ears to hear what his body is saying.
—Rollo May

Mindful eating and intuitive eating are two embodied approaches to eating that show potential for integration into the treatment of EDs. For example, both provide an alternative to maladaptive dietary restraint among the general population. Also, mindfulness-based eating awareness training was designed specifically for binge eating disorder (BED; Anderson, Reilly, Schaumberg, Dmochowski, & Anderson, 2016; Kristeller, & Wolever, 2010). A growing body of evidence suggests mindful and intuitive eating may help those with clinical EDs. Preliminary evidence suggests that intuitive eating can be successfully integrated into ED treatment for anorexia nervosa (AN), bulimia nervosa (BN), and ED not otherwise specified (Richards, Crowton, Berrett, Smith, & Passmore, 2017). A recent study found that, compared to healthy controls, individuals with EDs showed decreased engagement in direct experience when engaging in an eating task (Elices et al., 2017): those with EDs were more likely to process eating experiences analytically, perhaps related to the activation of dysfunctional cognitive schemas associated with the act of eating, which caused them to disengage from sensory experiences.

Mindful eating and intuitive eating are slightly different approaches to eating that share some common features (see Figure 12.1). Generally speaking, mindful eating approaches apply mindfulness techniques to the eating process with a goal of increasing awareness of body sensations related to eating and hunger and satiety cues (Anderson et al., 2016). Intuitive eating also encourages a turning inward and attention

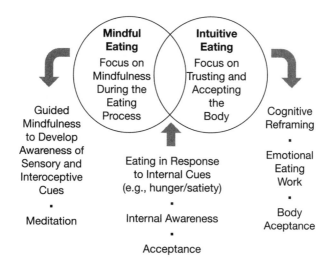

Figure 12.1. Mindful Versus Intuitive Eating

Source: Informed by Anderson et al. (2016) and Tribole and Resch (2017).

to hunger and satiety cues as well as encourages an increased trust in and acceptance of the body, while addressing emotional eating and cognitive distortions about eating and the body (Anderson et al., 2016; Tribole & Resch, 2017). Both are pathways to increased embodiment associated with eating. Depending on the overall treatment protocol, the approach can be specific to eating or it can be broader, integrating more facets of embodiment, such as body acceptance. Evelyn Tribole and Elyse Resch's (2017) broad approach to intuitive eating integrates cognitive distortions around dieting and the body, tackles media and cultural messages associated with eating and the body, offers guidance on nutrition and food choices, teaches to honoring of the body and its messages, and addresses healthy exercise and more.

In a study on the two approaches to eating, Anderson et al. (2016) asked 125 college students to complete a laboratory taste test and measured constructs related to mindful and intuitive eating. Intuitive eating accounted for significant variance in disordered eating and BMI. Specifically, elevated restraint in eating was associated with increased BMI and disordered eating, whereas increased intuitive eating was associated with decreases in both BMI and disordered eating. Mindful eating did not correlate with any of the outcome variables, although positive outcomes have been related to both approaches—effective mindfulness-based eating approaches tend to have broader, more comprehensive content addressing more than mindful eating as measured here. One possible implication of this study is that, to turn inward and attend to our internal cues, we must also combat other issues such as the cultural and media messages that obscure our relationship with our bodies.

Despite the promise, integrating mindful and/or intuitive eating into treatment should be considered carefully due to medical concerns related to malnutrition, physiological sequelae associated with bingeing and purging, and the critical role that nutritional counseling and meal planning play in preventing mortality and contributing to recovery. Whether or not to include these approaches in treatment is a complex and nuanced decision. I have worked with clients in recovery seeking to move away from their meal plans and to begin to attempt more intuitive eating—perhaps too quickly and without willingness to access resource supports—who experienced setbacks of weight loss and emotional struggle. I have worked with others who were able to move their eating smoothly toward more of a mindful connection with food and successful engagement in intuitive eating.

It is critical for therapists to honor the team approach to treatment, including ongoing coordination and consultation with both the medical team and the nutritionist. Any work related to the client's eating should be coordinated with everyone on the team and be aligned with the nutritional care plan. Moving outside the clear medical guidelines for the nutritional treatment of EDs would not be in the best interest of any client. Accordingly, integrating mindful and intuitive eating can occur only when a client is medically and psychologically stable, and you and the client have the support and cooperation of the treatment team. You must help your clients work within the medical recommendations, which involve external guidelines, weigh-ins, and mandated eating practices, all while you help them find their way back to their bodies with a sense of agency in and ownership of their recovery.

Mindful Eating

Mindful eating involves integrating mindfulness—present-moment awareness, curiosity, nonjudging, and a nonconceptual knowing—into the process of eating (Cook-Cottone, 2015b). There is a basic mindful practice called mindful eating, and a more comprehensive intervention that teaches clients to pay attention to their internal and external sensations while eating, to develop a more mindful approach to eating overall.

At its most basic level, a mindful eating practice is like mindful walking (Kabat-Zinn, 2013). Conducted in this manner, mindful eating is often a component of mindfulness-based programs for the general population (Kabat-Zinn, 2013). Often, participants eat a raisin or some other small food item, being mindful of the sensations of touch, smell, hearing, and taste as they mindfully eat (Cook-Cottone, 2015b; Kabat-Zinn, 2013). Clients with disordered eating often have substantial difficulty being in the present moment and engaging in a relationship with food that is nonjudgmental and sensational (i.e., based on the sensory experience). Mindful eating is a being-with practice for recovery.

Mindful eating is both a formal practice, in which the food item is the object of concentration in a concentration meditation, and an informal practice, simply adding mindfulness to the meal, bringing the sensory experiences to the forefront of awareness. In both practices, external stimuli are minimized by choosing a quiet place, turning off media, and eliminating conversation during the meal (Cook-Cottone, 2015b). When used in mindfulness training for the general population, the formal form of mindful eating practice is often done at the beginning of the course (Kabat-Zinn, 2013). See Script 12.1 for mindful eating that you can share with your clients.

As an intervention, mindful eating applies mindfulness practices to turn awareness to internal sensations such as hunger and satiety while correspondingly increasing nonjudgmental, present-moment awareness to other body sensations, emotions, and cognition (Anderson et al., 2016; Kristeller, Baer, & Quillian-Wolever, 2006; Musada & Hill, 2013). Mindful eating is also intended to decrease overeating via identification with external triggers for eating (Anderson et al., 2016; Masuda & Hill, 2013).

There is no agreed-upon protocol for mindful eating interventions, and many approaches are available, with a wide range of groundedness in empirical support. Books I recommend on the topic are Albers (2012) and Tsui (2018). The Center for Mindful Eating, a nonprofit international organization, has resources to educate professionals and individuals in the practices and principles of mindful eating (see Center for Mindful Eating, 2019). Its work centers on the principles of mindfulness, mindful eating, and the individual characteristics of someone who eats mindfully.

Research on the topic, directed mainly at the general population, not specific to ED prevention or treatment, has evolved from studies finding associations between mindfulness and healthier eating to more sophisticated mindful eating protocols. For example, in a series of four studies on college students, Jordan, Wang, Donatoni, and Meier (2014) found a positive relationship between mindfulness and healthier eating, with mindfulness associated with less impulsive eating, reduced calorie consumption, and healthier snack choices. They also found a causal effect of mindfulness on healthier eating with an experimental manipulation of state mindfulness, leading to participants consuming fewer calories in a spontaneous eating task. Hepworth (2010) completed a 10-week intervention in an out-patient setting designed to use mindfulness and mindful awareness to help patients enhance awareness around hunger and satiety cues. There was no control group, but the patients demonstrated significant reductions in disordered eating symptoms, with no significant difference between diagnoses.

Hendrickson and Rasmussen (2017) studied a 50-minute mindfulness workshop as applied to eating, for adolescents and adults from the general population, addressing the pace of eating and awareness of the sensations related to food (e.g., sight, smell, touch; Hendrickson & Rasmussen, 2013). Compared with controls, participants exhibited more self-controlled choices for food, but not money, suggesting that mindful eating may be a uniquely beneficial strategy for reducing impulsive food choices.

Mindfulness-based eating awareness training (MB-EAT) is a program that addresses BED. Research has shown that those who struggle with binge eating have an imbalance and oversensitivity to external and nonnutritive cues for eating, including social, emotional, or conditioned craving for certain foods, which occurs with a corresponding desensitization to internal cues, especially satiety (Kristeller & Wolever, 2010). The MB-EAT program integrates the concepts of wisdom, forgiveness, and self-acceptance. Clients learn to observe and decrease judgmental reactions to personal variance from internalized norms. Forgiveness is believed to be critical in interrupting the dysfunctional cycles of bingeing → self-recrimination → overrestraint → bingeing. The MB-EAT program involves psychoeducation (e.g., binge triggers and relapse prevention), mindfulness meditation practices (e.g., body scan and satiety meditations), eating exercises (e.g., food choices), and other activities such as yoga. Homework involves such exercises as mini-meditations before meals and eating all meals and snacks mindfully (which begins at the seventh of nine sessions; Kristeller et al. 2006; Kristeller & Wolever, 2010).

Overall, mindful eating is a mindfulness practice in and of itself, a popular approach to preventing dieting and overeating from an embodied perspective, as well as a series of research protocols ranging from brief 50-minute interventions to extensive mindfulness-based interventions for individuals with BED. When considered from its core principles (see Figure 12.1), mindful eating is distinct from intuitive eating in its focus on mindfulness and mindful meditation as a pathway to mindful eating. In practice, I find that working with mindful eating practices can be a good first step in exploring with clients sensations and subjective experiences while eating. Working from the outside in (i.e., taste and smell to hunger satiety) can be a manageable pathway for clients to become aware of and attend to body cues while eating.

Intuitive Eating

Tracy Tylka and Jennifer Wilcox (2006) described intuitive eating as "eating based on physiological hunger and satiety cues rather than situational or emotional cues" (p. 474). In their intuitive eating workbook, Tribole and Resch (2017) describe it as the practice of utilizing internal cues while deciding what to eat, when to eat, and how much to eat. The academic definition has four components: (1) trusting hunger and fullness cues; (2) unconditional permission to eat when hungry, a cognitive shift; (3) reducing emotional eating; and (4) increasing body acceptance (Anderson et al., 2016; Tribole & Resch, 2017). This definition highlights the strong connection with, understanding of, and eating in response to internal physiological hunger and satiety cues that occur within the context of low preoccupation with food (Anderson et al., 2016; Avalos & Tylka, 2006; Tribole & Resch, 1995; Tylka, 2006).

Intuitive eating is grounded in the belief that most of us are born with the wisdom of knowing exactly what we need to eat, when to eat, and how much of it to eat (Resch & Tylka, 2019). It is theorized that, as we develop, we shift away from our own body's cues for hunger and satiety toward external rules regarding how much food we should eat (e.g., portion sizes, calories, or macronutrients per day), the quality of the food we should eat (e.g., food becomes good and bad, healthy and unhealthy, acceptable and unacceptable), and when we should eat (e.g., "Breakfast is the most important meal"; Resch & Tylka, 2019). Over time, the embodied experience of nourishing ourselves shifts to an intellectualized and judgment-filled experience in which we no longer feel we can trust our bodies (Resch & Tylka, 2019).

Intuitive eating is now a standardized program developed by dietician Evlyn Tribole and nutrition therapist Elyse Resch, based on a set of 10 principles (see Table 12.1). Their website (https://www.intuitiveeating.org) has much information on trainings and certifications, resources, and a community that clients can join. Their *Intuitive Eating Workbook* (Tribole & Resch, 2017) is a self-help book that can be easily integrated into practice with clients seeking to explore intuitive eating.

A substantial body of research on intuitive eating among the general population and those at risk for ED, is reviewed by Resch and Tylka (2019). Intuitive eating is associated with psychological well-being, flourishing, self-compassion, mindfulness, emotional awareness, distress tolerance, life satisfaction, and more. Further, intuitive eating is inversely related to negative constructs such as depression, negative affect, anxiety, stress, and self-silencing. However, these findings cannot be easily generalized to those with ED, as their experience with the body is qualitatively different from those in the general population.

In a two-year pilot study, Richards et al. (2017) evaluated the effectiveness of an intuitive eating program for clients in an ED treatment center. The clients in the study first had meal plans plated by staff and then transitioned to family-style self-plated meals. After clients demonstrated the ability to plate as well as eat, to appropriately and accurately assess hunger/fullness, and manage ED impulses, they advanced to intuitive eating. Throughout the process, clients were closely monitored to assess the integration of intuitive eating principles. Clients with BN had the lowest mean intuitive eating score upon admission and showed the greatest improvement at residential transition and discharge. Clients with AN had the highest intuitive eating scores at intake and demonstrated modest improvement at residential transition and discharge. Those with ED not otherwise specified had average intuitive eating scores upon admission and displayed steady improvement at transition and discharge.

Overall, study findings indicate that clients can develop skills of

Table 12.1: The Ten Principles of Intuitive Eating

- **Reject the diet mentality:** Understanding, resisting, and challenging external influences often propagated by the media, family, and friends that can be internalized as such thoughts as "I need to lose this weight," "I should be on a diet," and "This is a cheat food/day."
- **Honor the hunger:** Eating when hungry as manifested in hunger cues accessible through body and interoceptive awareness.
- **Make peace with food:** Having unconditional permission to eat food. Food is not good or bad, or safe or unsafe; it is just food, a neutral construct.
- **Challenge the food police:** Letting go of restrictive and overly rigid beliefs about food and eating. Watch for words like *always* and *never*, and seek a flexible relationship with food.
- **Feel the fullness:** Turning inward toward internal satiety cues to decide when to finish eating and not because of portion size or prescribed ideas about food and how much should be eaten. (Note that, for those with eating disorders, this can be challenging, and the disorder can complicate perceptions of feelings of fullness when clients are highly symptomatic. Further, if they are on a meal plan as part of their program, they need to follow the meal plan unless other accommodations have been made with the treatment team.)
- **Discover the satisfaction factor:** Allowing eating to be a source of pleasure; eating what is really wanted at a pace that allows for mindful awareness and presence to each aspect of the food and the eating process.
- **Cope with emotions without using food:** Identifying emotional triggers for eating when not hungry and learning new ways to cope that have nothing to do with food.
- **Respect the body:** Accepting the body as it is, having gratitude for its functionality, engaging in self-care, stopping negative body talk, doing positive body image work, etc.
- **Exercise:** Engaging in healthy, noncompensatory physical activity as a way to partner with the body.
- **Honor health:** Choosing foods that align with and are attuned to the body's needs for energy and nutrition in a flexible and adaptive manner.

Sources: Definitions and clarifications informed by Tribole and Resch (2017) and Tylka and Resch (2017).

intuitive eating. Further, the ability to eat intuitively was associated with positive treatment outcomes for each diagnosis.

CONCLUSION

Mindful and intuitive eating are potentially viable approaches of increasing embodiment for those with disordered eating. Ranging from the most basic mindfulness activity (i.e., mindful eating practice) to more complex protocols (i.e., MB-EAT and intuitive eating), there is still a lot to be understood about which practices are key to embodiment and recovery, and what are the best approaches for each disorder, at various stages of illness and recovery, and across treatment settings and level of care. It is likely that some of the key mechanisms include: mindfulness; development of body sensation and interoceptive awareness; discernment of physical hunger and satiety cues from other sensations and experiences, such as emotions; emotional regulation work; integration of healthy exercise; methods for combating the diet culture and media ideals; and moving toward a partnership with the body in terms of respect, care, and gratitude. It is recommended that practitioners who would like to integrate this work might engage in the advanced or specialized training that is available in both mindful and intuitive eating. Further, use of the resources available on the web pages as well as in the recommended texts should support your work. As always, consult with the treatment team and integrate these practices only within the context of the team being informed and aligned with the plan.

Script 12.1 Mindful Eating

Have on hand a bowl of dried fruit, bowl of dark chocolate chips, and napkins, enough for your group with a few extra. Sometimes participants do not process the instructions and eat their food item right away, so they will need a new food item with which to practice. Offer participants napkins and the bowls of dried fruit and dark chocolate chips. Ask them to select a few pieces of dried fruit or chips and place them on their napkin.

Find a comfortable seated position. Be sure your feet or legs can ground on the floor and your sitting bones are pressed into your chair or the floor. Engage your core and extend your spine, reaching through the crown of your head. Now, settle into a steady even breath and relax. (*pause*)

Begin by simply looking at your dried fruit or chip. Pretend that you have never seen a dried fruit or a chocolate chip before. This is your first time. Notice the color, the texture, the shape, ridges, contours, and how it is resting on your napkin. See the raisin or chip as it is right there on your napkin. (*pause*) What do you notice? (*pause*)

Shift the dried fruit or chip on your napkin. What do you see now? Does the light fall in new ways on it? Do you see new contours or shades of color? (*pause*)

As you practice concentration on your dried fruit or chip, also notice your mind and body, as thoughts, memories, ideas, sounds, and other sensations arise and fall away. Try to simply notice any thoughts, judgments, cravings, and bodily sensations and then bring your awareness back to your object. (*pause*)

Next, pick up your dried fruit or chip with your fingers. Lift it closer to your eyes so you can see it in yet another way. Bring your attention to what your object feels like. Is it soft or hard, smooth or rough? Does it melt or get softer? Is it cold? (*pause*) What do you notice? (*pause*)

As you explore the touch sensation of your dried fruit or chocolate chip, also notice the sense impressions coming from your body in other areas. Maybe the room is cold, or your chair is hard. Maybe your legs are tingling as you sit very still. Work on just noticing the sense impressions that come to mind. You will also notice thoughts, feelings, and distractions. Perhaps you are wondering how this activity might help someone who struggles, or you wonder where the dried fruit or chips were purchased. Simply notice these mental events and bring your attention back to your dried fruit or chip. (*pause*)

Bring your dried fruit or chip to your nose. What do you smell? Do you smell the earthy fruitiness of the dried fruit, an essence of fruit? Do you smell chocolate? What if you had never smelled these smells before? How would you describe the smell you are smelling right now? Remember you can't say, "I smell chocolate" or "I smell dried fruit." Without these words, how would you describe what you are smelling right now? As before, notice any other sense impressions or mental events as they arise and fall way. (*pause*)

Now, bring the dried fruit or chip to your mouth. Let it touch your lips so that you can feel the texture and smell the essence. Slowly place the object in your mouth without chewing. Let the object rest on your tongue. What do you taste? Find the words to describe the taste without using the words *dried fruit* or *chocolate*. What comes up for you? (*pause*) What do you notice?

Slowly move the dried fruit or chocolate around in your mouth. Experience the taste and sensations. When you are ready, chew your dried fruit or chocolate. Has the taste changed? Did the texture change? Be aware of how your body, your mouth, your saliva respond to the dried fruit or chocolate in your mouth. Once you are ready to swallow, notice any shifts in awareness. With intention, swallow your dried fruit or chip. Notice your mouth, your nose, your hands now. (*pause*) What do you notice?

Take a moment to offer gratitude for the dried fruit or chip, for your awareness, and for the opportunity to explore mindful eating.

Adapted from Cook-Cottone (2015b) and informed by Davis et al. (2019), Kabat-Zinn (2013), and Stahl and Goldstein (2010).

CHAPTER 13

Embodied Connections
Mindful and Supportive Relationships

Relationships are essential. From neurons to neighborhoods, we are webs of interconnectedness.

—Grace Bullock, *Mindful Relationships*

We are deeply interconnected and interdependent beings (Bullock, 2016). Beyond our basic physiological needs (e.g., food, clothing, shelter), and perhaps more primitive than our existential needs (e.g., meaning and purpose), we have relational needs. As embodied beings, we need to be seen, heard, connected, and to belong (Miller, 2015). Embodiment is not fully possible in isolation—as "webs of interconnectedness," how we experience our embodiment is always in the context of the people, communities, and cultures with whom and within which we are embodied (Osher, Cantor, Berg, Steyer, & Rose, 2018). In fact, a portion of the risk for or protection from ED comes from this interconnection and interdependence with others.

Research tells us that relationships are uniquely important for those with disordered eating. For a variety of reasons, many of those with EDs have engaged in behaviors that are relationally bound, including having successfully internalized social messages about appearance, social acceptance, and worthiness of love from others (Chernin, 1998; Cook-Cottone, 2015b; Culbert et al., 2015). Often, they have failed to internalize nurturing behaviors such as the appropriate provision of food and care for the body (Chernin, 1998; Cook-Cottone, 2015b). Many with ED present with behavioral symptoms that, without words, either push those around them away (e.g., isolating, secretive, and intentionally deceptive behaviors) or draw them in (e.g., such a low weight that loved ones are compelled to be deeply involved; Chernin, 1998; Cook-Cottone, 2015b).

As described by Treasure et al. (2008), when a family member has an ED, a variety of emotions, thoughts, and behaviors shape the interpersonal interactions within a family, such as rigidity, compulsivity, and preoccupation with details. Together family members have difficulty stepping back to see the bigger picture, and clients and their caregivers share an overly analytical focus. The shared inflexibility reduces effective problem solving, and the family gets lost in details (e.g., macronutrients in breakfast). Caregivers of those with EDs have higher levels of expressed emotion, emotional overinvolvement, criticism, hostility, and overprotection, which are also associated with higher levels of anxiety. Expressed emotion is believed to interfere with treatment outcomes, with some research suggesting that families with high expressed emotion have better outcomes when they do separated family therapy. Caregivers also experience substantial guilt, shame, and stigma, which is known to be highly characteristic of parents who have their own eating struggles. Caregivers can reinforce ED symptoms through a variety of accommodation and enabling behaviors, such as allowing the ED behaviors to dominate the relationship or household, which may occur through explicit or implicit "emotional blackmail" or threatening from clients. As the family worries about the client's "fragile state," they accommodate the client.

Relational work means helping clients identify, secure, cultivate, and nurture relationships in which they no longer need to serve internalized, disordered beliefs and can be authentically be seen and heard and feel safe, supported, and even empowered when engaged in health-promoting behaviors. We are malleable, ever-changing processes of interconnectedness, and our patterns of development remain responsive to relationships throughout our life courses, offering opportunities to buffer and overcome certain risk factors throughout our lifetime (Osher et al., 2018). Our interconnections can change and, correspondingly, change us. How we manage these interactions can help us become the architects of our own interpersonal and social landscapes.

This is a substantial change in orientation from a looking outward to self-regulate to an inward sense of agency and self-determination. Many of my clients seem to have an externalized orientation to the management of self, often so attuned to what others need and want that they have no sense of their own experience (Cook-Cottone, 2006). It is a disembodied way to interact with the world. Rather than sense, feel, and take actions from an internal sensory experience that informs

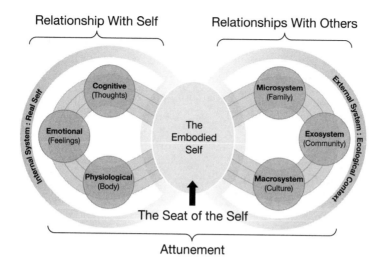

Figure 13.1. Embodied Relationships

(See insert for color.)

how we experience and interact with the world, those who struggle are self-regulating in accordance with the varying, ever-changing, objectifying, and skewed external world delivered through unhealthy appearance-focused or disordered relationships and social and traditional media. Mary Pipher (1994) called this phenomena "empathy sick." With this external orientation, clients' inner world is constructed of and functions around the demands of the external world, right down to the size their waist should be or what they would like to eat.

Therapy, then, must include not only how to self-regulate, or be in relation with self, but also how to remain true to the self in relations with others—peers, family, community, and cultures (see Figure 13.1). To be well requires attunement and an ongoing awareness of both inner and outer experiences and effective responses to both. The true seat of the self is in the midst of it all, honoring our own needs, desires, and purposes while not empathy sick or twisting ourselves to be, feel, or do something that is not attuned to who we are for some superficial sense of acceptance, connection, and love.

Given their role in symptomatology, risk, and maintenance of disorder, in many ways relationships can make or break recovery. Relationships and family systems can form around the premise that there needs to be an identified sick person, or that the only way the person with the ED is acknowledged, seen, or heard is if that person is sick. Addressing relationships and relationship skills in practice can be a substantial part of the recovery process. Clients must know how to manage their relationships with others as well as their relationships with themselves. Skills for relational work include self-regulation skills and, within the relational context, skills in interpersonal effectiveness, embodied intimacy, navigating culture and the media, and social justice.

EMBODYING RELATIONSHIPS FROM THE INSIDE OUT

Work with relationships begins with work with the self. As clients develop skills for identifying and managing physical sensations, body states, emotions, and thoughts, they are also developing relationship skills. As those skills develop, they can be turned outward to notice the physical, emotional, and cognitive experiences of others and how those experiences are impacting their own bodies in the here and now.

The body can be a resource in relationships as a source of self-attunement, "being the change," and embodied relational awareness. Self-attunement involves clients becoming aware of and meeting their own needs in a nurturing and loving manner. As they practice skills for being-with and working-with their experiences, honoring the effort, and engaging in consistent mindful self-care, they ultimately meet many of their own needs while increasing their capacity to handle what occurs within the context of relationships. Clients become the source of their own validation, compassion, and acknowledgment—the practice of self-attunement.

A quote attributed to Gandhi says, "Be the change you want to see in the world." Clients who frequently ignore their own needs, punish themselves for perceived missteps, and live within a rigidly perfectionistic or horribly chaotic relationship with themselves are, perhaps unintentionally, inviting others into their lives who are aligned with their dysfunction. If clients believe that they are only their symptoms (e.g., "I am an anorexic"), their relationships reflect that belief. As clients learn embodied self-regulation skills, they began to model them for significant people in their lives. This can be a slow and sometimes painful process, but seeing how good it feels to have a new way of being with their body can motivate clients in recovery. As their self-care grows and symptoms decrease, and they express feelings of empowerment, and agency—they can become the change they want to see in those around them.

To apply embodied mindfulness to relationships, I encourage clients to become mindful of their relationships and their roles in them in the same way they work to be mindful of sensations and emotions while meditating or doing yoga (Bullock, 2016). Our bodies are wired to help us make choices about other human beings. It is important to consider how the body feels when spending time with a person or group of people. The emotional responses that arise when interacting with others speak volumes about the person and the relationship, which may or may not align with the words being said.

With my clients I use the listening to intuition, heart, and mind practice (see Script 13.1) to help them consider, from an embodied place, what it is like to be in a particular relationship, by listening to how their intuition, heart, and mind react. Once they are aware of their embodied responses to the relationship, they have space for choice and effective action. For the practice, your clients might want to have their journal next to them to write down the answers or responses to any of the questions considered during the meditation. You can also do the meditation in session and process it after.

Once the meditation is complete, or if you are reviewing it as homework, ask your clients what they noticed. When all three of the sources—the mind, the heart, and the intuition—line up, your client can have a good sense of what direction to take. If the three sources do not line up, that is a good source for discussion and inquiry. Encourage your clients not to discount any one line of input but to notice and engage in inquiry around it all. They may discern that a particular person reminds them of someone who was unsafe or difficult in their past. By holding the information from the body and heart as valid and important, therapeutic work around the relationship becomes richer in affect and less of an intellectual discourse.

Before the embodied work begins, it can be helpful to explore and identify cognitive beliefs that can get in the way of interpersonal effectiveness, such as "I am not worthy" or "I might make someone upset if I ask something of them" (Linehan, 2015; Lynch, 2018). It can be helpful to assess your clients' readiness to do the work by walking through their list of beliefs. Include beliefs about others, such as thinking that other people should already know what they want, how others should behave, and what others deserve in terms of treatment (Linehan, 2015).

Practice Guide 13.1 can help you and your clients explore beliefs that can get in the way of relationship work. It guides them through their embodied awareness associated with one particular relationship, explores beliefs about that relationship and about relationships in general, and provides space to explore which beliefs support and impede the work.

EMBODIED PRACTICES THAT BALANCE SELF AND OTHERS

In the embodiment of self model (see Figure 13.1), there is a place in the middle that is equally centered between the internal and external experiences of self (Cook-Cottone, 2015b). Here a set of practices can help with both self-regulation and negotiation of the external work, involving integrity; safety and trust; kindness, compassion, allowing; and social justice work.

Integrity in a relationship can be an extremely challenging practice. This is especially true for clients who have been struggling with disorders that involve hiding and discounting authentic experiences of the self. Integrity in relationships means clients no longer hide who they are. It requires learning a careful balance between communicating their true self as expressed through their words and behaviors, and honoring their own need for a private and personal space for growth. The integrity questions, introduced in Chapter 11, are useful to check in with clients and in discussions around specific people in their lives:

1. Generally, how hard has it been to be honest with yourself?
2. Generally, how hard has it been to be honest with others?
3. How honest have you been with yourself?
4. How honest have you been with others?

Ask if there is some aspect of the relationship that allows them to be or not to be in integrity, and why this might be so. Have your clients consider strategies of embodying integrity in all relationships in a manner that is both authentic and self-protective.

Safety and trust are two sides of a coin. When we are a safe person for other people, we can be trusted. When we have worked on our own embodied self-regulation, we have a sense of trusting ourselves, and it is much easier to feel and know that trustworthiness in others. Trust is based on an aggregate of experiences with self and others and is deeply tied to living a life of integrity and asking the same from others in meaningful relationships. Trust is not something that should be easily granted and taken away when it is breached; it is something that evolves over time though hundreds of interactions. Trust can be signaled in therapy by offering clients training in the tools to make a decision and then letting them know that you have faith in their ability do what is right for them (Lynch, 2018). Trust is not treating the other as fragile or incompetent through micromanagement, walking on eggshells, or solving problems for them; it means speaking the truth and expressing feelings with humility, trusting the other to find a solution to their challenges—at times, it can mean offering a little more confidence in the person than they have in themselves (Lynch, 2018).

It is important to consider that for many clients safety often extends beyond the individual relationships to how a person feels in the world. Rachel Calogero, Tracy Tylka, and Daniel Siegel (2019) explain that personal safety is a pillar of positive embodiment, without which we cannot feel totally at home in our bodies. They explored this issue through the lens of women in a sexually objectifying world in which they experience high rates of sexual assault and violence. They posited that the erosion of personal safety for women has created more opportunities for negative embodiment, under an illusion of what they describe as paternalizing protection and sexual dependency that is seemingly safe (Calogero et al., 2019).

Personal safety lies at the intersection of race, gender, sexual orientation, weight, size, shape, age, socioeconomic status, and mobility/ability (see Buchanan, Settles, & Woods, 2019). It is important to explore each perspective as it relates to your clients. As you explore safety and trust with your clients, ask them to consider each of these constructs regarding to their relationships, as well as their sense of self in community. Help them develop embodied ways of knowing if a relationship embodies safety and trust. You can adapt the script for the intuition, heart, and mind practice (Script 13.1) to address both safety and trust issues with a particular individuals or groups of people. Work with clients to process what they are noticing and how they might use this information to direct their informed, intentional choices.

Kindness, compassion, and allowing are integral to safe and trusting relationships (Cook-Cottone, 2015b; Lynch, 2018). They can be difficult to practice because reacting and judging can feel very satisfying, especially when we believe we have been wounded or wronged in some way. Our negative implicit memory systems grow much faster than our positive implicit memory systems (Hanson and Mendius, 2009). In relationships, this translates into remembering more about negative words and actions of others than the positive ones. Orienting toward others with kindness, compassion, and allowing helps us neutralize or override the negativity bias and gives our relationships a chance (Cook-Cottone, 2015b; Linehan, 2015). See Script 13.2 for kindness, compassion, and allowing that you can use with your clients as they explore their relationships.

Social justice is the distribution of wealth, opportunities, and privileges within a society or culture. It is a deeply felt and experienced phenomenon and, like all of the influences on disordered eating, has a rich and deep history intersecting with race, ethnicity, weight, shape, age, gender, sexual orientation, socioeconomic status, mobility, and ability. Social justice can effectively link with the purpose and mission work you explore with your clients, as well as how their unique experience of self is included, supported, and celebrated in their relationships, community, and culture. Table 13.1 lists potential topics for discussion as you approach social justice with your clients. Discussions can be done in combination with journaling and feeling work in the body. For some, social justice is a critical aspect of the path to recovery, and for others it is not. If it is aligned with what the client would like to work on, draw this work back to a revision of mission and purpose work.

EMBODYING RELATIONSHIPS WITH OTHERS

Once your clients have embodied awareness, they can then choose, in an informed and intentional manner, how they would like to interact within the relationships in their life. Because skills increase choices and effectiveness, it is important to support the development of relational skills with your clients. In dialectical behavioral therapy this skill set is referred to as interpersonal effectiveness (Linehan, 2015). Building on this work, and integrating mindfulness and yoga-based practices, this section details several key practices/competencies for working with others in relationship that incorporate the principles discussed above, such as integrity, safety, and trust

Table 13.1: Topics to Explore Related to Social
Justice and Access to Positive Embodiment

Gender	Race/ethnicity	Immigration status
Sexual orientation	Gender identity	Socioeconomic status
Shape bias	Weight bias	Size bias
Inclusion in yoga spaces	Inclusion in fitness spaces	Apparel sizing
Inclusion in marketing	Objectification	Personal safety
Weigh-ins	Weight-related bullying	Ability
Mobility	Weight/fat stigma	Diet, fitness, and health talk
School policies	Public policies	Business practices and policies
Insurance reimbursement for EDs	Research funding	Funding for prevention work

Validation

It is important to remember that humans are hard-wired to be hyper-sensitive to signs of social exclusion (Lynch, 2018). Validation signals inclusion. In a broad sense, validation means that we understand a person and we communicate that understanding (Lynch, 2018). Relationships are reciprocal entities. They require your clients to act in ways they hope to be treated themselves. To invite validation into their lives, they need to know how to offer it. Validation is an acceptance of others, exactly as they are. It is not an attempt to change another person's emotional experience or direction (Lynch, 2018). Table 13.2 lists many ways you can help clients develop validation skills.

Balancing Self and Others

Clients often struggle to balance their needs with what is expected or demanded of them (Astrachan-Fletcher & Maslar, 2009). The ED is frequently a dysfunctional way to steady the balance, and I have seen

Table 13.2: Validation Practices for Your Clients

- **Use validation microskills:** Make eye contact and nod head to show you are listening; mimic facial expressions, and integrate a half smile.
- **Attend to others as if they were an object of meditation:** If you become distracted by thoughts or other distractions, simply notice this and then bring your full awareness back to the person.
- **Practice reflective listening:** In conversation, after a person finishes what he or she is saying, see if you can say it back: "What I hear you saying is . . ."
- **Practice reflective listening for feeling:** In conversation, after a person talking finishes what he or she is saying, see if you can reflect back the emotional content you noticed: "You are feeling (angry, frustrated, happy, loved)."
- **Acknowledge the efforts of those around you:** Notice them trying, and let them know you see this.
- **Let other people know when you appreciate them or are grateful:** Do this with words and small gestures as simple forms of acknowledgment: "I really appreciate how you supported me when I was . . ."

clients in recovery begin to manifest risk for relapse when they start losing this balance. The intuition, heart, and mind practice (Script 13.1) can help you check in on how they are feeling about each task they do for others. Practice Guide 13.2 offers a practice guide for balancing self and others that you can use to help your clients process their activities and choices.

Embodied Intimacy

Many clients with EDs have created a false, accommodating self that is not a true representation of who they are. No one can ever really like or love them because they do not know who they really are. Intimacy is a risk—it means not hiding, being full of integrity, and showing up to others as you are (Cook-Cottone, 2015b; Lynch, 2018). Being close to others requires practice in intimacy, and this requires vulnerability (Lynch, 2018). Intimacy is deeply tied to trust and safety (Lynch, 2018).

Embodied intimacy requires letting others get close. It means balancing your needs and desires for intimacy with theirs, and working within the context of safety and developing a sense of trust. The intuition, heart, and mind practice (Script 13.1) can help your clients pay attention to how it feels to be close to another person and the signal they get that this other person is feeling safe too.

Embodied intimacy is something reserved for those who are closest to us—friends, family members, and partners. For friends and many family members, it is an ongoing process of connecting, enjoying one another, and supporting one another. It is important to explore with clients their beliefs about intimacy, friends, and family members. Some clients have been raised to assume that being a family member equals intimacy. This is not necessarily true for many families. Some family members struggle to maintain healthy boundaries, while others have never really been close. Table 13.3 lists qualities of genuine friendship, which you can use to help your clients consider their relationships and what qualities they are presenting as they develop intimacy (Lynch, 2018). Your clients might have other qualities they'd like to add to the list.

Sexuality is another form of embodied intimacy. Satinsky and Winter (2019) refer to attuned sexuality as a pathway to positive embodiment within the context of sexual intimacy. They define attuned sexuality as

Table 13.3: Qualities of a Positively Embodied Friendship

- It feels safe to be together.
- You feel a sense of trust.
- You know that this person will look out for you and you will look out for this person.
- You share acceptance of each other, not trying to change each other.
- Your friendship is not conditional.
- You are kind to each other, even when disagreeing.
- You respect and maybe even admire each other's differences.
- You make repair when you have been unkind or hurtful to each other, although this is not a regular occurrence.
- You give each other the benefit of the doubt when exploring motives for behavior.
- You seek to understand each other's perspectives, especially during disagreements.
- You enjoy time together and get excited when you make plans.

Source: Informed by Lynch (2018).

an ideal state where an individual's sexual self-concept and experiences encompass desired levels of sexual connection, desire, self-concept, functioning, and expression. . . . Attuned sexuality includes not only positive body image, but also positively constructed notions of sexual agency and function, access to one's sexual desires, use of protective strategies to protect and nurture one's body, and the ability to tune mindfully into bodily pleasures in sexual contexts. (p. 91)

Working with clients in this area includes addressing negative body image, self-objectification, and disrupted sexual attunement (Satinsky & Winter, 2019).

In a review Castellini, Lelli, Ricca, and Maggi (2016) reported that there is a clear association between sexual problems and ED psychopathology. Pubertal timing and its hormonal consequences are related to the onset of disorder: in females, the earlier secondary sexual characteristics begin to develop, the more likely an ED would develop, whereas with males, the later the onset of puberty, the greater the body dissatisfaction and risk. Sexual abuse, especially childhood sexual abuse, are well-recognized factors in the risk for and development of EDs. Individuals with ED can show tendencies to engage in either hypersexuality or decreased sexuality. Sexual orientation and sexual identity are also related to ED symptoms, which may be related to the family, community, and cultural stressors associated these domains (Castellini et al., 2016). Transgender persons may be particularly at risk for body dissatisfaction, which has been associated with increased risk for ED. Coordinating care with someone who works as a specialist with transgender individuals is important, as many programs typically do not address in depth ED treatment and the experiences of trangendered individuals.

It can be helpful for clients to work on developing positive sexual agency, function, and desire. This includes seeing oneself as a sexual being, capable of experiencing sexual desire, self-determination and agency, and appreciation for the sexual functions of the body (Satinsky & Winter, 2019). If a client has a high level of sexual dysfunction, it is important to partner with a colleague who has advanced training in this area, or a trauma specialist if there is a traumatic history of sexual abuse or assault. Table 13.4 describes the areas to explore with your clients regarding sexual attunement.

Table 13.4: Exploring Issues Related to Sexual Attunement

- Develop a sense of sexual agency in which those in recovery have permission to follow sexual desire.
- Review and practice the verbal consent process as related to partnered sexual experiences.
- Help those in recovery explore the embodied sensations and emotions associated with giving and not giving consent.
- Reinforce the right to say no to sexual acts.
- Reinforce rights to sexual pleasure from self and partners.
- Explore intersectional experiences of self (e.g., race, ethnicity, gender identity, and objectification) and their role in access to sexual agency and pleasure.
- Review mindfulness as applied to bodily sexual pleasure (e.g., sensate focus).
- Encourage ongoing and open communication between partners as related to sexual and emotional intimacy and sexual decision making within the context of the relationship.

Source: Informed by Satinsky and Winter (2019).

Embodiment Within the Family and in Difficult Relationships

Families are powerful socializing agents. Many families have internalized patriarchal cultural norms that tend to preserve positive embodiment for boys and men and dismantle embodiment for girls and women (Tylka, 2019). Informed by Piran (2016), Tylka (2019) posits that family environments that intentionally encourage positive embodiment for all family members can be cultivated. Table 13.5 lists practices that you can recommend to clients' families to support positive embodiment at home.

Notably, no matter how hard a family works to cultivate an environment that encourages positive embodiment, there may be individuals who have internalized body-shaming messages. It is important to help clients develop a strategy for dealing with difficult people. I typically help them set up a strategy during a session. Many techniques can be used, including counting negative body talk comments, verbally labeling negative body comments, and structuring visits with difficult people so that they are short and followed with self-care activities.

Table 13.5: Practices for Cultivating Family
Environments That Support Embodiment

- Use positive self-talk that counters adverse social messages and body image threats.
- Accept all body types, sizes, and weights.
- Model positive body talk that celebrates function and acceptance.
- Do not use fat or diet talk.
- Do not engage in appearance-related teasing or criticism.
- Compliment physical attributes associated with self-expression or a sense of style.
- Shut down fat and diet talk or appearance related comments when they are overheard.
- Avoid appearance-related complements (e.g., "You are so very pretty").
- Promote healthy behaviors, such as physical activities.
- Engage in mind-body activities, such as yoga, dance, or tae kwon do.
- Encourage learning new physical skills, such as gardening, archery, or swimming.
- Encourage self-expression through voice, art, and acting.
- Create an "all opinions welcome" zone in the house.
- Be open for discussion and healthy debate.
- Rotate chores and tasks based on preferences, availability, and shared experience, rather than historical gender roles.
- Allow expression of self outside of traditional gender roles in costumes, dress, and play.
- Encourage participation in sports for fun and not just for elite or highly competitive performance.
- Embrace and even celebrate developmental changes, such as puberty, within the context of agency and self-determination.
- Celebrate the pleasures of eating by offering a wide variety of foods and following intuitive eating guidelines (see Chapter 12).
- Acknowledge and normalize sexual desire.
- Practice and model mindful self-care (see Chapter 7).
- Model and encourage inhabiting the body as a subjective site (rather than as an object).

Source: Informed by Tylka (2019).

Embodying the Self in Community and Within This Culture

Often, media and culture work is reserved for prevention programs, yet it can also be a critical part of treatment. Exploring media and cultural messages with your clients is important. Chelse Roff's Eat, Breath, Thrive yoga-based adjunct for EDs has an entire unit on media and cultural messages (see https://www.eatbreathethrive.org). A simple Google search will locate several TED and TEDx talks on body image, which I like to watch with clients in session or assign as homework and then talk about their impressions.

Relationship work must include work on the self, just as work on the self inherently involves relationship work. The self navigating and managing the outside world is most effective with an authentic and empowered voice, speaking through actions and words, and aligned with the needs and desires of our inner experience. This is an authentic representation of self. Also, how we manage relationships, community, and culture is most effective when it does not require a sacrifice of any one part of the internal experience (i.e., the psychological, emotional, or cognitive self).

THE EMBODIED THERAPIST: YOUR RELATIONSHIP WITH YOURSELF AS A THERAPEUTIC TOOL

The Latin proverb "Nemo dat quod non habet" translates literally to "No one gives what they do not have." The origins of this phrase are legal and related to ownership, sales, and rights. Essentially, it is like this: if someone sells you something that they do not own, whether it be a thing or rights, you too do not have legal ownership. That is, when a person gives or sells a thing they do not own in the first place, what they offer is compromised. I think this serves as a perfect metaphor for what can happen in therapy, especially in regard to embodied practices. There is no authentic way to offer guidance in a practice that you do not have. If you play at offering embodied practices without doing the work, you will be delivering a commodity that you do not fully own. What you ultimately share with your patients will be surface level at best. You can use all the methods, all the worksheets, and it will still be inherently distinct from the embodied wisdom that is shared by someone deep in the work. I urge you to live the question, "How might my ability to serve my patients be increased if I work to develop and support my own embodiment?"

It is in the turning toward our own embodiment with curiosity, care, respect, and loving-kindness that we are empowered as we endeavor outward (Cook-Cottone, 2017). You and your patients are worth the effort. In a field plagued with underfunding, relatively high mortality rates, a lack of compassion from laypersons or the media, and few empirically-supported treatments, our embodiment and fierce self-care will help us foster the resilience we need to press the boundaries of what is.

Presenting as hopeless, overworked, exhausted, depleted, and overly self-sacrificing, even if not spoken, does not inspire (Cook-Cottone, 2017). As world-renowned therapist Irvin D. Yalom (2002) asked, "What is the therapist's most valuable instrument?" The answer: "the therapist's own self" (p. 40). You and I can be the change we seek in this challenging and fulfilling field. Your embodiment practices allow you to bring a healthy and positive presence to your work, in addition to bringing resilience to your life (Cook-Cottone, 2015, 2017; Siegel, 2010). Siegel (2010) says it this way, "Caring for yourself, bringing support and healing to your own efforts to help others and the larger world in which we live, is an essential daily practice—not a luxury, not some form of self-indulgence" (p. 3). We owe it to ourselves and to our patients to tread the path, to do the work, and to embody this one beautiful, precious life.

The embodied self is the work of balancing both the internal and external worlds effectively without harming ourselves or others, and ideally flourishing with a powerful sense of mission supported by the stabilizing proactive mindful self-care. Table 13.6 summarizes the strategies presented in this chapter for embodying the self from the inside out, to help you help your clients establish healthy relationships with themselves, their bodies, their friends and family, and the culture in which they live, love, and breath. As Grace Bullock said, "We are webs of interconnections." Learning how to be interconnected and well is key to recovery.

Table 13.6: Practices for Embodying the Self From the Inside Out

Relationship With Self	Balancing Self and Others	Relationships With Others
• Self-attunement • Being the change • Embodied relational awareness • Beliefs about relationships	• Integrity (not hiding) • Safety and trust • Kindness, compassion, and allowing • Social justice	• Validation • Embodied intimacy • Embodiment in family and within difficult relationships • Embodying self in community and culture

FINAL THOUGHTS

I encourage you to use these tools with your clients and in your own life. Approach this work with a humble, yet steadfast honoring of the body as your most valuable resource. You will see in your work with clients and in your own unfolding; positive embodiment is possible for each of us. I'd like to close, as I have before, with a quote that was one of my mother's favorites: "What lies behind us and what lies before us is nothing compared to what lies within us." I tried to find out who wrote this first, as it has been attributed to many famous people with no definitive author. So, I leave it for you here with the one source of which I am sure (*Notes from my Mom*, Elizabeth G. Cook, 1940–2015).

Practice Guide 13.1: Your Beliefs About Your Relationships

Getting clarity on your beliefs about relationships can be helpful as you work to embody effective relationships skills and actions. You can use this practice guide to examine one relationship at a time. For your first attempt at this, choose a relationship that is mildly challenging, rather than your most difficult relationship. As you practice and work with your therapist, you can move to more challenging relationships.

STEP 1: Listening to Intuition, Heart, and Mind Practice

First, with your therapist, complete the Listening to Intuition, Heart, and Mind practice (Script 13.1), focusing on what your intuition, heart, and mind tell you about the person in the relationship you would like to examine. Then, answer the questions below:

When I think about this relationship, my beliefs about my worthiness and value tell me I deserve _____

_____

_____

_____

_____

When I think about this relationship, my beliefs about what it means to ask for support are that I should (beliefs about self) _____

_____

_____

_____

_____

And that they should (beliefs about this person) _____

_____

_____

_____

_____

STEP 2: General Beliefs About Relationships

Now consider your beliefs about relationships in general. Below are a few sentence starters. Complete the ones that resonate with what you believe—one of them, all of them, or none of them. If a sentence starter does resonate with one of your beliefs, indicate why in the lines below it.

Overall, when I think about this relationship, it reminds me of some things I believe are true about everyone, or most people (if it does not resonate with you, explain why):

I should not have to _____

_____

_____

_____

_____

Everyone always _____

_____

_____

_____

_____

Everyone should _____

_____

_____

_____

_____

There is no point because _____

_____

_____

_____

_____

STEP 3: Listing Your Beliefs

Reviewed Steps 1 and 2 with your therapist, and together make a list of the beliefs that are going to be helpful and another list of beliefs that are not going to be helpful in your relationships with this person and with people in general. As you add each belief to one list or the other, write a quick note about what will or will not be helpful. If you need more space, use your journal or a blank piece of paper.

These beliefs *will* be helpful in my relationships:

Belief   **Reason Why**

_____   _____

_____   _____

_____   _____

_____   _____

_____   _____

These beliefs *will not* be helpful in my relationships:

Belief   **Reason Why**

_____   _____

_____   _____

_____   _____

_____   _____

_____   _____

Practice Guide 13.2: Balancing Yourself and Others

Balancing your needs and wants with what others expect or need form you can be a critical part to your recovery and critical to maintaining the giant steps you have made. This practice guide is designed to help you and your therapist consider your balance.

STEP 1: Examine What You Are Doing

Fill out the balance sheet below, listing what you do that serves your needs and wants and what you do to meet the needs and expectations of others. If you can, estimate your weekly commitment by hours and minutes.

For example, to serve your own needs and wants, you might go to yoga class three times a week (for a total of 3 hours). To serve others' needs and expectations you might drive your friends to work when they don't have gas (2 hours). For the "a little of each" column in the middle you might take your grandmother grocery shopping each week (2.5 hours), adding that you love grandmother and the time you spend with her.

Things I do to serve my needs and wants (estimate time per week):	Things I do that are a little of each (self *and* others)	Things I do to serve others' needs and expectations (estimate time per week):

STEP 2: Develop a Plan

Review this sheet with your therapist. You might also notice where you have taken on too much or the balance is off. Make a plan for how you might address the imbalance. Are there things you might need to wait to do when it is a better time? Are there people with whom you need to practice saying "No"?

Script 13.1: Listening to Intuition, Heart, and Mind

Either in a seated position or lying on your back, place a hand on your belly and the other hand on your heart. If you'd like, close your eyes or soften your gaze. Begin to breathe, perhaps saying to yourself, "Breathing in, I know I am breathing in, and breathing out, I know I am breathing out." Take four cycles of deep breaths, tracking your breaths with your words. (*long pause*)

Bring to mind the relationship or the person you would like to consider in the practice. Imagine they are sitting about three feet away from you in a chair. They are simply sitting there. You do not need to interact with them. You are simply considering their presence. Think about the clothes they might be wearing, their posture, hair, eyes, and mannerisms. Bring them into your awareness as clearly as you can. (*pause*) Breathe here with this person in your awareness.

Now, bring your awareness to your belly where you have placed one of your hands. Breathe gently and simply notice. Consider the person and notice your belly. You might ask a question such as, "Is this person a positive influence in my life?" or "Is this person a negative influence in my life?" If a story comes to mind, gently coax your awareness back to your belly. Your belly is the seat of your intuition. It's your gut instinct. Listen to the messages that might come from your belly. (*pause*) It's okay if you don't feel anything, or if you feel a lot. Simply notice. Keep asking the same questions and notice. (*pause*)

Now, bring your awareness to your heart, where you have placed one of your hands. Breathe gently and simply notice. Consider the person and notice your heart. You might ask a question such as, "Is this person a positive influence in my life?" or "Is this person a negative influence in my life?" If a story comes to mind, gently coax your awareness back to your heart. Your heart is the seat of your emotions. Listen to the messages that might come from your heart. (*pause*) It's okay if you don't feel anything, or if you feel a lot. Simply notice. Keep asking the same questions and notice. (*pause*)

Now, keeping your hand on your belly and the other hand on your heart, bring your awareness to your head. Breathe gently and simply notice. Consider the person and notice your thoughts. You might ask a question such as, "Is this person a positive influence in my life?" or "Is this person a negative influence in my life?" See what stories come up. Are they defensive, supportive, or rationalizations? Pay more attention to the patterns or qualities of your thoughts than the thoughts themselves. Do they align with your belly and your heart? Listen to the messages that might come from the patterns of your thoughts. (*pause*) Simply notice. Keep asking the same questions and notice. (*pause*)

Using all three of your sources of embodied wisdom, the intuition in your belly, your emotions, and your thoughts, ask yourself this question, "Am I my best when I am with this person? What are my actions like when I am with this person? What is my state of being like when I am with this person?" Ask the questions, and check in with your belly, your heart, and your thoughts. Breathe and notice for about five deep breaths in each location. Then, see if the messages from your belly, heart, and mind align. (*long pause*)

Using all three of your sources of embodied wisdom, the intuition in your belly, your emotions, and your thoughts, ask yourself, "What do I feel like after I have spent time with this person? Am I energized, depleted, exhausted, or inspired? What does my body feel like, what does my heart tell me, and what are the contents and patterns of my thoughts?" Ask the questions and check in with our belly, your heart, and your thoughts. Breathe and notice for about five deep breaths in each location. Then, see if they align. (*long pause*)

Take some time to let the information settle. Breathe five breaths with extended exhales. (*long pause*) When you are ready, bring your awareness back to this room and slowly open your eyes if they were closed. Find something in the room on which you can anchor your gaze and then slowly broaden your awareness to the room. Offer gratitude to you belly, your heart, and your mind for their wisdom. Write down any thoughts or observations you might have in your journal.

Script 13.2: Their Path—Kindness, Compassion, and Allowing

Find a comfortable position in which your feet and sitting bones are grounded and you can extend through your spine. If you'd like, close your eyes or soften your gaze. Bring your awareness to your breath and take five deep, mindful breaths, extending the exhale. Breathing in for 1, 2, 3, 4 and breathing out for 1, 2, 3, 4, 5. Repeat this four more times. (*long pause*) If you notice any thoughts or distractions, simply notice them and label them, "That is a thought," or "That is a distraction." Bring your awareness back to your breathing.

Bring to mind someone in your life with whom you are having a difficult time. Choose someone who is not where you would like them to be in terms of their own growth and awareness. Hold this person in your mind, getting a sense of what this person is wearing, the expression on their face, so you can fully experience this person. (*pause*)

Now, with this person in mind, offer loving kindness:

"May you be happy.
May you be well.
May you be peaceful and at ease."

Hold this person in your mind's eye and maybe even in your heart, and repeat those words again.

"May you be happy.
May you be well.
May you be peaceful and at ease."

Now consider that this person has needs and wants just like you. This person struggles to be their best self, just like you. (*pause*) Hold this person in your mind's eye and maybe even in your heart and say these words:

"This person has a body and sensations just like me.
This person has feelings and emotions just like me.

> This person has, in their life, been hurt by another person,
>   disappointed, angry, frustrated, and afraid just like me.
> This person has wondered if they were worthy or good enough,
>   just like me.
> This person has longed to be seen and heard, just like me.
> This person is figuring out life, just like me.
> This person wishes for contentment and healing, just like me.
> This person wishes to be safe and happy, just like me,
> This person wishes to be loved, just like me." (*pause*)

Now consider that you have the ability to allow this person their own journey, their own path. Their path doesn't need to be on your terms or anybody's terms. It is this person's path, just like your path is yours. Offer this freedom to this person:

> "This person is on a journey, a path, just like me.
> This person will unfold exactly as they are intended,
>   just like me.
> This person will find their way in their own time, just like me.
> I offer this person the freedom to find their way, just like I
>   honor my freedom to find my way. (*pause*)
> I allow."

Hold this person in your mind's eye. Offer this person love and kindness. Hold how you and this person share a breadth of what we call common humanity—the need to love and the experience of pain. Last, offer this person freedom to find their own way at their own pace, one more time:

> "You are on a journey, a path, just like me.
> You will unfold exactly as you are intended, just like me.
> You will find your way in your own time, just like me.
> I offer you the freedom to find your way, just like I honor my
>   freedom to find my way. (*pause*)
> I allow."

When you are ready, bring your awareness back to your breath. Take two deep breaths here. (*pause*) Slowly bring your awareness back to the room, opening your eyes, if they were closed, find an object in the room upon which to anchor your gaze. Now, broaden your gaze to the whole room. Offer gratitude for the time and for your own willingness to do this important work.

REFERENCES

Abeyta, A. A., Routledge, C., Juhl, J., & Robinson, M. D. (2015). Finding meaning through emotional understanding: Emotional clarity predicts meaning in life and adjustment to existential threat. *Motivation and Emotion, 39*, 1–11.

Abril, L. (2014). *The epilogue.* Whales, UK: Dewi Lewis.

Adolphs, R., & Anderson, D. J. (2019). *The neuroscience of emotion: A new synthesis.* Princeton, NJ: Princeton University Press.

Ainley, V., Maister, L., Brokfeld, J., Farmer, H., & Tsakiris, M. (2013). More of myself: Manipulating interoceptive awareness by heightened attention to bodily and narrative aspects of the self. *Consciousness and Cognition, 22*, 1231–1238.

Akrawi, D., Bartrop, R., Potter, U., & Touyz, S. (2015). Religiosity, spirituality in relation to disordered eating and body image concerns: A systematic review. *Journal of Eating Disorders, 3*, 29.

Albers, S. (2012). *Eating mindfully: How to end mindless eating and enjoy a balanced relationship with food.* Oakland, CA: New Harbinger.

Allen, K., & Schmidt, U. (2017). Risk factors for eating disorders. In K. D. Brownell & B. T. Walsh (Eds.), *Eating disorders and obesity: A comprehensive handbook* (3rd ed., pp. 254–259). New York, NY: Guilford Press.

Allen, M., & Friston, K. J. (2018). From cognitivism to autopoiesis: Towards a computational framework for the embodied mind. *Synthese, 195*, 2459–2482.

Alleva, J. (2017). Shapeshifting: Focusing on body functionality to improve body image. *Journal of Aesthetic Nursing, 6*, 300–301.

Alleva, J. M., & Martijn, C. (2019). Body functionality. In T. Tylka & N. Piran (Eds.), *Handbook of positive body image and embodiment: Construct, protective factors, and interventions* (pp. 33–41). New York, NY: Oxford University Press.

Alleva, J. M., Sheeran, P., Webb, T. L., Martijn, C., & Miles, E. (2015). A meta-analytic review of stand-alone interventions to improve body image. *PLoS One, 10*, e0139177.

Allison, K. C., Spaeth, A., & Hopkins, C. M. (2016). Sleep and eating disorders. *Current Psychiatry Reports, 18*, 92.

American Institute of Stress (2019). *Take a deep breath.* Retrieved July 5th, 2019, from https://www.stress.org/take-a-deep-breath

American Psychiatric Association. (1980). *Diagnostic and statistical manual of mental disorders* (3rd ed.). Washington, DC: Author.

American Psychiatric Association. (1994). *Diagnostic and statistical manual of mental disorders* (4th ed.). Washington, DC: Author.

American Psychiatric Association. (2000). Practice guideline for the treatment of patients with eating disorders (revision). *American Journal of Psychiatry, 157*(1 Suppl.), 1–39.

American Psychiatric Association. (2013). *Diagnostic and statistical manual of mental disorders* (5th ed.). Arlington, VA: American Psychiatric Publishing.

Anderson, L. M., Reilly, E. E., Schaumberg, K., Dmochowski, S., & Anderson, D. A. (2016). Contributions of mindful eating, intuitive eating, and restraint to BMI, disordered eating, and meal consumption in college students. *Eating and Weight Disorders, 21,* 83–90.

Astrachan-Fletcher, E., & Maslar, M. (2009). *The dialectic behavior therapy skills workbook for bulimia: Using DBT to break the cycle and regain control of your life.* Oakland, CA: New Harbinger.

Attia, E. (2017). Anorexia nervosa. In K. D. Brownell & B. T. Walsh (Eds.), *Eating disorders and obesity: A comprehensive handbook* (3rd ed., pp. 176–181). New York, NY: Guilford Press.

Avalos, L. C., & Tylka, T. L. (2006). Exploring a model of intuitive eating with college women. *Journal of Counseling Psychology, 53,* 486–497.

Avalos, L. C., Tylka, T., & Wood-Barcalow, N. (2005). The Body Appreciation Scale: Development and psychometric evaluation. *Body Image, 2,* 285–297.

Bahji, A., Mazhar, M. N., Hawken, E., Hudson, C. C., Nadkarni, P., & MacNeil, B. A. (2019). Prevalence of substance use disorder comorbidity among individuals with eating disorders: A systematic review and meta-analysis. *Psychiatry Research, 273,* 58–66.

Beahan, R. C. (1982). *Bulimarexia: A college outreach and self help project* (Unpublished doctoral dissertation). California State University, Northridge, CA.

Beck, T., Riedl, D., Schöckel, A., Reddemann, L., Exenberger, S., & Lampe, A. (2017). Measuring self-soothing ability in patients with childhood trauma—Psychometric evaluation of the Self-Soothing Scale in a clinical sample. *Zeitschrift für Psychosomatische Medizin und Psychotherapie, 63,* 405–416.

Becker, C. B., & Stice, E. (2017). From efficacy to effectiveness to broad implementation: Evolution of the Body Project. *Journal of Consulting and Clinical Psychology, 85,* 767.

Benelam, B., & Wyness, L. (2010). Hydration and health: A review. *Nutrition Bulletin, 35,* 3–25.

Benson, H., Beary, J. F., & Carol, M. P. (1974). The relaxation response. *Psychiatry, 37,* 37–46.

Bhat, D., & Carleton, J. (2015). The role of the autonomic nervous system. In G. Marlock, H. Weiss, C. Young, & M. Soth (Eds.), *The handbook of body psychotherapy and somatic psychology* (pp. 615–632). Berkeley, CA: North Atlantic.

Biasetti, A. S. (2018). *Befriending your body: A self-compassionate approach freeing yourself from disordered eating.* Boulder, CO: Shambala.

Bien, T. (2006). *Mindful therapy: A guide for therapists and helping professionals.* Boston, MA: Wisdom.

Boon, B., Stroebe, W., Schut, H., & Jansen, A. (1998). Food for thought: Cognitive regulation of food intake. *British Journal of Health Psychology, 3,* 27–40.

Bora, E., & Köse, S. (2016). Meta-analysis of theory of mind in anorexia nervosa and bulimia nervosa: A specific impairment of cognitive perspective taking in anorexia nervosa? *International Journal of Eating Disorders, 49*, 739–740.

Boskind-Lodahl, M., & White, W. C., Jr. (1978). The definition and treatment of bulimarexia in college women—A pilot study. *Journal of American College Health Association, 27*, 84–97.

Bottaccioli, A. G., Bottaccioli, F., & Minelli, A. (2019). Stress and the psyche-brain-immune network in psychiatric diseases based on psychoneuroendocrine immunology: A concise review. *Annals of the New York Academy of Sciences, 1437*, 31–42.

Boudette, R. (2006). Yoga in the treatment of disordered eating and body image disturbance: How can the practice of yoga be helpful in recovery from an eating disorder? *Eating Disorders, 14*, 167–170.

Bowen, S., Chala, N., & Marlatt, A. G. (2010). *Mindfulness-based relapse prevention for addictive behaviors: A clinician's guide.* New York, NY: Guilford Press.

Brach, T. (2017, September 5). Deconditioning the hungry ghosts: Bringing mindfulness and self-compassion to craving and addiction. *Psychology Today.* Retrieved from https://www.psychologytoday.com/us/blog/finding-true-refuge/201709/de-conditioning-the-hungry-ghosts.

Braun, T. D., Park, C. L., & Gorin, A. (2016). Self-compassion, body image, and disordered eating: A review of the literature. *Body Image, 17*, 117–131.

Brown, D. (2015). Body meditation in the Tibetan Buddhist and Bon traditions. In G. Marlock & H. Weiss (Eds.), *The handbook of body psychotherapy and somatic psychology* (pp. 921–928). Berkeley, CA: North Atlantic.

Brown, K. W., & Kasser, T. (2005). Are psychological and ecological well-being compatible? The role of values, mindfulness, and lifestyle. *Social Indicators Research, 74*, 349–368.

Brown, K. W., Ryan, R. M., & Creswell, J. D. (2007). Addressing fundamental questions about mindfulness. *Psychological Inquiry, 18*, 272–281.

Brown, R. P., & Gerbarg, P. (2012). *The healing power of breath: Simple techniques to reduce stress and anxiety, enhance concentration, and balance your emotions.* Boulder, CO: Shambala.

Brownell, K. D., & Walsh, B. T. (Eds.). (2017). *Eating disorders and obesity: A comprehensive handbook* (3rd ed.). New York, NY: Guilford Press.

Bruch, H. (1962). Perceptual and conceptual disturbances in anorexia nervosa. *Psychosomatic Medicine, 24*, 187–194.

Bruch, H. (1973). *Eating disorders: Obesity, anorexia nervosa, and the person within.* New York, NY: Routledge and Kegan Paul.

Buchanan, N. T., Settles, I. H., & Woods, K. G. (2019). Black women's positive embodiment the face of race × gender oppression. In T. L. Tylka & N. Piran (Eds.), *Handbook of positive body image and embodiment: Constructs, protective factors and interventions* (pp. 191–200). New York, NY: Oxford University Press.

Buckley, T., Punkanen, M., & Ogden, P. (2018). The role of the body in fostering resilience: A sensorimotor psychotherapy perspective. *Body, Movement, and Dance in Psychotherapy, 13*(4), 225–233. https://doi.org/10.1080/17432979.2018.1467344

Bullock, G. (2016). *Mindful relationships: Seven skills for success.* Pencaitland, UK: Handspring.

Brumberg, J. J. (2000). *Fasting girls: A history of anorexia nervosa.* New York, NY: Vintage.

Byrne, S., Wade, T., Hay, P., Touyz, S., Fairburn, C. G., Treasure, J., . . . Crosby, R. D. (2017). A randomised controlled trial of three psychological treatments for anorexia nervosa. *Psychological Medicine, 47,* 2823–2833.

Caldwell, C. (1996). *Getting our bodies back: Recovery, healing, and transformation through body-centered psychotherapy.* Boulder, CO: Shambala.

Caldwell, C. (2015). Movement as and in psychotherapy. In G. Marlock & H. Weiss (Eds.), *The handbook of body psychotherapy and somatic psychology* (pp. 426–435). Berkeley, CA: North Atlantic.

Caldwell, C. (2018). *Bodyfulness: Somatic practices for presence, empowerment, and waking up in this life.* Boulder, CO: Shambhala.

Calì, G., Ambrosini, E., Picconi, L., Mehling, W., & Committeri, G. (2015). Investigating the relationship between interoceptive accuracy, interoceptive awareness, and emotional susceptibility. *Frontiers in Psychology, 6,* 1202.

Calogero, R. M. and Pedrotty, K. N. (2010) Incorporating exercise into the treatment and recovery of eating disorders: Cultivating a mindful approach. In M. Maine, D. Bunnell, & B. H. McGilley (Eds.), *Treatment of eating disorders: Bridging the research-practice gap* (pp. 425–442). Cambridge, MA: Academic Press.

Calogero, R., Tantleff-Dunn, S., & Thompson, J. K. (2011). *Self-objectification in women.* Washington, DC: American Psychological Association.

Calogero, R., Tylka, T. L., McGilly, B. H., & Pedrotty-Stump, K. N. (2019). Attuned with exercise (AWE). In T. Tylka & N. Piran (Eds.), *Handbook of positive body image and embodiment: Construct, protective factors, and interventions* (pp. 80–90). New York, NY: Oxford University Press.

Cameron, O. G. (2001). Interoception: The inside story—A model for psychosomatic processes. *Psychosomatic Medicine, 63,* 697–710.

Cappuccio, F. P., Cooper, D., D'Elia, L., Strazzullo, P., & Miller, M. A. (2011). Sleep duration predicts cardiovascular outcomes: A systematic review and meta-analysis of prospective studies. *European Heart Journal, 32,* 1484–1492.

Castellini, G., Lelli, L., Ricca, V., & Maggi, M. (2016). Sexuality in eating disorders patients: Etiological factors, sexual dysfunction and identity issues. A systematic review. *Hormone Molecular Biology and Clinical Investigation, 25,* 71–90.

Center for Mindful Eating. (2019). *The principles for mindful eating.* Retrieved July 16, 2019, from https://www.thecenterformindfuleating.org/Principles-Mindful-Eating

Chernin, K. (1994). *The hungry self: Women, eating, and identity.* Upper Saddle River, NJ: Harper Perennial.

Chernin, K. (1994). *The hungry self: Women, eating, and identity.* Upper Saddle River, NJ: Harper Perennial.

Chernin, K. (1998). *The woman who gave birth to her mother: Tales of transformation in women's lives.* London, UK: Penguin Books.

Chodron, P. (2013). *Living beautifully: With uncertainty and change.* Boulder, CO: Shambhala.

Chodron, P. (2019). *Tonglen Instruction.* Retrieved July 11, 2019, from http://static1.

squarespace.com/static/57b4bb3a6b8f5b5b2c74b3d0/t/57bcde9f03596ed5
dc891229/1471995552506/TONGLEN+INSTRUCTION+by+Pema+Chödrön.
pdf%C2%A0%C2%A0

Clements-Croome, D., Turner, B., & Pallaris, K. (2019). Flourishing workplaces: A multisensory approach to design and POE. *Intelligent Buildings International*, 1–14.

Cohen, R., Fardouly, J., Newton-John, T., & Slater, A. (2019). #BoPo on Instagram: An experimental investigation of the effects of viewing body positive content on young women's mood and body image. *New Media and Society.* http://doi. org/10.1177/1461444819826530

Cook, B., Wonderlich, S. A., Mitchell, J., Thompson, R., Sherman, R., & Mccallum, K. (2016). Exercise in eating disorders treatment: Systematic review and proposal of guidelines. *Medicine and Science in Sports and Exercise, 48*, 1408.

Cook-Cottone, C. P. (2006). The attuned representation model for the primary prevention of eating disorders: An overview for school psychologists. *Psychology in the Schools, 43*, 223–230.

Cook-Cottone, C. (2013). Dosage as a critical variable in yoga therapy research. *International Journal of Yoga Therapy, 23*, 11–12.

Cook-Cottone, C. P. (2015a). Incorporating positive body image into the treatment of eating disorders: A model for attunement and mindful self-care. *Body Image, 14*, 158–167.

Cook-Cottone, C. P. (2015b). *Mindfulness and yoga for self-regulation: A primer for mental health professionals.* New York, NY: Springer.

Cook-Cottone, C. P. (2016). Embodied self-regulation and mindful self-care in the prevention of eating disorders. *Eating Disorders, 24,* 98–105.

Cook-Cottone, C. P. (2017). *Mindfulness and yoga in schools: A guide for teachers and practitioners.* New York: Springer.

Cook-Cottone, C. P. (2018). Mindful self-care and positive body image: Mindfulness, yoga, and actionable tools for positive embodiment. In E. A. Daniels, M. M. Gillen, & C. H. Markey (Eds.), *Body positive: Understanding and improving body image in science and practice.* Cambridge, UK: Cambridge University Press

Cook-Cottone, C. P. (2019a). Mindful attunement. In T. L. Tylka & N. Piran (Eds.), *Handbook of positive body image and embodiment: Constructs, protective factors, and interventions* (pp. 68–79). New York, NY: Oxford University Press.

Cook-Cottone, C. P. (2019b). Yoga as a pathway to positive embedment in the prevention and treatment of eating disorders. In H. L. McBride & J. L. Kwee (Eds.), *Embodiment and eating disorders: Theory, research, prevention, and treatment.* New York, NY: Routledge.

Cook-Cottone, C. P., Anderson, L., & Kane, L. (2019). *Elements of counseling children and adolescents.* New York, NY: Springer.

Cook-Cottone, C. P., & Boys, K. (2019). *The peace on purpose curriculum: Creating mindfulness and resilience for humanitarian workers.* Washington, DC: United Nations Foundation.

Cook-Cottone, C., Childress, T., & Harper, J. C. (2018). Secularity: Guiding questions for inclusive yoga in schools. *International Journal of Yoga Therapy, 29.* https://doi.org/10.17761/2019-00007

Cook-Cottone. C. P., & Douglass, L. L. (2017). Yoga communities and eating disorders: Creating a safe space for positive embodiment. *International Journal of Yoga Therapy, 27.*

Cook-Cottone, C. P., Giambrone, C., & Klein, J. E. (2017a). Yoga for Kenyan children: Concept mapping with multidimensional scaling and hierarchical cluster analysis. *International Journal of Educational and School Psychology, 6,* 151–164. http://doi.org/10.1080/21683603.2017.1302852

Cook-Cottone, C. P., & Guyker, W. M. (2018). The development and validation of the Mindful Self-Care Scale (MSCS): An assessment of practices that support positive embodiment. *Mindfulness, 9,* 161–175. https://doi.org/10.1007/s12671-017-0759-1

Cook-Cottone, C. P., Kane, L., Keddie, E., & Haugli, S. (2013). *Girls growing in wellness and balance: Yoga and life skills to empower.* Stoddard, WI: Schoolhouse Educational Services.

Cook-Cottone, C. P., LaVigne, M., Guyker, W., Travers, L., Lemish., E., & Elenson, P. (2017b). Trauma-informed yoga: An embodied, cognitive-relational framework. *International Journal of Complementary and Alternative Medicine, 9,* 00284. https://doi.org/10.15406/ijcam.2017.09.00284

Cook-Cottone, C. P., Talebkhah, K., Guyker, W., & Keddie (2017c). A controlled trial of a yoga-based prevention program targeting eating disorder risk factors among middle school females. *Eating Disorders, 25,* 392–405.

Cook-Cottone, C. P., Tribole, E., & Tylka, T. (2013). *Healthy eating in schools: Evidenced-based interventions to help kids thrive.* Washington, DC: American Psychological Association.

Cook-Cottone, C. P., & Vujnovic, R. (2018). *Mindfulness for anxious kids: A workbook to help children cope with anxiety, stress, and worry.* Oakland, CA: New Harbinger.

Cooper, M. J. (2011). Working with imagery to modify core beliefs in people with eating disorders: A clinical protocol. *Cognitive and Behavioral Practice, 18,* 454–465.

Corn, S. (2013). *Yoga teacher training.* Toronto, ON: 889 Yoga.

Costarelli, V., & Patsai, A. (2012). Academic examination stress increases disordered eating symptomatology in female university students. *Eating and Weight Disorders, 17,* e164–e169.

Csikszentmihalyi, M. (2002). *Flow: The classic work on how to achieve happiness.* New York, NY: Random House.

Culbert, K. M., Racine, S. E., & Klump, K. L. (2015). What we have learned about the causes of eating disorders—A synthesis of sociocultural, psychological, and biological research. *Journal of Child Psychology and Psychiatry, 56,* 1141–1164.

Cumella, E., Lutter, C. B., Smith-Osborne, A., & Kally, Z. (2014). Equine therapy in the treatment of female eating disorder. *SOP Transactions on Psychology, 1*(1). https://doi.org/10.15764/STP.2014.01002

Czekierda, K., Banik, A., Park, C. L., & Luszczynska, A. (2017). Meaning in life and physical health: Systematic review and meta-analysis. *Health Psychology Review, 11,* 387–418.

Dana, D. (2018). *The polyvagal theory in therapy: Engaging the rhythm of regulation.* New York, NY: Norton.

Daubenmier, J. (2005). The relationship of yoga, body awareness, and body responsiveness to self-objectification and disordered eating. *Psychology of Women Quarterly, 29,* 207–219.

Davis, L. L., Fowler, S. A., Best, L. A., & Both, L. E. (2019). The role of body image in the prediction of life satisfaction and flourishing in men and women. *Journal of Happiness Studies,* https://doi.org/10.1007/s10902-019-00093-y

Davis, M., Eshelman, E. R., & McKay, M. (2008). *The relaxation and stress reduction workbook* (6th ed.). Oakland, CA: New Harbinger.

de Beauvoir, S. (1940). *The second sex.* New York, NY: Vintage.

Devlin, M. J. (2017). Binge eating disorders. In K. D. Brownell & B. T. Walsh (Eds.), *Eating disorders and obesity: A comprehensive handbook* (3rd ed., pp. 192–197). New York, NY: Guilford Press.

Devonport, T. J., Nicholls, W., & Fullerton, C. (2019). A systematic review of the association between emotions and eating behaviour in normal and overweight adult populations. *Journal of Health Psychology, 24,* 3–24.

Dilberto, T., & Hirsch, D. (2019). *Treating eating disorders in adolescents: Evidence-based intervention for anorexia, bulimia, and binge eating.* Oakland, CA: Context Press.

Dingemans, A., Danner, U., & Parks, M. (2017). Emotion regulation in binge eating disorder: A review. *Nutrients, 9,* 1274.

Dolan, P., & Metcalfe, R. (2012). Measuring subjective wellbeing: Recommendations on measures for use by national governments. *Journal of Social Policy, 41,* 409–427.

Dollar, E., Berman, M., & Adachi-Mejia, A. M. (2017). Do no harm: Moving beyond weight loss to emphasize physical activity at every size. *Preventing Chronic Disease, 14.* https://doi.org/10.5888/pcd14.170006

Domingues, R. B., & Carmo, C. (2019). Disordered eating behaviours and correlates in yoga practitioners: A systematic review. *Eating and Weight Disorders,* 1–10.

Douglass, L. (2011). Thinking through the body: The conceptualization of yoga as therapy for individuals with eating disorders. *Eating Disorders, 19,* 83–96.

Dunaev, J, L, & Markey, C. H. (2018). Better than before: Individual strategies for body image improvement. In E. A. Daniels, M. M. Gillen, & C. H. Markey (Eds.), *Body positive: Understanding and improving body image in science and practice* (pp. 189–207). Cambridge, UK: Cambridge University Press.

Dunkle, E., & Dunkle, B. (2016). *Elena vanishing: A memoir.* San Francisco, CA: Chronicle Books.

Duyff, R. L. (2011). *American Dietetic Association complete food and nutrition guide.* New York, NY: Houghton Mifflin Harcourt.

Elices, M., Carmona, C., Narváez, V., Seto, V., Martin-Blanco, A., Pascual, J. C., . . . Soler, J. (2017). Direct experience while eating: Laboratory outcomes among individuals with eating disorders versus healthy controls. *Eating Behaviors, 27,* 23–26.

Equine Assisted Growth and Learning Association. (2019). *How it works.* Retrieved July 8, 2019, from https://www.eagala.org/model

Esplen, M. J., Garfinkel, P. E., Olmsted, M., Gallop, R. M., & Kennedy, S. (1998). A randomized controlled trial of guided imagery in bulimia nervosa. *Psychological Medicine, 28,* 1347–1357.

Evans, G. W., & McCoy, J. (1998). When buildings don't work: The role of architecture in human health. *Journal of Environmental Psychology, 18,* 85–94.

Fairburn, C. G. (2008). *Cognitive behavioral therapy and eating disorders.* New York, NY: Guilford Press.

Fairburn, C. G. (2013). *Overcoming binge eating: The proven program to learn why you binge and how you can stop* (2nd ed.). New York, NY: Guilford Press.

Fairburn, C. G. (2017). Cognitive behavioral therapy and eating disorders. In K. D. Brownell & B. T. Walsh (Eds.), *Eating disorders and obesity: A comprehensive handbook* (3rd ed., pp. 284–289). New York, NY: Guilford Press.

Fairburn, C. G., Bailey-Straebler, S., Basden, S., Doll, H. A., Jones, R., Murphy, R., . . . Cooper, Z. (2015). A transdiagnostic comparison of enhanced cognitive behaviour therapy (CBT-E) and interpersonal psychotherapy in the treatment of eating disorders. *Behaviour Research and Therapy, 70,* 64–71.

Favaro, A., Tenconi, E., & Santonastaso, P. (2010). The interaction between perinatal factors and childhood abuse in the risk of developing anorexia nervosa. *Psychological Medicine, 40,* 657–665.

Feliu-Soler, A., Pascual, J. C., Elices, M., Martín-Blanco, A., Carmona, C., Cebolla, A., . . . Soler, J. (2017). Fostering self-compassion and loving-kindness in patients with borderline personality disorder: A randomized pilot study. *Clinical Psychology and Psychotherapy, 24,* 278–286.

Ferreira, C., Pinto-Gouveia, J., & Duarte, C. (2013). Self-compassion in the face of shame and body image dissatisfaction: Implications for eating disorders. *Eating Behaviors, 14,* 207–210.

Fleche, S., Smith, C., & Sorsa, P. (2012). *Exploring determinants of subjective wellbeing in OECD countries: Evidence from the World Value Survey.* OECD Statistics Working Papers 2012/01. OECD Publishing. http://doi.org/10.1787/5k9ffc6p1rvb-en

Foucault, M. (1986). The subject and power. *Critical Inquiry, 8,* 777–795.

Frankl, V. (1969). *The will to meaning: Foundations and applications of logotherapy.* New York, NY: World Publishing.

Frankl, V. E. (1978). *The unheard cry for meaning.* New York, NY: Simon and Schuster.

Frankl, V. (2006). *Man's search for meaning.* New York, NY: Beacon Press.

Frederickson, B. (1998). What good are positive emotions? *Review of General Psychology, 2,* 300–319.

Fredrickson, B. L., & Joiner, T. (2018). Reflections on positive emotions and upward spirals. *Perspectives on Psychological Science, 13,* 194–199.

Fredrickson, B. L., & Roberts, T.-A. (1997). Objectification theory: Toward understanding women's lived experiences and mental health risks. *Psychology of Women Quarterly, 21,* 173–206.

Fritz, M. M., Armenta, C. N., Walsh, L. C., & Lyubomirsky, S. (2019). Gratitude facilitates healthy eating behavior in adolescents and young adults. *Journal of Experimental Social Psychology, 81,* 4–14.

Gaete, M., & Fuchs, T. (2016). From body image to emotional bodily experience in eating disorders. *Journal of Phenomenology, 47,* 17–40.

García-Alandete, J., Ros, M. C., Salvador, J. H. M., & Rodríguez, S. P. (2018). Psychometric properties of the Purpose-in-Life Test and age-related differences among women diagnosed with eating disorders. *Psychiatry Research, 261,* 161–167.

Germer, C. K., & Neff, K. D. (2013). Self-compassion in clinical practice. *Journal of Clinical Psychology, 69,* 856–867.

Ghaderi, A., Odeberg, J., Gustafsson, S., Råstam, M., Brolund, A., Pettersson, A., & Parling, T. (2018). Psychological, pharmacological, and combined treatments for binge eating disorder: A systematic review and meta-analysis. *PeerJ, 6,* e5113.

Giambrone, C. A., Cook-Cottone, C. P., & Klein, J. E. (2018). The Africa Yoga Project and well-being: A concept map of students' perceptions. *Applied Psychology, 10,* 149–170.

Giovinazzo, S., Sukkar, S. G., Rosa, G. M., Zappi, A., Bezante, G. P., Balbi, M., & Brunelli, C. (2019). Anorexia nervosa and heart disease: A systematic review. *Eating and Weight Disorders, 24,* 199–207.

Godfrey, K. M., Juarascio, A., Manasse, S., Minassian, A., Risbrough, V., & Afari, N. (2019). Heart rate variability and emotion regulation among individuals with obesity and loss of control eating. *Physiology and Behavior, 199,* 73–78.

Goldberg, J. (2017). *The dark side of love: The positive role of negative feelings.* New York, NY: Routledge.

Golden, N. H., Katzman, D. K., Sawyer, S. M., Ornstein, R. M., Rome, E. S., Garber, A. K., . . . Kreipe, R. E. (2015). Update on the medical management of eating disorders in adolescents. *Journal of Adolescent Health, 56,* 370–375.

Gordon, R. A. (2017). The history of eating disorders. In K. D. Brownell & B. T. Walsh (Eds.), *Eating disorders and obesity: A comprehensive handbook* (3rd ed., pp. 163–167). New York, NY: Guilford Press.

Grabbe, L., & Miller-Karas, E. (2018). The trauma resiliency model: a "bottom-up" intervention for trauma psychotherapy. *Journal of the American Psychiatric Nurse Association, 24,* 76–84.

Grabovac, A. D., Lau, M. A., & Willett, B. R. (2011). Mechanisms of mindfulness: A Buddhist psychological model. *Mindfulness, 2,* 154–166.

Greenleaf, C., & Hauff, C. (2019). Environments that cultivate positive embodiment through mindful movement. In T. Tylka & N. Piran (Eds.), *Handbook of positive body image and embodiment: Construct, protective factors, and interventions* (pp. 119–128). New York, NY: Oxford University Press.

Guarda, A., & Redgrave, G. W. (2017). Weight restoration in anorexia nervosa. In K. D. Brownell & B. T. Walsh (Eds.), *Eating disorders and obesity: A comprehensive handbook* (3rd ed., pp. 176–181). New York, NY: Guilford Press.

Guillaume, S., Jaussent, I., Maimoun, L., Ryst, A., Seneque, M., Villain, L., . . . Courtet, P. (2016). Associations between adverse childhood experiences and clinical characteristics of eating disorders. *Scientific Reports, 6,* 35761.

Hadden, B. W., & Smith, C. V. (2019). I gotta say, today was a good (and meaningful) day: Daily meaning in life as a potential basic psychological need. *Journal of Happiness Studies, 20,* 185–202.

Hanh, T. N (1975). *The miracle of mindfulness: An introduction to the practice of meditation.* Boston, MA: Beacon Press.

Hanh, T. N. (2007). *True love: A practice for awakening the heart.* London, UK: Shambala.

Hanson, R., & Hanson, F. (2018). *Resilient: How to grow an unshakable core of calm, strength, and happiness.* Danvers, MA: Harmony Press

Hanson, R., & Mendius, R. (2009). *Buddha's brain: The practical neuroscience of happiness, love, and wisdom.* Oakland, CA: New Harbinger.

Harper, J. C. (2013). *Little flower yoga for kids: A yoga and mindfulness programs to help your children improve attention and emotional balance.* Oakland, CA: New Harbinger.

Harris, R. (2009). *ACT made simple: A quick start guide to ACT basic and beyond.* Oakland, CA: New Harbinger.

Hart, M. (2016). The importance and elements of healthy nutrition. *Advances in Eating Disorders, 4*, 14–30.

Hayes, S. C., Luoma, J. B., Bond, F. W., Masuda, A., & Lillis, J. (2006). Acceptance and commitment therapy: Model, processes and outcomes. *Behaviour Research and Therapy, 44*, 1–25

Hayes, S. C., Strosahl, K. D., & Wilson, K. G. (2012). *Acceptance and commitment therapy: The process and practice of mindful change.* New York, NY: Guilford Press.

Hayes, T. (2015). *Riding home: The power of horses to heal.* New York, NY: St. Martin's Press.

Hebb, D. O. (1949). *Organization of behavior: A neuropsychological theory.* New York, NY: Wiley.

Heidegger, M. (1962). Being and time. 1927. *Trans. John Macquarrie and Edward Robinson. New York: Harper.*

Hendrickson, K. L., & Rasmussen, E. B. (2013). Effects of mindful eating training on delay and probability discounting for food and money in obese and healthy-weight individuals. *Behaviour Research and Therapy, 51*, 399–409.

Hendrickson, K. L., & Rasmussen, E. B. (2017). Mindful eating reduces impulsive food choice in adolescents and adults. *Health Psychology, 36*, 226–235.

Hepworth, N. S. (2010). A mindful eating group as an adjunct to individual treatment for eating disorders: A pilot study. *Eating Disorders, 19*, 6–16.

Hietanen, J. K., Glerean, E., Hari, R., & Nummenmaa, L. (2016). Bodily maps of emotions Across child development. *Developmental Science, 19*, 1111–1118.

Hilbert, A., Vögele, C., Tuschen-Caffier, B., & Hartmann, A. S. (2011). Psychophysiological responses to idiosyncratic stress in bulimia nervosa and binge eating disorder. *Physiology and Behavior, 104*, 770–777.

Hirshkowitz, M., Whiton, K., Albert, S. M., Alessi, C., Bruni, O., DonCarlos, L., . . . Hillard, P. J., A (2015). National Sleep Foundation's sleep time duration recommendations: methodology and results summary. *Sleep Health, 1*, 40–43.

Hopkins, M. E., Davis, F. C., VanTieghem, M. R., Whalen, P. J., & Bucci, D. J. (2012). Differential effects of acute and regular physical exercise on cognition and affect. *Neuroscience, 215*, 59–68.

Hutcherson, C. A., Seppala, E. M., & Gross, J. J. (2008). Loving-kindness meditation increases social connectedness. *Emotion, 8*, 720.

Impett, E. A., Daubenmier, J. J., & Hirschman, A. L. (2006). Minding the body: Yoga, embodiment, and well-being. *Sexuality Research and Social Policy, 3*, 39–48.

Impett, E. A., Schooler, D., & Tolman, D. L. (2006). To be seen and not heard: Femininity ideology and adolescent girls' sexual health. *Archives of Sexual Behavior, 35*(2), 129–142.

Irving, L. M. (1999). A bolder model of prevention: Science, practice, and activism. In N. Piran, M. Levine, and C. Steiner-Adair (Eds.) *Preventing eating disorders: A handbook of interventions and special challenges* (pp. 63–84). Oxford, U.K.: Taylor and Francis Group.

Irwin, M. R., Olmstead, R., & Carroll, J. E. (2016). Sleep disturbance, sleep duration, and inflammation: A systematic review and meta-analysis of cohort studies and experimental sleep deprivation. *Biological Psychiatry, 80*, 40–52.

Jackman, P. C., Hawkins, R. M., Crust, L., & Swann, C. (2019). Flow states in exercise: A systematic review. *Psychology of Sport and Exercise*, 101546.

Jacobson, H. L., & Hall, E. L. (2018). The developmental theory of embodiment: Implications for treatment and prevention of eating disorders. In H. L. McBride & J. L. Kwee (Eds.), *Embodiment and eating disorders: Theory, research, prevention, and treatment* (pp. 77–89). New York, NY: Routledge.

Jenkinson, P. M., Taylor, L., & Laws, K. R. (2018). Self-reported interoceptive deficits in eating disorders: A meta-analysis of studies using the eating disorder inventory. *Journal of Psychosomatic Research, 110*, 38–45.

Jennings, P. A. (2015). *Mindfulness for teachers: Simple skills for peace and productivity in the classroom*. New York, NY: Norton.

Johnston, A. (2000). *Eating by the light of the moon: How women can transform their relationship with food through myths, metaphors, and storytelling*. Carlsbad, CA: Gurze Books.

Jones, A., Lindekilde, N., Lübeck, M., & Clausen, L. (2015). The association between interpersonal problems and treatment outcome in the eating disorders: A systematic review. *Nordic Journal of Psychiatry, 69*, 563–573.

Jordan, C. H., Wang, W., Donatoni, L., & Meier, B. P. (2014). Mindful eating: Trait and state mindfulness predict healthier eating behavior. *Personality and Individual Differences, 68*, 107–111.

Juarascio, A., Manesse, & Espel, H. (2016). Acceptance and commitment therapy for anorexia and bulimia nervosa. In A. F. Haynos, E. M. Forman, M. L. Butryn, & J. Lillis (Eds.), *Mindfulness and acceptance for treating eating disorders and weight concerns* (pp. 26–44). Oakland, CA: Context Press.

Juarascio, A. S., Manasse, S. M., Schumacher, L., Espel, H., & Forman, E. M. (2017). Developing an acceptance-based behavioral treatment for binge eating disorder: Rationale and challenges. *Cognitive and Behavioral Practice, 24*(1), 1–13.

Kabat-Zinn, J. (1990). *Full catastrophe living: Using the wisdom of your body and mind to face stress, pain, and illness*. New York, NY: Delacorte Press

Kabat-Zinn, J. (2013). *Full catastrophe living: Using the wisdom of your body and mind to face stress, pain, and illness*. New York, NY: Bantam Books.

Kabatznick, R. (1998). *The Zen of eating: Ancient answers to modern weight problems*. New York, NY: Berkley Publishing.

Keel, P. (2017). Bulimia nervosa. In K. D. Brownell & B. T Walsh (Eds.), *Eating disorders and obesity: A comprehensive handbook* (3rd ed., pp. 187–191). New York, NY: Guilford Press.

Kendall, E., Maujean, A., Pepping, C. A., Downes, M., Lakhani, A., Byrne, J., & Macfarlane, K. (2015). A systematic review of the efficacy of equine-assisted interventions on psychological outcomes. *European Journal of Psychotherapy and Counselling, 17*, 57–79.

Kendall, E., Maujean, A., Pepping, C. A., & Wright, J. J. (2014). Hypotheses about the psychological benefits of horses. *Explore, 10,* 81–87.

Khalili-Mahani, N., Smyrnova, A., & Kakinami, L. (2019). To each stress its own screen: A cross-sectional survey of the patterns of stress and various screen uses in relation to self-admitted screen addiction. *Journal of Medical Internet Research, 21,* e11485.

Khoury, B., Knauper, B., Pagnini, F., Trent, N., Chiesa, A., & Carriere, K. (2017). Embodied mindfulness. *Mindfulness.* https://doi.org/10.1007/s12671-017-0700-7

Kirberger, K. (2003). *No body's perfect: Stories by teens about body image, self-acceptance, and the search for anxiety.* New York, NY: Scholastic.

Klein, J., & Cook-Cottone, C. P. (2013). The effects of yoga on eating disorder symptoms and correlates: A review. *International Journal of Yoga Therapy, 23,* 41–50.

Klein, J. E., Cook-Cottone, C. P., & Giambrone, C. (2015). The Africa Yoga Project: A participant-driven concept map of Kenyan teachers' reported experiences. *International Journal of Yoga Therapy, 25,* 113–126. https://doi.org/10.17761/1531-2054-25.1.113

Korb, A. (2015). *The upward spiral: Using neuroscience to reverse the course of depression, one small change at a time.* Oakland, CA: New Harbinger.

Kristeller, J. L., Baer, R. A., & Quillian-Wolever, R. (2006). Mindfulness-based approaches to eating disorders. In R. A. Baer (Ed.), *Mindfulness-based treatment approaches: Clinician's guide to evidence base and applications* (pp. 75–91). San Diego, CA: Elsevier Academic Press.

Kristeller, J. L., & Wolever, R. Q. (2010). Mindfulness-based eating awareness training for treating binge eating disorder: The conceptual foundation. *Eating Disorders, 19,* 49–61.

Kumano, M. (2018). On the concept of well-being in Japan: Feeling *shiawase* as hedonic well-being and feeling *ikigai* as eudaimonic well-being. *Applied Research in Quality of Life, 13,* 419–433.

Kyle, S. D., Morgan, K., & Espie, C. A. (2010). Insomnia and health-related quality of life. *Sleep Medicine Reviews, 14,* 69–82.

Lakoff, G., & Johnson, M. (1999). *Philosophy of the flesh: The embodied mind and its challenge to Western thought.* New York, NY: Basic Books.

Larocca, M. (2018). *Starving: In search of me.* Coral Gables, FL: Mango Publishing.

Lasswell, H. D. (1939). The contribution of Freud's insight interview to the social sciences. *American Journal of Sociology, 45,* 375–390.

Lattimore, P., Mead, B. R., Irwin, L., Grice, L., Carson, R., & Malinowski, P. (2017). "I can't accept that feeling": Relationships between interoceptive awareness, mindfulness and eating disorder symptoms in females with, and at-risk of an eating disorder. *Psychiatry Research, 247,* 163–171.

Launeanu, M., & Kwee, J. L. (2018). Embodiment: A non-dualistic and existential perspective on understanding and treating disordered eating. In H. L. McBride & J. L. Kwee (Eds.), *Embodiment and eating disorders: Theory, research, prevention, and treatment* (pp. 35–52). New York, NY: Routledge.

Lavender, J. M., Wonderlich, S. A., Engel, S. G., Gordon, K. H., Kaye, W. H., & Mitchell, J. E. (2015). Dimensions of emotion dysregulation in anorexia nervosa and bulimia nervosa: A conceptual review of the empirical literature. *Clinical Psychology Review, 40,* 111–122.

Leehr, E. J., Krohmer, K., Schag, K., Dresler, T., Zipfel, S., & Giel, K. E. (2015). Emotion regulation model in binge eating disorder and obesity—A systematic review. *Neuroscience and Biobehavioral Reviews, 49*, 125–134.

Le Grange, D., & Eisler, I. (2017). Family therapy and eating disorders. In K. D. Brownell & B. T. Walsh (Eds.), *Eating disorders and obesity: A comprehensive handbook* (3rd ed., pp. 296–301). New York, NY: Guilford Press.

Lelwica, M. (2010, March 22). The spiritual dimensions of recovering from an eating disorder: Transforming suffering and finding new sources of meaning. *Psychology Today.* Retrieved June 11, 2019, from https://www.psychologytoday.com/us/blog/the-religion-thinness/201003/the-spiritual-dimensions-recovering-eating-disorder-transforming

Levine, P. (2008). *Healing trauma: A pioneering program for restoring the wisdom of your body.* Boulder. CO: Sounds True.

Levine, M. P., & Piran, N. (2004). The role of body image in the prevention of eating disorders. *Body image, 1*(1), 57–70.

Levinson, C. A., Zerwas, S., Calebs, B., Forbush, K., Kordy, H., Watson, H., . . . Bulick, C. M. (2017). The core symptoms of bulimia nervosa, anxiety, and depression: A network analysis. *Journal of Abnormal Psychology, 126*, 340.

Linardon, J., & Wade, T. D. (2018). How many individuals achieve symptom abstinence following psychological treatments for bulimia nervosa? A meta-analytic review. *International Journal of Eating Disorders, 51*(4), 287–294.

Linehan, M. M. (1993). *Cognitive-behavioral treatment of borderline personality disorder.* New York, NY: Guilford Press.

Linehan, M. M. (2015). *DBT® skills training manual* (2nd ed.). New York, NY: Guilford Press.

Lim, J., & Dinges, D. F. (2010). A meta-analysis of the impact of short-term sleep deprivation on cognitive variables. *Psychological Bulletin, 136*, 375.

Liska, D., Mah, E., Brisbois, T., Barrios, P., Baker, L., & Spriet, L. (2019). Narrative review of hydration and selected health outcomes in the general population. *Nutrients, 11*(70), 257–265. https://doi.org/10.1016/j.genhosppsych.2015.03.007

Lloyd, E. C., Frampton, I., Verplanken, B., & Haase, A. M. (2017). How extreme dieting becomes compulsive: A novel hypothesis for the role of anxiety in the development and maintenance of anorexia nervosa. *Medical Hypotheses, 108*, 144–150.

Lock, J., La Via, M. C., & AACAP (American Academy of Child and Adolescent Psychiatry) Community on Quality Issues. (2015). Practice parameter for the assessment and treatment of children and adolescents with eating disorders. *Journal of the American Academy of Child and Adolescent Psychiatry, 5*, 412–425.

Lynch, T. R. (2018). *The skills training manual for radically open dialectical behavior therapy: A clinician's guide for treating disorders of overcontrol.* Oakland, CA: Context Press.

Macht, M. (2008). How emotions affect eating: A five-way model. *Appetite, 50*, 1–11.

Maddi, S. R. (1996). *Personality theories: A comparative analysis* (6th ed.). Pacific Grove, CA: Brooks/Cole.

Mahlo, L., & Tiggemann, M. (2016). Yoga and positive body image: A test of the embodiment model. *Body Image, 18*, 135–142.

Manlick, C. F., Cochran, S. V., & Koon, J. (2013). Acceptance and commitment therapy for eating disorders: Rationale and literature review. *Journal of Contemporary Psychotherapy, 43*, 115–122.

Marco, J. H., Cañabate, M., & Pérez, S. (2019, January 20). Meaning in life is associated with the psychopathology of eating disorders: Differences depending on the diagnosis. *Eating Disorders.* https://doi.org/10.1080/10640266.2018.1560852

Marco, J. H., Cañabate, M., Pérez, S., & Llorca, G. (2017). Associations among meaning in life, body image, psychopathology, and suicide ideation in Spanish participants with eating disorders. *Journal of Clinical Psychology.* https://doi.org/10.1002/jclp.22481

Marco, J. H., Pérez, S., & García-Alandete, J. (2016). Meaning in life buffers the association between risk factors for suicide and hopelessness in participants with mental disorders. *Journal of Clinical Psychology, 72*, 689–700.

Marco, J. H., Pérez, S., García-Alandete, J., & Moliner, R. (2017). Meaning in life in people with borderline personality disorder. *Clinical Psychology and Psychotherapy, 24*, 162–170.

Marrero, L. A. (2013). *The path to a meaningful purpose: Psychological foundations of logoteleology.* Bloomington, IN: iUniverse.

Masuda, A, & Hill, M. L. (2013) Mindfulness as therapy for disordered eating: A systematic review. *Neuropsychiatry, 3*, 433–447.

Maté, G. (2010). *In the realm of hungry ghosts: Close encounters with addiction.* Berkeley, CA: North Atlantic.

McBride, H. L. (2018). Embodiment and body image. In H. L. McBride & J. L. Kwee (Eds.), *Embodiment and eating disorders: Theory, research, prevention, and treatment* (pp. 6–16). New York, NY: Routledge.

McMahan, E. A., & Estes, D. (2015). The effect of contact with natural environments on positive and negative affect: A meta-analysis. *Journal of Positive Psychology, 10*, 507–519.

Menzel, J., & Levine, M. P. (2007, August). *Female athletes and embodiment: Development and validation of the Athlete Body Experiences Questionnaire.* Poster presented at the annual convention of the American Psychological Association, San Francisco, CA.

Menzel, J. E., & Levine, M. P. (2011). Embodying experiences and the promotion of positive body image: The example of competitive athletics. In R. M. Calogero, S. Tantleff-Dunn, & J. K. Thompson (Eds.), *Self-objectification in women: Causes, consequences, and counteractions* (pp. 163–186). Washington, DC: American Psychological Association.

Menzel, J. E., Thompson, J. K., & Levine, M. P. (2019). Development and validation of the Physical Activity Body Experiences Questionnaire. *Bulletin of the Menninger Clinic.*

Merleau-Ponty, M. (2002). *Phenomenology of perception* (C. Smith, Trans.). New York, NY: Routledge.

Merleau-Ponty, M. (2012). *The phenomenology of perception* (D. A. Landes, Ed.). New York, NY: Routledge.

Meule, A. (2015). Back by popular demand: A narrative review on the history of food addiction research. *Yale Journal of Biology and Medicine, 88*, 295–302.

Miller, M., & Clark, A. (2018). Happily entangled: prediction, emotion, and the embodied mind. *Synthese, 195*, 2559–2575.

Miller, M. N., & Pumariega, A. J. (2001). Culture and eating disorders: A historical and cross-cultural review. *Psychiatry, 64,* 93–110.

Miller, R. (2015). *The iRest program for healing PTSD: A proven-effective approach to using yoga nidra meditation and deep relaxation techniques to overcome trauma.* Oakland, CA: New Harbinger.

Mountford, V., & Waller, G. (2006). Using imagery in cognitive-behavioral treatment for eating disorders: Tackling the restrictive mode. *International Journal of Eating Disorders, 39,* 533–543.

Moya, P. (2015). Habit and embodiment in Merleau-Ponty. *Frontiers in Human Neuroscience, 9,* 226–232.

National Center for Complementary and Integrative Health. (2019). *Relaxation techniques for health.* Retrieved July 15, 2019, from https://nccih.nih.gov/health/stress/relaxation.htm

National Eating Disorder Association. (2019). *Common health consequences of eating disorders.* Retrieved June 7, 2019, from https://www.nationaleatingdisorders.org/health-consequences

National Eating Disorder Assocation (2019). What are eating disorders? Anorexia Nervosa Retrieved June 10, 2019 https://www.nationaleatingdisorders.org/learn/by-eating-disorder/anorexia)

National Eating Disorder Assocation (2019). What are eating disorders? Bulimia Nervosa Retrieved June 10, 2019 https://www.nationaleatingdisorders.org/learn/by-eating-disorder/bulimia.

National Institute for Health and Care Excellence. (2017). *Eating disorders: Recognition and treatment.* NICE Quality Standard No. NG69. Retrieved from https://www.nice.org.uk/guidance/ng69

Neff, K. D. (2011). Self-compassion, self-esteem, and well-being. *Social and Personality Psychology Compass, 5,* 1–12.

Neff, K., & Germer, C. (2018). *The mindful self-compassion workbook: A proven way to accept yourself, build inner strength, and thrive.* New York, NY: Guilford Press.

Norcross, J. C., & Guy, J. D. (2007). *Leaving it at the office: A guide to psychotherapist self-care.* New York, NY: Guilford Press.

Nummenmaa, L., Glerean, E., Hari, R., & Hietanen, J. K. (2014). Bodily maps of emotions. *Proceedings of the National Academy of Sciences of the United States of America, 111,* 646–651.

Nummenmaa, L., Hari, R., Hietanen, J. K., & Glerean, E. (2018). Maps of subjective feelings. *Proceedings of the National Academy of Sciences of the United States of America, 115,* 9198–9203.

Ogden, P., & Fisher, J. (2015). *Sensorimotor psychotherapy: Interventions for trauma and attachment.* New York, NY: Norton.

Ogden, P., Minton, K., & Pain, C. (2006). *Trauma and the body: A sensorimotor approach to psychotherapy.* New York, NY: Norton.

Oh, B., Lee, K. J., Zaslawski, C., Yeung, A., Rosenthal, D., Larkey, L., & Back, M. (2017). Health and well-being benefits of spending time in forests: Systematic review. *Environmental Health and Preventive Medicine, 22.*

Oldershaw, A., Lavender, T., Sallis, H., Stahl, D., & Schmidt, U. (2015). Emotion generation and regulation in anorexia nervosa: A systematic review and meta-analysis of self-report data. *Clinical Psychology Review, 39,* 83–95.

Osher, D., Cantor, P., Berg, J., Steyer, L., & Rose, T. (2018). Drivers of human development: How relationships and context shape learning and development. *Applied Developmental Science*, 1–31. https://doi.org/10.1080/10888691.2017.139 8650

Osso, L. D., Abelli, M., Carpita, B., Pini, S., Castellini, G., Carmassi, C., & Ricca, V. (2016). Historical evolution of the concept of anorexia nervosa and relationships with orthorexia nervosa, autism and obsessive-compulsive spectrum. *Neuropsychiatric Disease and Treatment, 12*, 1651–1660.

Park, C. L. (2010). Making sense of the meaning literature: An integrative review of meaning making and its effects on adjustment to stressful life events. *Psychological Bulletin, 136*, 257–301.

Park, J., & Baumeister, R. F. (2017). Meaning in life and adjustment to daily stressors. *Journal of Positive Psychology, 12*, 333–341.

Parsons, E., & Betz, N. (2001). The relationship of participation in sports and physical activity to body objectification, instrumentality, and locus of control among young women. *Psychology of Women Quarterly, 25*, 209–222.

Perry, C. J., & Bond, M. (2017) Addressing defenses in psychotherapy to improve adaptation. *Psychoanalytic Inquiry, 37*, 153–166.

Piaget, J. (1952). *The origins of intelligence in children.* New York, NY: International Universities Press, Inc.

Pipher, M. (1994). *Reviving Ophelia: Saving the selves of adolescent girls.* New York, NY: Riverhead Trade.

Piran, N. (1999). Eating disorders: A trial of prevention in a high risk school setting. *Journal of Primary Prevention, 20*, 75–90.

Piran, N. (2017). *Journey of embodiement at the intrsecion of body and culture.* Cambridge, MA: Academic Press.

Piran, N. (2002). Prevention of eating disorders. *Eating disorders and obesity: A comprehensive handbook*, 367–371.

Piran, N. (2016). Embodied possibilities and disruptions: The emergence of the experience of embodiment construct from qualitative studies with girls and women. *Body Image, 18*, 43–60.

Piran, N. (2019). The developmental theory of embodiment: Protective social factors that enhance positive embodiment. In T. Tylka & N. Piran (Eds.), *Handbook of positive body image and embodiment* (pp. 105–117). New York, NY, Oxford University Press.

Piran, N., & Teall, T. L. (2006). *The embodiment scales for women.* Unpublished manuscript.

Piran, N., & Teall, T. L. (2012). The developmental theory of embodiment. In G. McVey, M P., Levine, N. Piran, & H. B. Ferguson (Eds.), *Preventing eating-related and weight-related disorders* (pp. 169–197). Ontario, CA: Wilfred Laurier University Press.

Porges, S. W. (2018). Polyvagal theory: A primer. In S. W. Porges & D. A. Dana (Eds.), *Clinical applications of the polyvagal theory: The emergence of polyvagal-informed therapies* (pp. 50–69). New York, NY: Norton.

Poulsen, S., Lunn, S., Daniel, S. I., Folke, S., Mathiesen, B. B., Katznelson, H., & Fairburn, C. G. (2014). A randomized controlled trial of psychoanalytic psychotherapy or cognitive-behavioral therapy for bulimia nervosa. *Journal of the American Academy of Child and Adolescent Psychiatry, 12*, 450–458.

Preyde, M., Watson, J., Remers, S., & Stuart, R. (2016). Emotional dysregulation, interoceptive deficits, and treatment outcomes in patients with eating disorders. *Social Work in Mental Health, 14,* 227–244.

Reel, J. J., Galli, N., Miyairi, M., Voelker, D., & Greenleaf, C. (2016). Development and validation of the intuitive exercise scale. *Eating Behaviors, 22,* 129–132.

Reindl, S. M. (2001). *Sensing the self: Women's recovery from bulimia.* Cambridge, MA: Harvard University Press.

Resch, E., & Tylka, T. L. (2019). Intuitive eating. In T. Tylka & N. Piran (Eds.), *Handbook of positive body image and embodiment: Constructs, protective factors, and interventions* (pp. 68–79). New York, NY: Oxford University Press.

Reynolds, J. M. (2017). Merleau-Ponty, world-creating blindness, and the phenomenology of non-normate bodies. *Chiasmi International: Trilingual Studies Concerning the Thought of Merleau-Ponty, 19.* 419–434

Richards, P. S., Crowton, S., Berrett, M. E., Smith, M. H., & Passmore, K. (2017). Can patients with eating disorders learn to eat intuitively? A 2-year pilot study. *Eating Disorders, 25,* 99–113.

Roach, G. M., & McNally, C. (2005). *The essential yoga sutra: Ancient wisdom for your yoga.* New York, NY: Double Day.

Ronen, T., & Ayelet (1988). *In and out of anorexia: The story of the client, the therapist, and the process of recovery.* Philadelphia, PA: Jessica Kingsley.

Rudolph, C. (2015). *The art of facilitation with 28 equine assisted activities.* Tehachapi, CA: Rising Moon Ranch

Salamon, S. I. (2019). Insight and responsibility: A psychodynamic-existential approach to psychotherapy. *Humanistic Psychologist, 47,* 52–75.

Salzberg, S. (2017). *Real love: The art of mindful connection.* New York, NY: Flatiron Books.

Sandoz, E., Wilson, K. C., & Dufrene, T. (2010). *Acceptance and commitment therapy for eating disorders: A process-focused guide to treating anorexia and bulimia.* Oakland, CA: New Harbinger Press.

Sanford, M. (2008). *Waking: A memoir of trauma and transcendence.* Emmaus, PA: Rodale Books.

Satinsky, A., & Winter, V. R. (2019). Attuned sexuality. In T. L. Tylka & N. Piran (Eds.), *Handbook of positive body image and embodiment: Constructs, protective factors and interventions* (pp. 91–101). New York, NY: Oxford University Press.

Sayrs, J. H. (2012). Mindfulness, acceptance, and values-based interventions for addiction counselors: The benefits of practicing what we preach. In S. C. Hayes & M. E. Levin (Eds.), *Mindfulness and acceptance for addictive behaviors: Applying contextual CBT to substance abuse and behavioral addictions* (pp. 187–215). Oakland, CA: Context Press.

Schiweck, C., Piette, D., Berckmans, D., Claes, S., & Vrieze, E. (2019). Heart rate and high frequency heart rate variability during stress as biomarker for clinical depression. A systematic review. *Psychological Medicine, 49,* 200–211.

Schore, A. N. (2015). *Affect regulation and the origin of the self: The neurobiology of emotional development.* New York, NY: Routledge.

Scime, M., & Cook-Cottone, C. P. (2008). Primary prevention of eating disorders: A constructivist integration of mind and body strategies. *International Journal of Eating Disorders, 41,* 134–142.

Scritchfield, R (2016). *Body kindness: Transform your health from the inside out—And never say diet again.* New York, NY: Workman.

Searight, B. K., & Searight, H. R. (2011). The value of a personal mission statement for university undergraduates. *Creative Education, 2,* 313.

Seligman, M. E. P. (2011). *Flourish: A visionary new understanding of happiness and well-being.* New York, NY: Simon and Schuster.

Shapiro, F. (2017). *Eye movement desensitization and reprocessing (EMDR) therapy: Basic principles, protocols, and procedures* (3rd ed.). New York, NY: Guilford Press.

Shapiro, S. L., & Carlson, L. E. (2009). *The art and science of mindfulness: Integrating mindfulness into psychology and the helping professions.* Washington, DC: American Psychological Association.

Shaw, G. (2019). *Anorexia: The body neglected.* Retrieved June 7, 2019, from https://www.webmd.com/mental-health/eating-disorders/anorexia-nervosa/features/anorexia-body-neglected#1

Shin, H., Park, Y. M., Ying, J. Y., Kim, B., Noh, H., & Lee, S. M. (2014). Relationships between coping strategies and burnout symptoms: A meta-analytic approach. *Professional Psychology: Research and Practice, 45,* 44–56.

Siegel, D. (1996). *The developing mind: Toward neurobiological understanding of relationships.* New York, NY: Guilford Press.

Siegel, D. J. (1999). *The developing mind: Toward a neurobiology of interpersonal experience.* New York, NY: Guilford Press.

Siegel, D. (2010). *The mindful therapist: A clinician's guide to mindsight and neural integration.* New York, NY: Norton.

Siegel, D. (2015). *The developing mind: How relationships and the brain interact to shape who we are* (2nd ed.). New York, NY: Guilford Press.

Sinclair, S., Bryan, C. J., & Bryan, A. O. (2016). Meaning in life as a protective factor for the emergence of suicide ideation that leads to suicide attempts among military personnel and veterans with elevated PTSD and depression. *International Journal of Cognitive Therapy, 9,* 87–98.

Singer, M. (2007). *The untethered soul: The journey beyond yourself.* Oakland, CA: New Harbinger Press.

Slade, E., Keeney, E., Mavranezouli, I., Dias, S., Fou, L., Stockton, S., . . . & Fairburn, C. G. (2018). Treatments for bulimia nervosa: A network meta-analysis. *Psychological Medicine,* 1–8. https://doi.org/10.1017/S0033291718001071

Smith, A., & Cook-Cottone, C. (2011). A review of family therapy as an effective intervention for anorexia nervosa in adolescents. *Journal of Clinical Psychology in Medical Settings, 18,* 323–334.

Smith, J. (2017). *Embodiment: A history.* New Yok, NY: Oxford University Press.

Stahl, B., & Goldstein, E. (2010). *A mindfulness-based stress reduction workbook.* Oakland, CA: New Harbinger Press.

Stankovskaya, E. (2014). *Embodiment: Thoughts from an existential-analytic perspective.* Moscow, Russia: National Research University Higher School of Economics.

Sutterfield, J. (2013). Self-care as a foundation for social action: How to thrive and sustain personal well-being in the field of yoga service. *Journal of Yoga Service, 1,* 33–37.

Svenaeus, F. (2013). Anorexia nervosa and the body uncanny: A phenomenological approach. *Philosophy, Psychiatry, and Psychology, 20,* 81–91.

Swami, V., Barron, D., & Furnham, A. (2018). Exposure to natural environments, and photographs of natural environments, promotes more positive body image. *Body Image, 24*, 82–94.

Swami, V., Barron, D., Weis, L., & Furnham, A. (2016). Bodies in nature: Associations between exposure to nature, connectedness to nature, and body image in US adults. *Body Image, 18*, 153–161.

Sysko, R. (2017). Self-help treatments and eating disorders. In K. D. Brownell & B. T. Walsh (Eds.), *Eating disorders and obesity: A comprehensive handbook* (3rd ed., pp. 284–289). New York, NY: Guilford Press.

Tatham, M. (2011). The role of imagery-based techniques in cognitive-behavioural therapy for adults with eating disorders. *Clinical Psychology Review, 31*, 1101–1109.

Taylor, S. R. (2018). *The body is not an apology: The power of radical self-love.* Oakland, CA: Berrett-Koehler.

Taylor, S. R. (2019). *Bodies as resistance: Claiming the political act of being oneself.* Retrieved July 13, 2019, from https://www.tedxmarin.org/sonya-rene-taylor/

Tchanturia, K., Dapelo, M. A. M., Harrison, A., & Hambrook, D. (2015). Why study positive emotions in the context of eating disorders? *Current Psychiatry Reports, 17*, 1–12.

Thomas, L., & Lytle, M. (2016). *Transforming therapy through horses: Case stories teaching the EAGALA model in action.* Santaquin, UT: Equine Assisted Growth and Learning Association.

Tiggemann, M., & Kemps, E. (2005). The phenomenology of food cravings: The role of mental imagery. *Appetite, 45*, 305–313.

Treasure, J., Sepulveda, A. R., MacDonald, P., Whitaker, W., Lopex, C., Zabala, M., . . . Todd, G. (2008). Interpersonal maintaining factors in eating disorder: Skill sharing interventions for carers. *International Journal of Child and Adolescent Health, 1*, 331–338.

Tribole, E., & Resch, E. (2017). *The intuitive eating workbook: Ten principles for nourishing a healthy relationship with food.* Oakland, CA: New Harbinger Press.

Tribole, E., & Resch, O. (1995). *Intuitive eating.* New York, NY: St. Martin's Griffin.

Trottier, K., & MacDonald, D. E. (2017). Update on psychological trauma, other severe adverse experiences and eating disorders: state of the research and future research directions. *Current psychiatry reports, 19*(8), 45. https://doi.org/10.1007/s11920-017- 0806-6

Tsui, V. (2018). *The mindful eating workbook: Simple mindfulness practices to nurture a healthy relationship with food.* Antonio, TX: Althea Press.

Tylka, T. L. (2006). Development and psychometric evaluation of a measure of intuitive eating. *Journal of Counseling Psychology, 53*, 226–240.

Tylka, T. L. (2019a). Body appreciation. In T. Tylka & N. Piran (Eds.), *Handbook of positive body image and embodiment: Constructs, protective factors, and interventions* (pp. 165–276). New York, NY: Oxford University Press.

Tylka, T. (2019b) Cultivating positive embodiment through the family environments. In T. L. Tylka & N. Piran (Eds.), *Handbook of positive body image and embodiment: Constructs, protective factors and interventions* (pp. 233–243). New York, NY: Oxford University Press.

Tylka, T. L., Annunziato, R. A., Burgard, D., Daníelsdóttir, S., Shuman, E., Davis, C., & Calogero, R. M. (2014). The weight-inclusive versus weight-normative approach to health: Evaluating the evidence for prioritizing well-being over weight loss. *Journal of Obesity.* http://doi.org/10.1155/2014/983495

Tylka, T. L., & Augustus-Horvath, C. L. (2011). Fighting self-objectification in prevention and intervention contexts. In R. M. Calogero, S. Tantleff-Dunn, & J. K. Thompson (Eds.), Self-objectification in women: Causes, consequences, and counteractions (pp. 187–214). Washington, DC: American Psychological Association.

Tylka, T., & Piran, N. (Eds.). (2019). *Handbook of positive body image and embodiment: Constructs, protective factors, and interventions.* New York, NY: Oxford University Press.

Tylka, T. L., & Wilcox, J. A. (2006). Are intuitive eating and eating disorder symptomatology opposite poles of the same construct? *Journal of Counseling Psychology, 53,* 474.

United Nations Mental Health Strategy Steering Group. (2018). *A healthy workforce for a better world: United Nations system mental health and well-being strategy.* Retrieved June 15, 2019, from https://www.unsceb.org/CEBPublicFiles/mental_health_well_being_strategy_final_2018 _may_25th_english.pdf

Utay, J., & Miller, M. (2006). Guided imagery as an effective therapeutic technique: A brief review of its history and efficacy research. *Journal of Instructional Psychology, 33*(1), 40–43.

van der Kolk, B. (2015). *The body keeps the score: Brain, mind, and body in the healing of trauma.* London, UK: Penguin Books.

van Manen, M. (2014). *Phenomenology of practice: Meaning giving methods in phenomenological research and writing.* New York, NY: Routledge.

Vos, J., Cooper, M., Hill, C. E., Neimeyer, R. A., Schneider, K., & Wong, P. T. (2019). Five perspectives on the meaning of meaning in the context of clinical practices. *Journal of Constructivist Psychology, 32,* 48–62.

Waalkes, P. L., Gonzalez, L. M., & Brunson, C. N. (2019). Vision boards and adolescent career counseling: A culturally responsive approach. *Journal of Creativity in Mental Health, 2,* 205–216.

Wallace, B. A. (2011). *Minding closely: The four applications of mindfulness.* Boulder, CO: Snow Lion Press.

Walsh, B. T. (2017). Classification of eating disorders. In K. D. Brownell & B. T. Walsh (Eds.), *Eating disorders and obesity: A comprehensive handbook* (3rd ed., pp. 169–175). New York, NY: Guilford Press.

Walter, F. A., Gathright, E., Redle, J. D., Gunstad, J., & Hughes, J. W. (2019). Depressive symptoms are associated with heart rate variability independently of fitness: A cross-sectional study of patients with heart failure. *Annals of Behavioral Medicine, 53*(11), 955–963. https://doi.org/10.1093/abm/kaz006

Westwood, H., Kerr-Gaffney, J., Stahl, D., & Tchanturia, K. (2017). Alexithymia in eating disorders: Systematic review and meta-analyses of studies using the Toronto Alexithymia Scale. *Journal of Psychosomatic Research, 99,* 66–81.

Wildes, J. E., & Marcus, M. D. (2016). Emotion acceptance behavior therapy for anorexia nervosa. In A. F. Haynos, E. M. Forman, M. L. Butryn, & J. Lillis (Eds.), *Mindfulness and acceptance for treating eating disorders and weight concerns: Evidence-based interventions* (pp. 45–70). Oakland, CA: New Harbinger.

Wilfey, D. E., & Eichen, D. M. (2017). Interpersonal psychotherapy. In K. D.

Brownell & B. T. Walsh (Eds.), *Eating disorders and obesity: A comprehensive handbook* (3rd ed., pp. 290–295). New York, NY: Guilford Press.

Wilson, K. G., Sandoz, E. K., Kitchens, J., & Roberts, M. (2010). The Valued Living Questionnaire: Defining and measuring valued action within a behavioral framework. *Psychological Record, 60,* 249–272.

Wolfe, W. L., & Patterson, K. (2017). Comparison of a gratitude-based and cognitive restructuring intervention for body dissatisfaction and dysfunctional eating behavior in college women. *Eating Disorders, 25,* 330–344.

Wood-Barcalow, N. L., & Augustus-Horvath, C. L. (2018). Clinical applications of positive body image. In E. A. Daniels, M. M. Gillen, & C. H. Markey (Eds.), *Body positive: Understanding and improving body image in science and practice* (pp. 235–261). Cambridge, UK: Cambridge University Press.

Wong, P. T. P. (2012). *The human quest for meaning: Theories, research, and applications* (2nd ed.). New York: Routledge.

World Health Organization. (2014). *Mental health: A state of wellbeing.* Retrieved June 15, 2019, from https://www.who.int/features/factfiles/mental_health/en/

World Health Organization. (2019). *How much physical activity is recommended?* Retrieved July 7, 2019, from https://www.who.int/news-room/fact-sheets/detail/physical-activity

Zeeck, A., Herpertz-Dahlmann, B., Friederich, H. C., Brockmeyer, T., Resmark, G., Hagenah, U., Ehrlich, S., Cuntz., Sipful., S. & Hartmann, A. (2018). Psychotherapeutic treatment for anorexia nervosa: A systematic review and network meta-analysis. *Frontiers in Psychiatry, 9,* 158. 10.3389/fpsyt.2018.00158. eCollection 2018

Zipfel, S., Giel, K. E., Bulik, C. M., Hay, P., & Schmidt, U. (2015). Anorexia nervosa: Aetiology, assessment, and treatment. *Lancet Psychiatry, 2,* 1099–1111.

INDEX

Note: Italicized page locators refer to figures; tables are noted with a *t*.